BATTLE

BATTLE

A History of Combat and Culture

JOHN A. LYNN

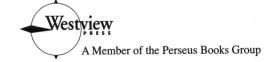

A Member of the Perseus Books Group

Published in 2003 in the United States of America by Westview Press, 5500 Central Avenue, Boulder, Colorado 80301–2877, and in the United Kingdom by Westview Press, 12 Hid's Copse Road, Cumnor Hill, Oxford OX2 9JJ.

Find us on the world wide web at www.westviewpress.com.

Westview Press books are available at special discounts for bulk purchases in the United States by corporations, institutions, and other organizations. For more information, please contact the Special Markets Department at the Perseus Books Group, 11 Cambridge Center, Cambridge, MA 02142, or call (617) 252-5298, (800)255-1514 or email j.mccrary@perseusbooks.com.

Text design by Jeff Williams
Set in 11-point Adobe Garamond by the Perseus Books Group.

Library of Congress Cataloging-in-Publication Data

Lynn, John A. (John Albert), 1943–
    Battle : a history of combat and culture / John Lynn.
      p. cm.
Includes bibliographical references and index.
    ISBN 0-8133-3371-7 (hardcover : alk. paper)
1. War. 2. Military history. 3. Combat. 4. Sociology, Military. 5. War and society.
6. Military art and science—Effect of technologicalinnovations on.   1. Title.

U21.2.L95 2003
303.6'6'09—DC21

2003006401

The paper used in this publication meets the requirements of the American National Standard for Permanence of Paper for Printed Library Materials Z39.48–1984.

10   9   8   7   6   5   4   3   2   1

CONTENTS

This book is dedicated to my

MARINE CORPS STUDENTS

at the University of Illinois at
Urbana-Champaign

and the

Marine Corps
University,
Quantico.

ACKNOWLEDGMENTS

Every project finds me in debt to friends and colleagues, but *Battle* has left me with the longest list of obligations to date. Writing a broad-based comparative history required that I leave the comfortable confines of my own expertise and undertake a long and difficult journey. Luckily for me there were a lot of grand people who helped me along the way by making suggestions, reading chapters, and pointing out areas for improvement. I will now do my best to name and thank them all. However, so many people aided me in one way or another that I am bound to leave somebody out. So, please, forgive me for any oversight. I wrote this book on my own, to be sure, but it was still very much a communal effort.

Let me first thank Fred Jaher, a fine historian and editor, who has once again proven his friendship by going over every word and every argument in this volume. His keen intelligence, sound judgment, and fine eye for language are much appreciated. He also read key chapters in formative versions, notably Chapters 7 and 8 and the Epilogue. I occasionally help him out, too, but nowhere near as much as he comes to my rescue.

In the latter stages of work on this volume, I benefited from the efforts of a superb research assistant, Michael Hughes. He not only did the obligatory hard work for me but also read and critiqued several chapters. The world will soon discover what a good historian Mike is, but I already know. Another first-rate research assistant, Lauren Heckler, helped in securing permissions for the illustrations.

I am fortunate to have two university venues, the University of Illinois at Urbana-Champaign, where I hang my hat, and the Ohio State University, where as adjunct professor I make yearly trips to lecture and counsel students. *Battle* first saw light as lectures at Ohio State over a period of several years. I enthusiastically express my gratitude to colleagues there, Allan R. Millett, Geoffrey Parker, John F. Guilmartin, Jr., and Mark Grimsley. They offered knowledgeable commentary and, above all, made me feel that I mattered. Thanks as well to the graduate students there who discussed my ideas and provided their insights. Go Bucks!

Back at home, my colleague John Buckler helped me by reading an early draft of Chapter 1. His corrections saved me from errors and slips. Chapter 2 became a cross-country project. Ralph D. Sawyer, whose translations and commentaries I used extensively, was kind enough to read the discussion of ancient China. Kai-wing Chow, a Confucian scholar at Illinois, also reviewed the Chinese section. Along the way I also gave an address at a conference on Chinese military history at Christchurch, New Zealand. My thanks to Nicola Di Cosmo, who invited me to participate there; I learned much and incorporated some of it in Chapter 2. My long-time colleague Blair King read and made valuable suggestions concerning the Indian half of the chapter. Pradeep Barua of the University of Nebraska at Kearney, who once was my student, but has always been my teacher, not only read the South Asian section but supplied me with his chapter on ancient India in his soon-to-be-published *The State at War in South Asia.*

Chapter 3 benefited from the reading and critique of Kelly DeVries, Mike Pedrotty, and Sharon Michalove. Chapter 4 went through many hands in draft. I presented it to the early Europe reading group at Illinois, which means that Clare Crowston, Lauren Heckler, Caroline Hibbard, Craig Koslofsky, David O'Brien, Dana Rabin, Brian Sandberg, Adam Sutcliffe, and others helped me sharpen my ideas. The fine French scholar Jean Chaginot also read the chapter and gave me the benefit of his great knowledge in correcting some errors. Azar Gat also looked over Chapter 4 in an earlier form. An abridged version of this chapter appeared in *MHQ, The Quarterly Journal of Military History,* winter 2003.

Chapter 5 also initially came under scrutiny as a presentation to a group of scholars at a conference organized by Emily O. Goldman and Leslie C. Eliasson, and it appears in the book that came out of that meeting, *Diffusion of Military Knowledge, Technology and Practices: International Consequences of Military Innovations* (Palo Alto, CA: 2003). Thanks to all those who attended and contributed to that joint effort. In addition, Blair King, Pradeep Barua, David Prochaska, and Antoinette Burton read and commented upon the manuscript of Chapter 5.

I received the expert help and criticism of Azar Gat on Chapter 6. His published works were essential to this chapter. I not only learned a great deal from them but also mined them for sources.

Because I was determined to display special care in dealing with the sensitive issues of American racism, the excesses of the Pacific War, and the dropping of the atomic bomb on Japan, I was particularly careful to confer with a broad range of scholars concerning Chapter 7. My thanks go to Allan Millett and Mark Grimsley at the Ohio State University—what a pleasure to gain from such expertise. Robert Rush, then a grad student at Ohio State and now with the U.S. Army Center of Military History, offered valuable comments. Three of my colleagues at Illinois, Fred Jaher, Poshek Fu, and Kristin Hoganson, pointed out weaknesses of the chapter for my further attention. I believe the final result is much better for their criticisms.

Chapter 8 enjoyed an advantage from the start, as Kenneth Pollack supported my work from day one. Years ago, he gave me a copy of his dissertation, which eventually saw light as *Arabs at War* (Lincoln, NE: 2002). Chapter 8 comes the closest of any part of *Battle* to being a conduit for someone else's work. Ken also took the time to read over an early draft of the chapter. I must also thank Ken Cuno, a historian of Egypt at the University of Illinois, for pointing out where I needed to revise my efforts substantially. He was immensely helpful.

The epilogue first appeared as a paper for a conference on terrorism held at the University of Illinois in October 2002. Thanks to Mark Steinberg for letting me take part and for reading my words. I should also thank my sister, Janice Lynn, for surveying the manuscript and making suggestions. Also, I owe thanks to Buffy Sainte-Marie for discussing the meanings of her song "Universal Soldier" and suggesting that I emphasize its appeal for responsibility.

I also owe recognition and thanks to two institutions at the University of Illinois. First, the Research Board once again supported my work by providing me with funds for research assistants. Second, the marvelous and varied collections at the Library at the University, a true wonder, greatly eased the task of pursuing comparative work.

This has been a long list, but it needs to be even longer, because the authors whose books and articles I discuss in *Battle* were all congenial colleagues, even when my only contacts with them were their words on a page. These scholars explained the past and pointed the way to many other studies and original sources.

I must also express my gratitude for the support I have received from Westview Press. Peter Kracht encouraged me to take on a "big" project and sponsored *Battle* with the press before he left for Greenwood. My current editor, Steve Catalano, has not only been unflaggingly cheerful and supportive but shown himself to be a very, very perceptive editor. He has done much to make this a better book.

Let me close once again with thanks to my wife, Andrea, my sons, Nathanael and Daniel, and my daughter-in-law, Amy, who have had to endure my endless one-way conversations about *Battle* and who have even been able to force a word in edgewise once in a while. I assure you I was listening.

Well, on to a new life and a new book—Andrea knows what I mean.

JOHN A. LYNN

PREFACE

Requiem for the Universal Soldier

He's five feet two and he's six feet four
He fights with missiles and with spears
He's all of 31 and he's only 17
He's been a soldier for a thousand years
He's a Catholic, a Hindu, an atheist, a Jain,
a Buddhist and a Baptist and a Jew
and he knows he shouldn't kill
and he knows he always will
kill you for me my friend and me for you
. . . He's the universal soldier and he really is to blame.

—*"Universal Soldier" by Buffy Sainte-Marie*

THE UNIVERSAL SOLDIER ENDURES through time—the unchanging agent of pillage, destruction, and death. He carries a torch, but not as a beacon to mankind, for he deals in fire and blood. He thrives in popular imagination, perpetuated by the fear of war itself. Song and art give him breath as the eternal, faceless killer. Even historians consecrate the universal soldier when they assert that only weapons and tactics have changed, not the men who have wielded them.[2] But does he really exist?

The universal soldier seems uniform and invariable because we view him far away. Separated from him by time and distance, unable to see his face or hear his words and, thus, unable to recognize his individuality or penetrate his thoughts. Standing so distant, we only make out his deadly actions, and these usually look very much the same.

Across gaps of time, space, and knowledge, we often have described past warriors in one of two flawed manners. On the one hand, we generalize too broadly and posit that everyone is essentially alike—consequently, the universal soldier. On the other hand, we build a false dichotomy between ourselves and everyone else. This is really only a slight variation on the theme of the universal soldier, since it again offers broad and essentially static characterizations. The discussion of our military past has been distorted by both these tendencies.

Battle suggests that by adopting a cultural approach to the study of war and combat, we better appreciate the variety and change that have typified military institutions, thought, and practice over the ages. A cultural interpretation is most likely to grant individuals and peoples their full personal, social, and cultural character. And it encourages historians, and in their wake military professionals and the informed public, to question assumptions and take care in generalizing about war and warriors.

This is not to deny that certain important constants characterize the nature of war. War brings havoc and suffering. The soldier, an agent of that destruction, also becomes a victim of it. Fear grips the warrior as he, or she, faces discomfort, danger, and death. As a casualty of his own war, pathos also unifies soldiers' experience over time. Yet so does his courage, which coexists with danger. War demands endurance, self-sacrifice, and heroism, but conceptions of cowardice and courage or brutality and compassion are hardly constants across human societies; one culture's bravery is another's bravado and one's mercy is another's meekness. Neither are those values and identities that compel and inspire warriors in combat consistent across age and place.

This volume has come to bury the universal soldier, not to praise him. Only if this concept of universality is put to rest can those men and women who bore the toil and combat of war escape from obscurity and reclaim their different and distinct human faces. We must recognize that they perceived and understood things in ways specific to time, place, and culture. Once we grant this fact, everything changes, and we rediscover the lives and passions of past warriors and soldiers. They are not always admirable, but they are real. Such is the proper task of the military historian, not building monuments of stone or effigies of straw.

The Cultural Study of War

Battle is not the first call for a cultural approach to the history of warfare, nor is it the first book that has sought to answer that call. In some form or another, cultural histories of war published as articles or books have been with us for some time, but our best studies have confined their discussions to specific times and places. We still lack a sound and convincing, cross-cultural study that adopts a cultural method without going awry. Still, because there have been historical works that already pursue cultural themes, *Battle* often engages in dialogues with other historians. I will discuss the works of such notable scholars as John W. Dower, Azar Gat, Victor Davis Hanson, Richard W. Kaeuper, John Keegan, Geoffrey Parker, Kenneth M. Pollack, Ralph D. Sawyer, and Ronald Takaki, but I have no intention of concentrating my efforts primarily on debating the historical literature. *Battle* is meant primarily as a series of discussions devoted to the past, not to what historians have said about that past. *Battle* will follow its own agenda.

Nevertheless, it is very important to give credit where credit is due. Working in this volume outside my usual specialty of early modern Europe, as most of the chapters require me to do, I am very much indebted for information and argument supplied by others. Moreover, some historians have served as inspiration or as valued and respected foils. As its title implies, *Battle* is often contentious, but those with whom I cross pens are all worthy.

In pursuing cultural themes, *Battle* will not forget that the ultimate fact of military history is combat, actual fighting with all its danger and its heavy costs. We have learned much from studies that do not deal directly with combat, but we cannot turn the history of war solely into the social history of military institutions or some other bloodless inquiry. Here I take exception to certain works of the "new military history." Also, I believe we ought to go beyond simply recounting the reactions of soldiers to combat. An entire genre of works about war discusses not the conflict of arms but what can best be called "the experience of war"—that is, what it was like or how it felt to be there. Such stories possess great human interest and often have much to say, but there are instances when concentrating on the experience of war can lead us away from understanding the nature of the fighting and the conduct of the war. For example, I believe this to be the case with Dower's discussion of race hatred in the Pacific during World War II.

For me, John Keegan's now classic *Face of Battle,* published in 1976, began modern studies of war and culture.[3] He does not explicitly attack the concept of the universal soldier, but the logic of his argument certainly does. Keegan argues that in the usual discussion of battle, military units are considered as if they were blocks on a map. They appear as uniform and faceless bodies of troops that move in response to their commanders' decisions as they attack or defend. Keegan insists that these units are composed of real men who are not identical and not constant from age to age. Soldiers bring different motivations, attitudes, and values to the field, just as they bear different arms and serve different masters. Keegan has done more than anyone else to redefine the way we regard battle, and for this the entire historical profession owes him gratitude. Yet, when Keegan took on a great cross-cultural sweep through time in his *A History of Warfare* (1993), he produced an idiosyncratic and unsatisfying study. This explicitly cultural history strongly, and correctly, contests Clausewitz's dictum that war is politics by asserting that war "is always an expression of culture, often a determinant of cultural forms, in some societies the culture itself."[4] Keegan errs, however, in advocating and extending the cultural thesis proposed by Victor Davis Hanson.

Hanson has become the leading historical author proposing a cultural approach to war through the publication of his *Western Way of War* in 1989 and the works that have followed it, most notably his *Carnage and Culture: Landmark Battles in the Rise of Western Power,* which came out in 2001.[5] He insists that the classical Greeks created a new form of warfare that has typified the West for 2,500 years. He emphasizes Western "civic militarism," warfare by willing citizens who understood their rights and responsibilities in a consensual, constitutional regime. Ultimately, Hanson replaces the notion of an all-encompassing universal soldier not with variety and change but with a universal and eternal *Western* soldier and, by implication, with an equally universal and stereotyped non-Western, or "Oriental," warrior. In his *A History of*

Warfare, Keegan makes this explicit by defining a non-Western form of warfare as the "other" juxtaposed to the Western: "Oriental warmaking, . . . as something different and apart from European warfare, is characterized by traits peculiar to itself. Foremost among them are evasion, delay and indirectness."[6] Not only John Keegan but the renowned Geoffrey Parker picked up this theory, giving it his imprimatur. There are aspects of Hanson's argument that appeal to me, including his emphasis on culture, but ultimately I find it deeply flawed.

A very different kind of cultural military history has been offered up by Azar Gat, who has written a series of books on the evolution of military thought.[7] These works, which appeared from 1989 to 2000, provide an impressive history of military theoreticians as representative of their environments. His volumes, particularly the first, which deals with the Enlightenment through Clausewitz, are models of the intellectual history of an immensely practical field. He does not deal in the new cultural history, because he focuses on great issues and great minds, not the flotsam and jetsam of daily existence. His works are essential for understanding military writings over the last 250 years.

My intentions differ vastly from those of Keegan and Hanson, and my subject matter is much more varied than Gat's, although our analyses converge from time to time. In *Battle,* conclusions do not run through the entire volume, growing in mass and velocity from chapter to chapter in order to maximize impact. Rather, the arguments are specific to each chapter. *Battle* holds together because of its theme, the importance of conceptual factors in determining military history. To make this point, it offers a range of examples from across the globe and across the centuries. Each case study differs, sharing only its own cultural emphasis with preceding and succeeding chapters.

CHALLENGING TECHNOLOGICAL DETERMINISM IN HISTORY AND POLICY

Battle constantly argues against the dominance of material factors in war, particularly technological determinacy. This is implicit in my cultural approach, since it by nature advocates the importance of the conceptual over the material.

Unfortunately, a desire to explain styles of warfare simply as a response to weaponry has long afflicted our view of battle. After World War II, the galactic importance of atomic and thermonuclear bombs and the fast pace of technological change have made such explanations even more attractive. Yet watershed advances in military technology have been relatively rare in recorded history. The West knew only a few before the Industrial Revolution—essentially, the breeding and harnessing of horses for war, the transition from bronze to iron, the evolution of the successful war galley, the refining of gunpowder and its weaponry, and the arrival of the broadside-firing sailing vessel. The other great transitions in warfare, and there were many, are better explained as political, social, and cultural.

Of course, after the Industrial Revolution exerted its influence on war after 1850, advances in weaponry came at a much more rapid rate. However, even then the most critical aspect of change has not been the technology alone but the choices that different militaries have made concerning it. Technological advance in the last century and a half has brought breakthroughs to developed countries at approximately the same time. In such a situation, technological improvement has been a tide that raises all boats. With similar menus of technology, it is, indeed, the conceptual choices that matter most.

Interwar tank development provides an excellent example of different selections from the same available menu. With relatively similar technology, the French and the Germans developed dissimilar armored vehicles. French tanks fit the French concept of a slow-moving, methodical battle along continuous fronts. These armored vehicles, designed to support foot-slogging infantry and fight with the aid of powerful artillery, mounted larger guns and carried heavier armor but were slower-moving. They had few radios and one-man turrets that required a single individual to load and fire the gun while also commanding the tank. All this rendered French armor less capable of dealing well with the challenges of a fluid battlefield. In contrast, German tanks fit a style of war we have come to call blitzkrieg, rapid-paced and intent on deep penetration into enemy territory. More lightly gunned and armored in 1940, German vehicles were faster, with radios and two-man turrets that allowed tank commanders to worry solely about directing the crew and coordinating the tank with others in the whirl of battle. The same technology produced very different weapons, which corresponded to contrasting professional discourses on war. The key German advantage was conceptual not mechanical.

Historians who have tried to explain victory and defeat simply in terms of technological difference have generally erred. Historically, such analyses work only when considering societies with radically different technological bases, such as sub-Saharan Africans confronted by nineteenth-century Europeans armed with weapons born of the Industrial Revolution. Moreover, even wise scholars who credit technology with compelling radical change in the broad sweep of military development run into real trouble. Geoffrey Parker has argued that the Military Revolution of early modern Europe came largely as a response to the rise of a new style of fortification, the *trace italienne,* but the subsequent debates have not been kind to his contention.

Of course, technology mesmerizes modern militaries, which now talk of Military Technical Revolutions or Revolutions in Military Affairs. Success in the Gulf War and later "victories" have tempted strategists and statesmen to believe that military hardware surpasses all other factors in war. Again, it is prudent to adopt and stretch technological advantages, but choosing, integrating, and exploiting new weaponry remain essentially a conceptual task. And the ability to maximize new technology depends very much on civil culture, such as religious, social, and political values.

THE DISCOURSE AND REALITY OF WAR

Battle suggests a way of pursuing a cultural approach by examining the relationship between the discourse and the reality of war. Today, one of the main thrusts of academic historical studies, perhaps *the* main thrust, is the "new cultural history." Cultural approaches of great sophistication practically define the field of history in American universities. The issues that so fascinate historians have little to do with the "high" culture of major intellectual figures. No, the "new cultural history" focuses on mass or popular culture and often concerns itself with "daily life issues," aspects of the past once regarded as trivial.

This book attempts to apply the basic concerns of the new cultural history without being guilty of its excesses. Those who pursue the new cultural history apply elaborate theories borrowed from anthropology and literary studies. Unfortunately, this theoretical discussion, specialized vocabulary, and references tend to make such histories inaccessible to all but the cognoscenti. This book consciously avoids arcane language as much as possible. In the discussion of the new cultural history, the very term "culture" takes on complex meanings, and obviously we must define it here. For my colleagues, the term covers a very broad spectrum encompassing practices and even objects— "material culture"—as well as ideas, but the essential value of using a cultural approach in military history is precisely in distinguishing the mental from the material. The discussions presented in these pages try to differentiate between the conceptual and the concrete and argue for the importance of the former. Therefore this volume emphasizes what could be termed "conceptual culture," that is values, beliefs, assumptions, expectations, preconceptions, and the like. Chapters also strongly differentiate thought from reality, although extreme proponents of cultural history might dispute the very existence of a reality, since all is perception to them. In the realm of military history, such airy discussions become foolish. Thousands dead and wounded as a result of battle is the kind of hard fact that defies intellectual games.

Observers of the military, both in uniform and in academe, already use a cultural vocabulary, and some of it appears here. In general three cultural realms receive attention: societal, military, and strategic. Many aspects of societal culture impact upon the military, matters such as religion and masculinity, for example. Armed forces also create their own cultures, influenced by, but distinct from, those of society. John Keegan claims to have originated the term "military culture" to encapsule ways in which different armed forces do things in different ways for reasons that are not simply dictated by reality. As well as the way in which armies think about themselves, I broaden "military culture" to include conceptions of war and combat within a military. Both societal and military cultures combine in strategic culture, a useful category comprising the way a state's political and military institutions conceive of and deal with armed conflict. Strategic culture derives from civil values and practices as well as from military conceptions and capabilities. Thus, in considering U.S. strategic culture, one must look at the presidency, Congress, and popular attitudes toward war as well as doctrine and strategic thought. Given its focus on combat, this volume concentrates on societal and military culture, although much that it says will bear, at least tangentially, on strategic culture as well.

The case studies presented in the following chapters suggest a way of describing the relationships between conception and reality in warfare. As an aid to my own understanding, I constructed a model to express these relationships, and I offer it as an applicable framework. However, explaining a theoretical model necessarily requires dense prose, so I have relegated a formal exposition and graphic representation of the model to the Appendix, which the reader may, or may not, choose to read. In this Preface, I intend only to block out its central elements.

We begin by differentiating between the reality of war and the way in which a culture conceives of war. These seem destined to be quite distinct, the one not matching the other. Despite my resolve to eschew the language of cultural theory, I have found it convenient to borrow the term "discourse" for the conceptual pole of the model. Here, the term signifies the complex of assumptions, perceptions, expectations, and values on a particular subject. Many cultural historians include those practices that reinforce values, expectations, and so on, in the definition of discourse, but I would like to keep action separate from conception for the purposes of this volume. It is also necessary to point out that a single society can harbor several discourses on war that vary by class, gender, and profession—the last an important differentiation with the emergence of a professional military. Thus, aristocrats might think of war very differently than peasants do, men than women do, and career soldiers than civilians do.

For a number of reasons, the discourse on war tries to modify reality to more nearly resemble conceptions of how war *should* be. Thus societies impose conventions and laws on the conduct of war. In addition, discourse must adjust to reality, if for no other reason than survival. So heroic ideals of warfare as Europe spiraled toward World War I had to give way to much grimmer notions to cope with the reality of the trenches. In fact, it is often this feedback between discourse and reality that most interests me, but its operation is not always a simple matter of recognition and reaction.

Two categories of more complex feedback pose particular challenges to societies and militaries. If a great gap separates the ideal from real, and if reality cannot be modified to match conception, then a society might very well spin off an artificial and highly ritualized form of military behavior that better matches the discourse on war. Such a perfected version of reality could take the form of a kind of mock combat, such as the medieval tournament, or the less war-like, but more deadly, practice of dueling. A need for the artificially perfect may also explain the survival of archaic drill and ceremony in modern militaries. Violent sport may even qualify as a perfected form of warfare.

On the other hand, if the actual practice of combat fundamentally clashes with a society's definitions of war or of the warrior and, consequently, cannot be accepted as war, then a society might reject it as such and create an alternative discourse to deal with it. In other words, it constructs a very different set of expectations, values, and so on outside the normal conception of war. As it does so, however, this alternative discourse abandons the conventions usually associated with armed conflict and, therefore, justifies a more extreme reality of war with few if any restraints. If, for instance, an enemy's behavior is considered utterly barbaric, then that enemy may be regarded as having forfeited any human consideration, and massacre replaces battle.

The simplicity of this model must of necessity fall short of the true labyrinth of reality, but the virtue of such intellectual maps is to reduce complexity to an understandable level by highlighting the most important processes and results. I hope that it will be of some aid or interest to the reader.

METHODS AND THEMES

The chapters presented in this volume find unity in their common emphasis on the importance of the discourse, or discourses, on war, but they vary in time period, geographical setting, and focus. Works on military history tend to dwell on the recent past and neglect more remote eras. Here I have attempted to balance the studies better, with chapters addressing ancient, medieval, early modern, and late modern periods. I have also bridged the continents rather than remaining within the Western world; therefore, the chapters present case studies from East Asia, South Asia, and the Middle East, as well as Europe and America. As the chapters span the ages and the globe, there is no attempt to fill in all gaps; the history offered here is intended to be instructive and provocative, not definitive.

This is not so much a work about the *why* of war but the *how* of war. The main focus is not explaining why peoples, nations, or states resorted to the clash of arms, but how they carried on those conflicts. This is a story of combat and of the cultural influences that led men and women to fight in the ways that they did. To establish and maintain its focus on the central fact of war, each chapter begins with an account of a battle.

Efforts at broad comparative history force an author to move away from his or her own comfortable ground of specialization. This requires relying heavily on other historians for information and insight. I have borrowed and built upon their works, accepting some and debating with others. By taking in the broad sweep, one becomes a lightning rod attracting bolts of criticism. Experts in particular epochs or areas demand a level of sophistication in discussing their specialties that only a lifetime of narrowly concentrated study can provide. They also often want a richness of detail that would turn each chapter into a book in its own right.

As a brief outline of the chapters makes clear, the range of cultural factors considered here encompasses philosophy, religion, aesthetics, popular culture, community values, and more. Different chapters deal with different mixes of these factors. While the chapters play off one another, they also stand alone, although I hope the whole adds up to more than the sum of its parts.

Chapter 1, "Written in Blood: The Classical Greek Drama of Battle and the Western Way of War," examines phalanx warfare as conducted by the independent city states of classical Greece. Combat in this era provides a strong example of the way in which societies impose conventions upon warfare in accord with their concept of what war should be. This chapter then critiques Victor Davis Hanson's provocative claim that the classical Greeks originated a style of combat that then came to typify Europe during the coming millennia. This volume simply must address his assertion of a Western Way of War, because if correct, that thesis would set the terms for the cultural history of war.

Chapter 2, "Subtleties of Violence: Ancient Chinese and Indian Texts on Warfare," contrasts Greek concepts of warfare with those proposed in ancient China and India. There, the literature on combat diverged from the Greek, preferring deception and diplomacy to direct confrontation. Warfare was different but not in a way that justifies Hanson's theory. Here the wonderfully rich and complete translations of ancient Chinese military texts and the commentaries upon them by Ralph D. Sawyer have proved essential. The differences between the Chinese and the South Asian discourses on war also establish that there was no one "Oriental" way of war to contrast to the Western. Because Chapter 2 emphasizes the ancient texts, it confronts the discourse on war far more than it defines reality.

Chapter 3, "Chivalry and *Chevauchée:* The Ideal, the Real, and the Perfect in Medieval European Warfare," returns to Europe in order to examine the contrast between the formalized and elegant discourse of chivalry and the exceptionally brutal reality of warfare during the Late Middle Ages, exemplified in the armed raids, or *chevauchées,* of the Hundred Years' War. But perhaps equally interesting is the fact that the medieval aristocracy created an artificial, but perfected, form of combat in the tournament to meet chivalry's cultural needs for combat. At the same time, the papacy preached the Crusades, which offered a different kind of perfected war. The chapter takes advantage of the fine works produced by Maurice Keen and Richard Kaeuper.

Chapter 4, "Linear Warfare: Images and Ideas of Combat in the Age of Enlightenment," examines the role played by aesthetics and style in warfare, focusing on the conscious mixture of fashion and function that reflected European tastes, rather than simply responding to military effectiveness. This chapter centers on my own particular expertise, Western Europe, particularly France, during the ancien régime, 1660–1789. Considering a potpourri of military practices, from apparel to organization to operations, this discussion ultimately suggests that the parameters of limited warfare were conceptual as much as or more than they were technological and material.

Chapter 5, "Victories of the Conquered: The Native Character of the Sepoy," observes the transmission of eighteenth-century European military institutions and practices to the Indian subcontinent. First the French and then the British created effective armies of native soldiers, sepoys, who fought with European weaponry and tactics. Tradition explains the sepoy's effectiveness on the battlefield as a result of his Western military practice, but this essay insists that his real power derived from motivations native to South Asian culture.

Chapter 6, "The Sun of Austerlitz: Romantic Visions of Decisive Battle in Nineteenth-Century Europe," examines the influence exerted by high culture on military thought and practice in nineteenth-century Europe. This inquiry probes the relationship between the dominant form of philosophy, literature, and art—Romanticism—and the systematized analysis of Napoleonic warfare formulated by Clausewitz. The arguments and conclusions presented here owe much to Peter Paret but are most strongly influenced by Azar Gat. Clausewitz, regarded today as the finest Western military writer since the ancient world, often receives the kind of deference usually reserved only for Holy Scripture, as military commentators quote him chapter and verse. Yet Clausewitz was a product of his times, and his resurrection of decisive battle was definably Napoleonic and of questionable relevance for other ages, including our own.

Chapter 7, "The Merciless Fight: Race and Military Culture in the Pacific War," argues that racial prejudice, regarded as a paramount factor for the last twenty years, was of less importance than scholars currently insist. This explicitly questions the cultural arguments of such noted scholars as John W. Dower and Ronald Takaki. To be sure, racial animosity typified American and Japanese attitudes on the home front and in the field, but racial stereotyping recognized a profound contrast in military cultures between the United States and Japan. The difference was cultural, not racial, but it did exist. Moreover, calling upon other historians, most notably Richard B. Frank, Chapter 7 denies that the race thesis explains U.S. doctrine or strategy, including the dropping of atomic bombs on Japan.

Chapter 8, "Crossing the Canal: Egyptian Effectiveness and Military Culture in the October War," examines Egyptian military culture to explain repeated failures in maneuver warfare, 1948–1967. In this chapter, tactical and operational analyses provide the methodology to uncover cultural traits. The arguments presented rely upon the important, if controversial, works of Kenneth M. Pollack, who regards the shortcomings revealed as typical not only of Egyptians but of Arab militaries as a group. The Egyptian commander Isma'il 'Ali carried off the single greatest triumph of Arab armies since World War II, the crossing of the Canal in 1973, precisely by recognizing his troops' inherent difficulties in maneuver warfare and overcoming them by designing a set-piece battle, which initially defeated Israeli counterattacks.

The Epilogue, "Terrorism and 'Evil': Framing a New Discourse on War at the Dawn of the Twenty-First Century," surveys assumptions at the foundation of the U.S. approach to war and Terrorism. Examples from other chapters suggest a view of Terrorism that U.S. policy makers might find hard to fit with U.S. notions of al Qaeda's "evil." In any case, it is clear that we must reshape our discourse on war to take into account new threats and new responses.

The universal soldier does not exist; he is wholly an imagined being born of fear and projection, a cultural construction. It is time to intone his requiem. Let us replace that unchanging, faceless warrior with real flesh and blood: a Greek hoplite, an Indian mahout, a Chinese charioteer, an English knight, a French fusilier, a Bengal sepoy, a Prussian jaeger, a Japanese pilot, a Marine rifleman, or an Egyptian military engineer. Each differed from one another in fundamental ways as they endured, triumphed, and perished. In their differences we find the substance of military history.

Notes on the Opening Illustration for the Preface

The resolute figure in this poster from the last months of World War I reminds his fellow Frenchmen that he defeated the Germans twice on the Marne in 1914 and 1918 and demands that his civilian comrades show the same firmness against the "Boche." He rises up out of the ground in tattered, decaying trench gear to represent both the fallen and those who fight on. Like the universal soldier, he is a generalized, faceless creation of the imagination that embodies the power and suffering of the warrior. But unlike any universal apparition, this haunting presence is definable in time and place: He is the son and soul of a defiant France.

(Library of Congress)

CHAPTER ONE

Written in Blood

The Classical Greek Drama of
Battle and the Western Way of War

PAGONDAS, THE THEBAN LEADER, urged the hearty Boeotian farmer-war-riors assembled at Tanagra to fight the Athenians, even though that hostile army had begun to withdraw back to Attica from Boeotia. Some days before, the Athenians, led by Hippocrates,[1] had trespassed into Boeotia and fortified Delium. Threatened by its powerful neighbor, Thebes and its Boeotian com-rades had allied with Sparta against Athens in this, the Peloponnesian War. Pagondas insisted that even though the Athenians were homeward bound now, the act of erecting a fortress and detailing a garrison at Delium could not be permitted. "So much more have we to fear from this neighbour than from another. . . . [M]en whose glory it is to be always ready to give battle for the liberty of their own country, and never unjustly to enslave that of others, will not let [the enemy] go without a struggle."[2] The Boeotians rallied to his argument, broke camp, took up their arms, and marched on the Athenians, reaching the enemy host near Delium late in the day. Little time remained before dark, but it was time enough to fight and die.

Brandishing their spears, encased in armor, and bearing their great round shields, or *aspides* (sing. *aspis*), the two opposing phalanxes first lumbered and then thundered toward each other. Many ranks deep, the two great walls of metal, flesh, and fury collided; iron spear points struck home through oak and bronze, shafts splintered, and shields ground against shields. As the two phalanxes drove into each other, these Greek warriors, hoplites, jabbed with their weapons and clawed with their hands; men stationed in the rear ranks put shoulder to shield and shoved forward, adding their might to the force of their comrades to the front. Those who stumbled or fell wounded in the crush had little chance on the ground, where they could be trampled in the press of men or dispatched where they lay by downward thrusts with the butts of spear shafts capped with a spike for this deadly purpose.

The Athenian right, fighting eight men deep, surrounded the Thespians on the left of the Boeotian phalanx and cut them down, but the Thebans, who marshaled "twenty-five shields deep" on the Boeotian right, drove the Athenians back. Seeing his left collapse, Pagondas dispatched a small cavalry force to support it, and when, in the heat, dust, and confusion, the Athenians believed this to be another army closing in on them, they broke and began to flee. The battle dissolved into pursued and pursuers. Knots of Athenians struggled against fear and exhaustion to maintain their order in retiring. One group gathered around a sturdy and resolute stonecutter, Socrates, who was "calmly contemplating enemies as well as friends, and making very intelligible to anybody, even a great way off, that whoever attacked him would be likely to meet with a stout resistance."[3] Socrates would virtually found European philosophy, but now he manifested pride in his weapons, not his words.

Like countless other clashes of rival Greek armies before it, the battle of Delium, 424 B.C., maximized the fury of battle in a brief but exceptionally costly drama that demanded the most of courage and endurance. The yeomen who fought and died in the phalanx defined a form of battle that purchased decision with blood.

It was a matter of choice. The men who stood in phalanx to defend their Greek city state, or polis, fought in a manner that they had decided was right and proper, as war was supposed to be. The Greeks set the terms of combat by conventions agreed to through a de facto consensus of the community of Greek poleis. No style of combat provides a stronger example of the way in which a discourse on war can set the terms for war's reality. As its first priority, this chapter will explore the influence of conception on the life-and-death matter of hoplite battle.

The second task will be to consider the influence of that convention-based combat on the conduct of war in the West during the succeeding millennia. In his provocative volumes, *The Western Way of War* and *Carnage and Culture,* the noted classical scholar Victor Davis Hanson maintains that the Greek manner of fighting established a pattern that has endured for 2,500 years in the West.[4] The implications of his thesis are profound. If it is correct, then a form of combat that appeared no later than the seventh century B.C. can explain the European conquest of the globe and the continued military pre-eminence of the West to the dawn of the twenty-first century. Hanson's thesis challenges us to examine what is essential and distinct about Western warfare, and we gain by the effort even should we ultimately find its bold conclusions wanting.

CLASSICAL GREEK WARFARE

During the Lyric Age, 800–500 B.C., the Greeks developed a distinct and decisive form of warfare. While the mountainous topography of Greece would seem to favor light armed troops who could exploit the rugged terrain for cover and concealment while plying bows, darts, and slings, this was not the case. Instead, Greeks fought as heavy infantry in tightly packed linear formations suited only for flat land, the agricultural valleys bounded by the rugged hills and mountains of Greece. Warfare focused on brief but bloody battles between armies composed primarily of yeoman farmers and artisans.

One argument traditionally employed to explain hoplite pitched battle insists that the Greeks fought in order to keep enemy forces from doing irreparable damage to the agricultural land of the polis. However, Hanson, an expert on Greek agriculture, rejects it, arguing that farming based on grapes, olives, and grains remained relatively immune to destruction.[5] Vines could only be eliminated by uprooting them, which required too much time and labor for a marauding army. The unusually robust olive tree was blessed with a very hard wood and quite often a wide girth that defied the axe. This left the possibility of torching an enemy's grain fields, yet grains were only susceptible to burning immediately before harvest, when they had dried from green to brown. Certainly crops could be burned, but yeoman farmers raiding the fields of a hostile polis just before the harvest had to be concerned with bringing in their own crop back home. Time would be limited.

For Hanson, agricultural raids did not compel pitched battles, but instead battle evolved as a matter of principle and, thus, of conceptual culture. "Infantrymen marched out not to save their livelihoods nor even their ancestral homes, but rather for an *idea:* that no enemy march uncontested through the plains of Greece, that in Themistocles' words, 'no man become inferior to, or give way, before another.'"[6] Battle grew out of the Greek sense of equality, independence, and intense civic and personal pride.

It should be mentioned that Hanson's conceptual explanation of Greek battle is highly controversial, and the older assertions that the classical Greeks were compelled not by some idealized notion of equality, but rather by the practical necessity of defending farms and crops, retains its proponents. This list includes a specialist on Thebes and its wars, John Buckler, who has criticized Hanson's work from the start.[7]

The Conventions of Greek Warfare

Traditional conventions circumscribed the fighting between Greek poleis (the plural of polis). It was essentially war by agreement in accord with the dominant discourse, as long as Greek fought Greek, although the rules did not apply when fighting non-Greeks. While no absolute list of conventions exists, quite a few protocols and limitations generally were observed.[8]

- War should be officially declared.
- Fighting should not take place at certain times, such as during sacred truces, as that for the Olympic games.
- Certain places and certain people should be exempt from violence, such as sacred sites, those who served the gods there, and heralds.
- Noncombatants should not be the primary targets of war.
- Adversaries must accept the verdict of battle, resolving the issue at stake.
- Battles should occur during the summer campaign season.

- Battle should be preceded by a ritual challenge and the acceptance of that challenge.
- The use of missile weapons, such as bows, in battle should be limited.
- Pursuit of the defeated by the victor after battle should be limited in duration.
- By constructing a trophy of arms on the battlefield the winners announce their victory.
- Enemy dead should be returned to the defeated, and requesting the return of the dead recognizes one's own defeat.
- Those who surrender should not be punished harshly.
- Prisoners should be offered for ransom, not summarily killed or mutilated.

Underlying all these conventions was the desire for decisive battle. In important respects, these conventions appealed to the needs and mentality of yeoman hoplites. Summer, the traditional time for Greek warfare, demanded that farmers not be gone from their own fields for long, so they could ill afford campaigns that dragged on for months. Fighting that might hold out the chance for lower casualty rates, such as hit-and-run skirmishes, would not resolve things soon. Battle settled affairs in an hour or two.

Conventions as to weapons are particularly interesting, as they fit the scheme of decisive combat. By limiting missile weapons such as bows and arrows, hoplites opted for weapons that inflicted the kind of fatal blows that won battles rather than those that were more likely to wound and wear down an enemy. In the first century A.D., the geographer Strabo reported seeing a pillar of great age that bore an inscription banning the use of missile weapons in war on the Lelantine Plain during the eighth century B.C.[9] Polybius noted that the Greeks "entered into a convention among themselves to use against each other neither secret missiles nor those discharged from a distance, and considered that it was only a hand-to-hand battle at close quarters which was truly decisive."[10] In fact, the convention concerning missile weapons may not have been absolute, but it placed such restrictions on the use of such arms that they could not compromise the clash of heavy infantry.

The highly ritualized contest between poleis followed the dictates of martial discourse. Both sides abided by a common code and fought as mirror images of each other. This similarity began with arms and armor and extended to all aspects of war.

Arms and Armor

The hoplite bore a heavy panoply of arms and armor, *hoplon*; current estimates of the weight of these range from forty to seventy pounds. The latter is about the maximum carrying capacity of a man at war.[11] He was heavy infantry in the literal sense of the word. His panoply weighed so much that the hoplite brought a servant or slave on campaign to help him carry the burden.

The key item of *hoplon* was the shield, or *aspis,* for it expressed the ultimate communal obligation of the phalanx warrior. The round *aspis,* about a yard in diameter, weighed perhaps sixteen pounds. Hard wood made up the body of the shield, although it might be covered with a skin of bronze. A hoplite carried his shield on his forearm, first slipping his arm through a broad ring in the center of the shield, the *porpax,* and then grasped a leather handhold near the rim, the *antilabe.* The form of the *aspis* was more that of a bowl than a disk. So concave was the interior of the shield that a hoplite could lever his shoulder under the lip of the shield either to take the weight off his forearm or to put his entire force behind the *aspis* when driving forward.

The *aspis* protected more than the hoplite who carried it, because it overlapped with others to form a shield wall that covered the front of the entire phalanx. In particular, the left portion of one man's *aspis* sheltered the right shoulder and arm of the hoplite standing to his left. Other parts of the panoply protected the individual hoplite, but in a sense, his *aspis* guarded his comrade and the phalanx as a whole, because a gap in the line could prove fatal in battle. Plutarch put it directly: "Men wear their helmets and breastplates for their own needs, but they carry their shields for the men of the entire line."[12] A hoplite who panicked might discard his shield to rid himself of its burden so that he could better flee the fighting. Greeks regarded casting aside the shield, *rhipsaspia,* as a form of cowardice; if done in the crush of battle, it practically amounted to treason. In carrying his *aspis* into battle and maintaining the shield wall, the hoplite expressed his dedication to family, community, and the polis itself. Thus, the well-known stern farewell of Spartan mothers to their sons: "Come back bearing your shield or on it."[13] Bringing back the shield meant one had fought bravely, not abandoning it in battle, and coming back on it meant that one had died fighting, because the concave shield was so large that a body could be wedged into its dish and carried as on a stretcher.

The personal armor of the hoplite also included helmet, greaves, and breastplate. Ancient Greek helmets of this time, particularly those of the

"Corinthian" design, encased the head in bronze. These helmets were so sculpted as to be virtually works of art. Eye openings allowed a limited field of vision, and cheek pieces wrapped around the face nearly completely, leaving only a narrow slit in the front for breathing. A lack of ear holes made hearing difficult. In the heat of a Greek summer, the helmet, weighing at least five pounds, must have been oppressive. In the same way that the helmet protected the warrior above his *aspis,* greaves guarded him below it, covering the shins from kneecap to ankle. Bronze possessed enough flexibility that the greaves could be bent and snapped into place, with a final squeeze for a tight fit.

The breastplate, or cuirasse, constituted the heaviest item of the hoplite's panoply; the upper estimate for the weight of this piece of armor ranges as high as forty pounds. With front and back plates lashed snugly together, the cuirasse completely encased the hoplite's upper torso. At the waist, the bronze flared out to keep the cuirasse from digging into the warrior's flesh; this flare gave the armor a slight bell shape, so we know it as the bell cuirasse. Hoplites donned the bronze cuirasse for centuries, but during the 400s B.C., this part of their bronze cocoon was lightened or replaced by quilted armor that allowed greater mobility. In this case, the *aspis* simply increased in importance, since it alone would be stout enough to stop deadly spear thrusts. As with the helmet, the bell cuirasse was stifling in hot weather, and it is clear that hoplites waited until the last minute to don their armor.

Hoplites relied on spears as their primary weapons. They regarded it as morally superior to close in with the spear than to shoot from a distance with the bow. The archer was seen as a coward and inferior to the hoplite, as Diomed charges in the *Iliad:* "Bowman, reviler, glorious in your curling locks, you ogler of girls! I wish you would make trial of me man to man in armor; then would your bow and your swift-falling arrows help you not."[14] To charge, spear in hand, implied the greatest courage. This weapon was not a light javelin meant to be thrown, but a more substantial weapon primarily intended to be grasped and thrust at the enemy. The wooden shaft, six to nine feet long, was only about an inch in diameter; thus, it might splinter on forceful impact. The broad iron spearhead, a large double-edged blade, narrowed to a menacing tip. A bronze spike capped the butt end of the spear; this could be used for downward thrusts to dispatch a fallen enemy. At the start of battle, as phalanx rushed toward phalanx, the front ranks might grasp their spears underhand to strike beneath the *aspis* at thighs or groin. With the impetus of the initial rush magnified by a strong arm, the iron spear point could penetrate or split an *aspis* and drive into the bell cuirasse, which provided relative, not absolute, protection. In the thick of the fight, the first three ranks of hoplites could ply their spears against the enemy. In the push of phalanxes, hoplites necessarily grasped their spears overhand, striking at exposed necks and the vulnerable openings in the helmet. Hoplites also carried iron swords as well, but they served as secondary weapons, to be drawn when spears shattered.

The hoplite's arms and armor prepared him for a vicious battle, but it would not allow him to go too far or fight too long. Carrying seventy pounds of wood, bronze, and iron, and confined in metal armor, even a hearty warrior fatigued quickly. Phalanx warfare suited the impatient hoplite, for victory or defeat, or death, came with little delay.

Hoplite Decisive Battle

Arms and armor fit the convention that armies would fight only on level ground, which, in ancient Europe's most mountainous country, is most extraordinary. The battle came as the final act to a scripted scenario. Greeks frowned on trick or deception. Invaders would cross into enemy territory during the summer and ravage farms and lands. In response, the beleaguered polis would send out its citizen muster of hoplites to face the invader in the field; siege warfare played a lesser role. Both sides would draw near each other on suitable ground. Each army afforded the other time to prepare for battle, as hoplites donned their cumbersome armor.

Hoplites marshaled in a thick, unbroken linear formation, the phalanx. Traditionally, they stood eight ranks deep, but circumstance or the lay of the land might require a different depth. A phalanx could stretch from hundreds of yards to over a mile, depending on the number of hoplites assembled. The commanding general had little to do but carry out certain religious preliminaries, speak to his troops before the charge, and then provide a potent example by fighting in the front rank.

The actual battle began with an advance by both the opposing phalanxes; this began at a walk, but finished at a run. The armored hoplite could endure a rush of perhaps 200 yards before becoming too exhausted to fight. As the lines advanced, each tended to slip to the right, as hoplites sought to protect themselves better by inching a bit more under the shields of their comrades. Thucydides reported: "All armies are alike in this: on going into action they get forced out rather on their right wing, and one and the other overlap with this the adversary's left: because fear makes each man do his best to shelter his unarmed side with the shield of the man next to him on the right, thinking that the closer the shields are locked together the better will he be protected."[15]

At the moment when the lines collided, the combatants delivered their most powerful blows, as momentum joined with arm strength to penetrate shields and armor. After the collision, the two phalanxes ground into each other in the push, or *othismos*. The opposing first ranks shoved into each other, impelled not only with their strength but by the rear ranks as well. This deadly scrum compressed the phalanx; men whose spears had shattered stabbed with swords or grabbed at one another with bare hands. To fall in this mêlée ensured injury or death. At some point one phalanx or the other gave way, and when an army started to break, the collapse came quickly. The victorious phalanx rushed forward to cut down those who had turned to run. Small groups of hoplites tried to ensure their retreat by maintaining some cohesion, although this effort limited the speed of their flight. Pursuit could continue with what cavalry forces were available. Casualties among the losing army could be heavy but were not usually crippling to the polis.

Hoplites fought in a manner as deadly and intense as Iron Age technology allowed. Deadly it was, but it asked only modest skill of the citizen militia, composed primarily of full-time farmers and artisans who were only occasional hoplites. The only exception to this pattern of amateur warriors comes from Sparta, where, by enslaving the Helots to do their agricultural labor, the Spartans freed themselves to devote all their efforts to training. Herodotus reports that foreigners found the Greek way of war incomprehensible; he portrayed Mardonius, the Persian commander, explaining the odd character of Greek combat to his king, Xerxes:

> And yet, I am told, these Greeks are wont to wage wars against one another in the most foolish way, through sheer perversity and doltishness. For no sooner is war proclaimed than they search out the smoothest and fairest plain that is to be found in all the land, and there they assemble and fight; when it comes to pass that even the conquerors depart with great loss: I say nothing of the conquered, for they are destroyed altogether.[16]

The key point is that by their sacrifice, the hoplites achieved decisive battle. But it is important to recognize that battle was decisive precisely because both sides agreed that it would be, that they would not challenge the result of that one great clash.

Citizenship and the Warrior Role

The Greek city state, or polis, based its defense on a citizen militia, composed of free men of moderate means. Over a thousand independent Greek poleis dotted Greece, the Aegean islands, and the Ionian coast, as well as Greek colonies around the Black Sea and the western and eastern Mediterranean. While some Greeks were far better off than others, poleis were not dominated by a small, monied elite. Around Athens, for example, there was no farm larger than one hundred acres.[17] The majority of hoplites were farmers of moderate means, joined by artisans and by men of greater wealth. They could not be poor, because they bore the substantial expense of supplying their own arms and armor. In general, hoplites constituted a substantial minority of the polis, on average 20–40 percent of the free adult male population.[18]

By the close of the Lyric Age, the hoplites had exerted the leverage afforded them by their warrior role to achieve citizenship, including the right to determine state policy in polis assemblies. Bronze Age Greece had been ruled by kings, as described in the works of Homer. The form of warfare then was individualistic, as opposed to the communal tactics of the phalanx. One spoke of great heroes, an Achilles or an Odysseus. After the decline and disintegration of Bronze Age Greece, about 1200–1100 B.C., we cannot reconstruct Greek history in detail. Among the skills lost in the Dark Age that followed was writing, so our record of events disappears until the Greeks begin to create literary monuments again in the Lyric Age. During the Dark Age, aristocratic government by a small elite of wealth and status replaced the monarchies. Kings might still exist, but as war or religious leaders, not as absolute rulers. Power had changed hands. During the Lyric Age, the phalanx style of warfare emerged, as all men carried the same weapons and were of essentially equal value as warriors. This military fact gave hoplites the logic and the leverage to gain political rights as a consequence of their military role. The government of the polis broadened to encompass all hoplites as participants. In Athens, the process that extended political participation to the hoplite militia is most associated with the well-born lawgiver Solon, who instituted constitutional reform in 594 B.C.

Men in the ranks enjoyed full political rights in a consensual government with a regular constitution that prescribed powers and practices. In this regular and restrained government, hoplites could both vote and hold office. Thus, hoplites had a voice in matters of war and peace, decisions that they must carry out. Their motivations derived from neither coercion nor hope for material reward but from their own civic values, based on the good of the community and their families.

Hoplite-based government produced not complete democracy but broad-based oligarchy—not one-man-one-vote but one-shield-one-vote. However, some historians misstate the case, as does John Keegan when he writes, "Democracy and pitched battle were, of course, two sides of the same coin."[19] Hoplite oligarchies may have granted much wider representation than had the aristocracies that preceded them, but they were not yet true democracies.

Reliance on a fleet, rather than an army, led coastal and island poleis to establish democracies that encompassed all free male citizens. This move to democracy followed very much the same logic that created hoplite oligarchies: Those who fought should have the right to vote. For land-based poleis dependent upon their militia armies for defense, this extended the franchise to those who stood in the phalanx. But for poleis that saw security in their galley fleets, all those who rowed deserved political rights. Ancient galleys were rowed by free men, not slaves, and because the naval value of an oarsman derived only from the strength of his body, rather than expensive personal armament, rowers could be poorer men. In Athens, the steps toward democracy, which limited the influence of the well-born and opened up offices to the lower classes of free men, came with constitutional restructuring designed by Cleisthenes in 508 and later reforms pursued by Pericles, who held office from 461 until his death in 429.

Among the testimonials to Athenian democracy, one of the most interesting flowed from the grudging pen of a disgruntled elitist known only as the Old Oligarch. He preferred government by society's betters but conceded that the role played by common men in the fleet justified their political rights:

> First I want to say this: there the poor and the people generally are right to have more than the highborn and wealthy for the reason that it is the people who man the ships and impart strength to the city . . . far more than the hoplites, the high born, and the good men. This being the case, it seems right for everyone to have a share in the magistracies, both allotted and elective, for anyone to be able to speak his mind if he wants to.[20]

Among the inland poleis, only Thebes evolved democracy, and it did so through a unique set of circumstances.

Greek democracy required direct participation, unlike today's popular governments that ask voters simply to choose representatives to act for them in legislative assemblies. In Athens, the best known of democratic poleis, a citizen attended the assembly personally in order to vote. Athenians also insisted that power be shared between economic and social classes, and that all take a hand by holding offices. Because election by vote would tend to select primarily the well-known, most offices were filled by lot. That is, those eligible to serve would scratch their names on pot shards, or ostraca, and put them in the container from which the winning lot would be drawn. In addition, so jealous were Athenians of their participatory democracy that they instituted a system to banish anyone who they believed threatened their government or their state. Citizens voted by again inscribing a name on a shard, and the individual whose name appeared on the most ostraca was "ostracized," sent away for ten years, after which he could return.

Classical Greeks tied political participation to military and naval service, citizenship to the warrior role. These were cultural choices made all the more imperative because of the hard character of Greek warfare. Greek conventions of battle did not imagine a restrained, less violent ideal, but rather constructed a kind of warfare that made tremendous demands on the individual. Such awesome burdens won for the hoplite, and eventually for the rower, full political rights. Consequently, the relationship between the discourse on war and the reality of war in classical Greece is of towering importance, for it explains the origin of our most cherished political ideal.

THE THESIS OF AN
ENDURING WESTERN WAY OF WAR

A discussion of Greek polis warfare in and of itself establishes certain basic tenets of this book: the role of culture in shaping combat, the secondary role of technology in determining military practice, and the strong relationship between military and civil culture. However, our consideration of classical combat cannot stop here, because hoplite battle has become the basis for a much broader thesis about the nature of Western warfare and its perseverance and influence. Victor Davis Hanson claims that the Greeks established parameters for warfare in the West that have endured for 2,500 years, and his theory has set the terms for considering war and culture today. He broached his ideas first in his *The Western Way of War,* arguing that the classical Greeks created a style of fighting based on shock infantry combat by armies intent on seeking battle to gain a rapid decision in war. Then he extended his theory in *Carnage and Culture* beyond combat style, to include the political, social, and intellectual context of Western armies. For him, this enduring mix of combat and culture explains the Western military dominance of the world. "This 2,500-year tradition explains not only why Western forces have overcome great odds to defeat their adversaries but also their uncanny ability to project power well beyond the shores of Europe and America."[21]

A book on war and culture written in the opening years of the twenty-first century cannot avoid Hanson's thesis, for it is the most intellectually grand theory on the subject currently circulating. He certainly has won adherents for his ambitious claims, including John Keegan and Geoffrey Parker. *Carnage and Culture* even hit the *New York Times* Extended Best Seller List. Notwithstanding such impressive supporters, this theory concerning the enduring influence of Greek warfare is full of gaps where it claims to see an unbroken record.

Defining the Western Way of War

In its mature form, as stated in *Carnage and Culture,* Hanson's Western Way of Warfare theory asserts a unique and continuous military culture that is dependent for much of its character on a societal and political culture that is equally unique and continuous. The conjunction of the two created "the singular lethality of Western culture at war in comparison to other traditions that grew up in Asia, Africa, and the Americas."[22] In short, it made "Europeans the most deadly soldiers in the history of civilization."[23]

The manner of fighting remains basic to the theory. The Greeks developed a style of heavy infantry battle that relied on shock combat, toe-to-toe, shield-to-shield, spear-to-spear. "Foot soldiers . . . who take and hold ground and fight face-to-face, are a uniquely Western specialty."[24] Classical Greeks "invented decisive infantry battle" and then passed on to their successors a strong resolve to actively seek battle, even though such fighting demanded a high cost in lives.[25] The Romans added the ideal of total war, which also ranks as "a particularly Western concept largely unfamiliar to the ritualistic fighting and emphasis on deception and attrition found outside Europe."[26] Romans also raised discipline to new levels of rigor and effectiveness. Such discipline, "very early on in Western culture . . . was institutionalized as staying in rank and obeying the orders of superior officers."[27] This was not slavish obedience, however; individualism and initiative were always part of the formula. "From the Greeks onward, Westerners have sought to distinguish moments of individual courage and obedience to leaders from a broader, more institutionalized bravery that derives from the harmony of discipline, training, and egalitarian values among men and officers."[28]

The effectiveness of Western warfare is linked to, and explained by, social, political, and cultural foundations summed up in the term "civic militarism." The Western soldier is the citizen of an ultimately consensual government. Hanson is most at home in the Greece of oligarchic or democratic poleis or in republican Rome, where voting citizens also stood to arms: "In the West those who fight demand political representation."[29] Greece started this political/military ideal, but Rome became far more inclusive, creating "the modern expansive idea of Western citizenship and the plutocratic values that thrive in a growing and free economy."[30] The constitutional protections of Western governments included freedoms of speech, action, and inquiry. He claims political freedom to be "an idea found nowhere outside the West."[31] Economic liberty is also essential to European military success, because, among other things, it ensured the flow of plentiful weaponry of high quality. Capitalism, which he argues began in Greece and remained the economic pattern in the West, stayed basic to the Western Way of War. Rational, scientific inquiry produced improved weaponry in a way other cultures could not and so provided the ever better blueprints that could then be produced by capitalist enterprise.

For Hanson it all flows together seamlessly: "Western civilization has given mankind the only economic system that works, a rationalist tradition that alone allows us material and technological progress, the sole political structure that ensures the freedom of the individual, a system of ethics and a religion that brings out the best in humankind—and the most lethal practice of arms conceivable."[32] In his review of *Carnage and Culture,* Edward Rothstein perceptively argues that what distinguishes this approach is its combining of "two visions of the West that have themselves been at war during the last 30 years: the celebration of the West for its democratic vision of human liberty, and the condemnation of the West for militarism and imperialism." Instead of seeing these as irreconcilable or incompatible, "Mr. Hanson argues that the reverse is true: they are inseparable. Democratic ideals have led to greater military power."[33]

Hanson's conception is so imposing that it is hard to know where to begin a critique. In order to cut to the heart of the matter, I will consider only some of the basics here, focusing on a short list of military and political elements: shock infantry combat, decisive battle, battle-seeking operations, and civic militarism. The thesis of a Western Way of War really cannot be maintained in its most fundamental assertions—the claim that it has maintained a continuity from the Greeks to the present day and its assertion that Western military practices are, in fact, unique.

Continuity?

It is easy to draw a direct line of continuity between the tactical and political traditions of classical Greece and those of republican Rome, but the line already begins to be less sure with imperial Rome. To claim that classical traditions then proceeded through the barbarian armies that defeated the western empire and survived in the various medieval European forces that followed is not at all convincing. And although there is no question that some details of ancient military practice were studied and revived during the Renaissance, they were adapted to the technological, social, and political context of early modern European armies. Breathing life back into the complete complex of the Western Way of War was beyond the alchemy of the age. The time would not be right for resurrecting the military and political principles of Greco-Roman warfare until the close of the eighteenth century.

The tactics of republican Rome evolved from those of the phalanx, which seems to have been the initial Roman style of combat. Over centuries the very different methods of the legions emerged. In its highest form, legionary tactics relied upon the short sword wielded by superbly trained and drilled troops fighting in formations that were more articulated and adaptable than the phalanx. For most of the republican period, 509–527 B.C., legionaries were citizen soldiers, a militia called out in wartime and quickly returned to civilian life when not on campaign. This is sanctified in the legend of Lucius Quinctius Cincinnatus, the Roman general who left his plow to lead armies against Rome's enemies, and then put down his considerable authority to return to his farm to finish planting his crops. Roman society was less egalitarian than the Greek polis, yet over the years, common Roman legionaries extended their political rights through appeal to their role as defenders of the people and the state. The Romans also exercised their political genius by expanding Roman citizenship to wider and wider sectors of people, not only in Rome but in Italy and eventually the Mediterranean world. Hanson's paradigm holds both as to combat and civic militarism in the case of republican Rome.

The evolved legionary style of fighting survived and thrived as it passed from the republic to the empire, but the nature of civic militarism was not so robust. Late in the republic, ca. 100 B.C., the demands of foreign wars became so great that the Roman army ceased to be a citizen militia and became a professional mercenary force. Farmers and artisans could not afford to be away from their livelihoods for the periods of time necessary to fight enemies far from home, so Rome raised its forces by enlisting paid volunteers who willingly became long-service professionals. Such men made effective troops, but they fought for themselves and their generals, and in doing so fueled the Roman civil wars that undermined the republic and led to its demise. A professional army linked to the state no longer by civic militarism but rather by self-interest was a legacy of the republic to the empire. Emperors had above all to command the army's loyalty, and most were successful generals. Early in the empire, emperors ruled through the army, but later the army ruled through the emperors. At its worst, the era of the Barracks Emperors brought a series of wars fought by rival generals at the head of their mercenary legions and gave Rome twenty-two emperors in fifty years, A.D. 235–285. This period of turmoil gravely wounded the empire and so weakened it that it began to succumb to a series of barbarian invasions within a century.

The Germanic peoples that swept into the western half of the Roman Empire after the victory of the Visigoths at the battle of Adrianople (A.D. 378) and continuing through the sixth century were not of one kind. Some, like the Goths, came out of the steppes and fought on horseback; some, like the Franks, came down from the northern forests and fought on foot. They brought with them different social and political traditions. Some leaders would ape the trappings of Roman rule, and their peoples would eventually mix with original populations, but the old practices and institutions of the Roman Empire either disappeared rapidly or eroded with the generations. Tribal societies may have been roughly egalitarian and governed by custom, but to see in them a continuation of Greek and Roman republican consensual government is dubious.

Instead of developing his continuity with care and evidence, Hanson offers his readers bold but debatable claims. Consider this sweeping assertion of continued allegiance to civic militarism:

> With the transition to empire and Rome's subsequent collapse . . . republicanism for a time would all but disappear from Europe. Western armies would at times become every bit as mercenary as their adversaries and often in some areas as tribal. Nevertheless, the idea of a voting citizen as warrior and the tradition of an entire culture freely taking the field of battle under constitutional directive with elected generals were too entrenched to be entirely forgotten.[34]

He apparently is willing here to admit discontinuity while papering it over with a promissory note assuring us that the West would get back to civic militarism at some unspecified time in the future.

Advancing to the High and Late Middle Ages, military and political institutions further deny a continuity in the conduct of war and civic militarism. It is difficult to square an infantry-based ideal with the importance of cavalry in the Middle Ages. Heavy aristocratic cavalry, knights, dominated the imagination of medieval warfare, at least from the Norman Conquest of England. It may be debated if they equally towered over the battlefield itself, but they certainly played a central role on campaign. Keegan tries to make knights seem like Greeks by pointing to their bravery in shock combat, "a continuation, in an elaborated form, of the code of the phalanx fighter,"[35] but it is pounding a round peg into a square hole to force a mounted medieval aristocrat into the pattern of a classical citizen hoplite on foot. Medieval battles mixed cavalry and infantry in different combinations, but the old offensive, close-order shock infantry tactics were hard to find. Some urban militias used them as did Swiss pike squares, but these were responses to the military realities of the times, not primarily the result of studying Greek precedent. In any case, they were not the rule. In the Hundred Years' War, for example, it is hard to find the phalanx or the legion, even in instances when most of the fighting was done on foot, as at the battle of Agincourt.

Feudal armies were made up of aristocratic heavy cavalry serving a fixed period of days in compensation for the land they held from their lords. To this would be added some paid mercenaries and peasant levies composed of serfs. This was not a mix of citizen soldiers. Even when monarchs grew rich enough to hire more mercenaries and rely less on feudal obligations, that did not increase the level of civic militarism. Only toward the end of the Middle Ages did regular representative institutions emerge to rule with European monarchs, but such assemblies as the English Parliament or the French Estates General were hardly egalitarian assemblies but rather bodies created and maintained either to extend the authority of the king or to assert the rights of the privileged elites. They might later evolve into democratic legislatures, but they were hardly that in the Middle Ages.

When we reach the age of the Renaissance, Hanson may take some comfort in the conscious attempt to copy classical military methods. There is no question that European military reformers looked to classical examples as inspiration and guides, in something we might fairly call a military Renaissance. Francis I of France wanted to re-create legions but failed.

Dutch reformers of the House of Nassau, particularly Maurice, incorporated classical solutions to modern problems—drilling troops, marching in
step, and employing the Roman countermarch to systematize the firing of
arquebuses and muskets in combat. Maurice even borrowed his checkerboard formation for Dutch battalions from Roman example.[36] I am prone to
analyze these changes as refinements in a military system that evolved step
by step from late medieval precedents and from the introduction of firearms
and artillery.[37] Nevertheless, classic-inspired reforms were important. But
even if we grant a classical revival of sorts in tactics, there are two other matters that forestall claims of a persistent Western Way of War: Military operations were usually battle-averse, and a return to civic militarism was still in
the future.

The Western Way of War posits more than close-order infantry tactics.
Campaigns are supposed to be battle-centered, with commanders seeking
quick decisive clashes as the preferred method of combat. Hanson identifies
this as the "Western notion of seeking out the enemy without deception, to
engage in bitter shock action."[38] However this may have typified the Greeks,
it was not standard medieval or early modern fare. During the High Middle
Ages, armies were more likely to avoid than to seek a confrontation in the
open field. It is a truism that battles were relatively rare during the medieval
period, and raiding and sieges were the rule. Battle-averse armies typified the
early modern period as well. Sixteenth-century *condottieri,* Italian mercenary
commanders, Paolo Vitelli and Prospero Colonna, hardly stressed battle, arguing that "wars are won rather by industry and cunning than by the clash of
arms."[39] Armies of the late seventeenth and eighteenth centuries may have
formed up their infantry in ways that looked classical, but they clashed comparatively rarely, and when they did, battles were anything but decisive.
Admittedly the frequency of battle varied from theater to theater on the
Continent, but in the cockpit of Europe, the Netherlands, the Rhineland, and
northern Italy, sieges dominated, and wars dragged on for years. As Roger
Boyle, first earl of Orrery, put it, "We make war more like foxes, than like
lyons; and you will have twenty sieges for one battell."[40] Armies fought battles
when it was advantageous to do so, or when compelled; these were not Greeks
who marched right at the enemy and fought furiously by agreement. In contradiction to such aggressive operations, Louis XIV once instructed Marshal
Luxembourg to avoid infantry battles because they were costly but not decisive.[41] Occasionally, commanders such as Frederick the Great saw their salvation in battle, but the full battle-seeking pattern of the Western Way only

returned to Europe with Napoleon and became enshrined in military literature by Clausewitz.

Interestingly enough this coincides with the return of civic militarism. Continental Europe would only see the reemergence of the enfranchised citizen soldier with the French Revolution. Until then, Europe was ruled by monarchs born to their thrones and who usually strove to increase their authority limited mainly by a hereditary aristocracy. Intellectuals might praise the Greeks and Romans while dreaming of representative government, but it was a long way from dreams to reality. The ideal of "a voting citizen as warrior and the tradition of an entire culture freely taking the field of battle under constitutional directive" was not truly realized until the Declaration of the Levée en masse of 1793. In it, the freely elected representatives of the French people declared: "From this moment until the enemy has been chased from the territory of the Republic, all the French are in permanent requisition for the service of the armies."[42] Historians have long summed up the transition in warfare at this time as going from limited war fought by kings to total war fought by peoples. In fact, Hanson's mature theory, with its complex of elements, works best when one jumps from the late Roman republic to the nineteenth century. From Marius to Robespierre is a gap of nearly 1,900 years in a claimed continuity of 2,500 years, making it no continuity at all. Even if we credit the Roman Empire with civic militarism, which seems to be wrong, the hole would gape for 1,400 years or more.

Asian Contrast?

Arguments that there were no real non-Western parallels for Western military practices result all too much from our ignorance of non-Western warfare. We know precious little about the facts of South Asian military history before the arrival of the Islamic invaders. We know more about ancient China, but that understanding does not rival our command of Greek and Roman military history. Still, what we do know suggests that proponents of the Western Way of Warfare overstate the differences and may well be flat wrong. For example, Hanson sees discipline and drill as a defining characteristic of Western armies, but during the Warring States Period (403–221 B.C.), rival Chinese rulers formed huge disciplined armies of conscripted peasant landholders. Discipline is a great advantage to any large military force, and there is no reason to believe that discipline was any less important in ancient Chinese armies than it was in medieval European hosts.

Comparison with China points to another dubious aspect of Hanson's theory: his claims for Western capitalism. During the Warring States Period, single states could have fielded as many as 600,000 troops, and there were several contending states at one time.[43] We do not know for a fact, but it seems likely that Vedic India also mobilized large infantry armies. The Mughal Emperor Aurangzeb is supposed to have campaigned with an army of several hundreds of thousands ca. 1700. Hanson believes only Western capitalism could produce enough effective arms for great armies. Clearly the Chinese and Indians turned out sufficient arms and armor for great numbers of soldiers. We cannot exactly measure their quality, but we know that East Asian elite arms could be truly excellent—consider the swords carried by samurai. We also know that Chinese technology was sophisticated. For example, the West developed great seagoing vessels, but so did the Chinese. And Chinese junks boasted the most efficient of sails and hulls divided into watertight compartments.

Fundamental contrasts between Western and "Oriental" military cultures and styles of warfare are most boldly drawn by John Keegan, who asserts: "Oriental warmaking, . . . as something different and apart from European warfare, is characterized by traits peculiar to itself. Foremost among them are evasion, delay and indirectness."[44] Tactically, this kind of combat avoided direct confrontation, wore down the enemy, and only closed for the kill.[45] Keegan argues that the forms of war based on massed horse archers, most notably the horse peoples of the Central Asian steppes, best typify this "Oriental warmaking." Among other criticisms that can be leveled against Keegan's definition of "Oriental" combat, one could reply that such warriors did not constitute the main forces of Chinese or South Asian armies for much of their history, as will be seen in Chapter 2. In fact, it is doing injury to history to posit a single dominant "Oriental" way of war or to see its characteristics as uniquely "Oriental." In fact, Western military practice often followed Keegan's characterization of "Oriental" warmaking. Military cultures are far more varied than Keegan's dichotomy allows.

European Success and Asian Failure?

One test of the truth of the thesis of a Western Way of War might be to tally Western victory and defeat, for, according to its proponents, this form of warfare bestowed great lethal advantages upon Europeans and their descendants. "Ultimately," Hanson points out, "wars are best decided by men who approach each other face-to-face, stab, strike, or shoot at close range, and physically drive the enemy from the battlefield."[46] If the Greeks alone created this form of battle, the non-West never mastered it, and the West enjoyed a continuity of 2,500 years with it, should not the West have enjoyed an amazing string of successes?

There is no doubt that the Romans were world-class conquerors, as much because they held what they took as because they took so much, but after them the military record of the West is not all that impressive. The Romans lost their empire in the western Mediterranean to a series of Germanic invasions after A.D. 378. Around 450 the Huns swept in, another horse people of the steppes. They were beaten back, but in general Western Europe would suffer from a series of armed migrations, invasions, and raids for over 600 years. After Germans and Huns, Avars and Magyars attacked from the east; Muslims of various loyalties swept up from North Africa and the Mediterranean itself; and Vikings, then pagans outside the Western Christian sphere, raided and invaded by sea from the north. Muslims took Spain, and Christians only reconquered the last of it in 1492. Vikings grabbed large parts of England (the Danelaw) and France (Normandy). The Western Europeans may have held on, but only after losing territory. Were they possessed of a greatly superior form of warfare, they should have been able to do more than simply hunker down.

Europeans seized the offensive again with the Crusades, but not for long. The First Crusade (1096–1099) reacted to the conquests of the Seljuk Turks in the Near East and succeeded in taking Antioch and Jerusalem and in setting up a series of Catholic states in the Holy Land. The Second Crusade (1147–1149) was a total disaster, with several Christian armies defeated or utterly wiped out by Turks. Then, led by the strong and capable Kurd Saladin, Muslim forces retook Jerusalem (1187). The Third Crusade (1189–1192) took Acre and won the battle of Arsouf but failed to recapture Jerusalem. The Crusader states continued to dwindle, eventually falling to Egyptians, who took Antioch in 1268, leaving but a few scattered holdings in Christian hands. Europeans occupied Jerusalem for only 90 years and Antioch 170. Even employing the vaunted Western Way of War, the Crusader states fell to Turks, Mongols, and Mamelukes.

Ottoman Turks established themselves in Anatolia in the thirteenth and fourteenth centuries and then swept into the Balkans, eventually taking Greece. Constantinople fell to the Ottomans in 1453, eliminating the last of the Christian Byzantine Empire. Ottomans would reach and besiege Vienna in 1529 and 1683. Europeans reconquered much of what the Ottomans had taken in Europe, but only after a good deal of time. Greece, the birthplace of the Western Way, only became an independent state in 1829–1830.

Of course, Spain, Portugal, England, France, and the Netherlands enjoyed considerable success in colonial expansion after 1500. This success was immediately most apparent in the Americas, where the Spanish laid low great pre-Columbian nations, above all the Aztecs and the Incas. Their destruction was truly phenomenal, a product of amazing leadership, armed force, and disease. It is worth remembering, however, that Native Americans possessed only Stone Age technologies, particularly in weaponry, and in what is now the United States and Canada, the native population was rather thin on the ground.

Europeans were notably less successful in mainland Asia. Consider the fate of India as discussed in Chapter 5 of *Battle*. Western triumph came initially only at sea, where Europeans took control early; for example, the Portuguese naval victory at Diu in 1509 established European naval preeminence in the Indian Ocean. However, for centuries, European presence on land amounted to no more than trading outposts perched on the coasts. When Europeans ventured inland, as in 1686–1688 when the English first tried to take parts of Bengal, they met defeat. The Western Way of War may have provided victories for small numbers of Europeans against great empires in the Americas, but not in South Asia. It would not be until after 1740 that the British began an impressive conquest of South Asian states, and then only after enlisting native South Asian troops, which may have employed European tactics but were not inspired by civic militarism.

In fact, for most of human history, the greatest conquerors were not Western at all but came out of Central Asia. They typified Keegan's "Oriental" warmaking, which he regards as inferior to the Western Way. Nomadic Parthians from south central Asia took Persia in the third century A.D., bedeviling the Romans with their horse archers—and the famous Parthian shot. Western Europe experienced the Mongol onslaught as early as the mid-fifth century, when Attila led the Huns into Europe. Other Mongol raiders, the Avars and the Magyars, broke into eastern Europe in the sixth and the ninth centuries respectively. Turkish peoples who at times fled or fought alongside the Mongols rode in the eleventh century into the Near East to stay. These Seljuk Turks were eventually defeated, only to be replaced by Ottoman Turks. Meanwhile, Turkish Ghaznis struck down into Afghanistan and raided India in the eleventh century, where they were later defeated by Ghurids who founded the Delhi Sultanate in the early thirteenth century.

Genghis Khan (1162?–1227) united the tribes of Mongolia and began to expand their domain; after his death, his grandson, Kublai Khan (1215–1294), conquered China and set up the Yuan dynasty. The historian of China John K. Fairbank calls the period from about the fourth to the fourteenth centuries the "millennium of the mounted archer," which he argues peaked with "the Mongol conquests of Persia, South Russia, and China."[47] To that list I would add South Asia. Tamerlane (1336–1405) terrorized much of the known world from Russia in the north to Persia and India in the south. A direct descendant of Genghis Khan and Tamerlane, Babur (1483–1530) brought his cavalry army to India and defeated the Delhi Sultanate at the battle of Panipat in 1526 to establish the Mughal Empire, which survived until its remnants fell to the British in the eighteenth century. Mongols and Turks were the horse archers of Keegan's "Oriental" warfare, and they represented the most successful military tradition in history, measured by the span of the globe that they dominated before the modern era.

Thus, any confident assertion of inherent Western advantages in land warfare deserves to be reevaluated and reinterpreted. In military terms, the West experienced hard times from the decline of the Roman Empire until the American conquests of the sixteenth century at least. Naval, not land, warfare was the real forte of the Europeans until they began their run of Asian and African land conquests in the eighteenth and nineteenth centuries. On land, Western warfare experienced a hiatus in forms and in success from the end of the Roman Empire until the mid-eighteenth century, with the only major exceptions being the triumph of the First Crusade and the amazing conquests in Mexico and South America by the likes of Cortéz and Pizarro. These are certainly notable conquests but not ones that undermine the concept of a hiatus in Western success in land battle.

CLASSICAL MILITARY LITERATURE: VEGETIUS

Denying the continuity of a Western Way of War does not rule out the endurance of elements of the classical tradition, and the most important of these was the constant availability of military literature from ancient Greece and Rome. However, this literature did not necessarily act as an agent of a Western Way of War. No ancient European text was more important than *De re militari,* written by Flavius Vegetius Renatus in the late fourth century A.D. It was perhaps the most influential military volume in the West until *On War* by Clausewitz.[48] This volume was more than the work of one author, for it

compiled the wisdom of several previous military authorities, including Cato
the Censor, Cornelius Celsus, Frontius, Praternus, Julius Caesar, Augustus,
Trajan, and Hadrian. It thus represented a body of knowledge going back for
centuries. Vegetius's magnum opus was widely read in the Middle Ages; it
appeared in the library of Duke Evrard of Friuli during the ninth century, was
read by the great knight William the Marshal in the twelfth, and was owned
by Sir John Fastolf in the fifteenth.[49] It is worth noting that in the medieval
and modern eras, Western military readers turned more to Rome than Greece
for examples. It is equally true that medieval readers approached that ultimate
Roman spokesman, Vegetius, in their own way; some editions were titled as
handbooks on chivalry. They could read there about courage and hardiness—
"Valor," he informed them, "is superior to numbers"[50]—and they could take
lessons from him about prowess and deception in warfare. However, it was
one thing to read about classical militaries and another to resuscitate them.
Because it was such a different cultural, social, political, and military environment, medieval Europe really could not create a Greek phalanx or a Roman
legion.

With the Renaissance of the late fifteenth and early sixteenth centuries,
classical texts from the arts to philosophy to history became more important
in European cultural life. And, as already mentioned, Vegetius and other classical authors inspired military reformers. The reference to classical texts as the
source for practical reform justifies the claim for a military Renaissance, an
attempt within that great intellectual movement to learn and apply classical
precedent to armies as others had applied it to architecture.

It is important, however, to note that *De re militari* did not simply trans-
mit the Western Way of War in the Renaissance or later. For example, Vegetius
did not preach a battle-hungry style of warfare with a penchant for decisive
battle. He did declare that "a battle is commonly decided in two or three
hours, after which no further hopes are left for the worsted army." But he then
immediately cautions against it: "Every plan, therefore, is to be considered,
every expedient tried and every method taken before matters are brought to
this last extremity. Good officers decline general engagements where the danger is common, and prefer the employment of stratagem and finesse to destroy
the enemy as much as possible in detail and intimidate them without expos-
ing our own forces."[51] Battle, or a general action, is to be avoided if possible
because of its cost and risk: "fortune has often a greater share than valor."[52]
Skilled generals find other ways of defeating an enemy: "Good generals never
engage in a general action unless induced by opportunity or obliged by neces-

sity."[53] Rather than leading an army into combat, sword in hand, "To distress the enemy more by famine than the sword is the mark of consummate skill."[54]

Vegetius carried a message to those conducting campaigns, but it was more that of the fox than of the phalanx. Early modern military commentators of the seventeenth and eighteenth centuries, such as Puységur and de Saxe, would echo Vegetius's sense of battle as a theater of loss and risk that should be eschewed by the able general. It was better to win by other means that a commander could manipulate and control by his intelligence and skill. Using military literature alone, one could argue that maneuver, attrition, and avoidance of pitched battle was quite common in the Western tradition and not simply an attribute of "Oriental" warmaking.

CONCLUSION: SOCRATES IN THE RANKS

Greek hoplite warfare highlights the influence of discourse in imagining and designing battle. The Greeks opted to fight as they did; in the last analysis, they made cultural choices over other alternatives. When Mardonius explains the seeming insanity of Greek warfare he comments:

> Now surely, as they are all of one speech, they ought to interchange heralds and messengers, and make up their differences by any means rather than battle; or, at the worst, if they must needs fight one against the another, they ought to post themselves as strongly as possible, and so try their quarrels.[55]

City walls might also have held off the enemy and made war too lengthy or costly for the attacker, posing a powerful deterrent. But this is not what the Greeks resolved to do. They were moved by a sense of moral outrage that their homes and ancestral lands were being violated, and even more by a keen sense of individual worth and independence. Battle became a consequence of values rather than necessity.

However, claims that a Western Way of Warfare extended with integrity for 2,500 years speak more of fantasy than fact. No overarching theory can encompass the totality of Western combat and culture. This is a varied and rich treasury of discourse and reality to be unearthed at many places on maps of space and time.

But even if a Western Way of War does not bind together the European experience by a continuous filament, Greek and Roman precedent has provided us with ideas, myths, and a vocabulary of war. Heroism, for example, is often dressed in classical attire. Achilles, Hector, the Spartans at Thermopylae, Horatius at the bridge—all represented heroic martial values. This powered imagination and emulation when further buttressed by more recent and immediate examples. Not surprisingly, the symbol of the United States Military Academy at West Point is a Greek Corinthian helmet. Classical example even penetrated to popular culture. The eighteenth-century military tune, still a much-heard march today, "The British Grenadiers," begins, "Some talk of Alexander and some of Hercules,/ of Hector and Lysander and such brave men as these."[56] Schools still christen their athletic teams "Spartans"; the British called one of their most successful tank designs the "Centurion." Societies require heroic myths, and the West still clings to those of the classical past as significant elements of Western military culture.

Perhaps the most important of these heroic paragons is the citizen soldier. The citizen militias of classical Greece and republican Rome stand as ideals, although history did not give those ideals an unbroken path to the present. Professional Roman legionaries, Germanic tribal levies, mounted medieval aristocrats, and disenfranchised mercenaries of early modern Europe had little in common with the yeoman hoplites of the phalanx. Only at the end of the eighteenth century did revolutionary transformations resurrect true citizen soldiers. Then the references abound. American officers form the Society of the Cincinnati in memory of the Roman general who returned to his plow. François Rude's sculptural group known as *La Marseillaise* on the Arc de Triomphe portrays the departure of the volunteers of 1792 for the front as the resolute march of an ancient militia, clad in Greek and Roman armor not in the actual uniforms of the French Revolution.

One supposition concerning the citizen soldier remains the notion that the freedom of a society must be maintained by the commitment of the common people to take up arms in their own defense. In the citizen militia, morality and responsibility meet in an ideal of civic virtue. Only in such an environment could the individual achieve his or her highest potential. Hanson praises the Greek polis for creating "a culture that could produce warrior-intellectuals."[57] This point helps explain one of the more startling observations by the great nineteenth-century art critic John Ruskin: "No great art ever yet arose on earth but among a nation of soldiers."[58] There should be no surprise then that Socrates stood in the ranks at Delium or that the dramatist Aeschylus chose to be remembered on his tombstone not for his plays but for the fact that he had fought at Marathon.[59] The link between philosophy, art, and combat is also part of the ever-present legacy of Greek warfare in the Western military tradition.

Notes on the Opening Illustration for Chapter One

This seventh-century B.C. Corinthian vase provides our earliest image of a classic Greek phalanx. Two rival forces approach; the heavily armored hoplites overlap their shields to form a wall as they raise their spears to thrust at their adversaries. A musician plays to pace the advance and raise the spirits of the embattled hoplites.

(Copyright Scala/Art Resource, NY)

CHAPTER TWO

Subtleties of Violence

Ancient Chinese and Indian Texts on Warfare

THE TIME WAS NOT PROPITIOUS for battle at Chi-fu. Being the last day of the lunar calendar, Chinese armies would usually remain immobile, fearing the inauspicious balance between yin and yang. But the brilliant Wu general Ho-lü realized that, greatly outnumbered as he was by the Ch'u army before him, he must use surprise to defeat his enemy. Because his enemy would expect a quiet day, Ho-lü decided to attack the Ch'u that morning in 519 B.C.[1]

Months earlier, threatened as they were by the growing power of the state of Ch'u, Liao, king of Wu, and his great general had decided to strike first, driving into Ch'u territory and besieging Chou-lai. Ch'u marshaled a large host to oppose this invasion; not only did it send out its own sizeable forces, but it also bullied six small allied kingdoms to dispatch their armies. But as the polyglot Ch'u force gathered at Chi-fu to relieve the siege of Chou-lai, things went badly for them. Their commander died, leaving the army in disarray, and when Ho-lü learned of this he sprang to take advantage of the opportunity. He abandoned the siege and shuttled as many forces as he could by river toward the enemy, but he could not match the Ch'u numbers. Still he appreciated that his army was united, whereas the Ch'u forces were not. Moreover, the enemy's spirit, or *ch'i*, was shaken, but that of the Wu army was strong and aggressive.

On the day of the battle, the large Ch'u army stayed in its encampment, which was covered by the six smaller allied armies stationed facing the Wu adversaries. Ho-lü concentrated on the three allied forces that held the center of the enemy line. Against these, he prepared a great ambush—his infantry and what chariots he could muster formed a three-sided square with the open face toward the enemy. The terrain disguised this deployment, a valley of death for any who entered. He then ordered a body of 3,000 ill-trained and expendable convict-troops to bait the trap by attacking the enemy line. As expected, Ho-lü's convict unit broke and fled back toward the main Wu dispositions. Flushed with their initial success, the Ch'u allies raced forward, losing their cohesion and order in the process. As they streamed into the killing zone, Wu troops cut them down. Soon, Ho-lü captured the three rulers of the allied states, and ordered them immediately executed at the head of his army in full view of the enemy. Seeing their kings beheaded multiplied the panic that swept the survivors back into the Ch'u encampment. Wu forces now charged, the center driving forward as the two flanks enveloped the Ch'u. Victory was complete.

A few years after the victory at Chi-fu, a stranger appeared at the Wu court; he would be remembered as Sun-tzu, whose great work *Art of War* ranks as the most honored of Chinese military classics. Sun-tzu at first advised King Liao, but when Ho-lü turned against Liao, killed him, and took his throne, Sun-tzu counseled the new ruler as well. The military wisdom of Sun-tzu would be valued and preserved not because he was the first great military mind of China but because the Chinese already boasted a rich military and intellectual tradition with sophistication enough to appreciate the genius of *Art of War*.

Chinese battle in the sixth century B.C. did not resemble the collision of polis phalanxes in Greece. To understand the range of warfare better, even its Western tradition, we must span continents to gain perspective. This chapter discusses military practice and thought in China and South Asia during a period roughly contemporary with classical Greece. A comparative approach promises two rewards. First, looking at several peoples and locales with roughly the same technologies emphasizes the differences imposed by conceptual culture. Second, case studies of China and South Asia demonstrate their contrast not only with Greece but also with each other, and thus undermine any simple concept of an "Oriental" way of war.

In the preceding chapter, we examined the highly conventionalized style of polis warfare; the discussion emphasized the reality of combat and the strong influence exerted upon it by the classical Greek discourse on war. The great variety of sources available concerning Greece allowed us to examine the interplay of discourse and reality. However, in discussing classical China and South Asia we are more restricted by the character of the historical accounts. We still lack a rich modern literature on the history of war in ancient Asia, and, more importantly, original source material is limited in quantity and biased in character. It is possible to sketch the reality of war to some degree, but the great bulk of material that has come down to us reveals conceptual culture rather than the actual details of combat. Ancient China produced an unsurpassed body of military theory and counsel, the crown jewel of which, Sun-tzu's *Art of War,* is widely read today. The legacy of ancient India lacks as extensive a professional military discussion, but important conceptual information can be gleaned from religious and literary texts. In addition, we can consider the *Manusmrti,* or book of laws of Manu, and the *Arthashastra,* ancient South Asia's major political text, both of which say a good deal about South Asian ideas concerning war. Accepting the nature of the sources, this chapter focuses on conception more than did Chapter 1.

The scarcity of material useful for reconstructing the reality of war and the abundance of texts valuable for elaborating the discourse challenge us to be careful and discriminating. Inevitably in such a situation, one calls upon the literature of discourse to flesh out the reality of combat, to fill in gaps in our knowledge left by the lack of other evidence. This promises to be a case study in the complexities and limitations of using prescriptive writings to establish how people actually behaved. These problems while particularly apparent when discussing Chinese and South Asian cultures are to a large extent universal.

The military thought revealed in texts from ancient China and South Asia is subtle in many senses of the word. Chinese classics exemplify subtlety in that they discuss the conduct of war by employing suggestive metaphors rather than direct maxims. Open to interpretation, the discussion fosters consideration rather than compliance. Chinese texts stress a subtlety on campaign, strongly advising generals to avoid the obvious and the direct and to adopt the veiled and the indirect. Such tactics expedite victory, husband resources, and save lives. Subtlety in the South Asian case carries greater connotations of being devious. The *Arthashastra* advocates assassination and subversion as superior to battle. We benefit much by turning to these Asian subtleties, for they represent a form of warfare intent on achieving objectives at minimum cost, a sensible concern of modern statesmen and war planners.

CHINA

China, a land of 1.3 billion today, was great in population and civilization in ancient times as well. The ancient Chinese achieved unity only in 221 B.C., by which time they already had a long and turbulent history. As a collage of kingdoms appeared, grew, declined, and disappeared, ancient China came to know war well. We are aware of this turbulent history, at least in outline, because the Chinese recorded their past. Historical annals, biographies, and chronologies have come down through the ages, along with works of religion, philosophy, and poetry, to say nothing of the rich literature on warfare. It is true that all these sources may mix the apocryphal and anachronistic with the authentic, but they still provide essential background when read carefully.

The epochs of Chinese history that most concern this chapter occurred from the sixth century B.C. through the second century A.D, but we should situate our discussion in the longer run of Chinese history as well. The earliest state for which we have good evidence was the Shang, ca. 1600–ca. 1050 B.C. The Shang state did not control a great deal of China, but its influence extended beyond its actual domain. In addition to being political and military leaders, Shang kings served as religious authorities in a religion that involved human sacrifice on a large scale. Under the Shang, bronze metalworking reached a high level as displayed in artwork and weaponry. The Western Chou (ca. 1050–770 B.C.) defeated the Shang and brought together northern China. A landed military aristocracy topped society during this era, when the state was not yet highly bureaucratic.

Control by the Western Chou eventually waned, yielding to political fragmentation and struggle, beginning with the essentially feudal Spring and Autumn Period (770–481 B.C.). Divided into as many as 150 small states, China witnessed an endless series of wars which continually consolidated this jumble into fewer and more powerful rivals. This process continued through the Period of the Warring States (403–221 B.C.), during which perhaps 110 states ceased to exist in the winnowing process.[2] Military forces grew immensely and changed in composition as rulers devoted their primary efforts to warfare.

Ultimately, the Ch'in defeated their adversaries and unified China, giving the country its name. From this point on, historians speak of imperial China. The period of Ch'in rule lasted but a few years, 221–206 B.C., but the Han dynasty soon triumphed and ruled over a united China for four centuries (202 B.C.–A.D. 220). Historians generally divide this last into two periods, the Former, or Western, Han (202 B.C.–A.D. 8) and the Later, or Eastern, Han (A.D. 23–220).

The Clash of Wen *and* Wu

An overarching struggle in Chinese history and historiography goes beyond battles between particular armies or states—it is a clash between principles. Those who praise the Chinese are apt to claim that *wen,* civilization or culture, triumphed over the *wu,* war and force. Some go so far as to speak of a dominant pacifistic strain in Chinese history, in contrast to the violent history of the war-like West. Such belief in the influence of *wen* over *wu* derives from the written historical record bequeathed by the past to the present. To gauge the objectivity of that record we must ask who wrote it and for what audience it was intended.

As first the Ch'in and then the Han unified China and established an imperial tradition; they created an effective bureaucracy staffed by an educated elite. With the Han, the primary military threat became not rival states within China but raiding peoples, the Hsiung-nu, along the frontiers. These forces of highly mobile mounted archers had to be confronted by troops stationed on the borders of the empire. War and the soldiers who fought it thus moved from the core to the periphery, and the bureaucracy occupied center stage of government and culture. Highest status belonged not to a violent military elite but to a scholarly bureaucratic elite.

It is common that the history of war is not written by those who command forces in combat, and the authors of chronicles usually write for their societies' most powerful and privileged classes. In Europe this meant telling the story of war in a way that complimented a warrior aristocracy; therefore, accounts had to bestow praise on military skill, prowess, and heroism or risk alienating the audience. But in the Chinese case, the bureaucracy, often steeped in a Confucian philosophy that was very critical of violence, could write for other similarly disposed scholar-functionaries who commanded the greatest prestige. This gives the literature of war a different cast, determined by the values of this bureaucracy—values of *wen*.

David Graff explains how during the T'ang dynasty (A.D. 618–907) the reports of wars reflected the men who wrote the record more than those who fought.[3] Chroniclers say almost nothing about heroic deeds or of actual combat; battles receive only cryptic accounts at best. Instead, the record reads as if war were primarily a mental exercise in which the commanders' native intelligence mattered most. Clever maneuvers and artful stratagems, not steel nerves and hard fighting, determined victory.

The primary focus of this chapter is the epoch before the emergence of imperial, bureaucratized, China during the Ch'in and Han dynasties. It is hard to believe that *wu* ranked below *wen* during these earlier centuries, for military success shaped the fate of rulers and states as battle raged in the heart of China. Much of our knowledge of pre-imperial China, however, was filtered or interpreted by the scholar-bureaucrats of imperial times before it reached us, a situation that even affects the classical military texts that serve as the subject of this chapter.

Stepping back from the official historical record and relying on reasonable surmise, we can conclude that *wu* was always an important factor in Chinese history and occupied a more central role in culture than the scholar-bureaucrats lead us to believe. Dynasties rose and fell following military success or failure; emperors maintained huge military forces, exceeding 1,500,000 at one point during the Sung (A.D. 907–1276): The costs of defense strained and even bankrupted regimes. The language of *wen* may turn our attention from such facts, but they remain.

The Evolution of Chinese Warfare

The limited amount of detail concerning combat thus far discovered in Chinese historical records hampers our knowledge of the hard facts of war. It is clear, however, that ancient China witnessed considerable evolution in the nature of war, the composition of military forces, and the conduct of battle. Shang warfare was closely tied to ritual, in several ways. The purposes of combat included the amassing of prisoners for sacrifice; in this way the Shang resembled the Aztecs. In one case, 600 individuals were sacrificed to hallow the construction of a single residence. Prisoners might also be killed at the close of a campaign, as one inscription reports: "The eighth day, 2,656 men were executed with the halberd."[4] The Shang state depended primarily on the military ability of the aristocracy, although peasant levies supplemented the nobility. Armies were raised through patriarchal clans. Some aristocratic warriors rode chariots, which were not native to China, but arrived from Central Asia, about 1300–1200 B.C. Burial pits show that the Shang chariots rolled on surprisingly modern, many-spoked wheels; early forms were drawn by two horses, but four-horse teams eventually became the rule. Still, the greater number of noble warriors fought as select infantry, which remained the primary fighting force throughout the Shang. Depending on the challenge, royal campaign armies could range from 5,000 to 13,000 men. Remains of chariots, horses, and men in a burial pit at Hsiao-t'un suggest that groups of five chariots made up the building blocks of the army, and each chariot would be surrounded by ten to twenty-five soldiers on foot. Already, Chinese armies seem to have been divided into three segments, right, center, and left. This practice predominated so much that texts refer to a single force as "three armies."

For these aristocratic armies, combat broke down into a number of duels by individual nobles. Formal, ritualistic constraints defined aristocratic combat. Offensive weapons during the Shang included dagger-axes and spears, along with daggers and hatchets. The most important shock weapon appears to have been the halberd. Mounted on a stout pole, the bronze head of this weapon combined a curved-bladed war axe with a piercing spear point in different designs. Charioteers favored the halberd for its reach. Archers carried compound bows firing bronze-tipped arrows, but crossbows were as yet unknown. Troops wore leather body armor and bronze helmets and carried large shields.

Warfare during the Spring and Autumn Period continued the ritualistic and largely aristocratic forms begun by the Shang, although without the emphasis on human sacrifice; some prisoners, however, may have been executed after battle, providing what the Chinese called "blood for the drums." Surmising from historical writing, rather than from purely literary sources, the conventions of war included divination by generals before battle, agreement between foes as to where and when to fight, and feasting on the captured enemies' food stores after battle.[5] As with the Greeks, conventional warfare implies a strong influence of discourse on reality. Armies, composed of elite charioteers and supporting infantry, were of modest size. Early in the Spring and Autumn Period, a respectable force might be composed of about 1,000 chariots and 10,000 infantry, but later armies grew, regularly mustering 4,000 chariots and 40,000 infantry. At this time, Chinese favored chariots that carried three men: a driver, an archer, and a halberdier. Armor worn by charioteers and infantry included bronze helmets, greaves, and bronze plates attached to the warrior's clothing front and back.

Battle involved the kind of chivalric bravado and stern warrior codes typical of aristocracy. For example, at the battle of An, Kao Cu rushed into the enemy host, overcame a charioteer, seized his chariot and rode before the enemy shouting, "If any man wants valor, he may buy what I have to spare."[6] Such taunting seems to have been a natural part of the clash. Brave words required brave action. In a chariot confrontation between Prince Ch'en of Sung and his rival Hua Pao, Ch'en's arrows first killed Pao and then his driver. The third man in the chariot, an archer, was also wounded and demanded to be killed by Ch'en, who was at first reluctant. The archer pleaded, "One who does not die, if in the same file or chariot [as those already dead],[earns] the gravest of military penalties." Ch'en granted the resolute archer his fatal wish.[7]

The Warring States Period holds the greatest interest for this chapter, if for no other reason than it produced an unsurpassed body of military literature, with Sun-tzu being simply one author among many, albeit the best known. In this era, the art of war in China was radically transformed in weaponry, strategy, and army size. Iron now provided stronger, more durable weapons. Early in the Warring States Period, the Chinese adopted the crossbow, raising it to a weapon of great sophistication. It was also during this epoch that cavalry replaced chariots as the primary mobile arm. Threats from nomadic horse people just to the west and north of the Chinese states encouraged the turn to cavalry. In fact, the king of the Choa reformed his cavalry dramatically in 307 B.C., ordering his soldiers to wear barbarian-style trousers and tight-fitting sleeves in place of robes and to ride horses and learn mounted archery.[8] These cavalrymen lacked stirrups until the end of the Han, and saddles were rudimentary; understandably, this hampered the effectiveness of men on horseback. Therefore, cavalry at first supplemented chariots rather than replacing them, but chariots eventually gave way. In another response to the barbarian threat, the Chinese began to employ earthwork walls, often manned by soldiers armed with crossbows. Such works would later be extended, elaborated, and linked to form the "Great Wall."

Ultimately, it was not technological advance but the expansion and reformation of armies themselves that constituted the most impressive change in Chinese warmaking. Armies swelled impressively during the Warring States Period. In the mid-third century, one Choa field army on campaign included 1,300 chariots, 13,000 cavalry, and 150,000 infantry.[9] Estimates of the greatest total army size during the third century climb as high as 600,000 men.[10] Larger forces demanded a greater participation of commoners, so armies ceased to be a noble preserve. States conscripted their peasantry to fill the ranks. Such armies were organized around infantry squads of five men and employed a mixture of shock and missile tactics.

At the end of the Warring States Period, the Ch'in emperor Shih Huang Ti became the first ruler of all China, and to suit his grandeur he ordered the construction of a mausoleum to honor and hold his remains. He conscripted 700,000 laborers to work on this monumental project. Part of this incredible monument to his success was understandably military. An army of thousands of life-size terra-cotta soldiers standing in ranks, formed for battle, occupied part of the tomb complex. In their variety of weapons for different purposes, rational order in neat lines, and obvious concern for command, they imply a high sophistication.

Han China brought another watershed in the history of Chinese military institutions. The factor that most drove Han military development was the shift in military threat to the frontiers. Containing incursions by the Hsiung-nu, or Huns, and conquests along the borders of China required new kinds of armies. At first the Former Han continued and regularized the great conscript armies that had first arisen during the Warring States. The Han required every free adult male from ages twenty-three to fifty-six to serve two years. Around A.D. 30, the Later Han abolished this system. Needs of economy and mobility drove the emperors to create new modes of defense. Instead of conscripted peasant armies, the state turned to military forces stationed on the frontiers and to barbarian allies. To stock its frontier armies, the Later Han drew a great many of its rank and file from convicts whose sentences had been commuted to military service. These troops could do well when fighting on their own terms, but, in mobile raiding warfare, Han troops could not keep up with the enemy, and so they set a barbarian to catch a barbarian. The Han fielded cavalry composed of nomadic horse peoples who had come to terms with the empire. These tribes in service to the Han differed little from the raiders they now fought.

The troops defending the empire ceased to be exemplary Chinese and became marginal types or simply non-Chinese. Changing the nature of the soldier implies a revolution in the discourse as well as the reality of war. The rising bureaucratic elite came increasingly to see war as someone else's job. War became an inferior and denigrated activity. *Wu* lost its prominence to *wen*.

Training, Discipline, and Performance

It is impossible to establish the level of training and coordination in Chinese forces with certainty, so the question remains as to whether Chinese troops constituted disciplined armies or something less. Did disciplined coordination rule among them or was that a Western monopoly? If conclusive evidence remains hard to find, inferential and anecdotal evidence suggests that Chinese troops were skilled, obedient, and effective. The very size of armies from the era of the Warring States and later implies obedience and control. Such large forces would have been impossible to manage and maintain without effective and systematic discipline in the ranks.

When armies expanded dramatically during the Warring States Period through peasant conscription, these recruits received military training. The legalist thinker Han Fei-tzu (d. 233 B.C.) described a good ruler: "He imposes military training on everyone in the land and makes his forces fight hard in order to capture the enemy," but, he cautions, this leads the people to "consider him violent."[11] During the Former Han, peasant conscripts served their first year in training and spent the second guarding the interior or garrisoning the frontier. Selected individuals received more intense training as crossbowmen and cavalrymen. Every year, those who had already served had to perform a month's labor duty, during which time their military abilities could be practiced and certified. Campaign armies were based on those individuals with special training, and the rest worked as porters and labor support. As Ying Shao insisted in the Later Han, "Sending men into battle without having trained them is nothing more than throwing them away."[12]

We do not know the details of their training, but the noted commander and theorist Chu-ko Liang (A.D. 181–234) advocated five aspects to such instruction. The initial two were to train the soldiers' eyes and ears to signals from flags, banners, drums, and gongs so as to march, advance, and retire as ordered. The next was to instruct them in punishments and rewards. The fourth was weapons training for combat, and the last was instruction in maneuvering in ranks.[13] All this supports the idea of coordinated and skilled armies that were obedient to their commanders, as do severe penalties for failure to follow commands quickly. As will be seen in the following pages, the Chinese military classics put a high premium on discipline. Mark Lewis concludes, perhaps prematurely, that during the Warring States Period, the spirited bravado of the warrior gave way before the disciplined conduct of the soldier: "The focus of military training was no longer skill but discipline, not the instruction and development of the individual's abilities but the perfection of a system to which individuals were forced to conform."[14]

What rare combat detail exists demonstrates the ability of Chinese infantry to hold off attacking cavalry, a capacity that proves cohesion and implies more. Coordination of a combination of arms—typically bows, crossbows, halberds, and spears—in close order and while marching suggests expertise of a kind created through drill. Han regular forces could do well against nomadic horsemen in the right circumstances, as Chao Cuo testified of the Former Han:

As for flat plains and easy terrain [suitable for] chariots and shock cavalry, there the hordes of the Hsiung-nu are easily scattered. As for powerful crossbows and long lances shot or cast from afar, the Hsiung-nu cannot match them. . . . If they dismount and fight on the ground, with swords and halberds clashing together, where if one pulls back the other presses in, then the Hsiung-nu's legs cannot keep them.[15]

We find undeniable tactical finesse and cohesion in a well-documented campaign conducted by Li Ling. In 99 B.C., with a band of 5,000 infantry, he faced off against tens of thousands of Hsiung-nu steppe cavalry. When he first confronted them, "He drew up his forces . . . the front ranks armed with halberds and shields and the rear ranks with bows or crossbows. His orders were to discharge at the sound of the drum and to hold the shooting when the bells were struck."[16] Li Ling fought off their charges and conducted a retreat for days, inflicting thousands of casualties on the Hsiung-nu. Only when wounds and deaths thinned his ranks and his crossbowmen ran short of bolts for their weapons did the Hsiung-nu overcome his troops. Certainly, the ability of cohesive infantry fighting in close order to withstand cavalry is not exclusive to the West. The conduct of Li Ling's infantry ranks with any stand of the few against the many in history.

The considerable military literature of the Warring States Period also illustrates greater professionalism in command as armies grew, employed more complex tactics, and required great skill of their leaders. Control of an army with drums, bells, and banners, rather than fighting in the first rank, became the true mark of a general. When offered a sword by his officers just before a battle, General Wu Ch'i refused it, explaining, "The general takes sole control of the flags and drums, and that is all. Approaching hardship he decides what is doubtful, controls the troops, and directs their blades. Such is the work of the general. Bearing a single sword, that is not a general's affair."[17] It is interesting to note that the officers portrayed in the terra-cotta army of Shih Huang Ti did not carry weapons.[18]

While the state of our knowledge cannot establish that Chinese armies usually fought as disciplined infantry in close order, the record certainly does not justify confident assertions that they lacked the ability to do so.

THE GREAT WORKS OF CLASSIC CHINESE MILITARY LITERATURE

Our most interesting, complete, and complex view of ancient Chinese warfare comes from the military classics written during the Spring and Autumn Period through the Former Han. *Wu* remained serious and important business, and excellent minds turned their attentions to it, producing a remarkable military literature. For moral, social, and political reasons, the discussion of warfare has been important to cultures throughout human history; the ancient Chinese have left us abundant and intriguing evidence of this principle.

Dating the texts that serve as the basis for this discussion is far from easy. One, *T'ai Kung's Six Secret Teachings,* claims to report advice given in the eleventh century B.C., but textual analysis reveals it to be a work of the Warring States Period. Long after these works appeared originally, scholars of the Sung dynasty (960–1126) assembled seven works as the *Seven Military Classics* ca. 1078 to serve as a basis for examinations, which had become the entrée to government civil and military posts by that time. To earlier works they appended one composed during the T'ang dynasty (A.D. 618–907), but this chapter will treat only the first six. Specifically, the texts employed here include Sun-tzu's *Art of War; Wu-tzu; The Methods of the Ssu-ma; Wei Liao-tzu; T'ai Kung's Six Secret Teachings;* and *Three Strategies of Huang Shih-kung.* In addition to these, it is also necessary to consider *Military Methods* by Sun Pin, another work of the Warring States Period. Thanks to the efforts of Ralph D. Sawyer, assisted by his wife Mei-chün, we now can read all these ancient works in English.[19]

Without their careful translations, intelligent commentaries, and informative introductions, a consideration of Chinese military theory would be largely restricted to Sun-tzu; with their labors, there is an entire world to explore.

When regarding the military classics discussed here, one must recognize that while they originated before the privileging of *wen,* the actual editions included in the *Seven Military Classics* were assembled by scholar-functionaries under the Sung dynasty and integrated into the examination system, a creation of the bureaucracy. Thus these discussions of *wu* passed through the filter of those who saw it as "unpropitious." This could possibly have influenced what we read today. The subject matter is war, that could not be altered, but perhaps, the moral tone of the works may reflect the sympathies of those who denigrated the *wu*. However, to me, the philosophical tone of the texts does not seem pasted onto the original; on the contrary, it appears as essential to the very discussion of command and combat. Therefore, it seems reasonable to see these as reflecting military thought at the time of their origin, not simply as reshaped under the Sung.

Of course thought is more reflective of discourse than reality. In reviewing the military classics, it is critical to remember that they express ideas rather than document practice.[20]

Philosophical Underpinnings of Chinese Military Thought

These intriguing military texts reflect not only the political realities and military practices of their day but cultural values as well. Chinese martial discussion is infused with philosophical and religious concepts—in contrast to ancient and modern Western military theory, which has usually considered war in pragmatic terms. (However, as will be seen in Chapter 3, medieval European discourses could be steeped in references to religion.) The Chinese treatises considered in this chapter have a strongly Confucian cast to them, although one treatise discussed here is more markedly Legalist and another decidedly Taoist. These three philosophies of life and government require some comment, because they are so fundamental to the military literature. Confucius, who lived 551–479 B.C., expressed and extended Chinese concepts of private and public morality. This near contemporary of Socrates (ca. 470–399) shared with the Greek his conviction that knowledge created wisdom that led to a finer life for the individual. Confucius praised involvement rather than withdrawal; at base he was a reformer.

Confucian teachings centered on his concept of *jen,* usually translated as benevolence, but meaning perfect goodness and humanity as well—a compelling concern for the welfare of others. When asked the meaning of *jen,* Confucius replied "love others."[21] Also essential for Confucius, the notion of *li,* or propriety, encompassed a concern for the proper forms of conduct, including ritual, a subject on which Confucius claimed considerable expertise. *Li* also included all those polite behaviors that signified a sense of appropriate place and status, and with that of responsibility and deference—"manners" in the most significant sense of the word. Confucian righteousness, or *i,* in a sense flowed from both *jen* and *li. I* required that one do the right thing at the right time, acting appropriately and giving all its proper due. Righteousness also comprised exerting authority correctly. In addition to *jen, li,* and *i,* Confucius put great stock in filial piety, or *hsiao,* the love and respect awarded to parents and elders, which he regarded as the wellspring of other virtues. He also ascribed great value to loyalty, reciprocity, and proper forms of music. No earthly sage has had greater influence over his people over the millennia than has Confucius, who never claimed divinity, special knowledge of divinity, or, in fact, great interest in it. His ethics and guides were of this world, not the next.

According to Confucian principles, governments were maintained by their moral weight, their capacity to promote welfare and justice. Such a virtuous government enjoyed the Mandate of Heaven, and dynasties fell when they lost this mandate. Consequently the moral corruption of a ruler provided a harbinger of his fall.

Legalism contrasted with Confucianism in its emphasis on authority, law, punishment, and reward. Confucius said: "If you govern the people legalistically and control them by punishment, they will avoid crime, but have no personal sense of shame. If you govern them by means of virtue and control them with propriety, they will gain their own sense of shame, and thus correct themselves."[22] He put his confidence in the potential goodness of humankind. Not so the legalists. For them official hierarchy demanded a system of rewards and punishments; order sprang from power rather than from moral example, as the Confucians held. Lord Shang (d. 338 B.C.) propounded the Legalist point of view, as did Han Fei-tzu, who advocated an authoritarian concept of rule. Given the necessity for hierarchy and obedience in the military, all military texts imparted some shade of a Legalist argument, embodied in the concept of awesomeness, *wei,* the ability to inspire a respect born of severity. Awesomeness could be tied closely to righteousness.

Taoism, or Daoism, provided another worldview. *Tao* means "way," a term common to other Chinese philosophies. For Confucians the *tao* was the correct or appropriate way, but for Taoists it was the way of nature, a force that surrounded and pervaded all. It lay beyond human comprehension, yet the highest good came from submitting to it. The greatest virtue was like water, flowing and forming to meet the surroundings. In a formal sense, then, Taoism proposed a more submissive and passive course for mankind. The basic work of Taoism, the *Tao Te Ching,* was composed by Lao-tzu in the third century B.C. The unknowable mystery of the *tao* contrasts with the more earthly codes of Confucianism and Legalism. "The Tao that can be followed is not the eternal Tao. The name that can be named is not the eternal name. The nameless is the origin of heaven and earth. . . . Therefore, always desireless, you see the mystery. . . . Mystery within mystery."[23] The highly active and brutally real world of military combat seems somehow inconsistent with Taoism, but this philosophy had some influence.

Major Conceptions of Virtue, the State, and War

The Chinese military classics regard the state as founded on virtue not simply power. Authority, punishment, and reward play a role as well, but a state without virtue lacks the Mandate of Heaven and will be unsuccessful in war. Asked by King Wen, "How does the ruler of the state and leader of the people come to lose his position?" T'ai Kung replies that the ruler must have the "six preservations"—benevolence, righteousness, loyalty, trust, courage, and planning.[24] The *Wei Liao-tzu* concludes, "Therefore a state must have the righteousness of the forms of etiquette *[li],* trust, familiarity, and love, and then it can exchange hunger for surfeit. The state must first have the customs of filiality, parental love, honesty, and shame, and then it can exchange death for life."[25] The *Three Strategies of Huang Shih-kung,* a work with a strong Taoist sense, simply adds to the concern for public ethics: "The Tao, Virtue, benevolence, righteousness, and forms of propriety—these five—are one body."[26]

Chinese emphasis on the state as a moral entity and on the ruler as the primary ethical actor gave the notions of corruption and subversion special meanings. Among the Chinese military texts considered here, only *T'ai Kung's Six Secret Teachings* explores the potential of corrupting an enemy; it is not an essential of Chinese martial thought. Nonetheless, the discussion of this subject in the *Six Secret Teachings* is particularly illuminating in that it differs considerably from the constant discussion of underhanded tricks in the South

Asian classic the *Arthashastra*. The *Six Secret Teachings* urges a just ruler to tempt his adversary to reveal his own evil nature. In showing himself to be corrupt, the adversary would lose the Mandate of Heaven and, therefore, the support of his people. The goal is not to subvert specific policies, ministers, or generals but to allow the opponent to undermine his own legitimacy. "[A]ssist him in his licentiousness and indulge in music in order to dissipate his will. Make him generous gifts of pearls and jade, and ply him with beautiful women."[27] While music occupied special spiritual importance in Confucian thought, "music" here probably also means "pleasure," as both were written with the same character. "Debauch him with beautiful women, entice him with profit. Nurture him with flowers, and provide him with the company of female musicians."[28] So vital is perceived virtue to power that moral short-comings threaten a king and the state itself.

The Moral Paradox of War

A fundamental paradox emerges in the necessity for an essentially ethical state to pursue war. As Sun-tzu insists, "Warfare is the greatest affair of the state, the basis of life and death, the Way to survival or extinction."[29] For Sun Pin, war, while brutal, is natural: "Now being endowed with teeth and mounting horns, [having] claws in front and spurs in back, coming together when happy, fighting when angry, this is the Tao of Heaven; it cannot be stopped. Thus those who lack Heavenly weapons provide them themselves."[30] Yet the Chinese military texts agree that war remains an evil. Confucius disparaged the profession of arms, the *wu*. The Taoist classic *Tao Te Ching* condemns weapons as "inauspicious instruments" and asserts that "Everyone hates them."[31] The *Wei Liao-tzu* agrees: "Thus weapons are evil implements. Conflict is a contrary virtue. The post of general is an office of death. Thus only when it cannot be avoided does one employ them."[32] Paradox lies in the necessity for the ethical state to resort to "inauspicious" means for survival. The *Wu-tzu* reminds its readers that virtue is not enough: "In antiquity the ruler of the Ch'eng Sang clan cultivated Virtue but neglected military affairs, thereby leading to the extinction of the state."[33] *The Methods of the Ssu-ma* concedes that "those who love warfare will inevitably perish," yet "Even though calm may prevail under Heaven, those who forget warfare will certainly be endangered."[34]

However evil and destructive the violence of war might be, Chinese military thought holds that virtue promotes victory. Treatises emphasize the commitment of the general population and the army to the war effort, and that commitment hinges on acceptance of the ethical legitimacy of the ruler and his policies. Victory in a just war demonstrates that a ruler still enjoys the Mandate of Heaven. The *Six Secret Teaching*s insists that "Warfare which is invariably in accord with righteousness is the means by which to incite the masses and be victorious over the enemy."[35]

Most of the classical military literature discussed here comes out of the Warring States Period, a time of mass conscript armies, so desire to involve the people in a war effort rings with rhetoric extolling the unity of the people with the ruler. For Sun-tzu, "The Tao causes the people to be fully in accord with the ruler. [Thus] they will die with him; they will live with him and not fear death."[36] The *Three Strategies of Huang Shih-kung,* which dates from the Han dynasty, counsels, "The essence of the army and the state lies in investigating the mind of the people and putting into effect the hundred duties of government."[37]

No theme appears in the Chinese military classics with greater consistency than the need for the people's support and concern for their spirit, or *ch'i*. *T'ai Kung's Six Secret Teaching*s insists:

> If you suffer the same illness as other people and you all aid each other; if you have the same emotions and complete each other; the same hatreds and assist each other; and the same likes and seek them together—then without any armored soldiers you will win; without any battering rams you will have attacked; and without moats and ditches you have defended. [38]

Ch'i is essential. It is spirit, but more; most fundamentally it is the energy of life, and for an army it is morale. For the *Wei Liao-tzu,* "Now the means by which the general fights is the people; the means by which the people fight is their *ch'i*."[39] The *ch'i* of the people may differ from civic militarism as extolled by Hanson or popular passion as emphasized by Clausewitz, but all three recognize the need for the population to be mentally committed to the state and its wars. In the Chinese classics, the mass of the people and the mass of the army seem indistinguishable, and their *ch'i* translates immediately into military power. "In general, in battle one endures through strength and gains victory through spirit."[40]

Warfare, Ethics, and Power

The ancient Chinese fought costly battles, but, not surprisingly, their military theory praises the bloodless victory. Here we may be seeing the discourse of *wen* polishing the rough finish of *wu*. Given the "inauspicious" nature of war, the military culture hopes to limit the extent of deadly violence. The great Sun-tzu recognizes the necessity of bloodshed, yet he rates highest a general who wins without killing. "Thus one who excels at employing the military subjugates other peoples' armies without engaging in battle, captures other peoples' fortified cities without attacking them, and destroys other peoples' states without prolonged fighting."[41] This is "the true pinnacle of excellence."[42] Therefore he reaches a conclusion quite in contrast with the Napoleonic and Clausewitzian goal of destroying one's enemies: "Preserving their army is best, destroying their army second best."[43]

Unlike a general leading a Greek phalanx, the Chinese commander should avoid the obvious and deadly frontal assault that pitted the strength of one army against the other. He is to mix orthodox warfare *(cheng)* with unorthodox *(ch'i)*. (Unfortunately, for the English reader, *ch'i* here takes on an entirely different meaning from the *ch'i* of energy.) Orthodox tactics and forces adopt more conventional and expected means. Unorthodox tactics and forces rely on the unexpected. Thus, an army might array its main body in a battle line to oppose an enemy army, while maneuvering a flanking force to envelop the foe. Sun-tzu assures his readers that the two approaches could phase into each other and back. An able general cannot exhaust the combinations and permutations of orthodox and unorthodox. As will be seen in Chapter 8, modern U.S. Marine Corps doctrine endorses this creative approach, rather than the head-on clash.

The ultimate key is to remain unfathomable and formless to the enemy, not to avoid him but to deceive and overcome him. In knowing your dispositions, movements, and intentions, your adversary could confront and confound you. *T'ai Kung's Six Secret Teachings* warns, "If you are fathomed, they will endanger you," and advises, "In planning nothing is more important than not being knowable."[44] In *Art of War*, "Warfare is the Way [Tao] of deception. Thus although [you are] capable, display incapability to them. When committed to employing your forces, feign inactivity. When [your objective] is nearby, make it appear as if distant; when far away, create the illusion of being nearby."[45] Above all, be formless. "Thus if I determine the enemy's dispositions of forces while I have no perceptible form, I can concentrate [my forces] while the enemy is fragmented."[46] "Subtle! Subtle! It approaches the formless. Spiritual! Spiritual! It approaches the soundless. Thus he can be the enemy's Master of Fate."[47] Sun Pin multiplies this advice: "Being unexpected and relying on suddenness are the means by which [to conduct] unfathomable warfare."[48] "Deliberate tactical errors and minor losses are the means by which to bait the enemy."[49] In fact, feigned flight, such as occurred at Chi-fu, was often praised as a cunning tactic.[50] Graff observes that in Chinese military thought, "The target of strategy is not so much the enemy army as the mind of the enemy commander."[51] Formlessness confuses or unhinges the opposing general.

The doctrine of the formed and formless plays back and forth with the concepts of orthodox and unorthodox warfare: "When form is employed to respond to form, it is orthodox. When the formless controls the formed, it is unorthodox."[52] Even the Taoist *Tao Te Ching* counsels the unorthodox in war: "With the orthodox govern the state; with the unorthodox employ the army."[53] Here orthodoxy carries with it the notion of predictability, essential to justice but deadly in war.

Chinese classics often express the need for armies to be both formless and flexible, by using the analogy of water. In *Art of War,* "Now the army's disposition of force is like water. Water's configuration avoids heights and races downwards. The army's disposition of force avoids the substantial and strikes the vacuous. . . . Thus the army does not maintain any constant strategic configuration of power; water has no constant shape."[54] The *Wei Liao-tzu* agrees, "The army that would be victorious is like water."[55]

The general should reflect virtues consistent with army command, but these include attributes beyond, or at least different from, those thought to be necessary in the West. Sun Pin argues that the general must be righteous, which implies a just severity, and benevolent. "The general cannot but be benevolent. If he is not benevolent then the army will not conquer."[56]

Chinese military classics award the general near absolute authority in the army and great independence from the ruler and his government, testifying to the loyalty and trust between general and ruler. "Military matters are not determined by the ruler's commands; they all proceed from the commanding general."[57] *The Methods of the Ssu-ma* allows what would be condemned as insubordination in other cultures: "When the general is with the army, there are orders of the ruler which are not accepted."[58] It is possible that these statements of the general's authority overstate the case. This literature was, after all, a discourse on war stating how things ought to be, and since it was most like-

ly read by professional military commanders or would-be commanders, assertions that power should be wielded by the general without interference were
what the readers wished to hear. Graff surmises thus: "The general's authority was probably never as unfettered as this prescriptive literature would have
it, but there is ample evidence from Warring States and Han that it was still
considerable."[59]

Perhaps the most famous story of a general asserting his authority over the
objections of the ruler comes from a tale told about Sun-tzu in the *Spring and
Autumn Annals of Wu and Yüeh*.[60] When Sun-tzu visits the court of Wu, King
Ho-lü is reluctant to send his armies against Ch'u. In discussing military matters with the king, Ho-lü asks Sun-tzu to demonstrate the effectiveness of his
methods, and he agrees to a test employing the king's concubines, a most
unlikely bunch of recruits. The three hundred women receive weapons, and
Sun-tzu asks the king to appoint his two favorite concubines as company
commanders. Then Sun-tzu explains his orders repeatedly and the penalties
for not complying. When he orders the women to drill at the command of the
drums, they simply giggle. He then takes the drum sticks in his own hand and
sounds the orders, and they again laugh. Furious, he commands that the exe-
cutioner's axes be brought to him and that the Master of Laws state the penalty for refusal to obey orders. "Execution" comes the reply. Sun-tzu orders the
two favorite concubines, as officers, to be beheaded. Now amazed, King Ho-
lü, a fine general himself, rushes a note down to Sun-tzu forbidding the executions. But Sun-tzu staunchly insists, "I have already received my commission as commanding general. According to the rules for generals, when I, as a
general, am in command of the army even though you issue orders to me, I
do not [have to] accept them." The women are beheaded in front of the king.
This act makes the other concubines fear Sun-tzu, and they drill with atten-
tive precision. At first shocked, the king regains heart and orders the attack on
Ch'u, which succeeds.

Commanders demanded obedience and enforced it by severe punishments.
Another tale concerning the discipline that a general should enforce comes
from the *Wei Liao-tzu*. One of Wu Ch'i's cavalrymen breaks ranks and charges
the enemy before receiving the order to advance, and in a display of prowess
beheads two of the enemy and brings their heads back to his unit as trophies.
Wu Ch'i orders this valiant but rash horsemen executed. Those around him
protest, pointing out the fact that he is an excellent warrior, but Wu Ch'i
remains unmoved, "He is indeed a fine warrior, but he disobeyed my orders."[61]
The *Wei Liao-tzu* suggests a staggering list of regular penalties to ensure disci-

pline and obedience. For example concerning a squad of five, the classic advises, "If they lose their squad leader without capturing or killing an enemy squad leader, they will be killed and their families exterminated."[62] Woe to drummers who strike the wrong signals for an army in battle: "If a drummer misses a beat he is executed."[63] The punishments prescribed in the *Wei Liao-tzu* remind us of the Roman practice of decimation, whereby one in every ten legionaries within a cohort that had performed poorly in battle would be executed. Such harsh measures further justify the impression that Chinese armies were disciplined forces.

The Chinese make a strong point about the necessary "awesomeness" of the general. As Ralph Sawyer observes, "Virtually all of the Legalists and military thinkers sought consciously to develop this awesomeness because of its critical role in governing men and causing the enemy to shiver and quake."[64] *T'ai Kung's Six Secret Teachings* advocates exactly the issue of using execution to create the kind of fear that inspired obedience: "The general creates awesomeness by executing the great, and becomes enlightened by rewarding the small. . . . Therefore if by executing one man the entire army will quake, kill him."[65] The author of the *Wei Liao-tzu,* perhaps himself a student of the Legalist master Lord Shang, reasons that if the army fears its general then it will not fear the enemy, a precursor of Frederick the Great's principle that the Prussian soldier should be more afraid of his officer than of the enemy. Even the Taoist author of the *Three Strategies of Huang Shih-kung* sounds very Legalist concerning awesomeness: "When rewards and punishments are clear, then the general's awesomeness is effected."[66]

In his desire to impose obedience through awe, the general should not, however, live separate from his troops. On the contrary, he must experience the same discomfort and danger as his men. *T'ai Kung's Six Secret Teachings* insists, "The general shares heat and cold, labor and suffering, hunger and satiety with the officers and men."[67] The *Wei Liao-tzu* would deny a general an umbrella in the heat or heavy clothing in the cold and insists that in difficult terrain he dismount and walk. He must be last to eat and last to rest.[68] The *Three Strategies of Huang Shih-kung* relates the story of a general offered a keg of sweet wine. "The general had it poured into the river and shared the drinking of the wine with the officers and men as it flowed downstream."[69] It is reminiscent of the story of Alexander the Great, who, when offered a helmet full of water in the desert where his troops were suffering from thirst, theatrically poured it on the ground because there was not enough for all to drink.

Another important attribute of a general was his skill in collecting and exploiting intelligence, in particular his ability to maximize the value of space. Sun-tzu argues, "Unless someone has the wisdom of a Sage, he cannot use spies; unless he is benevolent and righteous, he cannot employ spies; unless he is subtle and perspicacious, he cannot perceive the substance in intelligence reports. It is subtle, subtle! There are no areas in which one does not employ spies."[70] For Sun Pin, "One who does not use spies will not be victorious."[71] In fact, the Chinese literature puts a premium on gaining military intelligence and deceiving the enemy as to one's own intentions. Spies are part, but not all of this. Interestingly, the commander does not dispatch spies to check on the loyalty of his own troops, as the *Arthashastra* advises; the Chinese commander ensures loyalty by benevolence and obedience by awesomeness.

The Chinese classics provide counsel on conducting specific campaigns, but this advice is neither pervasive nor uniform. Sun-tzu dislikes besieging fortresses—"If you attack cities, [the army's] strength will be exhausted"—and thought long wars were inevitably disastrous—"No country has ever profited from protracted warfare."[72] Sun Pin, probably Sun-tzu's great grandson, writing a century later when things had changed and cities had become more important, accepts siege warfare, as does the *Wei Liao-tzu*. Of the works discussed here, Sun Pin speaks most of tactical dispositions. For example, he proposes deployments, "square, circular, diffuse, concentrated, Awl, Wild Geese, hooked, Dark Rising, incendiary, and aquatic." Interestingly, of these, only the "Wild Geese" is specifically designed "for exchanging archery fire."[73] And in contradiction to the notion that the Chinese did not use massed infantry, Sun Pin comments, "Solid formations and massed [battalions] are the means to attack an enemy's fiery strength."[74] But as a whole, the works are not tactical manuals and are more likely to discuss major issues of statecraft than to offer instructions for combat.

Chinese military classics, particularly the greatest of them, *Art of War*, are often enigmatic rather than definitive. They stir the reader to fathom the author's words, which may well be more metaphoric than precise. In the process, thoughtful consideration promises wisdom. Carl von Clausewitz's *On War* provides the most obvious comparison with the *Art of War*, although they are very different in assumptions, methods, and conclusions. One thing that the Chinese military classics and *On War* share, however, is the fact that they are both very closely related to the philosophical tenor of the times, although

On War is morally neutral, or amoral, in a way that the Chinese classics are not. In many ways I prefer Sun-tzu; Clausewitz may be brilliant, but he is also battering. Sun-tzu is far less sanguinary and far more subtle, to use his own language.

INDIA

Ancient South Asia lacked a body of military literature analogous to the Chinese military classics, a fact that reflects important cultural differences between the two Asian societies. It is not simply that South Asians failed to record their evolving discourses on war in as complete a manner as did the Chinese. The contrast is more profound; conceptions of history, morality, politics, and warfare differed between the two, just as both of them contrasted with cultures of the ancient Mediterranean. Such diversity between great Asian civilizations belies any attempt to identify a single "Oriental" way of warmaking. This chapter now directs its attention toward the unique realities and conceptions of war in South Asia, or India, as it was called by the historians of ancient Europe.

History

Ancient China regarded its history as precious and preserved its records, but ancient India largely failed to chronicle its own political and military past. Rich Indian classics that have come down through the ages are works not of history but of religion, law, and literature. Certainly these provide historical evidence, traces of bygone eras, but they supply no real narrative. Some of the best records of Indian kings and courts come from visitors from other cultures, such as the Greek Megasthenes. Military facts suffer. The first battle in South Asia for which we have eyewitness accounts was at the Hydaspes in 326 B.C., and then only because Alexander fought there and his actions were recorded by Greeks.

The epochs of South Asian history that figure in this exploration came after the fall of the Indus Valley Civilization, ca. 2600–ca. 1600 B.C., which built such cities as Harappa, with a population of perhaps 35,000, and Mohenjo-daro. What brought Indus Valley Civilization to an end remains a matter of speculation, but it seems likely that a series of earthquakes and floods struck the mortal blow.

About 1500 B.C., Indo-European-speaking Aryans migrated from their home between the Caspian and Black Seas across the Hindu Kush Mountains into India, a perilous but common path for invading peoples. They brought a new language, new beliefs, and new military practices. Historians still debate whether the Aryans simply migrated or stormed into India as armed invaders, extinguishing the Indus Valley Civilization. Aryan religion was a precursor of the Hindu faith, on a clear evolutionary track to it, giving Hindu South Asia a religious continuity dating back over three millennia. With the Aryan migration/invasion, South Asian history entered the Vedic Period, 1500–1000 B.C., so named after the religious texts, the Vedas, originating during this period, although our written versions come from later times. The Epic Age, 1000–500 B.C., which followed, receives its title from the great tales of gods and heroes going back to this era.

Ancient South Asia knew political unity only once, under the Mauryan Empire (322–184 B.C.), founded by Chandragupta Maurya. His empire grew in the wake of Alexander's incursion into India, 326–324 B.C.; in fact, Alexander may have encountered the young Chandragupta before that extraordinary Indian became emperor. Building on a base of the Indian state of Magadha, Chandragupta absorbed surrounding states and defended his throne and territory against Alexander's Macedonian successor, Seleucus Nicator. Eventually, the Mauryan Empire grew to include most of the Deccan, the triangular mass that juts south between the Arabian Sea and the Bay of Bengal.

The height of the Mauryan Empire lasted only a century, and after its decline, India returned to its more natural political condition, a series of rival states balancing one against the other. The closest that Hindu India would come to imperial unity again fell far short of Mauryan domains. Like the Mauryans before them, the founders of the Gupta Empire (A.D. 320–550) built from a base in the north Indian kingdom of Magadha. Chandra Gupta I (320–335), who was not related to the great Mauryan, extended Gupta control over the Ganges Valley; later rulers extended it further, although it never absorbed the Deccan as did the Mauryans. Hindu culture reached its peak under the Guptas, and the final form of works important to this study may have appeared as late as the Gupta Empire, although their origins could go back a millennium before. India would not again see the likes of the Mauryan and Gupta Empires until Muslim conquests established the Delhi Sultanate early in the thirteenth century, long after the concerns of this chapter. We will pick up that story in Chapter 5.

South Asian Texts Concerning War and Warriors

Many important ancient Chinese texts deal directly and at great length with the nature and conduct of war, but ancient South Asia provides no such body of military classics. Certain Indian religious and literary texts employed in this chapter cursorily discuss war and combat as part of religious mythology while focusing on wider matters. In addition, the *Manusmrti* and the *Arthashastra* provide more commentary but relatively little on the conduct of campaigns.

It is hard to attach dates to Indian discussions, descriptions, and directives. The sources, while dealing with earlier epochs, usually come down to us in later forms. For example, the great religious epics, the *Ramayana* and the *Mahabharata,* which contains the spiritually essential *Bhagavad Gita* and the more political *Santi Parva,* deal with events that may have occurred 1000–700 B.C., but the versions available to us now date from the first half of the first millennium A.D. The *Puranas,* tales of Hindu gods and heroes, appeared during a long stretch of time, roughly 500 B.C. to A.D. 500.

The *Manusmrti* has an ancient lineage but was probably only finalized in the second or third century A.D. This work of unknown authorship purports to detail the rules of life, society, and governance given to Manu, the progenitor of the human race, by the divine Brahma. The *Manusmrti* is the oldest of the *dharmashastras,* works on duty, right conduct, and law, primarily in a religious but also in a civil sense. Because Hindus defined the role of the warrior caste as fulfilling dharma and because kings might turn to force and warfare to uphold order and religion in the state, the *Manusmrti* deals with armies and warfare, albeit in a cursory manner.

Of special interest in this chapter is the *Arthashastra.* Tradition credits this work to Kautilya, the counselor of Chandragupta Maurya; this would date it at about 300 B.C. However, linguistic analysis of the text puts it at about A.D. 150.[75] It is quite possible that the ascription to Kautilya refers to an original core of the *Arthashastra* written by Kautilya and extended and embellished by later authorities. The word *arthashastra* means "science of material gain," and some translate it as "science of politics," which is closer to its subject matter. There was, in fact, a body of literature with this theme that predated Kautilya, and the *Arthashastra* expressly declared itself to be a complication: "This . . . has been prepared mostly by bringing together as many treatises on the Science of Politics as have been composed by ancient teachers for the acquisition and protection of the earth."[76] It is best to consider the *Arthashastra* as a

compendium of Indian political thought, making this work all the more valuable for our purposes because it represents the dominant discourse, not simply the idiosyncratic product of a single mind. It could be argued that the
Bhagavad Gita and the *Manusmrti* are intrinsically more important works, but
in order to compare Chinese and South Asian military thought, one must
emphasize the *Arthashastra,* because it is much closer in subject matter to the
Chinese classics and provides the most extensive discussion of warfare contained in any of the Hindu texts.

Armies and Styles of Combat in Ancient Indian Warfare

We know that the societies and states of South Asia produced huge armies
with considerable complexity, but we are less sure exactly how these armies
fought. The archeological evidence discovered from Indus Valley Civilization
suggests a style of warfare geared to the defensive, according to Pradeep
Barua.[77] Strong, thick walls made of baked mud brick and buttressed by stone
towers protected fortresses and town citadels. Defensive architecture on such
an order implies a threat, so it seems reasonable to see Indus Valley warfare as
having an offensive as well as a defensive side. Indus Valley arms are not particularly impressive. The most common weapons discovered have been baked
clay pellets and balls. Pellets seem to have been shot from slings, and the larger balls were almost certainly meant to be hurled from atop walls at attackers
below. Those copper and bronze weapons unearthed tend to be lightly made;
spear points, for example, are thin and flat without reinforcing ribs. Barua
concludes that the lack of evidence that Indus Valley warriors employed
swords and the absence of armor suggests that Indus Valley armies did not
normally engage at close quarters. The weapon of choice seems to have been
the bow, judging from the quantity and variety of arrowheads found.
Although Indus Valley Civilization knew horses, there is no evidence that they
were used for combat.

Aryans brought superior military technology and an aggressive and mobile
form of warfare. The Aryan elite arrived with horse-drawn war chariots. Such
chariots had been available since about 1700 B.C. in the Near East. The Vedas
mention the two-horse light chariot as the platform of the gods. The mighty
Indra, "mounter of the chariot at the neighing of his two bay horses," is "the
shatterer of even the steadfast."[78] From his chariot, god or hero plies the bow.
The *Artharva Veda* speaks of "ye divine arrows of men pierce my enemies."[79]
The bow reigned as the weapon supreme, as a classic text of the era makes clear:

[B]y the bow the contest may we win;
by the bow dread battles may we win;
the bow doth work displeasure to the foe;
by the bow let us win in all the quarters.[80]

An Indian bowman, by drawing an arrow to his ear instead of to his chest, maximized the power of his bow. One verse illustrates this, personifying the bow string as a woman: "Close to his ear, as fain to speak, she presses, holding her well loved friend in her embraces."[81] So essential was the bow to warfare that in the epics, the word for science of warfare is actually *dhanurveda*, or knowledge of the bow.[82] Archery combat ranked above all other forms of fighting, the *Agni Purana* declares, "Battles [fought] with the bows [and arrows] are excellent, those with darts are mediocre, those with swords are inferior and those fought with hands are still inferior to them."[83]

Obviously the elite archer in a two-man chariot had to possess considerable skill, but so did his driver, who piloted his chariot through the twists and turns necessary to give the archer good shots. As the *Mahabharata* described, "The warriors could be seen by the hundreds of thousands making intricate maneuvers with their chariots on the battlefield."[84] The driver could be a man of equal status to the elite, warrior-caste bowman; often they were related. The hero Arjuna's driver was of even higher status: the god Krishna. Elite charioteers wore armor in battle, but infantry in support of the chariots did not seem to wear any protection, although some carried shields. Infantry, who seem to have been primarily archers, appear in the texts as little more than victims of charioteer heroes who magnified their greatness by slaughter.

Judging by Vedic and Epic texts and by the *Manusmrti*, ancient South Asian warfare would appear to have been fairly ritualistic and bound by conventions.[85] Combat between heroes should be preceded by a challenge. Like should only fight like, equals confront equals; thus a charioteer should only combat with another charioteer, a warrior in armor with another so clad, a king with a king. Those who surrender should be taken prisoner and treated well. One should stop fighting when an opponent was disarmed by loss or damage to his weapon or disabled by wounds. A panicked, fleeing foe should not be relentlessly pursued. Poisoned or barbed arrows are banned. Should a *brahman* enter the field to stop the fighting, it must stop. Such conventions in South Asian warfare, as well as their presence in Chinese and Greek battle, suggest that during early stages of military development, combat is often, or even usually, conventionalized through the imposition of discourse.

South Asian conventions have the ring of idealized combat about them, or, in the language of my model, they seem like a "perfected reality." Trying to reconstruct real warfare from literary texts can lead us to imagine warfare as very different than it actually was. Considering the great difference between real warfare and the tournament in medieval Europe—see Chapter 3—it may be wise to suspect the description of combat in South Asian sources as representing a staged form of contest. The notion of a tournament is suggested not only by the conventions imposed on combat, but by the presence of male and female spectators. In fact, one of the revered restrictions on war forbade doing any violence to individuals who had come to observe the battle. One king even supplied spectators with entertainment, such as poets and singers.[86] Singh proposes that "warfare was reduced to the level of a large scale tournament and might even be something of a festive occasion."[87] To him this comment is an aside, but in the context of the present book, it poses profound questions. Did the perfected form of martial contest coexist with a far more stern and brutal reality of war? Whether the conventional quality of Indian warfare has more in common with the formalities of Greek polis battle or with the artificiality of the medieval tournament is an issue we may never be able to resolve.

During the Epic Age, the traditional *caturanga-bala*, or four-part army, emerged to become the pattern for South Asia. Such an army, composed of infantry, cavalry, chariots, and elephants, remained the archetypal Indian force during the coming centuries until chariots fell out of use by the seventh or eighth century A.D. Even then, the other elements continued until replaced by the military practices of Islamic invaders in the twelfth century. The size of armies and the balance of forces within them depended on the individual state and ruler. According to Diodorus of Sicily, at the time of Alexander's invasion, Porus commanded an army of 50,000 infantry, 3,000 cavalry, 1,000 chariots, and 130 elephants.[88] Arrian states that Porus, after leaving some troops and elephants in camp, marched against Alexander with a field force of 30,000 infantry, 4,000 cavalry, 300 chariots, and 200 elephants.[89] Megasthenes (ca. 340–282 B.C.), who visited the court of Chandragupta Maurya in 302 as a representative of the Macedonian Seleucus Nicator, estimated Chandragupta's total forces at 600,000 infantry, 30,000 cavalry, and 8,000–9,000 elephants; he was mute on chariots.[90] Even if Megasthenes exaggerated, the Mauryan army must still have been very formidable, and the infantry clearly outnumbered other troops by a very substantial margin.

Ancient literature and modern historians alike rate infantry as being of low utility within the *caturanga-bala*. Even if foot troops mattered more in rough country and in siege warfare, they are portrayed as marginal in battle on open ground. Infantry certainly was numerous and served as garrisons, guards, and laborers for the more prestigious elements of the army. Infantry remained poorly protected; bas reliefs at Bharut and Sanchi, dating from about 200 B.C., show troops in the traditional loin wrap *(dhoti)*, tunic, and little more.[91] Infantry carried shields and a variety of weapons, including swords, spears, battle axes, maces, and quoits, or discuses, for close combat, but its most effective weapon was the bow. Iron came into use for weaponry 1000–800 B.C., and arrowheads were now of iron in a variety of shapes. South Asian bow technique among infantry differed from that of the West, as the archer braced the lower end of the bow upon the ground with his left foot while drawing the bow.[92] Arrian provided a very interesting report on Indian archery, basing his information on an account from Megasthenes.

> Their infantry have a bow equal in length to the man who carries it. Placing this downward to the ground and stepping against it with the left foot, they discharge the arrow, drawing the string far back. Their arrows are little less than four and one-half feet long; and nothing can withstand one shot by an Indian archer, neither shield nor breast-plate nor anything else that is strong.[93]

In this passage, the power of the Indian longbow rivals that of the more famous English longbow. If this was true, the infantry archer may have been more important on the battlefield that the literature credits him with being. In any case, men on foot fought in their own all-infantry units and in small detachments to supporting chariots and elephants.

Cavalry did not enjoy great prestige in ancient India, and horsemen only drove out chariot-mounted warriors fairly late in the history of ancient warfare—much later than in Europe or China. Cavalry riding in support of chariots had been present in the Vedic era, but the lack of the stirrup limited its effectiveness. The epic literature frequently tells of horsemen falling from their horses.[94] It is possible that the Indians developed a true stirrup by about 1 B.C., because a bas relief at Sanchi seems to show a horse with saddle and stirrups.[95] If this is, in fact, the case, the development of the stirrup in South Asia predated its appearance in China by centuries. However, this evidence is pretty thin, and the lack of a great rise in the importance of cavalry may invalidate the theory. The continual problem of securing an adequate number of suitable horses also limited the use of cavalry. Smaller, less robust horses can be put to good use pulling chariots, but are inferior as mounts. This explains why chariots rode with armies before horses were bred up to a size and strength capable of carrying a man. On the whole, the Indian climate is not good for war horses, and even Islamic forces under the Delhi Sultanate and the Mughal Empire had to import them constantly to have enough mounts. The South Asians seem not to have relied to any great extent on horse archers before the arrival of the Muslims. Alexander had some horse archers with his army, but Arrian makes no mention of them at the Mauryan court; he describes cavalry as carrying throwing spears, or javelins. Some mounted archers were employed by the Gupta Empire, but their use died with that state about A.D. 600.[96]

The chariot arm initially enjoyed the highest status, as in Vedic and Epic times, but over the centuries reliance upon elephants increased, pushing aside the chariot. Chariots originally served as the vehicles of kings, but, by the time of the battle of Hydaspes, Porus rode to battle on an elephant. Throughout their military career, South Asian charioteers relied mainly on the bow in combat. After a long decline, chariots eventually disappeared, probably in the seventh century A.D. The Chinese traveler Hiuen-Tsang, who visited India in the first half of that century, talked of Indian infantry, cavalry, and elephants, but not of chariots.[97]

Of the four parts of the army, elephants inspired the greatest awe. To be sure, war elephants were formidable. On their backs they carried howdahs with sides high enough to protect archers and spearmen within. A Chinese traveler described Indian war elephants in 1178 A.D.: "When fighting, these elephants carry on their backs houses, and these houses are full of soldiers who shoot arrows at long range, and fight with spears at close quarters."[98] Another threat posed by elephants came not from the soldiers they carried but from their own weight and strength. As listed by the *Arthashastra*, one of the ways a war elephant accomplished its task was by trampling.[99] So fearsome was this death that being trampled by an elephant was also a mode of execution decreed for high crimes. These behemoths also played a role in siege warfare, by breaking down gates. Moreover, an elephant provided a high and impressive perch for a commander to survey the battlefield as the fighting surged around him. It was also of great importance for him to be seen by his troops; because Indian hosts were held together by the general or prince, the men needed to behold him like a banner. An elephant made an admirably visible perch.

But for all their impressive power, elephants also had serious drawbacks. In battle, a wounded elephant could go crazy with pain and turn on its own army in blind fear. Not only did they lack the steadiness of disciplined infantry, elephants lacked the speed of cavalry. They set a plodding pace for maneuver. On campaign, their appetites imposed a tremendous logistical burden on their armies, and during the dry season they normally could not campaign because of their prodigious need for water. And of course, they were extremely expensive to purchase, train, and maintain.

Elephants enjoyed a reputation as outsized as the beasts themselves, and one is left with the impression that the behemoth was not simply praised for its military utility but for its symbolic value as well. These great beasts were cultural icons. Elephants graced religious processions for the same reason that they accompanied armies, their majestic or awesome presence. They seemed to promise invincibility, and a great army could not be without them. The *Arthashastra* declares, "Victory for a king depends principally on elephants."[100] The *Visnudharmottara Purana* and the *Agni Purana* concur.[101] Other, later authorities ascribe almost miraculous powers to elephants; the *Nitisara* proclaims, "Each elephant . . . is capable of destroying a cavalry of six hundred horses."[102] It also concludes that elephants "constitute a stable support for the kingdoms of rulers," and this might encapsulate a greater truth.[103] Elephants advertised the grandeur of political authority, and perhaps the Indian populace expected authority to arrive on the back of an elephant.

The *Arthashastra* identifies and differentiates six different sources of troops. In descending order of quality, these include the following: permanent troops belonging directly to the ruler; hired native soldiers; militia levies; allied troops; enemies who had deserted or switched sides; and warriors from forest tribes.[104] True excellence is found in the hereditary troops: "Inherited from the father and the grandfather, constant, obedient, with the soldiers' sons and wives contented, not disappointed during marches, unhindered everywhere, able to put up with troubles, that has fought many battles, skilled in the science of all types of war and weapons."[105] At the other extreme, forest peoples could be useful but were unreliable and interested only in plunder. The best troops were not mobs but trained professionals.

The *Arthashastra* advises: "Infantry, cavalry, chariots and elephants should carry out practice in their arts outside [the city] at sun-rise, except on junction-days. The king should constantly attend to that, and should frequently inspect their arts."[106] The *Nitiprakasika* counsels, "The king should instruct his troops in those thirty-two movements of war, which are acknowledged by polity."[107] Sukracraya disregards the "untrained, inefficient, and raw recruits" as being "like balls of cotton. The wise should appoint them to other tasks besides warfare."[108] Again respect for training, drill, and discipline is not uniquely Western.

The *Arthashastra* offers some, but not particularly extensive, directions for disposing troops for battle; they concern only two short chapters of the volume.[109] This treatise allows a tight infantry formation for all-infantry units armed with spears and sword. These foot soldiers would stand only one sama apart, or 10.5 inches, which would allow roughly 3 feet to each man along the front, a close order, indeed.[110] Archers had much more room, with 7.5 feet between each man to give them enough space to use their weapon. Large combined units, such as a chariot "division," united a great many troops. In such a formation, six infantrymen surrounded each cavalryman, and five such cavalry units surrounded each chariot. The division was divided into five units of nine chariots each, with their supporting troops, and the five units arrayed themselves in a checkerboard formation to create the "division" of forty-five chariots, 225 cavalry, and 1,350 foot soldiers.[111] Elephant units employed the same pattern of surrounding horse and infantry. The *Arthashastra* suggests different ways of echeloning the main units of an army: "Foot soldiers in the wings, horses on the flanks, elephants in the rear, chariots in front, or a reversal of this in accordance with the enemy's array."[112] Battle formations intricately linked together elephants and/or chariots with supporting infantry and cavalry must have limited the army's pace to that of its slowest troops. The army could advance or deploy in a deliberate manner, but rapid movements were probably outside its repertoire.

South Asian armies maintained the *caturanga-bala* style of army and its ponderous tactics from the late Epic Age through the conquest of north India by the Mughals. The only major changes came with the increasing importance of elephants and the decline and extinction of chariots. Judging from literary accounts, armies took elaborate formations and then lumbered forward. The actual fighting across the army's front seems to have been a swirling and disorganized clash, as chariots darted out from the mass to duel with one another. Battles were not typically fought toe to toe; infantry were simply not armed for such a clash. Arrian writes that battle "at close quarters" was "a thing which very rarely happens to be the case between Indians."[113]

Barua blames the conservative preservation of awkward battle tactics in large part on the geographical isolation of South Asia; Indian states could keep their traditional ways of fighting because they did not often have to fight outsiders. He also posits that the weakness of the Indian states did not allow them to form professional armies and break the mold of South Asian forces.

I will hazard another, entirely speculative, hypothesis. Perhaps the texts upon which we place so much reliance give us only a partial and prejudiced view of South Asian warfare. Indian armies might have been more effective than we normally believe; the actual battle record, sparse as it is, may indicate this. Porus met defeat at the hands of Alexander the Great, but Alexander was one of the greatest generals in history, and his fight at the Hydaspes may have been his hardest battle. And while we do not know how Chandragupta Maurya defeated Alexander's successor, Seleucus Nicator, we do know he was victorious. One key to success may have been the much-maligned Indian infantry. Although sources continually downplay the value of the plebeian infantry, these accounts were written for consumption by privileged religious and military elites. Social prejudice could conceivably have warped discourse to hide reality in order to compliment the audience. If the Indian longbow was as potent as Megasthenes claims, could it not have been critical in combat? Powerful archery might have determined the form and result of battles. If literary sources slighted common-born archers, it would not be the last time this would occur. Neither Norman archers at Hastings nor English longbowmen at Crécy received their due, particularly among the aristocratic elite of France. The effectiveness of infantry archery might also go some way to explain the paucity of horse archers among the Indians. If infantry carried a superior bow that could outrange and overpower a short cavalryman's bow, then horsemen would do much better to avoid trading arrows with infantry.

This is all surmise, to be sure, but if nothing else, the Indian case illustrates the kind of problems that can arise when using literary sources to reconstruct the reality of war. Where evidence of reality is lacking, as in the case of ancient India, we are tempted to stretch our knowledge of discourse to cover the gap. This is intrinsically dangerous.

South Asian Thought on Caste, Ethics, Government, and War

Whereas the Chinese texts considered in this chapter discuss public ethics at length and relate these to the conduct of war, the moral focus of Hindu texts is markedly more pragmatic. The personal and caste ethics of the Hindu warrior attract a good deal of discussion, and rulers receive general counsel to be wise and just. However, the discussion of practical advice for the conduct of foreign relations and war is overwhelmingly restricted to one work, the

Arthashastra, and its directives are pragmatic. The survival and advancement of the state and the protection of its dynasty and its people constitute the ultimate good; the means toward those ends are subject to little ethical scrutiny.

The clearest moral imperatives concerning combat in Hindu texts concern the duties of the *kshatriyas* in battle. The traditional Hindu hierarchy of castes, or *varna* system, classified the population in four categories—*brahmans, kshatriyas, vaishyas,* and *shudras*—and those below or excluded from these, the untouchables. Although South Asian society would develop a far more elaborate system of groups defined by birth, profession, and marriage, the *jati,* ancient texts speak only of the *varna.* Ideally, *brahmans* were priests, *kshatriyas* warriors and rulers, *vaishyas* landholders and merchants, and *shudras* peasants and workers.[114]

As traditional warriors, the *kshatriyas* were instructed to fulfill their duty, or dharma, by fighting. The ethical universe of the *kshatriyas* encompassed determination and courage, along with skill at arms, but the casus belli receive only cursory attention. References to righteous war appear, but "righteous" in the ancient texts implies more "reasonable" or "proper" than "virtuous." The *Santi Parva,* a section of the *Mahabharata,* a fundamental Hindu text and the longest known epic poem, insists: "That *kshatriya* is said to be acquainted with duty who in battle makes the earth a lake of blood, having the hair of slain warriors for the grass and straw floating on it. . . . A *kshatriya,* when challenged, should always fight in battle, since Manu has said that a righteous battle leads to both heaven and fame on earth."[115] The *Bhagavad Gita,* another and more fundamental section of the *Mahabharata,* finds the god Krishna insisting that the *kshatriya* hero Arjuna take up arms against his own kinsmen for it is his calling. (More will be said about caste, *jati,* and the *Gita* as factors in defining South Asian senses of loyalty and duty in Chapter 5.) Combat is its own virtue, and the wounded and killed receive forgiveness and rewards. As the *Agni Purana* states, "They would be washed of their sins as blood flows from the bold warriors. The endurance of pain due to wounds is the excellent penance. Thousands of celestial women attend on a man killed in the battle."[116]

The *Manusmrti* also states the *kshatriya's* obligation to fight, to fulfill "the blameless, primeval law for warriors."[117] His rank should depend on valor.[118] While *kshatriyas* must fulfill their dharma of combat, they are also "commanded to protect the people."[119] Even his name must speak of this; the *kshatriya* male's first name should "be connected with power" and the second with "protection."[120] Power and protection are the attributes of kings, and the

Manusmrti speaks of rulers as *kshatriyas*. "A *kshatriya*, who has received according to the rule the sacrament prescribed by the Veda, must duly protect this whole [world]. . . . the Lord created a king for the protection of this whole [creation]."[121]

In the name of his duties both to caste and to his people, a king must be willing to fight. The *Matsya Purana* argues that because the king is *kshatriya*, he should not turn away from fighting.[122] The *Manusmrti* demands, "A king who, while he protects his people, is defied by [foes], be they equal in strength, or stronger, or weaker, must not shrink from battle, remembering the duty of *kshatriyas*."[123] There is little moral paradox in war for the Hindu sage, in contrast to the Confucian. As the historian A. L. Basham comments, "Positive condemnations of war are rare in Indian literature."[124]

Because *kshatriyas* were so invested in the very act of fighting, there is little wonder that treatises dealing with the creation of armies prefer *kshatriya* troops. The ancient texts speak constantly of *kshatriyas*, "who protect the earth," as the best soldiers, so that, for example, the *Arthashastra* defines the most excellent army as "consisting mostly" of them.[125] It should be noted, however, that military service was not limited to them; the other castes could supply troops, and even *brahmans* might serve if they did not find employment as priests. However, the *Arthashastra* warns that a *brahman* army could be won over by an enemy that would ritually prostrate itself before the *brahmans*. Thus, "A *kshatriya* army, trained in the art of weapons, is better, or a *vaishya* or *shudra* army, when possessed of great strength."[126] This inclusion of other castes is not unique; the *Agni Purana* states, "A *shudra* has the right to fight in case of an emergency if he had undergone training."[127]

As defined by the *Manusmrti,* the work of the king should be performed in an ethical manner. He must overcome his own baser instincts and refrain from sins that arise from love of pleasure or wrath. The condemnation of addiction to pleasures of gambling, sloth, and sexual excess are expected, but the criticism of "hunting . . . [an inordinate love of] dancing, singing, . . . music, and useless travel" seems harsh when one thinks of Western monarchies, which celebrated such enjoyments.[128] More relevant in the context of South Asian political thought, the *Manusmrti* forbids a monarch treachery and slander, which will become methods advocated by the *Arthashastra*. The king is also enjoined to appoint worthy ministers and consult with them. Ambassadors are also to be "loyal, honest, [and] skillful." The king should also pursue "the complete attainment of justice,"[129] but this does not mean that he eschews violence, which, in the form of punishment, is essential to the well-being of the state. "The whole world is kept in order by punishment."[130] Judicious use of punishment is the key to a healthy society, for if it "is properly inflicted after [due] consideration, it makes all people happy; but if inflicted without consideration, it destroys everything."[131] The key is wisdom, not simply intimidation or universal benevolence.

Religious texts and the *Manusmrti*, however, do not provide practical instruction for rulers and generals. To find a work that does and, thus, provides Hindu discussions of war that are similar in subject to those contained in the Chinese military classics, it is necessary to turn to the *Arthashastra*. In contrast to the high-minded *Manusmrti,* the *Arthashastra* reduces questions of war and peace to raw expediency. It regards a capable ruler's desire to conquer as natural and enmity between states as inevitable. Foreign policy aims at expansion rather than peace. In the words of the modern commentator Aradhana Parma, "the question of peace is not an ethical one but one of practical politics."[132] Reliance upon the *Arthashastra* here may slant our view of South Asian politics toward the seamy side, but given the fact that the *Arthashastra* alone among Indian classics deals extensively with politics and war, we must put it center stage.

The *Arthashastra* defines enmity not by action but by position; a neighbor is by nature an enemy. This fundamental assumption about the predatory nature of bordering states receives an elaborate development in the mandala, or circle, theory, which combines assertions of the inevitable armed rivalry between neighbors with the time-honored proposition that the enemy of my enemy is my friend. Book 6 of the *Arthashastra* develops this geometry of war.[133] Consider a particular state as the center of a series of circles. Any state sharing a border with the first is a potential antagonist. "Encircling him on all sides, with territory immediately next to his is the constituent called the enemy." By this logic a state on the next ring out, on the other side of the enemy, is a natural ally, being an enemy of the enemy. A state beyond this ally is an ally of the enemy, and so on. The treatise expands the series of rings to encompass twelve categories of potential enemies and allies.[134] In the context of rings beyond rings, a conqueror can attack a foe from both flanks: "The Conqueror shall think of the circle of states as a wheel—himself at the hub and his allies, drawn to him by the spokes though separated by intervening territory, as its rim. The enemy, however strong he may be, becomes vulnerable to harassment and destruction when he is squeezed between the conqueror and his allies."[135] The range of subtle variance in the mandala system can be played out at great length, but it remains essentially predatory and ultimately cynical.

The *Arthashastra* lays out the six measures of foreign policy in this predatory environment: "peace, war, staying quiet, marching, seeking shelter and
dual policy." Peace and war are obvious; "Remaining indifferent is staying
quiet. Augmentation of [powers] is marching. Submitting to another is seeking shelter. Resorting to peace [with one] and war [with another] is dual policy." Choices among these alternative courses correspond simply to the situation of a state and a ruler. Most centrally, "When in decline as compared to
the enemy, he should make peace. When prospering, he should make war."[136]

Types of War and Types of Conquerors

Given the fact that, as Parma insists, "The whole purpose of Kautilya's foreign
policy is to increase one's power, mainly at the cost of the natural enemy,"[137]
war is a matter of "when" not "if," of pragmatism not principle. The
Manusmrti might command a *kshatriya* ruler not to shrink from war, but the
Arthashastra advises him to embrace it. Conquerors are not megalomaniacs
but able rulers who have made their states strong enough to be the hunter
instead of the prey. "The king, endowed with personal excellences and those
of his material constituents, the seat of good policy, is the would-be conqueror."[138] All depends on one's relative strength; if stronger, fight the enemy,
but if weaker, hope to avoid open warfare and strive to increase one's own
strength. Some counsels of good government come not from ethical imperatives but from the desire to buttress the state. "If weak in might, he should
endeavor to secure the welfare of his subjects. The countryside is the source of
all undertakings; from them comes might."[139]

Conquerors can be righteous, greedy, or demoniacal; the righteous ask only
submission, the greedy demand land or goods, and the demoniacal want
everything, even the wives and sons of the king.[140] A weaker state must adopt
different policies toward the three: Submit to the first, buy off the second, and
yield land and goods to the last, while adopting surreptitious counter-meas-
ures.

Conflict can follow four patterns. The initial means would be diplomacy,
"war by counsel" or *Mantrayuddha,* pursued when a weaker state wants to
avoid actual fighting.[141] Beyond this, a state may turn to open, concealed, or
silent war. "Open warfare is fighting at the place and time indicated; creating
fright, sudden assault, striking when there is error or a calamity, giving way
and striking in one place, are types of concealed warfare; that which concerns
secret practices and instigations through secret agents is the mark of silent

war."[142] Open warfare, *Prakasayuddha,* would resemble a battle by Greek poleis, in that the time and place of the fighting were set in advance. The strong can appeal to *Prakasayuddha,* which the *Arthashastra* ranks above other forms: "Open warfare, however, in which the place and time [for the fighting] are indicated, is most righteous."[143] But even in *Prakasayuddha,* a wise commander makes use of devious methods; the *Arthashastra* defines one of the preconditions to engage in open fight as "when secret instigations are made [in the enemy's camp]."[144]

Concealed warfare, *Kutayuddha,* would be more familiar to the ancient Chinese or to a modern military in that it sought to outmaneuver or surprise an enemy. Secret war, *Gudayuddha,* is hardly war at all in the normal sense, for it employed covert violence to confound and subvert the enemy while assassinating his leaders. Such tactics verged on our concepts of Terrorism.

Spies

In reading the *Arthashastra,* one is struck by its emphasis on underhanded methods, not only the ample use of spies, but recourse to seedy characters, agents provocateurs, and assassins. Reliance upon spies to gain intelligence concerning enemy strength and plans seems nearly universal across time and geography, for, in war, knowledge is, indeed, power. The *Arthashastra* would have a king dispatch operatives to the courts of his allies and enemies: "A king shall have his agents in the courts of the enemy, the ally, the Middle and Neutral kings to spy on the kings as well as their eighteen types of high officials."[145] But the book goes beyond this; spies and secret agents could command no more central a role in political theory than they do in the *Arthashastra.* This pervasive recourse to espionage derives from two sources beyond the need for intelligence concerning the enemy: first, suspicion toward the king's own ministers and officers and, second, subversion as a favored form of conflict in lieu of battle. Throughout its pages, the *Arthashastra* concerns the selection and action of agents for "secret" and "silent" service.

Treachery never seems far from the surface. Steven Rosen argues that the fragmented and conflicting loyalties generated within a society segmented by caste limited fidelity and trust, leading to "low expectations of political loyalty to leaders when those loyalties are not supported by the obligations of the caste ideology."[146] Whether or not his analysis of its cause is correct, he hits upon an important reality. In such a world, a lack of confidence spawned distrust that required self-protection by fair means or foul. And, as opposed to the Chinese tradition in which the ruler places his confidence in the general and grants him authority even to disobey, the Indian ruler sets spies on his officials and officers.

A king must also challenge the loyalty of his servants. "After appointing ministers to ordinary offices in consultation with the councilors and the chaplain, he should test their integrity by means of secret tests."[147] The *Arthashastra* proposes elaborate tests for piety, greed, lust, and fear, all of which probe loyalty. For example, the king should invent a reason to imprison an official, and in prison he should plant a provocateur to urge that such an unjust king should be assassinated. The agent should insist others are for the plan and ask how stands the official. "If he repulses [the suggestion], he is loyal."[148]

The royal head seldom rests secure on its pillow or, for that matter, on its shoulders. A king must constantly survey all levels of his government. In the countryside, "The Administrator should station in the country [secret agents] appearing as holy ascetics, wandering monks, cart-drivers, wandering minstrels, jugglers, tramps, fortune-tellers, soothsayers, astrologers, physicians, lunatics, dumb persons, deaf persons, idiots, blind persons, traders, artisans, artists, brothel-keepers, vintners, dealers in bread, dealers in cooked meat, and dealers in cooked rice. They should find out the integrity or otherwise of village-officials and heads of departments."[149] Secret agents should test judges.[150] Neither should a ruler assume the loyalty of his army: "And secret agents, prostitutes, artisans and actors as well as elders of the army should ascertain, with diligence, the loyalty or disloyalty of soldiers."[151]

Obsession with spies and with suspecting those close is not unique to the *Arthashastra*. Even in the *Mahabharata,* the *Santi Parva* advises: "With proper attention, the king should set his spies upon all his counselors and friends and sons, in his city and the provinces, and in dominions of the chiefs under him."[152] The *Matsya Purana* insists that a king should use several spies for one job and never rely on a single agent; moreover the king should deploy spies to watch other spies.[153]

Subversion and the Art of the Underhanded

"Miraculous results can be achieved by practicing the methods of subversion," so the *Arthashastra* counsels the king.[154] In dealing with enemy states, subversion is less costly and potentially more effective than battle. The corollary of fear about the limited loyalty of one's supporters was confidence that an enemy's councilors and generals could be turned against him. Such confidence inspired efforts to foster antagonisms among powerful men in rival states: "In the case of all, secret agents close to them should find out [their] defects, and occasions for mutual hatred, enmity or strife among members of the oligarchy, and should sow discord." When fomenting discord among enemy officials and commanders, "[Agents] should urge the party worsted in the strife to go away elsewhere or to render help to their master."[155] In this clandestine warfare, rumors can overturn regimes: ". . . assassins should start quarrels among the followers of the chiefs in the oligarchy by praising the opponents in brothels and taverns, or by supporting seducible parties."[156] Having instigated revolt, a shrewd ruler then backs the rebels: "And in all cases of strife, the king should support the weak party with treasury and troops and urge them to kill the rival party."[157]

The *Arthashastra* advocates assassination: "An assassin, single-handed, may be able to achieve his end with weapon, poison and fire. He does the work of a whole army or more."[158] No subterfuge is too devious. Confronted by an enemy oligarchy: "Keepers of prostitutes or acrobats, actors, dancers or showmen, employed as agents, should make chiefs of the ruling council infatuated with women possessed of great beauty and youth. When passion is roused in them, they should start quarrels by creating belief [about their love] in one and going to another, or by forcible abduction [by the other]. During the quarrel, assassins should do their work, saying, 'Thus has this passionate fellow been slain.'"[159] Better to kill an enemy general than to fight him. Again, the *Arthashastra* prescribes using beautiful prostitutes to lure the target into lust and to create quarrels; and "Agents in the guise of ascetics shall administer poison to the infatuated army chiefs on the pretext of giving them love potions."[160] It is worth noting that some students of Terrorism today argue that assassination is a relatively humane form of dealing with enemies, because it targets leaders instead of killing the innocent in more large-scale military actions.[161] There are times when the *Arthashastra* reads like a handbook on Terrorism, both in undermining an enemy and in controlling one's own officials and people.

Generals made attractive targets because their troops became dependent upon particular commanders and looked to them alone for leadership. Cut off the head and the body falls. The *Agni Purana* insists that in battle, the commander of an army should be "surrounded by excellent warriors. . . . A commander is the life of a battle. [The army] would be destroyed if it is without a commander."[162]

Assassination plots attack treasonous officials of a king's own government as well as the enemy. If the king suspects treason from his major officers close to court or on the frontiers, the *Arthashastra* suggests specific surreptitious means to divide, subvert, or kill the offenders.[163] In one scenario, the king "should dispatch the treasonable high officer with a weak army containing assassins, for destroying foresters or an enemy's town" and "in the fight, taking place by day or night, assassins or agents appearing as highway robbers should kill him, announcing, 'He was killed during the attack.'"[164] The fact that the *Arthashastra* advises surreptitious assassination over arrest and trial speaks volumes about stability and loyalty within the state. The strongest rationale for assassination would be fear that the treasonous official commanded a faction that would revolt should he be apprehended.

The *Arthashastra*'s advocacy of intrigue, subversion, and murder as alternatives to combat comes out very clearly in the treatise's discussion of taking a fortress. The attacker is encouraged to instigate dissatisfaction within the enemy camp, lure the king and assassinate him, employ secret agents, and the like. Only when this fails should the attacker undertake a siege.

Chinese discussions of warfare probably strike the modern reader as more admirable than that offered in the *Arthashastra*. Yet the *Arthashastra* would achieve victory at a minimum loss of life. There are more subtleties in Asian styles of warfare than simply those of tactics. In fact, the questions posed by comparing Greek, Chinese, and Indian styles of warfare are as much moral as military. But, then, where life and death, loyalty and treachery are at issue, we must consider virtue and evil as well as victory and defeat.

Comparing Asian Experiences

Our inability to provide an authoritative, detailed description of the Chinese and South Asian combat, at least at this time, forbids definitive conclusions about the reality of war, but much can still be said. Both Chinese and South Asian sources indicate that in early eras, battle was highly conventional and ritualized, with some of the same characteristics found in Greek polis warfare, such as agreed forms of combat and restrictions on weaponry. Judging from the Chinese, South Asian, and Greek examples, it may be fair to conclude that at certain fairly early stages of military development, warfare is often, perhaps usually, circumscribed with convention and ritual, and thus very much a creature of discourse.

However, by the Warring States Period in China and the emergence of the Mauryan Empire in South Asia, these Asian civilizations had evolved large-scale warfare, far beyond the heroic forms of early literature. The Chinese fielded great armies composed of conscripts and capable of close-order infantry combat. These forces were trained and cohesive, although the level of discipline, ability to maneuver, and frequency of combat at close quarters are impossible to state with precision. In contrast, South Asian forces seem not to have preferred infantry combat with shock weapons. Such diversity belies broad generalizations about a single dominant Asian form of warfare. In addition, at least Chinese styles of combat probably had enough in common with European battle that confident assertions about the unique advantages of Western warfare are also uncertain at best.

Although materials that have come down to us allow only some modest statements about the reality of Asian warfare, our literary sources, from religious texts to political and military treatises, justify much firmer assertions about ancient discourses on war. The Asian discourses presented in this chapter contrast with one another, and both diverge from that of classical Greece. A reading of the Chinese classics and the more diverse Indian sources reveals an emphasis on stratagems and, at times, battle avoidance. Such emphases may seem to justify the stereotypes of "Oriental" warmaking offered by Keegan.

But this would be to misuse Western and Asian examples by comparing apples with oranges—that is, contrasting the reality of Greek warfare at a fairly early stage of development with more mature forms of Asian military discourse. The reality of phalanx warfare was highly conventional, with one of these conventions prescribing a direct rush to bloody battle. This record of actual combat is then put alongside a military literature generated at a very different stage in military evolution. There is no question that Chinese texts and the *Arthashastra* advise stratagems and exhausting an enemy rather than fighting toe-to-toe battle, and this certainly differs from warfare among the classic Greek poleis. But a fairer comparison for Chinese and Indian classics would be Roman literature on war. Rome's more mature form of legionary warfare was not conventional in the Greek sense, and the prescriptive literature generated during the empire, epitomized by Vegetius, counsels methods of warfare much more akin to the subtlety of Chinese texts than to the headlong charge of the phalanx. It is also worth noting that the extensive military literature of the seventeenth and eighteenth centuries in Europe, a discourse very much inspired by warfare as practiced in ancient Rome, espouses battle-averse campaigning typified by maneuver, stratagem, and siege. This will be discussed in Chapter 4. Put in proper context, a stark contrast between Western battle seeking and Asian battle avoidance evaporates.

But beyond any comparison with Western ideas, Asian discourses on war are above all interesting in their own right, as intriguing examples of distinct cultures and not simply as contrast with Western ideas. The highly ethical and metaphorical Chinese military classics serve as springboards for thought rather than offering conclusions and directives. These provocative classics still influence the discourse on war today, even to the point of shaping Marine Corps doctrine on maneuver warfare, as will be seen in Chapter 8. Indian religious texts mix the discussion of combat with consideration of dharma, of responsibility and action, which transcends the military context. The *Arthashastra* holds a fascination similar to Machiavelli's *The Prince,* to which the Indian classic is often compared, as an exploration of cutthroat political behavior in an unforgiving world.

General Ho-lü won decisively against a superior foe at the battle of Chi-fu by employing the unorthodox warfare so lauded by the Chinese military texts. Sun-tzu and other commentators would likely have scorned as wasteful the classical Greek tradition of frontal assault. The Chinese sought to win a campaign by carefully masking their intentions, by artfully maneuvering their forces, and by patiently wearing down their foes. The *Arthashastra* would also have rejected the directness of the phalanx, advising his king to avoid the costs of battle by ruthlessly subverting his rivals, as war became intrigue. "An arrow, discharged by an archer, may kill one person or may not kill [even one]; but intellect operated by a wise man would kill even children in the womb."[165]

In the introduction to their volume on Chinese military history, David Graff and Robin Higham write, "The difference between premodern warfare in China and the West was probably not as great as prescriptive texts such as the Chinese military classics might lead us to believe."[166] I would endorse this conclusion, but with a very different implication. Graff and Higham seem content to suggest that the East resembled the West envisioned by Hanson and Keegan. I would reverse this to argue that Western military thought and practice were often closer to Asian conceptions and methods than to those of classical Greece. Keegan characterizes "Oriental warmaking" as indirect.[167] But that description often fits the best of European campaigns as well, and Vegetius's maxims can resemble the counsel offered by Sun-tzu. In his book on military operations and strategy written shortly after World War II, the prominent theorist of armored warfare Basil Henry Liddell Hart advocated what he termed the "indirect approach."[168] In this he represented a strong *Western* tradition, which will be further revealed in the next chapters. Without doubt, many cultural differences separate Asian concepts of warfare from the Western, but the important contrasts are not as obvious as some would claim; they are, above all, subtle.

Notes on the Opening Illustration for Chapter Two

These life-size terra-cotta troops stand prepared to defend the first Ch'in emperor, who commanded this eternal army, composed of thousands of troops, to guard his tomb, circa 200 B.C. Their neat ranks, various arms, and distinction between men and officers speak to the sophistication and power of ancient Chinese military institutions.

(Copyright Erich Lessing/Art Resource, NY)

CHAPTER THREE

Chivalry and *Chevauchée*

The Ideal, the Real, and the
Perfect in Medieval European Warfare

IN PREPARATION FOR THE FRENCH ONSLAUGHT that he so much
desired, English King Edward III arrayed his army on a ridge that ran between
the villages of Crécy and Waldicourt. He chose his position wisely; the ridge
commanded both roads running northwest from Abbeville. The English
could adopt the defensive tactics that favored the longbowmen he brought to

the field, and he could count on the French, led by their King Philip VI, to hurl themselves at the forces astride their path. Ever since Edward had landed on the Cotentin Peninsula of Normandy in mid-July 1346, he had tried to bring the French out to fight this kind of battle; now he would have it. Edward had set in motion the monumental struggle we now call the Hundred Years' War (1337–1453) in order to lay claim to the French throne against the Valois prince, crowned at Reims as King Philip VI. This battle at Crécy, fought on 26 August 1346, would win the campaign for Edward, but the curse of war would last for generations.

The opposing forces at Crécy differed sharply. Edward raised the army he brought across the Channel as a professional force recruited from men who fought for pay and booty. It is true that some 2,700 knights and squires, men of aristocratic and landed backgrounds, accompanied Edward; however, they did not now fight alongside the king because of feudal obligations, that is requirements to serve their lord in exchange for land—a fief—that they received from him. No, even these men served as paid professionals. The other 12,500 men in his army were commoners, including 7,000 of the peasant longbowmen who would play such a great role in the Hundred Years' War. Philip VI led three times as many men in pursuit of Edward, but the French were a motley assembly: 12,000 men-at-arms, many called up to fulfill their service to lords who rode with the king, 6,000 mercenary Italian crossbow-men, and 20–25,000 other infantry, including urban and peasant militias.

The English had evolved a tactical system; the French would fight in an ad hoc manner. Edward had learned to dismount his cavalry for battle, turning his knights into heavily armed and armored, albeit loosely organized, infantry to stand among low-born spearmen along the center of the line. Flanking them stood peasant archers employing the longbow. This bow measured about six feet in length and required such strength to pull back the bowstring that only a man trained from an early age could properly unleash the killing force of its yard-long arrows. A skilled longbowman could fire rapidly and accurately and do harm at several hundred yards, although the bow became much more effec-tive at shorter ranges. As potent as was the English tactical combination of dis-mounted knights, common infantrymen, and longbowmen, to be effective, it had to stand on the defensive, not charge forward in the manner of Greek pha-lanx or Roman legion. English dismounted knights might gain solidity by compacting together, but they certainly sacrificed mobility. Longbowmen needed to maintain their own static cohesion, preferably protected by some natural or man-made obstacles. Scattered in an open field, they could be ridden down by cavalry. But Edward knew the tenets of French chivalry, and he could count on his foes to oblige him by attacking at Crécy.

Although several medieval chronicles describe the battle of Crécy, they conflict as to numbers and formations. Edward probably divided his army into the traditional three sections, or "battles," at Crécy. In these three battles, dismounted knights and spear-wielding infantry probably stood in line, one next to the other, on a ridge between Crécy and Waldicourt. At either flank massed longbowmen supported this great line of men on foot. The lay of the land on the ridge suited Edward's tactics perfectly, as it projected forward at each end, giving his archers the kind of flanking position they needed, "at the sides of the army almost like wings," to enfilade an enemy charge.[1] The English had established a wagon laager in the woods behind their line to corral their horses and better protect their baggage.[2] The English also brought a number of early firearms to the battle, including small "cannon," but these did little except make noise. The English put the time before battle to good use: "They quickly dug a large number of pits in the ground near their front line, each a foot deep and a foot wide, so that if the French cavalry approached, their horses would stumble in the pits."[3] Rain, which fell shortly before the battle, also probably muddied the field, making the ground itself an impediment to the attacker.

Philip's army left Abbeville that morning and its van only reached the battlefield late in the afternoon, with the rest of the French still strung out along the road. Certainly, he had reason to expect success. His forces greatly outnumbered Edward's, and the French boasted the most renowned chivalry in Europe. Nonetheless, it was the end of a long day and a long march, and Philip would have to send his tired men and horses uphill to reach the English at the crest. He might have been wise to hold back his troops until the next morning, but he could not. The French did not disappoint Edward's confidence in the rash spirit of their chivalry. According to Froissart, they pressed forward: "Those behind continued to advance, saying that they would not stop until they had caught up with the front ranks. And when the leaders saw the other coming they went on also. So pride and vanity took charge of events. Each wanted to outshine his companions."[4] Philip could not restrain his army, so he led it in the attack.

About 5 P.M., he began the fighting by sending his Italian—generically known as Genoese—crossbowmen to unsettle the English line, preparing it for assault by Philip's horsemen. The rain may have wet the Genoese's bow-strings and thus crippled their fire somewhat, but in any case, although the crossbow was a powerful weapon, the longbow outranged it and boasted a much more rapid rate of fire. Apparently these crossbowmen had not faced the longbow before, but now they learned the fatal truth. Uttering their war cries, the Genoese approached and fired, but "their crossbow bolts did not reach the English."[5] Immediately the longbowmen responded, withering the Genoese under a hail of English arrows. The large shields, or *pavisses,* that the crossbowmen usually hid behind while laboriously cocking their crossbows were still in the baggage train, so they lacked any cover.[6] Many fell on the spot; survivors, powerless and wounded, began to withdraw. Seeing this, Philip, enraged, called on his own knights to ride down and slay the Genoese: "Quick now, kill all that rabble. They are only getting in our way!"[7]

As the first charge trampled the retreating Italians, it came under fire from the longbowmen. Even at extreme ranges, arrows easily penetrated the flesh of unarmored horses, causing them to panic and rear, breaking the momentum and cohesion of the charge. When the thundering advance closed the range to the stout English, archers brought down armored men as well.[8] Hoping to avoid the deadly arrows coming from the English flanks, the mass of French horsemen shied away from the flanks and compressed together on their own center. In such a crush their numbers became a disadvantage as knights were pinned against one another, hardly able to wield their weapons. Once the wave of horsemen struck the English line and broke against its unyielding ranks, the French were cut down by the English knights and infantry, while continuing to be pierced by arrows.

When the initial assault fell back, lighter-armed infantry rushed forward from the English line to finish off the French wounded. Some foreign knights who accompanied Edward protested, "Sire, we wonder greatly that you allow so much noble blood to be shed, for you could make great progress in your war and gain a very great deal in ransoms if you were to take these men."[9] Chivalry and tradition normally required that vanquished or fallen knights be captured not slain; this both preserved aristocratic life and gained for the vic-tors sizeable ransoms for the prisoners. But this appeal did not move Edward. Knowing his army to be outnumbered, he realized that he could not spare men to take and guard prisoners; therefore, "fearing that his men would spend their whole time trying to capture nobles for ransom" he ordered that "no-one was to take prisoners on pain of death."[10]

On came the French again and again. Chroniclers report as many as fifteen charges against the English lines, but with the same results. Between attacks, spearmen dispatched survivors, and bowmen left their lines to retrieve arrows from fallen men and horses so that these missiles could find new victims.

No one could question French courage; tales of valor abound. King Philip had two horses killed under him and was wounded in the face by an arrow. The blind King of Bohemia, accompanying the French army that day, ordered his retainers to lead him into the thick of the fight, where he and his companions met their deaths.

As night fell, it was clear that the French cause had been lost beyond recovery, and the French began to desert the field. Philip tried to rally his men: "My lords, to where are you fleeing? Don't you see your king in the field, with his face towards his enemies?"[11] Finally Philip reluctantly rode off himself, led by Jean d'Hainault.

While Edward's victory at Crécy and the raiding campaign, or *chevauchée,* that preceded it displayed some of the panoply of chivalry, they also revealed the brutal character of campaigns fought during the High and Late Middle Ages. This chapter contrasts the elegant aristocratic discourse on chivalry with the harsh reality of war. Although some of the brutality was implicit in an ideal that stressed prowess with arms, a basic incompatibility separated warfare as imagined in the literature of chivalry and as actually fought in the field. So great was that contrast that it inspired the aristocratic elite to create an artificial, perfected kind of combat, the tournament, that more fully adhered to the ideal. However, chivalry and the tournament were not utterly irrelevant to the conduct of war in all its aspects, because they still influenced the style and etiquette of combat between socially elite knights and squires. We will have to distinguish between the usual conduct of campaigns and the special world of elite combat to correctly understand the martial role of chivalry.

If aristocratic warriors could insulate and perfect their notion of war in the tournament, the Church could not take the same course, which would sanction violence between fellow Christians. Instead, the Church sought its own means to control and divert the martial energies of Europe, first by imposing conventions on war through a peace movement and then by redirecting attention toward the Crusades, another perfected vision of warfare.

Medieval warfare presents us with an intricate tapestry of violence and vision, which interwove the ideal, the real, and the perfect in different complicated patterns.

GILDED IRON: THE DISCOURSE ON CHIVALRY

Chivalry, the codification of idealistic notions of warfare, the stuff of romances, practically defines the Middle Ages in the popular imagination. It evokes notions of reverence, honor, and virtue. It is, in fact, an elaborate and elegant discourse on war, carrying with it conceptions of combat and of proper conduct toward leaders, fellows, foes, and noncombatants. For all its brightly caparisoned courtliness, chivalry was ultimately about violence.

Strictly speaking, chivalry belongs only to the latter eleventh through the fifteenth centuries. Its lore and legends speak of King Arthur and Charlemagne, but its works actually date from a later era. While a surprisingly international aristocracy embraced the codes of chivalry, it flourished above all in France. Ultimately the discourse of chivalry was constructed by and for the military elite; it was for knights, their lords, their families, and their ladies. The ties between military role, class, and language come out more clearly in French than in English. The core word is *cheval*, or horse, and the mounted paragon of chivalry, the knight, is a *chevalier*, literally horseman. Thus, the French saying, *Il n'y a pas de chevalier sans cheval*—there is no knight without a horse—or as Malory wrote in English "What is a knight but when he is on horseback?"[12] *Chevalerie*, or chivalry, means the code of these mounted aristocratic men-at-arms or those knights themselves spoken of collectively. The parallels to the tales and principles of chivalry may be found in the literatures of other mounted, military aristocrats, such as the *kshatriya* of Hindu South Asia or the samurai of Japan.

While chivalry has enjoyed the attention of artists, philosophers, and scholars for centuries, superb studies that have appeared in the last two decades allow us to reappraise its essence and detail. We are particularly indebted to Maurice Keen and Richard W. Kaeuper, although others have also revealed the face of chivalric warfare.[13] These modern authors base their analyses on the wonderfully rich medieval literature of chivalry.

Of greatest literary interest are the *chansons de geste* and the romances. The former, literally "songs of great deeds," are epic poems, primarily French, that mix mythology and history dealing with Charlemagne, William of Orange, and a theme of barons' revolts. Our earliest surviving manuscripts of the chansons date from about 1100, but the actual origins of the chansons may be somewhat earlier. The *Chanson de Roland* ranks as the most famous of these. Generally of somewhat later origin, the romances are works of poetry or prose that tell of the exploits of great chivalric heroes. Here we find the Arthurian legends, with their rich variety. The late chivalric period produced treatises on chivalry, the most important being the *Book of the Order of Chivalry* written by Ramon Llull (d. 1316) and the *Book of Chivalry* by Geoffroi de Charny (d. 1356). But this does not exhaust the works on the subject; we must consider other sources, from the songs of troubadours and *trouvères* to medieval chroniclers. The discourse on chivalry was defined and reflected by such a large body of literature precisely because it was so fundamental to the European imagination, especially for the aristocracy. The literature of chivalry above all dealt with manly violence, but it also spanned a range of important subjects from religion to the relations between the sexes.

It is worth noting that the Middle Ages preserved and read works on the ancient Romans and Greeks and integrated these into the literature on chivalry. One of the three themes of chivalric literature was "the matter of Rome," that is, stories both from history and imagination of great ancient times and heroes, Troy, Alexander, and Caesar.[14] Medieval knights read the classic Roman military text *De re militari* by Vegetius, in fact the taste for Vegetius corresponded with the rise of chivalry. Lest this be taken as proof of the survival and dominance of the classical "Western Way of War," however, it should be recognized that medieval readers viewed Vegetius not as a tract on great, disciplined infantry armies, but as a work that counseled the kind of warfare that they were used to, one that stressed attrition and stratagems. In addition, with its emphasis on courage, *De re militari* could be and was read as a book on chivalry; in fact one translation of *De re militari* was entitled *Livre de chevalerie*.[15] Medieval armies in the field were not composed of free, enfranchised farmers, but of aristocratic knights and a far larger number of disenfranchised commoners, with the possible exception of some urban militias. They hardly conformed to Hanson's picture of the Western soldier, tactically or in terms of civic militarism.

Reflecting the omnipresent power of religion, a heavy veneer of piety overlies the discussion of chivalry. It appeals to God and Christ and stresses the protection of the Church. Perhaps the most honored of romances tells of the quest for the Holy Grail. Masters of the chivalric tradition defended knighthood on the basis of preserving order so that people could lead Christian lives. In fact, Kaeuper describes chivalry "as the male, aristocratic form of lay piety."[16] However, in revering God and His Church, chivalry was not subservient to the dictates of that Church or its clergy. So, for example, popes, councils, and theologians condemned tournaments, but this did not diminish aristocratic participation in these ultimate expressions of chivalry. Eventually the papacy sponsored the Crusades and religious orders of knights, such as the Templars, so it came to terms with the violence of knights, but this was the Church adapting to chivalry, not the other way around.

Warrior values of prowess, courage, honor, and loyalty provided the heart of chivalry. When the literature speaks of virtue, it fundamentally concerns *virtu,* manly power and excellence. Prowess with arms dominates, and this prowess is far more about force than forbearance. Tales of honored warriors praise the blow that hacks off an arm or cleaves helmet and head. Fighting in a tournament against fellow knights of the Round Table, Lancelot performs "great marvels of his prowess that he had proven in many places before, because he split knights and horses to the right and left."[17] The purest of knights, Galahad, demonstrates his prowess with his sword by mightily cutting through his opponent's "shield, the pommel of his saddle, and the horse's withers, so that half the horse fell one way and half the other."[18] In describing an actual campaign, Gerald of Wales awarded high praise to the knight Meyler Fitz Henry: "Meyler, thus left alone, and surrounded by the enemy on every side, drew his sword, and charging the band, boldly cut his way through them, chopping here a hand and there an arm, besides hewing through heads and shoulders, and thus rejoining his friends."[19]

Courage, always necessary in war, became all the more essential in this particularly bloody form of combat, with its fearsome actions and sights. The real knight had to embrace a particularly chivalric bravery, face great danger, and accept awesome risks. In fact, without courage there could be no prowess, because warriors would have fled combat.

Prowess and courage ensured honor. A complex idea, honor is best interpreted as reputation, and for the knight this meant appearing as an example of the warrior virtues. Aristocratic men of medieval and early modern Europe valued their honor so highly that they gambled their lives to maintain it even in what would seem to modern eyes as frivolous matters. Men could fight for no other reason than to avoid any suspicion of cowardice. In fact, a sense of masculine honor led to the common, almost casual nature of violence. Aspersions and insults could not be brooked for the sake of one's own dignity or that of one's family. A woman's personal honor had more to do with sexual propriety, of course.

Next within the chivalric code came loyalty, of immense importance in life and in combat. In what Philippe Contamine has termed the "feudo-vassalic system," individuals, "men and women, great and small, young and old, owed military service of various sorts to their lords for their fiefs."[20]

Historians today question older stereotypes about "feudalism," but these need not trouble us here. The essence was that the feudo-vassalic system cemented the relationships between lord and vassal with pledges of loyalty; dissolve loyalty and the edifice would fall. For Llull, the ultimate treacheries were to slay a lord, surrender his castle, or sleep with his wife.[21] In this context, we can see why Lancelot's sin with Guinevere was unforgivable. Obviously, loyalty on the battlefield meant life or death. Without it, armies disintegrated during combat and leaders faced their enemies alone. There was loyalty in love as well as in war. The statutes of the Order of the Band of Castille proclaims loyalty as "one of the greatest virtues that there can be in any person, and especially in a knight, who ought to keep himself loyal in many ways. But the principal ways are two: first to keep loyalty to his lord, and secondly to love truly her in whom he has placed his heart."[22] There will be more said about such love soon.

Beyond being warriors, knights exercised the powers of rulers on their own estates or as feudal barons; thus, they held the values of men of authority. Moreover, given the fact that the heyday of chivalry came in the high and late Middle Ages, as the great monarchies of Europe took form, chivalry promoted loyalty and service to those in power; and in legend and in fact, kings benefited from this. Knights are clearly defined as men in service to princes who deserve their labors and loyalties, but if the knight serves his prince, he is not blindly obedient. Pride and a sense that he deserves his own authority made the knight inherently independent, a man who reserved his judgment and his right to assert his own honor.

In his own authority and in supporting that of his lord or his king, the true knight had to seek and support justice. For Llull, "Chivalry is the disposition with which the knight helps the prince maintain justice."[23] As a master of violent force in his own land, the knight had to wield his arms not only bravely but rightly, or he would become a danger to his society and his prince.

Instead of employing his power to abuse, the knight must protect the helpless, as a good ruler protects his subjects. A knight's protection especially extended to widows and orphans, those who had no man to take care of them. The Mainz Pontifical, one of the fundamental texts for the dubbing ceremony that raised a man to knighthood, includes this blessing of the sword: "Bless this sword . . . so that it may be a defence for churches, widows and orphans, and for all servants of God against the fury of the heathen."[24] During the Hundred Years' War, Philippe de Mézières argued that the "laws of true chivalry, by which they ought to fight" required that knights protect "those who are under oppression and cannot defend themselves."[25] Thus the true knight was to defend the poor, honor women, and defend damsels. It is important to recognize that those most explicitly to be protected were of the noble class. In Thomas Malory's *Morte Darthur,* King Arthur requires an oath of his knights at Pentecost, which included a promise "always to do ladies, damsels, and gentlewomen and widows succor; strengthen them in their rights, and never to force them upon pain of death."[26] The terms "ladies, damsels, and gentlewomen" makes clear the class focus of this pledge. Still, there was an implication of a wider responsibility. One mid-fourteenth-century poem has the French captain Jean de Beaumanoir criticize the English knight Richard Bamborough for committing "a great sin" by abusing "the people who till the wheat" for if it was not for them, the nobles would have to work the land themselves "and suffer poverty."[27]

Beyond the *virtu* of warriors and views of men of authority, chivalry also espoused the values of court life. A lord had to be generous to those around him, particularly if the lord hoped to lead them. A great knight was to dispense largesse to the extent of his resources. In *The Story of Merlin,* King Arthur's vaunted conduct provides a literary example: "He sought out fighting men everywhere he knew them to be and bestowed on them clothing, money, and horses, and the poor knights throughout the country took him in such love that they swore never to fail him even in the face of death."[28] Without largesse, how could a knight or lord gain a following? Generosity extended beyond the giving of gifts to staging banquets, festivals, and tournaments. As in so much of medieval relations, there was a quid pro quo, but largesse seemed a path to inspiring, not buying, loyalty. Beyond this, largesse would socially separate the open-handed lord from the tight-fisted merchant. The aristocrat's seeming unconcern about personal wealth, as witnessed by his distributing it to others, marked him as above the bourgeois.

The proper knight also practiced the key virtue of courtesy. Certainly this involved proper manners, knowing how to act among the elite, but it was more as well. Courtesy in the normal sense certainly could tame the mighty warrior, or at least help him act tame in the right circumstances. Yet courtesy in a sharply hierarchical society of individuals jealous of their honor could help one avoid insult that could lead to injury. This may be considered in the same vein as the Confucian *li,* which was much more profound than etiquette; *li* signified treating a person correctly according to his or her station. In his *Romance of the Wings* (ca. 1210), Raoul de Houdenc suggested that prowess could only fly on two wings, the first being liberality, referring to largesse, and the second being courtesy, which required love of the Church and avoidance of pride, boasting, envy, and slander. It also led to the next and last element in this survey of chivalric tenets—"that he should be a lover and that he should love truly for love's sake."[29]

Courtly love, on the surface not very military, nevertheless raises the entire issue of how women relate to masculine codes of legitimate violence. Today scholars shy away from the term "courtly love" and prefer "courtliness," but I will use the older terminology, since it is the relationship between men and women and the role of sex as a reward for military success that most interest me here.

In its most idyllic form, courtly love entailed the notion of platonic affection, but even in the literature of chivalry it need not be so remote. The essence was that the love of a woman could both inspire a knight to deeds of valor and reward him for his noteworthy feats. In his *Parsifal,* Wolfram von Eschenbach put this notion in the speech by Willeham delivered on the eve of battle: "There are two rewards that await us, heaven and the recognition of noble women."[30] In *The Story of Merlin,* Merlin uses a kiss from Guinevere to drive young Arthur in battle: "Arthur, now we'll see what you can do here today. See to it that the kiss that your lady gave you is dearly paid for [by the enemy], so that it will be talked about all the days of your life."[31] Written during the Hundred Years' War, the biography of the French marshal Boucicaut insists: "Just as one reads of Lancelot, of Tristan, and of many others, who love inspired to good and to attain renown, in the same way the service of love has made many of our living nobles in France and elsewhere . . . valiant."[32]

The recognition Willeham mentioned can be enjoyed without being consummated, but clearly it often was and was known to be. In *Raoul of Cambrai,* the heroine Bernice speaks of her desire for the hero Bernier: "Oh God who judges all things, how fortunate one would be, to be the lover and the engaged bride of such a knight. Anyone who was allowed to kiss and embrace him would find it better for her than meat and drink."[33] Of course, this could lead to a cardinal breach of loyalty. One version of the Arthurian legend has Guinevere defend her betrayal of Arthur with Lancelot: "But the power of the love that led me to do it was so great that I could not resist it; and besides, what was calling me was the prowess of the finest of knights."[34] As would be expected, men were certainly driven by lust, and this need not be disguised. In one of the bawdier stories coming out of this tradition of courtly love,

Duke William IX of Aquitaine is said to have painted the image of his mistress on his shield to honor her, declaring that "he would serve under her ensign in battle as she did [under] him in the bedchamber."[35]

Women certainly enjoyed an honored, and tender, role in chivalric literature, but we need to be aware of some of the nuances that make their position less idealized. The sanctity of a woman might well be tied to her relationship with a man at arms. A knight might combat over his lady or her honor, but this may have been as much out of self-love as out of love. A woman could be an extension of the man who claimed her, almost property, and thus the knight might unsheathe his sword to assert himself rather than to defend her. This notion of woman as property emerges in Chrétien de Troyes's *Lancelot*, as the Lovesome Damsel explains to Lancelot:

> The custom and policy at the time were as follows: any knight meeting a damsel who is alone should slit his own throat rather than fail to treat her honourably, if he cares about his reputation. For if he takes her by force, he will be shamed forever in all courts of all lands. But if she is led by another, and if some knight desires her, is willing to take up his weapons and fight for her in battle, and conquers her, he can without shame do with her as he will.[36]

Here fighting wins sex, not as a willing submission but as conquest, even when a noblewoman is involved.

The direct involvement of women in chivalry was fundamental. Their attention, affection, and favors rewarded valor, and even if they did not bear the lance and sword themselves, they could appreciate combat. They grew up amidst the violence of the Middle Ages and sent fathers, brothers, lovers, husbands, and sons off to fight. Certainly, along with the honor of being adored by women came the shame of their disdain. Women were not decoration in the discourse on chivalry, they were important supporters of the code.

Taking the literature of chivalry seriously, the true knight would be a man of prowess and authority who was pious, brave, loyal, just, protective, generous, courteous, and courtly. The great medieval authority on chivalry, Llull, offered this definition: "A knight was a man chosen to ride on horseback to carry out justice and to protect and safeguard the king and his people so that the king could reign in such a manner that his subjects could love and know God."[37] Certainly such a lofty ideal could be attained rarely, but was it little more than an unreachable star? Kaeuper argues that the literature of chivalry was not so much descriptive as it was prescriptive; it was a literature of reform, expressing more how things ought to be than how they were. In other words it was a discourse of aspirations. The question then becomes, how outside the chivalric ideal was the real world of war? The *chevauchée* makes the contrast uncomfortably clear.

THE BRUTAL REALITY OF THE *CHEVAUCHÉE*

In profound contrast to the elegant aristocratic discourse on war, reality showed a vicious face. We have already seen some of that divergence on the field of Crécy, but the campaign leading up to that battle revealed the differences in a far more brutal manner. Before defeating Philip's army, Edward III had led a great *chevauchée* that ravaged France and compelled Philip to face him on that field of Edward's choice. Literally translated, *chevauchée* means a "ride," sharing as its base *cheval* just as does "chivalry." But a *chevauchée* was not a ride but a raid, typified by pillage, burning, rape, and murder. The term *chevauchée* was already in use long before the Hundred Years' War; it appeared, as *chevalchie*, in the *History of William the Marshal* in the early thirteenth century, for example.[38]

The English relied on *chevauchées* with devastating regularity during the Hundred Years' War. During the first four decades of that conflict, the English launched eleven such major raids—1339, 1342, 1345, 1346, 1355, 1356, 1359–1360, 1369, 1370, 1373, and 1380. These were not simply the affairs of small parties, but of entire armies cutting a path some five leagues to either side of the main line of march, meaning that they ravaged a swath about twenty-seven miles wide. This means that during the Black Prince's 1355 *chevauchée,* which covered 675 miles, the English devastated 18,000 square miles.[39] The herald of Sir John Chandos reported that King Edward's son and heir, Edward the Black Prince, "rode towards Toulouse; there were no towns which he did not lay waste. He took Carcassonne, and Béziers and Narbonne, and laid waste and harried all the countryside as well as many towns and castles."[40] Such repeated fury explains why the Hundred Years' War constituted a catastrophe of nearly unimaginable gravity for France. The great Italian poet and humanist Petrarch had visited this bountiful land shortly before the Hundred Years' War and was shocked when he returned a quarter century later in 1360; the English had "reduced the entire kingdom of France by fire and sword to such an extent that I . . . had to force myself to believe that it was the same country I had seen before."[41]

In a sense, the *chevauchée* was simply an extreme and Machiavellian extension of the kind of pillage endemic to medieval warfare as a result of the inflexible dictates of logistics and the ever-present problem of paying for an army.
The fact is that medieval armies had to take from the surrounding countryside in order to maintain themselves on campaign. At the very least, horses
had to be fed by gathering local forage.[42] A horse could consume daily about
twenty-five pounds of dry forage or fifty pounds of green forage freshly cut in
the field. A force of 5,000 chargers and draft horses would consume 62.5 tons
of dry or 125 tons of green forage each day, or 437.5 and 875 tons for a single
week. Such quantities were really beyond what a force like this could drag
along with it. Thus, forage had to be taken in the field, most conveniently out
of local barns along an army's path. Although there might be some effort at
compensation in friendly territory, in hostile territory fodder was simply
stolen. In fact, because armies generally could not pay their way, they regularly resorted to confiscation or theft. Men had to eat as well, and while there
was a better chance of a small army being able to cart food supplies, particularly bread, armies lived off the land to a greater or lesser extent on food found
or seized locally. The need for armies to live off the country forced troops into
predatory contact with the local population, making abuse virtually inevitable
even in the best of situations.

The fact that armies could only survive by living off the country also lent
special force to a scorched-earth strategy. By destroying the resources of the
countryside over and beyond what one army needed, that army hampered the
ability of its foes to survive. In Jordan Fantosme's *Chronicle,* Count Philip of
Flanders counsels: "Thus should war be begun: such is my advice. First lay
waste the land [so that] nothing is left [for the enemy] of which they could
have a meal."[43] And the logic of pillage went even further than this.

Medieval soldiers served with an army or band for a variety of reasons.
Knights and their retainers might well appear out of feudo-vassalic obligation.
Terms of such service varied widely and the tradition certainly waned in the
Late Middle Ages. A common, but by no means universal, period required a
vassal to serve his lord in arms for forty days. Lords might also call up local
peasant or town levies as well. In addition, armies might serve for pay and
plunder, as did Edward's troops at Crécy.[44] Given the limits of the princely
purse, pay could be insufficient or irregular or simply never appear. Not surprisingly, unpaid troops felt more than justified in taking some form of compensation from the unlucky villages and towns in their paths. One old French
captain argued the necessity of preying on his own king's subjects:

If it please the king, our lord, to supply us with victuals and money to sustain us, we will serve him in all his enterprises and obey all his orders—as indeed we must do—without levying or exacting anything from the inhabitants of the countryside here. If, however, other affairs, or false counsel, prevent him from provisioning us or paying us, we ourselves must raise victuals and finance both from persons in our own obedience and from enemies, as reasonably as we can.[45]

Medieval men of war also regarded war as a source of wealth through plunder. Today, we regard troop motivation primarily as the product of psychological rationale—nationalism, ideology, religion, or dedication to task—buttressed by the bonding between men in units, but this is a modern point of view. In ages past, both coercion and the hope for material rewards have compelled and driven men in war. Medieval warriors, be they noble or common, hoped for gain. So important was plunder to them that medieval military custom, varying from country to country, set out the principles of dividing spoils on campaign in great detail.[46] Some troops fought for nothing else but what they could take on campaign. *Routiers,* late medieval mercenaries with a bad reputation, could act like privateers—not paid directly by the crown, but licensed and legitimated to take what they could from the enemy. Still other bands of "free companies" or "free booters" operated like pirates, using their arms to plunder anyone at will.[47]

If the needs of supply made abuses probable and the lust for material gain made plunder inevitable, the goals of strategy made destruction desirable. Rampaging through an adversary's territory accomplished more than filling the attacker's wagons with booty; it undermined the foe. By devastating a foe's lands and plundering his people, an attacker could discredit the enemy prince. The fundamental obligation of a prince was to defend his own, so a rapacious *chevauchée* conducted against him could undermine princely legitimacy. This was all the more to the point in the case of Edward III, because he challenged Philip's claim to the throne of France. Moreover, by impoverishing an enemy's subjects, destruction also eroded that prince's ability to acquire further resources, either by taxation or requisition. By discrediting and weakening the enemy, the *chevauchée* could achieve victory through attrition, a common strategy of medieval armies. This certainly was the primary role of the *chevauchée,* but it also could be used to precipitate battle.

Devastation could compel an enemy who was safely ensconced behind castle walls to come out and fight. Modern students of medieval warfare are quick to point out that for all the discussion of battle in chivalric literature, major engagements in the field were relatively rare. Sieges and raids consumed the vast majority of campaigns. Defensive architecture was so strong that defenders could withdraw behind their walls, and attackers had to invest a great deal of time and resources in the doubtful enterprise of besieging such fortifications. It is a commonplace that the Middle Ages saw a superiority of the defense over the offense. The limited resources of a medieval army, and the fact that noble feudo-vassalic levies could rightfully leave after they had fulfilled their term of duty, meant that time worked in favor of the defender who could outwait the attacker. However, an attacker could pry the foe out of his castle and compel him to take the field, by attacking that foe's countryside. Edward III used his *chevauchée* in this calculated manner to force Philip to give battle in 1346.

Chevauchées colored medieval warfare with flame-red fury. Armies intent on keeping moving could rarely stop for systematic demolition, but they could enlist fire to do the work for them. Along with driving off livestock, burning proved the most effective means for a mobile army to ravage the countryside. Edward III said of one of his first campaigns, "We began to burn in the Cambrésis so that that country is clean laid waste as of corn and cattle and other goods."[48] Writing of the Black Prince, a master of the *chevauchée* himself, the Chandos Herald reports that "the English to amuse themselves put everything to flame. There were made many a lady a widow and many a poor child an orphan."[49] The medieval nobility developed a taste for war, and they enjoyed its garnishes. Henry V quite literally took relish in flames; he asserted with zest, "War without fire is as worthless as sausage without mustard."[50] Such sentiments were not restricted to the Hundred Years' War, of course; destructive raids had a long history. The twelfth-century author of the *Chanson de Gaydon* criticized knights' lust for having "no desire to make peace, they have always heard the war-cry, and they love war more than Nones or Compline. They would rather one town burned than two cities surrendered without a struggle."[51]

Along with fire rode murder and rape. Peasants and townsmen who defended themselves and their property, or simply wished to escape the torrent, fell to sword and fire. The Carmelite friar Jean de Venette reported that the English broke into a fortified church and massacred one hundred peasants at Orly on Easter Week during the *chevauchée* of 1360. Another nine hundred died at Chatre when raiders burned the church in which they were sheltering.[52] The same witness claimed that as the countryside sank into lawlessness, the local nobles provided no protection: "Rather did the burdens which bore so heavily upon the people seem to please the lords and princes."[53]

Women became plunder, and rape was common. The same force used to pillage could be turned to this particular violence. It was a demonstration of power, a gratification of lust, and a means of extorting money. Soldiers admitted to, or boasted of, "raping women and deflowering virgins."[54] Many a peasant faced the alternative of rape or ransom. One particularly vicious practice was to lock a man in a bin, while his wife was raped on the closed lid. He could only save the poor woman by revealing where he had stashed his money.[55] Women might be held for ransom and violated while confined. In his *Lay de guerre* (ca. 1429), the poet Pierre de Nesson has his she-devil War, "from the abyss of hell, the daughter of the felon, Lucifer," proclaim, "There will be neither old or young woman who is not taken, raped, and defamed."[56]

Soldiers, *routiers*, and freebooters demanded ransoms to spare individuals and communities from the horrors of war. Villages and towns would have to buy off a band by paying it *patis* to keep it at bay. However, offering one group of soldiers *patis* did not secure a town protection against other marauders, so it might have to pay *patis* to several bands at the same time. Should a village or town promise payment, but then come up short, it risked reprisal raids.[57]

Although the brutality of medieval warfare was not restricted to the *chevauchées*, the destruction they unleashed epitomizes its vicious reality. In a very real sense, the *chevauchée* represented a strategy of terror. It focused the fury of war on the civilian population to force the enemy prince to change his conduct of war. In the words of Clifford Rogers, a historian of the *chevauchée*: "Noncombatants were made the victims of attack because attacking noncombatants *worked*, because it could facilitate the conquest of a fortified region, compel an enemy to do battle in the field, or hamstring him economically or politically."[58]

Regardless of chivalric language of justice and protection, the rapacious reality of war struck hardest those with a limited ability to defend themselves. Honoré Bouvet wrote in the fourteenth century: "In these days all wars are directed against the poor laboring people and against their goods and chattels. I do not call that war, but it seems to me to be pillage and robbery. Further the way of warfare does not follow the ordinances of worthy chivalry or the ancient custom of noble warriors who upheld justice, the widow, the orphan and the poor."[59]

So much violence was directed at noncombatants that they did what they could to run or resist. It was not an equal contest by any means, but peasants both fled the predation of soldier bands and opposed them. The French crown authorized armed resistance, as in 1357 when the regent decreed, "We wish and command that anyone may resist them by any method which seems best to them, and to call for help from neighboring villages by the sound of bells."[60]

The easiest way to avoid pillaging bands was to flee, and peasants would try to escape with their animals and moveable goods to the forest. Also, where possible, peasants dug underground corridors with multiple secret entrances to hide from marauding troops. Such subterranean retreats seem to have been excavated in every province and were most abundant in Picardy.[61] Fortified churches provided more obvious, and more vulnerable, refuges. Such local strong points did not enjoy much success against full-scale armed raids like the *chevauchées* but could be quite effective against small bands of brigands. Whole villages and farms were also fortified, and some of these fortified farms still dot the French countryside today.

Story and legend celebrated peasant heroes who combatted raiders. The most famous of these was the giant Grandferré, celebrated by Jean de Venette: "One of his blows, aimed straight, never failed to cleave a man's helmet and to leave him prostrate, his brain pouring out of his skull."[62] In such harsh times, common people took to violence, but not always to resist brigands in the manner of the hearty Grandferré. Indeed, many peasants responded to the loss of their homes and livelihoods by becoming brigands themselves; they probably had little choice.

Local lords sometimes saw peasant resistance to raiders as undermining their own authority and threatening rebellion. The most extreme form of peasant action was precisely that. In 1358 the peasantry near Paris, burdened by unreasonable taxation by their own monarchy, which could not protect them from abuse by English *chevauchées,* rose up in a Jacquerie, a revolt that derived its name from the common appellation for a peasant, Jacques Bonhomme. This, the greatest of the medieval Jacqueries, lasted only two weeks from late May to early June, but it so challenged the landholding aristocracy that the nobles put down the rebellion with unequaled ferocity. The *chevauchée* seemed to have eroded the very foundations of society.

EDWARD'S *CHEVAUCHÉE* OF 1346

The *chevauchée* that led up to the battle of Crécy was as severe as any mounted by the English during the Hundred Years' War.[63] It offers a chilling example of the interplay of necessity and design that gave medieval warfare its rapacious character.

In 1346, Edward's campaign aimed at forcing Philip into a decisive engagement. The resultant fight, Crécy, would be an anomaly in a number of respects, such as in Edward's refusal to take prisoners. But the greatest anomaly was the nature of the clash itself. In an age that fought few battles and strongly preferred other forms of campaigning, Crécy was a decisive battle. Urging from Parliament goes a long way to explain Edward's need to bring off such an odd event. When Parliament conceded him money for the campaign, it pressured him to "make an end to this war, either by battle, or by a suitable peace," and to ensure that Edward would devote his full attention and skill to the campaign, Parliament required that Edward cross the Channel and lead the army himself.[64]

As anxious as Edward was to fight, he could afford battle only on his own terms. He must have good defensive ground and fight where and when the French *must* come at him; the English could not take the tactical offensive. The French were sure to outnumber Edward's army, so it must not stand where it could be surrounded and simply "besieged" until it starved. He had to have an open route to his rear for both supply and retreat; this meant that Edward dared not be trapped against a river, such as the Seine or the Somme. Edward trusted that a *chevauchée* would force Philip to give battle to the English on ground and in circumstances that fit Edward's purposes.

The English landed on the Norman Cotentin Peninsula on 12 July 1346, and the next day Edward declared that his troops would spare the persons and property of clergy, old people, women, children, and all those who would recognize him as rightful ruler and "enter his peace." Bands of his men, however, immediately disregarded his decree and began to pillage on 13 July; they "cheerfully and boldly set fire to the countryside around, until the sky itself glowed with a fiery colour."[65] Edward had apparently meant to hold the Cotentin as a friendly base, but his men had come to plunder. Barfleur was one of the first towns to fall victim: "The English, eager to make war on the enemy, ranged across various parts of the country on the 14th, and several reached the town of Barfleur, where they found an abundance of hidden rich-

es and returned unharmed with a number of prisoners, both citizens and peasants. But first they burned the town."[66]

On 18 July with his army at his back, Edward accepted the surrender of the
Cotentin town of Valognes and took it under his protection, promising that
it would not be burned. But the next day Valognes went up in flames despite
the royal will. The army now split into three divisions to cover a wider expanse
of ground during its advance. St.-Lô unwisely chose to resist the English and
paid the price. Taken by assault, it did not deserve the restraint owed a fortress
that had surrendered, so Edward let his soldiers have their way. Notable
inhabitants were imprisoned and sent off to England as hostages for ransom.
They were comparatively lucky to be imprisoned, because killing and rape
accompanied the looting of the town. Jean le Bel wrote of the plunder from
St.-Lô, "No man alive could imagine or believe the riches which were there
acquired and robbed, even if he were told of it."[67] Finally, the English set fire
to the town.

A tougher fight awaited Edward at Caen when the English attacked it on
26 July. After seizing it, the English also went on the rampage. Froissart
reports that "Several gallant English knights . . . prevented a number of evil
deeds and rescued many a pretty townswoman and many a nun from rape."[68]
All well and good, but many more suffered. Resistance from desperate towns-
folk resulted in injury or death for several hundred English, which infuriated
Edward, and he ordered the entire population put to the sword. Sir Godfrey
of Harcourt intervened and pleaded with the king:

> There are large numbers of people in this town who will defend themselves
> from house to house if they are attacked. To destroy the place might cost
> you dear and cripple your expedition. . . . We can be master of this town
> without further killing. Both men and women will be quite ready to give up
> everything they have to us.[69]

Edward ordered a stop to the rampage, and as Harcourt predicted, his soldiers were richly rewarded. "The town and the suburbs unto the bare walls of
all things that might be born and carried out, was robbed and despoiled."[70]
Lack of resistance, however, did not end all the mayhem, for despite the
efforts of commanders "there were many ugly cases of murder and pillage."[71]
The army sent this booty and prisoners, including "sixty knights and three
hundred wealthy citizens," to the fleet at Ouistreham, from which it sailed to

England.[72] Meanwhile, detachments pillaged and burned the surrounding countryside. Panicked towns, including Bayeux, offered their surrender.

Edward began his march again on 31 July spreading fire and terror. In marvelously medieval fashion, Edward dispatched a herald on 7 August to challenge Philip to battle, but Philip, safe on the far bank of the Seine, declined. Edward would have to do more to compel Philip to accept battle where and when the English wanted it, so he marched toward Paris, stopping to rebuild the bridge at Poissy. Edward continued to torch towns and villages within reach. The English were so bold as to set ablaze St.-Germain, St.-Cloud, and Retz just miles from Paris. Philip next challenged Edward to fight on 14 August, naming the battlefield. The English king responded: "We have come without pride or presumption into our realm of France, making our way towards you to make an end to war by battle."[73] However, Edward was not ready to accept Philip's conditions or fight on a field of his choosing, so Edward crossed the Seine on 16 August and marched for the Somme, which, as we know, he forded on 24 August with Philip in pursuit. Once north of the Somme, Edward was ready for battle, and Philip was compelled to give it at Crécy.

TOURNAMENT: A PERFECTED FORM OF WAR

The flames of Edward's *chevauchée* illuminate the conflict between ideal and real in medieval warfare; campaigning did not, and could not, conform to the aristocratic discourse on chivalry. Literally speaking, of course, chivalry was a code designed exclusively for and by the social/military elite, not the common everyman, but chivalric mythology portrayed proper warfare as honorable and just, as protecting rather than ravaging the innocent. In contrast, actual conflict brutally victimized those least able to defend themselves, and even when knight fought knight, they could not always obey the niceties of combat and capture. In the words of Johan Huizinga, "This illusion of society based on chivalry curiously clashed with the reality of things."[74] Yet although real warfare refused to match ideal conceptions, powerful cultural necessity required some form of chivalric combat to maintain the self-image and justify the privilege of the aristocracy. In this circumstance, the military elite created a far more perfect, although artificial, kind of combat in the tournament, which pitted knights against knights in an exclusive and controlled version of war.

The tournament evolved, so while it retained its essence as a perfected form of warfare, it changed during the centuries from its inception through its 500-year-long history. Some award Godefroi de Preuilly credit for inventing the tournament in 1062, but there were certainly earlier precedents.[75] The tournament took shape between the mid-eleventh and the mid-twelfth century as a very rough affair. Groups, "teams," of knights would square off against one another over a prescribed area, large enough to simulate real military action in the field and often encompassing villages. Early on, common foot soldiers might accompany the mounted aristocratic knights. Contemporaries viewed the tournament as a French creation—English commentators referred to it as *conflictus Gallicus,* or the French fight—yet tournaments spread across Europe. English ordinances for tournaments demonstrate a first stage in their evolution. In 1194, Richard I (r. 1189–1199) issued an edict licensing tournaments in five areas, each between two townships. The site and day of the contest would be chosen in advance and publicized; contestants paid a fee to take part. The battlefield was not enclosed, but warriors could enter roped-in sanctuaries, called "refuges," to catch their breath and rest their horses. Such ordinances at first stipulated little concerning weapons or tactics, although the use of bows and crossbows seems to have been restricted. A century later, under Edward I (r. 1272–1307), things had changed. Men on foot could no longer carry weapons, and those wielded by the knights had to be blunted, or bated, in some manner. A lord could only bring a limited number of retainers with him to the fray.

Even though tournaments became more stylized and less deadly contests over time, they remained dangerous. Speaking of a tournament held at Lagny-sur-Marne in 1179, the author of the *History of William the Marshal* reported, "Horses fell down there thick and fast, and the men who fell with them were badly trampled and injured, damaged and disfigured."[76] At the tournament of Neuss (1241), eighty knights were supposed to have died. The same year, Gilbert the Marshal fell in a tournament at Chalons.[77] Later tournaments might reduce the group fighting to the mêlée, fought by rival teams within a much smaller enclosed field. In this, knights would be forbidden to strike an opponent below the waist or to injure his horse. Still, knights bashing about, even with blunted weapons, left scars.

Throughout its existence, many of the practices of the tournament exactly copied real battle. Knights captured by their foes in a tournament forfeited their armor and horses to the victor. Captors could hold their prisoners for ransom and refuse to release them until it was paid.

In a way that real war could not, tournaments could restrict participants to members of elite society, those practitioners and consumers of chivalry. And while aristocratic men attended in order to fight, their ladies attended in order to observe and reward. Festivities followed the hard fighting of the day, allowing for further mixing of the sexes and further recognition of the valiant by the fair.

As the thirteenth century progressed, individual contests between opponents, jousts, became more popular. Jousting pitted one champion against another on restricted courses enclosed by fencing, or lists. Authorities on chivalry accepted the joust as valuable practice for men in arms, but did not consider it as important as the group fights. Eventually jousting served as a warm-up for the central business of the tournament, so at Chauvency (1285), two days of such mounted duels preceded the battle, which was the main event.[78] When jousting with lances, the winner achieved victory either by unseating his mounted opponent or by breaking more lances against him. A broken lance scored better than one that remained intact because a shattered lance indicated a solid hit and not simply a glancing blow. A tournament ordinance of 1466 proclaimed, "whosoever breaks the most spears . . . shall have the prize."[79] Jousting may seem more like sport than battle, but tournament contests mirrored the "jousts of war," fought to the death on campaign, when knights from opposing armies challenged each other to single combat.[80]

The highly staged *pas d'armes,* or passage of arms, constituted a late medieval elaboration of the joust.[81] *Pas d'armes* adopted a theme, often Arthurian, which involved props, such as magic fountains or islands. These comparatively rare contests went by grand titles, such as the *Rocher périlleux* (1445) or the *Arbre d'or* (1468). Champions announced their individual challenges by ceremoniously touching shields hung up in advance of the *pas d'armes* to bring out rivals. These shows took some time to organize and cost a great deal. *Pas d'armes* were particularly important in the fifteenth century, whereas simpler jousts predated them by centuries.

Proponents of the tournament defended it as necessary training for war. Men had to develop and practice skills, endurance, and toughness through combat. Roger of Hoveden tells how the sons of Henry II (r. 1133–1189) sought tournaments in France because "he is not fit for battle who has never seen his own blood flow, who had not heard his teeth crunch under the blow of an opponent, or felt the full weight of his adversary upon him."[82] Two centuries later, Ralph Ferrers still credited the tournament with being "where the school and study of arms is."[83] In his *Livre de chevalerie,* ca. 1350, the great French knight Geoffroi de Charny judged the honor to be awarded different forms of conflict. The joust, though honorable, stood lowest, then the tournament, and finally war.[84] This scale was not simply an ascending rank of prowess, but stages in the training of a knight. It is worth noting that this training would create a warrior, but not a disciplined soldier; it was not drill in which the individual subjects himself to command, but self-assertion through arms. Josephus's famous aphorism observed of the Romans: "Their drills were bloodless battles, and their battles bloody drills." Tournaments were bloody and very much like battles, but they were not drills.

Historians have often regarded the tournament as sport: Huizinga, "the warlike sport of the Middle Ages"; Kaeuper, "the ideal sport"; Barber and Barker, the knights' "favorite sport"; Nickel "*the* spectator sport" for six hundred years; etc.[85] Certainly it offered the chance to display athletic ability with weapons, and there is no necessary conflict between sports competition and preparation for war. Consider the way in which Greek athletics prepared men to serve as hoplites. However, the tournament, though eventually stylized, was too much like war to be just a game. Although, if it qualifies as sport, what does this say about the violent sports of later ages?

For all its practical value, the tournament was also culturally necessary. With martial values so essential to status and privilege, to the very definition of the military/social elite, they needed to be exercised in a highly public forum. The real business of campaigning did not approach the full letter and spirit of chivalric standards, and it simply could not bend to fit them. Therefore, the aristocracy created the tournament to achieve its violent ideals. The Limousin troubadour Girart de Borneth wonderfully contrasted the chivalric splendor of the tournament with the ugly reality of pillage: "I used to see the barons in beautiful armour, following the tournaments, and I heard those who had given the best blow spoken of for many a day. But now honour lies in stealing cattle, sheep and oxen, or pillaging churches and travelers."[86]

In the language of this essay, the tournament was perfected reality, warfare as it should be in accord with the aristocratic discourse on war. It was freed from the tyranny of logistics, defensive technology, or political complexity; in the tournament, combat was tailored to fit the dictates of chivalric culture. The tournament was the right kind of combat for the right kind of people. While early tournaments did involve commoners, later contests excluded the lowborn. Eventually, knights had to prove their pedigrees to be allowed to participate. A German regulation, ostensibly dating from the mid-tenth century but known later, stated "Whoever would come to tourney, and is not born a nobleman by his parents, and cannot prove to have four noble ancestors, he cannot justly participate in a tournament."[87] In addition, those who had broken the codes of chivalry would be excluded or humiliated. Again, in reference to Henry the Fowler's code, anyone who had spoken "in any way against the Holy Faith" would be barred as would those who had somehow dishonored or ravished "women or virgins," broken a sworn oath, robbed "churches, monasteries, widows, and orphans," or attacked a neighbor without a proper declaration of war would be considered unworthy and punished. [88] Arsonists would find themselves similarly excluded, regardless of pedigree.[89]

Above all, the tournament was a public stage for prowess, courage, and honor. Those attending would see knights shatter lances and strike with swords. Because these arranged combats presented less threat than real war, perhaps tournament courage stood lower, but contestants still faced real pain and danger.[90] In any case, the honor won could be great, since the forum was so public and the witnesses so numerous.

Tournaments also provided the talented and courageous a way to accumulate the wealth necessary for a proper lordly life, with its need for largesse. Successful young competitors would make the tournament circuit to earn their purses as well as their spurs. In one medieval debate, a lady thoughtfully argues, "It is not love that makes young knights brave, it is poverty."[91] On the tournament circuit, adventurous young knights full of courage but empty of pocket could also attract a sponsor by tournament victories. In another way, the tournament was itself a display of largesse, where hosts could advertise themselves and their qualities.

One of the most interesting facets of the tournament, at least by the late thirteenth century, was the opportunity to combine the values of war with those of court behavior, because in this case the courtly community came to the "battlefield." The assemblage of the aristocracy gave full play to that aspect of courtesy that was based on the proper recognition of place and power within the elite, as well as giving knights a chance to display polite behavior. But far more interesting is the leverage given to women through the tournament. If war is political, as Clausewitz insists, then those without a political voice, the disenfranchised, count for less, so the legal distance between women and power matters more. But if war is at base cultural, or if the cultural dimension remains great even in a political contest, then the role of women in fostering military values and behavior looms much larger. To the extent that mothers, wives, and lovers accepted the discourse on war, they became agents of its promotion and enforcement. The literature and practice of chivalry put the relationship between the sexes center stage and declared that adulation by women and their granting of sexual favors served as a primary motivation for prowess and courage.

Martial competitions at a tournament gave knights the chance to perform before the women of their class. Knights might ceremoniously receive their arms from a lady or carry her token. By bringing together both sexes around a display of martial skills, the tournament created a highly charged environment for chivalric strutting and the workings of courtly love. At times it was particularly blatant; a lady would offer herself as the prize to the winner of tournament or *pas d'armes*.[92] But the competition for women's favors was not limited to a few. Some tournaments included a rather silly attack on a castle of love, in which fair damsels defended mock battlements with flowers and rosewater against assaults by ardent knights. The imagery of women employing flowers and men swords is embarrassingly obvious. When the defenders finally capitulated, they ransomed themselves with kisses.[93] A tournament might end not only with the declaration of a champion of arms, but a queen of beauty as well.

In this emphasis on women, the tournament diverged from war. Battles could not be fought before audiences including aristocratic women, and in the field, male bonding mattered much more than female adulation. Knights suffered discomfort and disease on campaign that could not be imposed upon court ladies at a tournament, even if champions could risk the danger of combat before their appreciative eyes.

Banquets associated with tournaments provided opportunities to reinforce chivalric values through the relationships between men and women. Geoffroi de Charny contrasts the reflected glory won by a woman whose champion proved his worth in combat, with that whose lover failed in the field. His consideration also demonstrates that the woman has helped to make the man.

Which one of two ladies should have the greater joy in her lover when they are both at a feast in a great company and they are aware of each other's situation? Is it the one who loves the good knight and she sees her lover come into the hall where all are at table and she sees him honoured, saluted and celebrated by all manner of people and brought to favourable attention before ladies and damsels, knights and squires, and she observes the great renown and the glory attributed to him by everyone? All of this makes the noble lady rejoice greatly within herself at the fact that she has set her mind and heart on loving and helping to make such a good knight or good man-at-arms.[94]

Women such as this embraced the aristocratic discourse on chivalry, even with all its stress on the bloody proofs of manhood.

The link between martial success and sexual reward was not always seen as something positive. Jacques de Vitry (c. 1170–1240), cardinal of Acre and, later, Tusculum, believed that the tournament encouraged all the seven deadly sins, including lust. "They do not want for the seventh deadly sin, known to be lechery, while so striving to ingratiate themselves with shameless women, if they can prove their prowess in arms; some are even in the habit of bearing women's love tokens in place of martial banners."[95] The Church, in fact, condemned the tournament for much of its history. If piety was one of the cardinal virtues of chivalry, that piety need not require obedience to Church authorities.

DISCOURSES ON WAR AND ON BATTLE: THE *HISTORY OF WILLIAM THE MARSHAL*

Though it was not real war, the tournament may tell us something fundamental about destructive campaigning, the discourse on chivalry, and the rather special circumstance of aristocratic combat. An understandable frustration plagues those who might try to reconcile war and chivalry. This problem has provided the central theme of this chapter, but we must go further in order to understand the complicated quadrille between reality and discourse. Other questions present themselves. If war did not conform to chivalry, was there another, more brutal discourse on war that recognized and legitimated reality? And if there was, what was its relationship to the discourse on chivalry? We can move toward answering both these questions by examining one of the classic documents of both chivalry and war, the *History of William the Marshal*.

This biography was the work of an anonymous writer, a *trouvère*, who composed the 19,215-line poem at the request of William's son, shortly after the death of his father. The *History* stands out as the first vernacular biography of a layman in European medieval history. There are reasons to give the *History* some credence, since the author could consult with the marshal's squire and since the author probably witnessed some of the events toward the end of the great man's life. The key point for us, however, is not whether the *History* faithfully reported the facts, but that it was written and believed, since these constitute evidence of a discourse.

William was an exceptional knight; the archbishop of Canterbury called him "the best knight in the world."[96] Born about 1146, the younger son of John the Marshal, William had no land of his own at first and made his fortune in the tournament circuit, where he was a perpetual winner. On his deathbed, William confessed: "I have captured five hundred knights and have appropriated their arms, horses, and their entire equipment."[97] In 1170 he became head of the military household of Prince Henry, son of Henry II, until the young man's death in 1183. He received lands first from Henry II and then from Richard I, in the form of marriage to a landed heiress, Isabel de Clare. This would lead to his assuming the title Earl of Pembroke. Counselor to Henry II, Richard, and John, he eventually became regent for John's successor, Henry III, in 1216. William's victory over Philip II of France at Lincoln in 1217, when William was in his seventies, helped secure the young Henry III his throne. A paragon of both tournament and war, William serves as a light on both. It is important to realize that William was recognized as not only a great warrior but also as a teacher of military skills. This model knight died in 1219, by which time he had become one of the best-known figures in Europe.

The *History* portrays the raw character of real war, albeit with the gloss of heroic poetry. William's biographer leaves no doubt that raids and sieges far outweigh battle in the warfare of his day; William only took part in two pitched battles during fifty years of service. One notable piece of campaign advice he gave to Henry II, campaigning against Philip II in 1188, illustrates the true conduct of war:

> Philip has divided and disbanded his troops. I advise you to disperse your men too, but to give them secret orders to reassemble at a given time and place. From there they are to launch a *chevauchée* into the territory of the king of France. If this is done in force, prudently and promptly, then he will find he has to suffer far greater damage. . . . This will be a better and finer deed.[98]

William advocates tricking Philip, avoiding battle, and carrying out a *chevauchée* against now defenseless civilians as "a better and finer deed," to which the king answers, "By God's eyes, Marshal, you are most courteous [or chivalrous] and have given me good advice. I shall do exactly as you suggest."[99] It is clear from other passages as well that for the king and for the *History*, raids on civilians, with all the attendant brutalities we have already discussed, were reasonable, even good, actions of war. Elsewhere, the author demonstrates his understanding and approval of *chevauchées:* "For when the poor can no longer reap a harvest from their fields, they can no longer pay their rents and this, in turn, impoverishes their lords."[100] A reader of Vegetius, William the Marshal championed stratagems and ravaging enemy territory. The authority on Angevin warfare, John Gillingham, sums it up: "The kind of war William fought—and by definition this was the kind of war the best knights fought—was a war full of ravaging, punctuated quite often by attacks on strong-points but only rarely by pitched battles."[101]

Given that "the best knight in the world" counseled and commanded campaigns fought in this manner, we can accept that this was what war was *supposed* to be. Thus, the *History* evidences a well-accepted vision of war, even if it was different from the formal codes of chivalry. We should then conclude that, in addition to the aristocratic discourse on chivalry, there existed what we can call a "practical discourse on war," which sanctioned war as it truly was, without surprise or, apparently, much regret. Parallel discourses on war can operate in the same society at the same time.

Certainly the two discourses are different, but it is important to realize that they also overlapped. Reading the *History* shows that in some important ways, chivalry provided an important subset of the practical discourse. In combat between aristocratic knights, the code of chivalry could very much apply.

William is reported to have conducted himself during battle much as he did when engaged in that chivalric ideal, the tournament. Describing a tournament at Lagny-sur-Marne in 1179, where some 3,000 knights competed, the author declares: "I can tell you that that encounter was not a stealthy affair, indeed, there was great noise and tumult as all strove to deal mighty blows. There you would have heard such a great clash of lances, from which the splinters fell to the ground."[102] Capture of opponents was of first importance, and the method repeatedly described in the *History* was seizing the reins of an adversary's horse: "there you might have seen knights taken by the bridles of their horses."[103] "Prowess," we are assured, was "shown and displayed for all to see."[104] In this particular tournament, the king was almost taken captive, but William rescued him. William emerged a hero, but many came out of the furious fighting "injured, damaged and disfigured."[105]

The same behavior, and the same words, describe battle. At the fighting around Le Mans in 1189, when Philip II drove Henry II from the town, the

History declares, "If you had been there, you would have seen lances shattering on a great scale, and much clashing of steel swords on helmets."[106] At Lincoln, in 1217, "Had you been there, you would have seen great blows dealt, heard helmets clanging and resounding, seen lances fly in splinters in the air, saddles vacated by riders, knights taken prisoner."[107] One description of Lincoln seems to come directly from a tournament: "Robert of Roppesley picked up a lance to joust, and, whatever the cost might be to him, he dealt such a savage blow to the earl of Salisbury, as our story has it, that he broke his lance to pieces, after which he rode on past. As he rode back, the Marshal dealt him such a fierce blow between the shoulders that he almost knocked him to the ground. . . ."[108] William seemed always ready to break lances or strike mighty blows against foes, but through it all he was particularly eager to take prisoners. At Le Mans, he seized several, although he was not able to keep them all. "The Marshal stretched out his hand, took Sir Andrew de Chauvigny by the bridle, and led him away."[109] "During the fight the Marshal took two others by the bridle, joining these two together."[110]

The description of battle transmits the notion of a contest between worthy opponents in a noble contest, rather than a struggle against ruthless aggressors. The *History* characterizes one of the Marshal's prisoners at Le Mans as "a very fine knight from the company of the count of Poitiers."[111] At Lincoln, the French enemies were "men who in the past were accustomed to coming first in the tournament."[112] When the enemy commander, the count of Perche, died from a sword thrust through the eye-slit of his helmet, the *History* laments, "It was a great pity that he died in this manner."[113] At Lincoln, though the Marshal's men were outnumbered, the atmosphere is described as being that of a tournament: "All those who listened to the earl displayed their joy and disported themselves as merrily as if they were at a tournament."[114]

In an essential sense, while a tournament was a perfected battle, a battle was but an imperfect tournament. Chivalry mattered in real war; it was not simply irrelevant. When the right sort met in combat, the discourse on chivalry provided a pattern for the discourse on battle within the larger and nastier context of the practical discourse on war. One cannot understand medieval combat, even in the midst of war, without reference to chivalry, but one cannot understand the more encompassing conduct of war in terms of the discourse on chivalry alone.

CHURCH ATTEMPTS TO
MITIGATE VIOLENCE AND TO PERFECT WAR

The Church had little tolerance for the violence of real war in Europe. Obviously the horrors of killing, rape, and destruction transgressed against the better angels of a religion that spoke of love and peace. Not surprisingly the Church sought to ameliorate the inhumane character of war; however, it is no less surprising that this lofty campaign had only limited success. Eventually these attempts to restrain the worst excesses within Europe gained a powerful ally in the call to redirect that violence away from fellow Christians and toward infidel Muslims who dominated the Holy Land. Thus issued the summons for the Crusades, which would constitute a second form of perfected war, in contrast to the chivalric ideal of the tournament.

The Peace Movement

Witnesses to the costs of war, churchmen sought to blunt its blows; the pervasive character of warfare in the Middle Ages made this a compelling but frustrating task. The decay of royal authority in the ninth century, after the death of Charlemagne and with the assaults on Europe by Vikings, Magyars, and Islamic raiders, saw political and military power fragment, often down to the level of local lords in their castellanies, areas best defined militarily as small domains based on a fortified site, or castle. Fiercely independent lords and knights looked to their arms to achieve their ambitions and settle their feuds, and lesser folk became the victims of warring parties. The superb historian of violence and medieval society Richard Kaeuper puts it clearly and crisply, "[F]or the emerging group of *milites* [knights] the world took on an almost Hobbesian cast; at least there was for the time no judicial institution capable of enforcing peaceful behavior on them, no ironclad restraint on the feuding and greed of these mail-clad warriors."[115] Even in the twelfth century, as the great new monarchies were beginning to consolidate their power, the plague of private wars continued. Orderic Vitalis, writing ca. 1123–1137, condemned Robert of Vitot and his "almost forty kinsmen, all proud of their knightly status, who were continually at war with one another,"[116] and the infamous torturer Robert of Bellême, who "hid the talents with which Heaven had endowed him under a sombre mass of evil deeds." Bellême "engaged in many wars against his neighbours as a result of his arrogance and ambition."[117]

Confronted by this flood of destructive private warfare, Church leaders, notably bishops, tried to constrain the warrior nobility through the peace movement. This began with an attempt to protect certain classes of people from attack in such conflicts, a protection known as the Peace of God. Bishop Guy held the first of the councils that proclaimed this peace at Le Puy in 975. At a great open-air meeting of knights and peasants, he compelled the assembly to take an oath to respect the Church and the poor. The Council of Charroux (989 or 990) produced three canons that anathematized those who robbed from churches or the poor or assaulted unarmed clerics.[118] A number of councils held from 990 through the 1030s in France followed these in condemning violence against protected categories of churchmen, peasants, and merchants. This, in fact, was an important milestone in formally defining noncombatancy in war.[119]

The Truce of God brought another strategy to the peace movement. Rather than exempting certain classes of people from attack, it sought to impose moratoriums on fighting at certain times. The Council of Toulouges (1027) in Rousillon climaxed in an oath forbidding warriors to attack their foes from Saturday evening through Monday morning, "in order to enable every man to show proper respect for the Lord's Day."[120] Other councils soon increased the basic truce to Wednesday night to Monday morning and added holy days and periods of Church festivals. Eventually the Peace of God and the Truce of God merged to produce expanded pleas for protection blessed by the Church. Yves de Chartres exemplified the confluence of the two in his *Panormia* (ca. 1094):

> We prescribe that priests, clerics, monks, pilgrims, merchants going and coming, as well as peasants, with their working animals, their seed and their sheep, be always in security. And we prescribe that the truce be strictly observed by all, from sunset on Wednesday through sunrise on Monday, and from Advent through the week following Epiphany, and from the third Sunday before Lent through the week following Pentecost.[121]

These prohibitions would forbid private warfare for about two-thirds of the year.

Sanctions were explicitly religious, but the Church and its leadership appealed to powerful lords and princes to support the will of the Church in sparing the vulnerable from violence born of constant warfare. About 1033, the millennium of the Passion of Christ, Archbishop Aimo of Bourges even tried to enlist the entire male population in a "war against war" to enforce peace on those who dismissed the Peace and Truce of God.[122]

The Council of Narbonne brought the Church-led peace movement to a climax in 1054. The first canon coming out of this council espoused the lofty, if unattainable, ideal that "no Christian should kill another Christian, for whoever kills a Christian undoubtedly sheds the blood of Christ."[123]

The peace movement, which evidences a distinct Catholic discourse on war, did not end private conflicts in Europe, but it was not without important consequences. Great lords, princes, and kings incorporated the Peace of God and the Truce of God in their efforts to curb the excesses and independence of their own aristocratic warriors and to impose peace within their domains. Thus rulers co-opted the peace movement for their own purposes. Yves de Chartres when insisting on the Peace and Truce was, in fact, appealing to Louis VI (r. 1108–1137) to support Geoffrey de Nogent, bishop of Amiens, against attack by Count Enguerrand de Coucy and others. In response, Louis led a royal army to Picardy in 1115 for just this purpose. Louis spent much of his reign subduing robber barons, but his campaign of 1115 appealed to the Peace and Truce of God for justification. In fact, under him and his successor, Louis VII (1137–1180), the Peace of God became the king's or royal peace. This transition becomes particularly clear in the correspondence of Abbé Suger, the great churchman and regent of France when Louis was off on Crusade, 1147–1148.[124]

Church Condemnation of Chivalry and the Tournament

The Church's attempt to confine war within new conventions stood in direct opposition to the chivalric elite's own concept of a higher form of combat, the tournament. Noted churchmen regarded the tournament not as an answer but as simply another face of the enemy. Certainly religious consciousness pervaded chivalry, as it did all medieval life, and the proper respect must be shown to the true faith. The tournament regulation attributed to Henry the Fowler began by declaring, "What nobleman would speak or act in any way against Holy Faith, shall not be admitted to the tournament."[125] Thus, piety was proclaimed and defended, but chivalric devotion to the tournament, even as the Church repeatedly cursed the practice, demonstrates the independence of chivalric piety from obedience to the papacy.

Churchmen turned against the tournament from its inception. At the Council of Clermont in 1130, Pope Innocent II placed a ban on tournaments:

We completely forbid those detestable fairs or festivals where knights cus-
tomarily gather by agreement and heedlessly fight among themselves to
make show of their strength and bravery, whence often result men's deaths
and souls' peril. Should anyone of them die on such an occasion, he should
not be denied penance and the last rights if he asks for them; yet let him
not enjoy Church burial.[126]

Church councils, such as those of 1148, 1179, and 1215, continued to condemn
tournaments, reinforcing a ban that would last until 1316, when Pope John
XXII finally revoked it.

The notable puritanical churchman Bernard of Clairvaux (1090–1153), later
elevated to sainthood, condemned not only what he called "those accursed
tournaments," but chivalry as a whole, at least in its secular form.[127]

What then is the end or issue of this secular chivalry, which I should probably just call wickedness outright, if its murderers sin mortally and its victims perish forever? . . . What engenders such war and raises such strife
among you is nothing more than unreasoned anger, or lust for profitless
glory, or want of some trifling worldly good.[128]

The Crusades

A righteous path led from the peace movement, with its attempt to parry the
thrusts of chivalric prowess, to the creation of the Church's own form of perfected struggle, the Crusades. Attempts to reform the practice of violence
would be supplemented with calls to transform the purpose of violence by
redirecting it away from the Christian community of Europe and toward the
infidels who occupied the Holy Land. The papacy had adopted the peace
movement as early as Nicolas II, about 1059, and the very first canon of the
Council of Clermont in 1095 proclaimed the Peace of God. It was also at this
council that Urban II delivered his famous oration proclaiming the First
Crusade. In it, the pope condemned private warfare, but offered the alternative of redemption though arms in the Holy Land. The sinful knights must
seek salvation by defending the Church in the eastern Mediterranean:

You, girt about with the badge of knighthood, are arrogant with great pride;
you rage against your brother and cut each other in pieces. . . . You, the

oppressors of children, plunderers of widows; you, guilty of homicide, of sacrilege, robbers of another's rights; you who await the pay of thieves for the shedding of Christian blood—as vultures smell fetid corpses, so do you sense battles from afar and rush to them eagerly. . . . If, forsooth, you wish to be mindful of your souls, either lay down the girdle of such knighthood or advance boldly, as knights of Christ, and rush as quickly as you can to the defense of the Eastern Church.[129]

The Crusades complemented the peace movement by providing an outlet for the martial penchant of the aristocracy in the Holy Land.[130] Knights might remain violent and deadly, but they would channel this torrent of force toward purposes sanctioned by the papacy.

A generation after Urban II preached the First Crusade, Saint Bernard of Clairvaux condemned the knight in harsh terms reminiscent of that pope, "impious rogues, sacrilegious thieves, murderers, perjurers and adulterers."[131] Bernard advocated the Second Crusade and saw salvation for knights in the crusading orders, such as the Knights of the Temple, or Templars. He even drew up the rule for the Templars, basing it on that of his own Cistercian order of monks. The Church continued to view knights as dangerous but promised them redemption through the use of their swords. It might not be possible to eliminate brutal violence, but it could be refocused. In the words of Guibert de Nogent:

> In our own time God has instituted a Holy War, so that the order of knights and the unstable multitude who used to engage in mutual slaughter in the manner of ancient paganism may find a new way of gaining salvation: so that now they may seek God's grace in their wonted habit, and in the discharge of their own office, and no longer need to be drawn to seek salvation by utterly renouncing the world in the profession of the monk.[132]

The crusading movement, begun with Urban's call in 1095, continued through 1270. In that period Western Europeans launched eight Crusades to the eastern Mediterranean. These included the highly successful First Crusade (1096–1099), which took Jerusalem in 1099. The massacre of virtually the entire Islamic and Jewish population there demonstrated the bloody fury possible to chivalry in the name of righteousness. The First Crusade resulted in the creation of Latin principalities in the Near East; later Crusades sought to aid these as an Islamic reconquista threatened and eventually took them. The low point of the crusading movement came with the Fourth Crusade (1202–1204), which ended with the capture and sack of Christian Constantinople by the Crusaders, who stopped there rather than attacking Islamic domains. The Crusades may have fallen short of the ideal in practice, but the concept that drove them was one of harnessing and perfecting chivalry as a servant of the Church.

Bernard's advocacy of the crusading orders represented the most thorough path to faultless chivalry, for his knights combined a warrior's prowess with a monk's self-effacing piety—at least in theory. Bernard praised the Knights Templar as "Christ's knights," a "Christ's chivalry" that worldly "chivalry which so clearly does its chivalrous deeds not for God but for the devil, can take either as a model of emulation or as an indictment of its ways." Of course, such Christian knights live in joy without "wives or loose women" and "without private property."[133]

Bernard wanted to reform both practice and purpose, but most who went on Crusade did so without forsaking their secular lives. Conon de Béthune commented on crusading and courtly love: "There [in Syria] shall the knights great and small do deeds of chivalry. Thus a man shall win paradise and honour, and the love and praise of his beloved."[134] Guy, *châtelain* of Coucy, was even more carnal: "May God raise me to that honour, that I may hold her, in whom dwell all my heart and thought, naked in my arms once before I cross the sea to Outremer."[135] Though the Crusades unified prowess with piety, they did not transform the knight into a saint; they sent the devilry elsewhere.

European chivalry enjoyed its apogee in the first half of the fourteenth century; soon after Crécy, the catastrophe of the Black Death would paint Europe in far more somber tones than the bright colors of heraldry. By the time of the battle, the literature of chivalry, although not yet complete, was immensely rich. Those great secular fellowships of knighthood were then emerging; in Castile, Alphonso XI created the Order of the Band, and in 1348 Edward III himself would found the Order of the Garter. Tournaments had given chivalry an image of its secular ideal and the Crusades its religious perfection.

But perfection yielded to perversion in 1346. The aristocratic discourse on chivalry envisioned combat as aristocratic and heroic and portrayed knights as pious and protective, even in their prowess. But a practical discourse on war recognized that commoners marched along with nobles and that the weak suffered at the hands of both. Knights carried the torch as well as the sword. Even when Edward proclaimed his protection for those Normans who acknowledged his lordship, his troops plundered all, and did far worse to many. Not that the campaign was without its chivalric accoutrements. Repeatedly the two kings challenged each other to battle as at a gallant *pas d'armes*. But the adversaries fought at Crécy virtually without quarter in the heat of the fight. Philip rode down his own mercenary crossbowmen, and Edward sinned against chivalry's own traditions by murdering rather than capturing fallen French knights.

The campaign and battle of Crécy exemplified how varied, intricate, and, at times, apparently contradictory was the interplay between reality and discourse in medieval warfare. Part of that complexity arose from the cultural nature of war. Elite medieval society embraced violence openly, wearing it proudly like a lady's token on the armor of its civilization. Combat was not simply required by a brutal and unstable world, it rose to become a virtue. In such an environment, while war might also be a tool of princely policy, it was none the less a cultural necessity. With combat considered a virtue, men sought opportunities for fighting. Tournaments and *pas d'armes* provided venues, but as Geoffroi de Charny insisted, the highest glory was won by those who went to war. Is there any wonder that it was welcomed? And so the armies faced each other at Crécy with all the trappings of chivalry, but the journey that brought them to the field was marked with the smoking remains of villages and towns, with the sufferings of those who could hardly understand the issues for which their so-called betters fought.

Notes on the Opening Illustration for Chapter Three

This illumination, itself a characteristic cultural product of the Late Middle Ages, takes great liberties with the Battle of Crécy. It imagines the English knights on horseback, although they fought on foot. Archers exchange arrows at close quarters in the foreground, although the great range of the English longbow proved its value that day, a fact indicated by the arrow-pierced crossbowmen on the left. This colorful representation, like the tournament, is an idealized conception of combat.

(Copyright Snark/Art Resource, NY)

CHAPTER FOUR

Linear Warfare

Images and Ideals of Combat in the Age of Enlightenment

AT FONTENOY, during the early morning hours of 11 May 1745, the French army led by Marshal Maurice de Saxe beat back the initial allied attacks. An assault by Dutch troops on de Saxe's right shattered against entrenched infantry and artillery, while an attempt by British and Hanoverian battalions to clear the French from the woods that anchored de Saxe's left stalled. About 9 A.M., the frustrated allied general, the duke of Cumberland, changed focus and launched a mass of 15,000 infantry to batter through the French center. Drums beat as his red-coated battalions marched toward their enemy and eternity.

The complicated ebb and flow of the War of the Austrian Succession (1740–1748) brought the opposing armies to the field. France only entered the conflict outright in March 1744, although it had previously taken part in the fighting as an ally of Bavaria, when its prince challenged Maria Theresa for the inheritance of her father, Habsburg Emperor Charles II. As the war greatly expanded for the French, Louis XV made plans to invade the Austrian Netherlands—essentially what is today Belgium.

Louis chose Maurice de Saxe to lead his armies in this critical theater. Maurice, one of many illegitimate children of Augustus the Strong, Elector of Saxony, began his military career with Habsburg forces, but in 1721 he transferred to French service. Rising to the rank of marshal of France at the outbreak of war in 1744, Maurice proved himself the greatest French general from the accession of Louis XV to the rise of Napoleon, and the battle of Fontenoy would be Maurice's masterpiece.

The French offensive had begun in 1744, but the need to respond to threats elsewhere and the king's illness forestalled a great campaign that year. But 1745 would be different. The king and his son, the dauphin, joined Maurice at Maubeuge in April. Intending to commit his army of 70,000 troops to a siege of Tournai, Maurice skillfully deceived the allied forces arrayed against him under command of the duke of Cumberland, third son to Britain's King George II and a man of meager talents. Cumberland was taken in by Maurice's feigned threat to Mons and did not block the French army's advance on Tournai, which the French invested on 28 April. Recovering his balance, Cumberland assembled about 50,000 troops and marched to relieve Tournai. Learning of the allied advance, Maurice left 18,000 troops in the siege lines around Tournai and came out to face Cumberland.

Maurice prepared excellent defenses along an inverted "L"-shaped front from Antoing on the Schelde River to Fontenoy and then on to the Wood of Barry. Maurice buttressed the short stretch of the "L" on the right from Antoing to Fontenoy with three redoubts mounting cannon. The French also surrounded the entire village of Fontenoy with field fortifications. The long arm of the "L" extended to the left from the village to the Wood of Barry. Maurice detailed infantry to hold the wood and sited two redoubts just below it. Artillery stationed in one of these, the redoubt d'Eu, swept the ground between the wood and Fontenoy, where fire from another battery would catch any advancing troops in a deadly cross-fire. He did not build redoubts on the open ground from Fontenoy to the wood, as if he was tempting the enemy to attack there. On this left wing, he stationed the bulk of his infantry backed with two lines of cavalry. His reserves stood well behind these lines covering the rear of his position and guarding pontoon bridges he had thrown across the Schelde to ensure his retreat, should it be necessary.

After his failed efforts on the flanks, Cumberland drove his massed infantry assault against the gap between Fontenoy and the wood. Without firing a shot, the British and allied battalions marched steadily on, maintaining their straight ranks as best they could under heavy French artillery fire. Finally the first line, composed of British guard regiments, breasted a slight rise and stood within fifty paces of the French. The British stopped to fire withering volleys that blasted the French line, shredding it with lead. Having decimated the enemy's front, Cumberland advanced several hundred yards past its initial position.

This crisis struck at 1 P.M. Marshal de Saxe had been relegated to being carried about on a litter that morning because of a severe attack of edema, a product of his dissolute life, but he now took to horse. Louis XV inquired if the situation was lost; forgetting himself for a moment, Maurice thundered back, "Lost, lost, what ass says that?"[1] Already, French infantry and cavalry were slowing Cumberland's advance. Maurice quickly brought up his reserves, including the Irish Brigade of Wild Geese in French service, men itching to pull the trigger on Englishmen. Faced with mounting resistance, Cumberland halted, recoiled, and re-formed his infantry into a three-sided square between the wood and Fontenoy. The allied troops excelled at the disciplined volleys of eighteenth-century tactics, but fierce French counterattacks exacted a heavy toll on Cumberland's isolated foot soldiers. French infantry alternately fired into the allied mass or crossed bayonets with them; elsewhere in the fight, French cavalry attacks compelled the allies to keep ranks, making them better targets for Maurice's well-sited artillery. Unable to resume his advance and unwilling to suffer continued heavy losses, Cumberland began an orderly withdrawal about 2 P.M.

De Saxe and his troops had triumphed.

One can see the battle of Fontenoy as example and metaphor. Let us begin with two memorials to Fontenoy, one in paint and one in prose, bearing in mind that the reality of battle cannot survive the final shot, but memory endures.

Louis XV chose to commemorate his victories in paintings just as had his great predecessor, Louis XIV. Only a year after the battle of Fontenoy and well before the fighting was over in the Austrian Netherlands, his chief military artist, Charles Parrocel (1688–1752), visited the battlefield to make sketches for a canvas.[2] His student and successor, Pierre Lenfant (1704–1787), later painted a series of French victories, including Fontenoy, to decorate the new Ministry of War building constructed at Versailles. While Parrocel's painting no longer exists, Lenfant's work, first unveiled at the art salon of 1761, can still be seen in the Musée de l'armée in Paris.[3] Interestingly, their court painter was the father of Pierre-Charles L'Enfant, who laid out the rational, linear pattern of Washington, D.C. The painting by the older Lenfant tells us much about the aesthetic of war in the eighteenth century. In the foreground, the beautiful attire of Louis XV and his entourage advertises the elegance of war, as do the uniforms of the troops shown with full accoutrements. Lenfant marshals his army in straight and exact lines, not only the squadrons near the king, but also the troops heavily engaged with the allied square in the crucial fight that occupies the center of the canvas and the event. Some horsemen rush from foreground to the central combat, but this adds movement, not disorder. Lenfant painted an image of control and glory. Parts of the field are obscured by smoke, but none by blood. No wounded writhe upon the ground; no gaps break the linear perfection of the infantry. The word "linear" has two meanings; on the one hand it denotes lines, as the neat formations of troops in the painting, while on the other it refers to predictability, as in a linear equation. Both meanings apply to warfare in the age of the Enlightenment. Lenfant's geometric regularity pleases the eye and reassures the viewer. Certainly reality could not have been so clean and precise.

A much-repeated anecdote concerning the battle also buffs reality to an ideal gloss. No less a literary figure than the great Voltaire spread this story in his *Précis du siècle de Louis XV*. There he immortalized the tale of how, during the main allied attack, the British guards of Cumberland's first advancing line approached the French and Swiss Guards of de Saxe's front. The British officers doffed their hats in salute to the French officers, who returned the courtesy. Then Lord Charles Hay advanced before his regiment and gallantly invited the French Guards to fire first, "Gentlemen of the French Guards, fire." To which the count d'Anterroches shouted back: "Messieurs, we never fire first; fire yourselves."[4] A series of crashing British volleys followed quickly on the heels of this final pleasantry. Others have repeated this story with different variants: Hay pulled out a flask and toasted the French; the troops cheered; Hay taunted the French instead of inviting them to fire, etc.[5] This moment of bravado even became the subject of later paintings.[6]

The incident probably did not happen, at least in the form Voltaire reported, but it still reveals much about the Enlightenment discourse on war. Officers were aristocratic gentlemen of high spirits, who shared much though they fought for opposing armies. They regarded battle as a theater to display their values of honor and bravery, even chivalry. Troops took pride in withholding their fire rather than in taking first blood. Beyond the practical reasons for doing so, to be discussed later in this chapter, belief in the virtue of forbearance in battle guided military practice.

Such memorialization of war reflected the tastes and ideas of the age as much as it did the reality of combat; that is clear, easily grasped. However, this chapter makes a far more challenging claim concerning the importance of those tastes and ideas—that they shaped contemporary military practice from the trivial to the essential, from buttons to battles. To demonstrate the great range of choice and action affected by cultural preconceptions, we must highlight diverse categories of influence. This chapter begins by considering the power of early modern aesthetics, proposing that the look of things mattered even in the most practical concerns. It then will discuss the pivotal role of thought, the Military Enlightenment, in imposing rational and scientific forms on operations and tactics. Next, we will note the rise of international law, which fostered reasonable conventions restraining combat. We conclude by weighing the importance of a critical martial value, aristocratic honor, not only in determining the conduct of officers but in affecting the administration and even the size of the French army. The diversity of the subjects discussed here is itself the uniting theme of this chapter, the top-to-bottom impact of conceptual culture on early modern armies and warfare.

AESTHETICS OF WAR:
AN AGE OF APPEARANCES

More than most, the ancien régime was an age of appearances, when people put much stock in the way things looked. Historians date the ancien régime differently, with some not using that label until after the death of Louis XIV in 1715. However, judged by its military institutions, the ancien régime in France, the primary focus of this chapter, began with Louis XIV's accession to power in 1661 and extended through the reigns of Louis XV and Louis XVI until the onset of revolution in 1789. During this refined epoch, it was impossible to disregard the influence of aesthetics and taste, even in practical matters.

An Age of Uniforms

A glance at French military uniforms reveals a tyranny of fashion that warped an innovation meant to foster the well-being of troops into one of decidedly compromised value.[7] Before the innovations of the seventeenth century, a common soldier usually furnished his own clothing much as would a modern carpenter or electrician on the job, but, as the monarchy spent increasing amounts on training and maintaining its soldiers, the provision of adequate clothing seemed a reasonable expense to protect the health of this greater investment.[8] Apparel equated with survival, as the great French Marshal Turenne insisted in 1667, "Nothing is more necessary for them than clothing; many soldiers will perish there because of not having received it soon."[9]

Wise commentators have written a great deal about the psychological role of uniforms in improving drill, increasing cohesion, and boosting military effectiveness among the rank and file, but, without denying that there is something to all this, such benefits seem more the unintended consequences than the driving force behind the adoption of uniforms. In fact, this adoption initially grew out of the need of the state to control its officers; other benefits came later. Since at this time officers were responsible for furnishing their men with clothing, they might save money by scrimping on the cut or quality of the clothes they supplied. Early military ordinances only stipulate that the clothing be good. In 1647, a time when exigencies required the monarchy to request its cities to provide clothing for the army, the minister of war, Le Tellier, sent a sample coat to provincial administrators, not to create a true uniform but simply to serve as a pattern that would hold the clothing to a general standard: "I send you a *pourpoint* or *justaucorps* that has been made here to serve as a model for all those that will be furnished by the principal towns of the kingdom."[10] A 1668 instruction to the new French inspector general, the famous Martinet, who gave his name to a style of exacting military discipline, stated, "It is not at all necessary to ask officers to have their clothing all the same nor made at the same time . . . ; but you must not allow, no matter what, that the soldiers be badly shod or badly dressed."[11] The effort to ensure adequate clothing and close loopholes for abuse led the government to distribute sample items to regulate the cut but, interestingly, not the color of clothing.[12] Uniforms also promised another way to limit the monarchy's expenses, for as a commander of the chateau of Angers suggested, "Soldiers would have more trouble in deserting if they were all dressed in the same manner, because one could recognize them everywhere more easily."[13]

Any pressure to make soldier's clothing look alike came later than the insistence that it be adequate to ensure the soldier's well-being or that it be of similar pattern to guarantee that the government got its money's worth. Therefore, function preceded fashion. Uniform color and decoration followed before long, however. Although some units sported uniforms as early as the 1660s, this was the exception. Soldiers and troopers of French line regiments probably did not regularly wear clothing of uniform color until the 1680s. In 1673, the minister of war, Louvois, informed Marshal Luxembourg that it was not necessary to attire troops "in new clothes for this year, nor all in the same fashion."[14] And as late as 1682, Louvois instructed infantry that "His Majesty desires only that all the *officers* of the same regiment be dressed in the same color."[15] Yet in 1685, an ordinance finally prescribed particular colors for regiments in French service: blue for the French guards and the royal regiments, red for the Swiss, and gray-white for regular French infantry.[16] The first regulation stipulating the exact details of uniforms appeared in 1704.[17]

The spread of uniforms occupies a place in the broader story of fashion. The noted historian Daniel Roche speaks of a "clothing revolution" during the ancien régime, and the institution of military uniforms should be put in this context.[18] The first French journal devoted to clothing styles, the *Mercure galant*, appeared in 1672, declaring that "Nothing pleases more than fashions born in France."[19] A few years later, a piece in its pages asserted: "I answer . . . that I believe that men acknowledged the empire of fashion more than the most inconstant and most ridiculous of Parisian coquettes."[20] Officers announced their position by their appearance, often wasting money on costly garnishes. Fashion demanded extravagance in the matter of silver and gold lace trimming. In fact, a desire to stem such wasteful costs supplied some of the impetus behind clothing regulations. An ordinance of 1672 preached: "One of the things that contributes the most to the ruin of the king's officers is the luxury and the sumptuousness of their clothes."[21] However, so strong was the compulsion for display that regulations never halted lavish extremes. Moreover, because French officers regarded their companies and regiments as demonstrations of their own elite status, uniforms worn by their troops became a form of aristocratic conspicuous consumption. The social values of the nobility reinforced the pressure to follow fashion.

Rousseau condemned Paris as a city where "Everything is judged on appearances"[22]; in a similar manner, Marshal Maurice de Saxe wrote of French uniforms in 1732, "The love of appearance prevails over attention to health, and this is one of the most important points demanding attention."[23] He complained that owing to fashion, "Our uniform is not only expensive but very uncomfortable; the soldier is neither shod, nor clothed, nor covered."[24] Utility suffered in the effort to put men in stylish garments. The standard three-cornered hat of the eighteenth century is a case in point. Descended from a hat with a broad brim designed to shade and shelter the head, this headgear now pinned up the brim so that it could do neither very well. De Saxe suggested that a more functional helmet replace it.[25] The large clumsy cuffs of the uniform worn during the first half of the century must also must have been a hindrance, particularly in loading the musket, but they too followed a form dictated by civilian styles.

In its mixture of function and fashion, the soldier's uniform provides a metaphor for other military aspects of the ancien régime. His attire fulfilled the practical need to cover his body, but did so in a way that drew from contemporary vogues in male clothing and these concessions to fashion compromised the utility of the uniform. In other ways, military institutions and the conduct of war also followed styles characteristic of the era. Military practice was shaped by hard realities, to be sure, but also by aesthetic preferences, intellectual predispositions, and societal values.

Fortifications

Aesthetics also conspired with utility to shape fortifications, those essentials of ancien régime warfare. The form of bastioned design that dominated this era—what some call a "star fortress," what Geoffrey Parker has described as the *trace italienne,* and what I have termed the "artillery fortress"—emerged during the Italian wars of the sixteenth century.[26] It replaced the high thin walls of medieval fortifications with low thick walls constructed to resist artillery bombardment and to provide a suitable platform for defensive artillery. Military architects and engineers contoured angles of walls, bastions, and outworks to allow gunfire to rake the surrounding ditches and thus defend the fortress by gunfire, rather than by manpower alone. The resultant designs were marvels of geometry.

Without denying the effective nature of these designs, two observations remain: First, these plans appealed as aesthetic creations beyond their practical functions, and, second, they reflected and influenced the way contemporaries conceived of battle. Looking at the design of a fortress such as Neuf Brisach, it is impossible to see it only as a practical pattern of masonry and earth. This fortress, the masterwork of Sébastien le Prestre de Vauban, the greatest French military engineer of the era and a model for all Europe, was also a marvel of intriguing design. Like other bastioned fortresses, it approached in appearance those elaborately ornamental medals and orders awarded by monarchs to their noteworthy subjects. How could anyone look at these plans without appreciating their geometric beauty? Certainly Louis XIV could not. The fortress models he ordered constructed, the famous *plans en relief*, were not so much practical tools as displays, almost ornaments.[27] Vauban thought them a waste, at least at first.

Some might insist that all this intriguing geometry was a product of necessity, pure and simple. And certainly, fortress design did respond to the realities of ballistics and materials, but the classic bastioned fortress was not the only response possible. The different, and radically simpler, system of fortification advocated by Marc-René, marquis de Montalembert (1714–1800), in *La Fortification perpendiculaire* (1776) demonstrates that other roads might have been followed. More than accomplishing a practical task in a manner that engaged the eye, Vauban's plans also expressed the rational, scientific ideal of the age; he was even appointed to the Académie royale des sciences.[28] Louis XIV imposed order on nature, witness his gardens at Versailles, and the late seventeenth century was, after all, the culmination of the Scientific Revolution. Fashion, both aesthetic and intellectual, cannot be written off.

The geometric patterns of fortifications and the methodical practices of siege warfare so attracted the European eye and imagination that they were proposed as models for armies on the battlefield. The proven rational guidelines drafted by Vauban, with their Newtonian, systematized simplicity, seemed to promise similar resolutions for battle.[29] After all, if the most common face of war during the reign of Louis XIV could be reduced to rules and neat lines, why could not the same be done for that rarer aspect of war, the full-scale field battle? Turpin de Crisse asserted "that the principles which serve for the conducting of a siege, may become rules for forming the plan . . . of campaign."[30] No less a military figure than Frederick the Great of Prussia said much the same: "We should draw our dispositions for battle from the rules of besieging positions."[31]

An intellectual monument of the Enlightenment enshrined the conviction that geometry linked fortress design, siege warfare, and battle tactics. The

Encyclopédie, edited by Denis Diderot (1713–1784), was the grandest publica-tion project of the age.[32] That great compendium began with a discussion of intellectual progress and knowledge in general, and part of this presentation was the "Detailed System of Human Knowledge," a graphic classification of man's intellectual endeavors that supplies a striking visual example of the cli-mate of opinion. In this system, both military architecture and tactics appear under "Science of Nature," as a form of "Elementary Geometry."[33] This ten-dency endured for some time; Adam Heinrich von Bülow (1757–1807), a well-respected tactical authority who published his first major work in 1799, still tried to establish mathematical principles to explain and guide the con-duct of war.[34] And the widely read nineteenth-century authority Antoine-Henri Jomini (1779–1869) would also continue the emphasis on geometrical analysis.

Infantry Tactics

As advocated by military figures and intellectuals of the Enlightenment, French battlefield tactics shared important characteristics with fortifications and siege warfare. Eighteenth-century armies arrayed themselves for battle like lines drawn across a page in satisfying regularity. Infantry normally stood only a few ranks deep, shoulder to shoulder, stretching battalion after battalion. Cavalry regiments similarly marshaled in thin squadrons guarded the flanks, while artillery garnished the formation. Armies generally presented a first solid line toward the enemy with a second line, usually with gaps between battal-ions to facilitate maneuver, stationed some two hundred yards behind the first. There was something formal, almost courtly, about the linear battle tac-tics of the age. Diderot, commenting upon Lenfant's painting of the battle of Fontenoy at the 1761 salon, spoke of "these long parallel files of soldiers, of these oblong or square bodies of troops, and the symmetry of our tactics."[35]

Linear infantry reached its peak with the Prussian army of Frederick the Great; its renowned parade ground performances marshaled troops in battal-ions so straight that they seemed to form a single rod of steel. The French never matched that perfection, and their tactical convictions took into account not only the logic and aesthetics of the line, but their self-image as particularly suited to attacks with cold steel, or the *arme blanche,* as they called it. They opted for a relatively thick line, which varied in width during the cen-tury; at Fontenoy the standard line stood four ranks deep. The French pre-ferred a stouter line because they thought it better suited to shock action with the bayonet. In contrast, the fire-oriented British line under Wellington would stand only two ranks deep. So tactical variation had roots in cultural conviction.

Certainly, it would be going too far to insist that the only, or even primary, factor that determined ancien régime fascination with extremely formal linear tactics was some aesthetic obsession with geometric regularity. There is no question that weaponry played an absolutely central part in shaping battle, but tactical practice did not simply reflect the firearms of the day, as some technological determinists believe. In addition, the orderly combat formations of the ancien régime also derived from assumptions made by the aristocratic officers about the rank and file they commanded. In order to gauge the role of aesthetic preference in battle, we must briefly digress to consider the limits of technological necessity and the influence of social prejudice.

Technology

Compared with today's infantry firearms, those shouldered during the ancien régime were slow-firing and inaccurate, and it has become commonplace to ascribe the linear tactics of that age strictly to those limitations. However, more needs to be said, because the weapons of that day could have been, and eventually were, employed for different tactics. Technology did not dictate a single best use, but rather it presented alternatives, and the choices soldiers made within that range reflected their cultural values.

The basic infantry firearm changed very little from the 1690s through the 1830s, and artillery, although it enjoyed some significant advances, also remained relatively constant in its destructive potential. This stability makes the ancien régime a good laboratory in which to judge the claims of technological determinists. The question to ask is whether or not the limitations of smoothbore, muzzle-loading weapons obliged armies to mass their firepower in linear formations or could they have employed skirmishers, who relied on aimed fire, or other tactical alternatives before the advent of rifled weapons? The classic infantry weapon of the early seventeenth century, the smoothbore matchlock musket, gave way by that century's end to the smoothbore flintlock. In order to avoid confusion, let us call the latter weapon by its proper name, "fusil," to distinguish it from the matchlock musket. Smoothbore muzzle-loaders are by nature inaccurate, because the ball, which must be smaller than the bore of the weapon to be loaded, literally bounces in the bore on the way out, picking up an unpredictable spin that then curves the flight of the musket ball much as a baseball can curve in flight depending on its spin. A number of contemporary tests established that while the fire from fusils could carry beyond 240 yards, its accuracy fell off rapidly after eighty. On the test range, fusils that were shot at a very large target equal to the front of a deployed battalion, 100 feet by 7 feet, scored hits with 60 percent of the time at eighty yards, while only 40 percent struck at 160 yards and only 25 percent at 240 yards.[36]

Tests of eighteenth-century rifled weapons certainly revealed them to be more accurate, but rifles took much longer to load because the bullet had to be forced into the rifling down the length of the barrel. Prussian trials reported by the great staff officer Gerhard von Scharnhorst in the Napoleonic era revealed a surprising fact: On the battlefield fusils could be as effective as rifles. At 160 yards, the rifle was twice as likely to hit a "small" target as was a smoothbore fusil, but the rifle took 2.5 times longer to load, aim, and fire. Thus Scharnhorst concluded that, although the smoothbore would require more ammunition, "Rifled and smoothbore shoulder arms have approximately the same effect in the same time."[37] When fired against a "large" target, the fusil actually enjoyed an advantage, as it could hit the mark 7.5 times in the same time it took the rifle to strike home only four times.

This comparison between fusil and rifle refutes claims that the explanation for tactical reform late in the eighteenth century lies in the advent of rifled firearms. This is made all the more clear by the fact that although some German and British light infantry specialists adopted rifles, the French, who had great success with skirmishers, did not change over to rifles until well into the nineteenth century. The next chapter will have more to say about advances in European weaponry during the seventeenth and eighteenth centuries.

To be sure, the limited accuracy of fusils often made it advantageous to mass as many weapons as possible along a given front to maximize firepower through numbers, and this encouraged reliance on some form of linear formation with the men tightly packed in several ranks. Safety also required men in the same rank to be relatively well-aligned with each other to avoid injury from the pan flash that ignited the powder in the chamber and the backflash of that explosion through the touch hole. Yet technology did not dictate the Prussian-style penchant for aligning whole battalions with rigid geometrical precision; this became a matter of battlefield aesthetics, a cultural preference. Moreover, weapons technology presented a menu of possibilities other than the line. As will be seen in Chapter 6, the French added light infantry fighting in open order and close-packed columns to their repertoire as standard practice after 1789. Even before this day, the Russians employed both skirmishers and columns, and the Austrians fielded large numbers of light infantry. Therefore, while the line of battle may have made sense as a way of maximizing the effects of inaccurate and slow-firing weapons, the tactical possibilities were much more varied than those exemplified by the French and the allies at Fontenoy.

Officer Prejudice

Within the menu of tactical possibilities consistent with weapons technology, aesthetic tastes influenced the choices made, and that influence was reinforced by the social prejudices of the aristocratic officer corps. Such tactics not only massed as many fusils as possible toward the enemy, they also allowed for the close supervision of troops that their officers regarded as untrustworthy. Aristocrats who composed the officer corps were apt to see themselves as portrayed in Voltaire's story of the salute at Fontenoy—well-born men of courage, courtesy, and custom. This international elite entertained a lower opinion of the common soldiers they led than of fellow officers in opposing armies. The rank and file, they believed, were men were without honor who could not be trusted on the battlefield. The Enlightenment philosopher, or *philosophe,* Jaucourt, writing in the *Encyclopédie,* argued that "soldiers in the countries of Europe are truly . . . the most vile portion of the subject of the nation."[38] The French minister of war 1775–1777, the count de Saint-Germain, described his common soldiers as "the slime *[bourbe]* of the nation and all that is useless to society."[39] Frederick, as well, said disparaging things about his troops:

> All that one can make of common soldiers consists in giving them esprit de corps, that is a higher opinion of their regiment than of all the other troops on earth. Because officers must lead these soldiers into the greatest dangers, and the soldiers cannot be influenced by ambition, the rank and file should fear their officers more than all the dangers to which they are exposed. Otherwise, no one would be able to lead such soldiers into the attack as 300 cannon thunder against them. [40]

Such men had to be watched, lest they run in battle. They could not be trusted to disperse, take cover, and fire on their own initiative as skirmishers. They must stand in open, arrayed in linear tactics, and boxed in by sergeants and officers so that every man could be observed and controlled.

While misconduct and desertion under fire posed a threat to eighteenth-century armies, there is ample evidence to suggest that the French might well have employed other tactical alternatives without melting away.[41] In fact, the contempt felt by ancien régime French officers for their men was probably unwarranted. When asked to deliver more, common soldiers responded. During the Seven Years' War (1756–1763), Marshal Broglie experimented with dispersing infantry to fight in open order, and instead of balking or deserting they fought reliably. The French recognized this ability to a degree and, in the decade *before* the Revolution, created specialized light infantry companies in line battalions and some specialized light infantry battalions. Studies in primary group cohesion, discussed at greater length in Chapter 7, suggest that rank and file troops formed bonds that required comrades to display devotion and courage, at least toward each other.[42] This probably explains why light infantry experiments and innovations succeeded as well as they did before the Revolution. Honor among common soldiers was not expressed with the same nicety that it would be among officers, but it surely existed.

Aristocratic disdain for the enlisted ranks constituted a prejudice that legitimated the great privilege enjoyed by the nobility. Beyond tradition, the justification for aristocratic social, economic, and political advantage rested upon the assertion that they provided a special, and deadly, service to the state, the "tax in blood" nobles paid as officers. They believed themselves uniquely suited to rank by their sense of honor, which entailed courage and devotion to the king. Ascribing honor to the rural and urban poor who made up the enlisted ranks would undermine their claims.

This chapter does not claim that the geometrical aesthetics of battle overshadowed all other factors in defining linear tactics during the ancien régime. Even that age of appearances conceded to practical necessity when the well-being and effectiveness of military forces were at stake. However, armies made choices within menus of possibilities consistent with necessity and technology. Contemporary aesthetic tastes biased militaries for some alternatives and against others, and the tactical choices made under the influence of those biases could hinder armies from maximizing their effectiveness in combat. In explaining those straight lines of troops on the battlefield, and on Lenfant's canvas, the tastes of the Enlightenment must be taken into account, just as they help explain the uniforms of the men who stood in those serried ranks. In fact, the stylish clothing worn by mid–eighteenth-century European armies and the linear tactics they employed reveal a similar interplay of necessity and cultural choices. Beyond the obvious need to clothe the soldier, contemporary ideas of fashion influenced the cut of military attire, sometimes in a way that diminished its practicality. Social values also played a role in the fact that the uniforms worn by an officer and the troops he led could advertise the status, wealth, and taste of that commander. Linear tactics took advantage of some of the characteristics of the fusil and bayonet; however, at the same time they reflected preferences as to how an army ought to look on the field and predispositions for geometrical forms. Reinforcing these preferences and predispositions were the social prejudices of officers.

To go further in understanding the influence of conceptual culture on the reality of combat, this discussion must now go beyond the aesthetics of the visual and enter the realm of thought as expressed on the printed page.

THOUGHT ON WAR: THE MILITARY ENLIGHTENMENT

Ancien régime military literature reflected intellectual tenets of that immensely important movement, the Enlightenment, that took root and flourished in Paris more than in all its other European homes. At this time, the social elite encompassed a range of military topics within its intellectual interests, so it should come as little surprise that the Enlightenment generated a specialist discussion termed here the Military Enlightenment. Azar Gat has contributed the most impressive recent exploration of this period, and he reports that the second half of the eighteenth century brought a burst of military literature, with over 125 titles appearing from 1748 to 1789.[43] During this rush of publication, the most commonly discussed topics included battlefield tactics, military organization, and troop composition. Henry Lloyd (ca. 1718–1783) switched the primary focus from tactics to operations in his works, which began appearing in the late 1760s, but operations only became the central concern of the Military Enlightenment in the last decade of the eighteenth century. The movement gave an unmistakable stamp to the work of Antoine-Henri Jomini, so in a sense it continued well into the nineteenth century, long after the rise of Military Romanticism, the subject of Chapter 6.

The Military Enlightenment followed the program of the broader Enlightenment, which sought to pattern study and knowledge after the natural sciences. By doing so it hoped to provide simple but fundamental, almost Newtonian, empirical truths, even in the realms of human psychology and conduct. Science seemed basic to all understanding. Historian Erik Lund points out that "a scientific education and an inclination towards scientific experimentation was part of a spectrum of activities that together defined the public image of the gentleman soldier."[44] As the most prolific military author in the *Encyclopédie,* Guillaume Le Blond, declared, "Before entering into some detail on this subject, let us observe from the outset that war is an art which has its rules and principles," and these he said, in good scientific style, were "no more than the fruit of observations."[45] It is no accident that one of the most popular military books of the mid-eighteenth century was Jacques-François de Chastenet de Puységur's *Art de la guerre par principes et par règles.* Maizeroy (1719–1780) expressed the spirit of the times when he announced that tactics, unlike strategy, "is easily reduced to sure rules, because it is entirely geometrical like fortification." But even strategy, he says, has "certain general rules which one can propose with certainty and regard as an invariable base."[46] This faith in the existence and value of universal and immutable rules and principles continued into the nineteenth century among late proponents of the Military Enlightenment, such as Archduke Charles and Jomini. Writing early in the nineteenth century, Charles insisted, "The principles of the science of war are few and unchanging" and that they were "founded on mathematical, evident truths."[47]

It would be unfair to dismiss the confidence of the Military Enlightenment in rules and principles as naïve, for while these military writers pursued the aesthetics of scientific knowledge, they also recognized that the battlefield presented the commander with a complicated reality that required judgment and flexibility. Eighteenth-century military authors were not armchair theorists; most had campaign experience. For them, rules existed, but not exactly like those of physics. To interpret and apply principles, commanders required what the Military Enlightenment called "genius," which need not be extraordinary to be effective. Turpin de Crisse advised: "Of most other sciences the principles are fixed . . . but the study of war is of another kind . . . nothing but a mind enlightened by a diligent study can make a due application of rules to circumstances."[48] So this modest genius operated in tandem with, and within, rules and principles.

Classical authority also stood high in the Enlightenment, and it helped to define ancien régime tactics.[49] Tactical reformers looked directly to ancient Greek and, particularly, Roman authors for precedent and direction in order to solve military problems of the day. Reference to that enduring standard, Vegetius, and others inspired such military advances as battalion organization, firing by countermarch, and marching in step. This process was a later phase of that earlier intellectual phenomenon, the Renaissance. In the *Encyclopédie,* Le Blond stated flatly, "It is to the Greeks that one owes the first principles or the first writings on tactics. . . . The basis of modern tactics is composed of that of the Greeks and the Romans."[50] Also, long sections of entries devoted to contemporary military problems were given over to discussing classical antiquity. When considering the manner of forming troops for battle in his article "Ordre de bataille," Le Blond organized much of his treatment around the seven orders of battle outlined by Vegetius. This reverential culture permeated even arguments for change; Jean de Folard, a radical proponent of column formations, presented his new ideas in his *Comments sur Polybe* [Comments on Polybius] (1727–1730). De Saxe repeatedly refers to the Romans as if they held the key to reform. Other voices of the Military Enlightenment pictured the Romans as effective, orderly, and rational.

In addition to privileging rules and principles and revering classical examples, the Enlightenment also encouraged a particular French image of themselves in battle. One curious offshoot of contemporary thought posited a pseudo-anthropological belief in the different characters of peoples or nations. Montesquieu argued in his highly influential *Spirit of the Laws* that geography and weather often determined such differences in character. The search for the "essence" of a people, then, followed Enlightenment predilections. This extended to military characteristics, as the French believed that while they were at a disadvantage in firefights, they possessed a special affinity for the *arme blanche.* This cultural assumption, touted as a scientific observation, shaped tactical thinking. Voltaire announced in his *Dictionnaire philosophique:* "French artillery is very good, but the fire of French infantry is rarely superior and usually inferior to that of other nations. It can be said with as much truth that the French nation attacks with the greatest impetuosity and that it is very difficult to resist its shock."[51] De Saxe commented, "It is the nature of the French to attack," and the count de Guibert, the noted military reformer, held, "The French were without discipline, hardly suited to fire fights . . . , redoubtable in all attacks with cold steel and assaults on outposts."[52]

For the infantry, the offensive spirit soon claimed the bayonet as the weapon of choice. Marshal Claude Villars, the greatest French commander of the War of the Spanish Succession (1701–1714), praised "the air of audacity so natural to the French,"[53] and affirmed, "In my opinion, the best method for the French infantry . . . is to charge with the bayonet."[54] The French cult of the bayonet that would have such tragic consequences in World War I first emerged during the ancien régime.

The Battle Culture of Forbearance

The French cult complemented a more basic ancien régime military prejudice and practice, which demanded that attacking infantry advance without firing, to forbear enemy cannon balls and musketry. This view of combat emphasized not so much the power to inflict heavy losses on the enemy as it did the fortitude to maintain good order while sustaining such losses oneself. Such a conception deserves the title "the battle culture of forbearance." By the seventeenth century, increased firepower brought the triumph of suffering. Artillery inflicted death at long range, and infantry could do little about it except to cross the valley of death and take the enemy cannon. Defensive fire from muskets and fusils also could rip into attacking enemy formations without the attackers being able to answer in kind, for to do so they would have had to halt, fire, and reload, a pause that would waste the momentum of the assault.

Victory rewarded the stoic determination to press on and close with an enemy despite the cost. Louis XIV claimed, "Good order makes us look assured, and it seems enough to look brave, because most often our enemies do not wait for us to approach near enough for us to have to show if we are in fact brave."[55] And the great monarch's opinion was hardly unique. Marshal Catinat, a practical soldier who served the great Louis, in describing an assault, insisted that "One prepares the soldier to not fire and to realize that it is necessary to suffer the enemy's fire, expecting that the enemy who fires is assuredly beaten when one receives his entire fire."[56] Part of the force behind this argument approaches the boxer's taunt "Hit me with your best shot," for one gains moral ascendancy by remaining standing after absorbing the worst the opponent can dish out.

Such advice contained a good deal of common sense, because at a time when muzzle-loading weapons took so long to load, particularly under combat conditions, troops temporarily disarmed themselves by firing. Moreover, because the weapons were relatively inaccurate at long ranges, waiting to fire until the last moment maximized the effect of the volley. Vauban put it succinctly: "Usually, in man-to-man combat the advantage lies with those who fire last."[57] Thus one heard the typically eighteenth-century order "Don't fire till you see the whites of their eyes" or other variants of this counsel of restraint. They certainly were not restricted to the French. Frederick the Great argued that in attacking prepared enemy positions, "those attacking should not fire at all, but advance resolutely, gun on shoulder."[58] So counter-instinctual was the required forbearance that armies devoted great attention to teaching it through drill, a subject dealt with at greater length in Chapter 5.

The fixation with holding one's fire in a battle of forbearance provides the backdrop for the drama at Fontenoy, when Hay is supposed to have invited the French to fire first. This was a display of bravado in the mode of courtesy, but he was also tempting the French to commit a tactical blunder.

Even considering the advantages of holding one's fire, forbearance still demanded an odd psychology that put a premium on paying a heavy cost in casualties as an essential down payment on victory. Hanson's concept of a Western Way of War may take some comfort in this practice, although it hardly encouraged Enlightenment commanders to embrace battle—quite the opposite.

Forbearance guaranteed that battles were bloody, but it could not guarantee that they would be decisive. During the Nine Years' War, Louis XIV explicitly ordered his finest commander, Marshal Luxembourg, "[M]ake use of my cavalry rather than engaging yourself in an infantry battle, which causes the loss of a lot of men but which never decides anything."[59] In fact, the ancien régime provides few examples of battles that ended major wars; the presence of numerous fortified towns and the dependence on cumbersome logistics made it difficult to turn a victory into decisive military or political success. Conflicts tended to drag on until exhaustion settled the matter.

The Quest for Scientific Warfare

Given their conception of battle as universally bloody but only rarely decisive, it follows that the Enlightenment pundits advised against it and sought alternatives. The tendency of rulers and generals to eschew battle expressed a tenet of the age: reluctance to accept chance and preference for the predictable, characteristics that reflected Enlightenment concepts of reason and control. War by rules and principles disdained chaos; it was linear in the mathematical sense, as military action should produce an expected and knowable result.

The Military Enlightenment in France regarded chance with misgiving, and battle opened too many possibilities to the unforeseen and uncontrollable. De Saxe claimed that "War can be made without leaving anything to chance. And this is the highest point of perfection and skill in a general."[60] In a particularly revealing passage, another influential contemporary pundit, Puységur, argued, "Generals who do not have great resources of knowledge always prefer battles to other actions of war that are less hazardous but demand greater ability."[61] This statement rejects battles as "hazardous," meaning unpredictable as well as costly, and implies that a truly skilled general could and would avoid them. Confronting this issue head on, de Saxe declared, "I do not favor pitched battles, especially at the beginning of a war, and I am convinced that a skillful general could make war all his life without being forced into one."[62] Bülow repeated this sentiment: "It is always possible to avoid a battle."[63] This was Orrery's war of foxes. It is only fair to comment that pundits often followed such criticisms of battle with disclaimers stating that sometimes it was advantageous to fight. However, the overriding fact is that they did not regard battle as desirable, but usually as an inferior course of action, even as a last resort.

To be sure, while this opinion was widespread and influential, it fell short of being universal. Marlborough praised battle, but between 1702 and 1711 he fought only four or five battles while conducting thirty sieges. Early in his career, Frederick the Great wrote, "War is decided only by battles, and it is not finished except by them."[64] However, he also penned more conventional opinions on combat, as when he echoed Puységur by arguing, "[M]ost generals in love with battle resort to this expedient for want of other resources."[65]

The Siege as an Engineered Battle

Considering principles of the Military Enlightenment, it comes as little surprise that sieges became the preponderant form of combat, at least where fortifications lay thick on the ground. Although battles often won no real advantage, sieges promised tangible gains. Fortresses protected one's own resources while making enemy lands vulnerable to contributions, a serious matter in long wars of attrition. Commanding enemy territory by seizing fortresses also gave greater leverage in negotiations. The result was a battle-averse and siege-heavy form of warfare that hardly tallies well with the supposed Western desire for decisive battle.

Although the distinction between battle and siege is an important one, it may also hide a certain conceptual similarity. In many ways, the siege was the archetypal Enlightenment battle. It is not simply that men fought and died in attacking fortresses just as they did in the open field. Although military writers expressly argued that battle formations should be patterned on fortifications and siegecraft, it is also true that the siege became battle as refashioned in accord with parameters set by the Enlightenment. If the Military

Enlightenment mistrusted field battles because they were chaotic and open to the play of chance, the siege was suitably scientific and predictable. The geometric character of military practice in the siege could yield results on schedule, provided that attackers followed the proper procedure. Vauban laid down a system for what procedures were to be carried out on what day of a hypothetical siege, although he realized that the details of an actual attack would deviate from any ideal. The often fruitless character of field battles recommended the siege as yielding results in a way more sparing of casualties. Vauban urged his methodical practice of siege warfare with the admonition: "Let us burn gunpowder and spill less blood."[66] De Saxe expressed a similar desire to conserve the lives of soldiers, if for no other reason than that they represented an important investment. He counseled that in siege warfare, "It is better to defer [an assault] for several days, rather than to lose [rashly] a single grenadier, who has been twenty years in the making."[67] Fortress and siege rendered combat subject to rational control, giving combat an aesthetic and intellectual style more suited to the age.

Fortifications became ideal engineered battlefields. These fortresses themselves no longer consisted of walled enclosures rising above the surrounding terrain, because the old verticality meant vulnerability to modern artillery. Now crafted by science, fortresses secured for the defenders every conceivable advantage that a well-chosen and well-prepared battlefield could offer: excellent fields of fire, protected positions for infantry and artillery, and difficult obstacles to impede an enemy attack. Science limited the accidents of nature by transforming the surroundings into military perfection. In achieving benefits provided by geometry and construction, engineers sacrificed one key advantage to the enemy; fortresses would be surrounded. But even this eliminated another major embarrassment of the battlefield, open flanks.

To be sure, differences separated field from fortress. A great battle lasted hours, while a major siege could drag on for months. The battle of Fontenoy was over in nine hours; Maurice's siege of Tournai consumed four weeks. Attacks in the field advanced quickly over open ground, while besiegers dug their trenches forward methodically, as the shovel became the weapon of choice. All this is true, but the lines still blurred. Field fortifications played an important role in open battle; consider Malplaquet, Fontenoy, Leuthen, and a long list of other clashes. And modern readers are apt to forget that in the later stages of a siege, when the sappers had dug their trenches to close the distance between attackers and defenders, furious, often hand-to-hand fighting ensued between infantry battling to control outworks and breaches, and this often at night. There was ample opportunity for courage, even on this engineered battlefield.

LAWS OF WAR: REASONABLE CONVENTIONS

During this military ancien régime, the discourse on war incorporated another genre of constraint as never before, the international law of war. It constituted a "cultural regulation of war" that tried to pattern real war after an ideal.[68] Certainly discussion of "just" wars and attempts to limit combat go back at least to St. Augustine and became a European movement with the Peace and Truce of God, but the Europeans made a quantum leap in defining legality within the conduct of war during the early modern era. These efforts seem to have had some actual effect during the Enlightenment, often touted as an age of limited war.

From the first, the literature on the morality and legality of war broke down into two broad categories: the causes of war *(jus ad bellum)* and the conduct of war *(jus in bello)*. Being the more basic topic, *jus ad bellum* received the primary emphasis. The first great Christian thinker to turn his attention to this, St. Augustine (354–430), questioned the justice of war in his fundamental work of theology, *The City of God,* published after 412. His ideas would continue to shape the discussion of "just war" for centuries to come. Appealing to scripture, he defended the legitimacy of war but only if fought for the right reasons: "It makes a great difference by which causes and under which authorities men undertake the wars that must be waged."[69] For St. Augustine, a just war could only be fought by a legitimate ruler, and then it should only be directed toward righting an injustice. He also insisted that the suffering caused by war be less than that caused by the wrong one is combatting. For him, an unwinnable war could not be just, since it led to suffering without result. St. Thomas Aquinas (1225–1274) developed the matter further in his *Summa Theologica* (1267–1273). Appealing to biblical authority and St. Augustine, Aquinas again insisted that war could only be fought justly by a sovereign prince, "For it is not the business of a private person to declare war"—a charge against medieval private warfare.[70] Then he addressed just cause. Should sovereigns attack other parties, those assaulted "should be attacked because they deserve it on account of some fault." Those engaged in a war should also have "a rightful intention, so that they intend the advancement of good, or the avoidance of evil." Sheer territorial aggrandizement or a lust for power will not do.

The sixteenth and seventeenth centuries witnessed a good deal of writing on the law of war. Geoffrey Parker concludes: "Most of the modern conventions concerning restraint in war appeared in Europe between 1550 and 1700."[71] The list of important writers and works at this time includes: Franciscus de Victoria (1480–1546), *De indis et de ivre belli relectiones* (1557); Balthazar Ayala (1548–1584), *De jure et officiis bellicis et disciplina militari* (1582); and Alberico Gentili (1552–1608), *De jure belli* (1598). This literature brought together several strands: prescriptive religious texts, the Peace and Truce of God, articles of war designed to regulate armies in the field, and from the "customs of war," that is, the evolved conventions of combat.[72]

Building upon the contributions of his predecessors, Hugo Grotius (1583–1645) wrote his true classic of international law *De jure belli ac pacis* (1625). In his discussion of *jus ad bellum*, Grotius, like Augustine, stressed the right of the sovereign to fight. He accepts the legitimacy of turning to violence when no institutional legal recourse exists. "Where the power of law ceases, there war begins."[73] Grotius recognized the rights and powers of the sovereign, but allowed that the same lack of legal redress could justify private war for proper cause. He accepted what by then were traditional explanations of just war: "The justifiable causes generally assigned for war are three, defence, indemnity, and punishment."[74] It was, then, proper to fight against aggression, to seek redress for a wrong, and to punish a foe for a wrongful act.

Within the great variety of subjects treated by *jus in bello,* his views on prisoners of war and on siege warfare illustrate the increasing adoption of conventions in warfare in early modern Europe. He recognized historical precedents for massacres of captured troops and civilians, but he insisted on the modern right to surrender and good treatment. "More civilized manners having abolished the barbarous practice of putting prisoners to death, for the same reason, the surrender of those, who stipulate for the preservation of their lives either in battle, or in a siege, is not to be rejected."[75] Medieval practice had assumed the right of knight and squire to surrender and ransom, but it had denied this to commoners, who simply might be killed on the spot. Of course, this convention could break down, as at Crécy. From the late sixteenth century, European armies adopted an elaborate system of surrender and return. Adversaries signed agreements, cartels, detailing the conditions for exchanging and ransoming prisoners. Prisoners of equal rank were exchanged one for one, from common soldiers to exalted generals. Different ranks were also assigned differing ransom amounts to pursue release. For example, a *cartel d'échange* between France and Spain in 1675 set the values

of prisoners as follows: a soldier 7 livres 6 sous; a sergeant, 15 livres; a lieutenant, 35 livres; and a captain, 90 livres.[76] The state the soldiers served must
pay for their upkeep while being held prison or by the enemy. Officers might
be released on their word, their *parole,* that they would not rejoin their army
until they were formally exchanged. These were definite changes for the better, so influential that in 1703 the French marshal, Claude Villars, was indig-
nant at the suggestion that he slaughter prisoners to save food and the trouble of guarding them.[77]

The treatment of the garrisons and inhabitants of fortified towns also
improved. Medieval authorities agreed that towns that surrendered when
demanded would be spared further trials, but those that resisted forfeited their
goods and even their lives. Of course, medieval armies transgressed these principles—for example, as during Edward III's Crécy campaign in 1346.
Seventeenth- and eighteenth-century practice was more regular. Again, in theory the garrison and population of a town that refused to surrender by the
time the besieging army was in place and its artillery batteries set to fire forfeited consideration. However, a fortress that surrendered before the enemy
undertook the very costly task of storming the walls could expect good terms
that protected the lives and property of the citizens and allowed the garrison
to march out with "the honors of war" and even rejoin their army. As Grotius
explained, "In modern times it is the usual practice, before shells are thrown,
or mines sprung, to summon places to surrender, which are thought unable to
hold out and where places are stronger, such summons is generally sent, before
the storming is made."[78]

Until the mid-seventeenth century, fortified towns could suffer a terrible
fate if they resisted too long, if either the attackers had their blood up after
storming a breach, or if the commanding general thought there was something to be gained by brutality. General practice was that the soldiers be given
a free hand to plunder, rape, and kill for three days after assaulting a town.
Sometimes a brutal sacking could be a strategy of terror. By viciously savaging
a town, a victor could forestall potential resistance by other towns, which
would quickly surrender rather than suffer the fate of their neighbors. Such
was the case at Magdeburg in 1631 and Drogheda in 1649. Even Grotius
accepted the principle that "where very important advantages may attend
striking a terror . . . it may be proper to exercise the right of rigour in its full
extent."[79] By the eighteenth century, however, although the right of sacking a
town still existed, it was generally regarded as outside the pale.

The regularization of contributions also marked an amelioration in the conduct of war. Contributions were payments made by village, town, district, or even province to buy off an army from pillaging it. Such payments descended from the medieval practice of *patis*. *Patis*, however, simply bought off one band without gaining their protection against other raiders. Contributions, as became practice in the mid-seventeenth century, protected one from pillage by the army that demanded the contribution and gained that army's protection against other forces. Exaction of contributions became extremely regular, systematic, and bureaucratic. In the Spanish Netherlands, the French calculated payments on the basis of the peacetime taxes, used printed forms to demand sums, and offered other protective services. Those who had paid contributions to the French could deduct them from taxes owed to Spanish authorities. It all seemed very civil, unless a town refused to pay, in which case it was "executed," which meant that a raiding party would burn it out. In fact, it could get very nasty, with one army demanding contributions and another commanding peasants and townsmen not to pay. But it was usually a great deal better than medieval practice, and a world apart from the *chevauchée*.

During the eighteenth century, literature on the just war shifted in a manner characteristic of the Enlightenment, moving away from elevated but unresolvable issues to more practical matters. The important theorist of international relations Emmerich de Vattel (1714–1767) applied his understanding to *jus in bello*. His *Le droit des gens ou principes de la loi naturelle* or *The Law of Nations* appeared in 1758, practically a high water mark for the Enlightenment. Although this volume spent a good deal of time discussing *jus ad bellum*, providing much of what was by then a common argument, he put it aside. Each contending adversary, he observed, will appeal to the "necessary law of nature" to make its own case for a rightful cause. Thus, "Let us then leave the strictness of the necessary law of nature to the conscience of sovereigns."[80] This approach to legality simply conceded that both adversaries claimed and had equal justification, or "the same pretensions to justice as we ourselves have."[81] Vattel refocused his attention to the more practical "voluntary law of nations," by which a war could be judged "just" not by its *cause* but by its *conduct*—the issue at hand became one of *means*. "Thus, the rights founded on the state of war, the lawfulness of its effects, the validity of the acquisitions made by arms, do not, externally and between mankind, depend on the justice of the cause, but on the legality of the means in themselves."[82]

He then appealed for conflict far short of total war. "War would become too cruel and destructive, were all intercourse between enemies absolutely broken off."[83] There can be truces for given purposes. He addresses the matter of passports, safe conducts, ransoms of prisoners, etc., in the context of the voluntary law of nations.

Vattel exemplified the concept of limited warfare and for that reason has attracted those who believe that today we must curb the excesses of passion in combatting Terrorism. One such advocate, Caleb Carr, judges Vattel "enormously influential" and heralds the eighteenth century as an exemplary era of limited war.[84] How effective were such cultural restraints on combat at this time? Captured towns and prisoners were better treated, and hostage taking tailed off. As illustrated at Fontenoy, there was a more elegant and less brutal etiquette of battle. At the core of Europe, war did become less intrusive and savage. France and England suffered great rebellions in the seventeenth century, but between 1715 and 1789 they did not, with the exception of Scottish risings north of England. In general, large foreign armies did not penetrate the borders of France or England, with the minor exception of 1744 in France and the more serious threat of Bonnie Prince Charlie's ill-fated drive into England in 1745–1746. On the whole, international wars were shorter and less common than they had been during the seventeenth century. But that is not to say that war disappeared, for there were a number of international conflicts. While the demands of war were certainly limited on France, they were not on Prussia. At the periphery of Europe, Austrians and Russians fought wars with religious fury against the Turks. Yet surveying the entire balance sheet, war was less extensive, damaging, and brutal during the age of the Enlightenment. Reasonable constraints and conventions, as described by Vattel, certainly enhanced this amelioration.

VALUES AND WAR: ARISTOCRATIC HONOR

The discourse on war that shaped warfare and military institutions included not only aesthetic tastes, Enlightenment principles, and legal concepts but social values as well. We have already confronted aristocratic propensities for ostentatious display and prejudices against common soldiers, but we must now consider the far-reaching implications of a most fundamental military value, aristocratic honor. Not only does honor go a long way to explain aristocratic bravery, it also helps account for the survival of the purchase system and, quite probably, the size of the French army, the most important aspect of seventeenth-century military change under Louis XIV. The French army, which did not exceed a paper strength of 60,000 to 80,000 in the sixteenth and early seventeenth centuries, climbed to an official size of 440,000 troops in 1692–1693 and probably mustered about 350,000 men in reality.[85] A thirst for honor among young aristocratic men helps to explain how the French monarchy, with limited resources, could field such a gargantuan army. Through the Enlightenment, the ancien régime experimented with forward-looking, progressive thought, yet in codes of honor, the age maintained a more archaic, traditional influence that still bore the stamp of the Middle Ages. But if a modern observer sees a tension between precedent and progress, they harmonized quite well during the ancien régime.

The "Semi-Entrepreneurial" System: Purchase and Maintenance

In order to live up to their self-image and value system, French officers under-took considerable expense to exercise unit command. David Parrott has called the French system "semi-entrepreneurial," to distinguish it from the fully entrepreneurial soldier-capitalists of early modern Europe who built fortunes upon military command.[86] In the semi-entrepreneurial system, French colonels and captains owned their regiments and companies, but exercised command only under strict regulation by the state. Officers purchased their commands, so it was not enough to be talented, one had to possess wealth in order to stand at the head of troops. But the financial costs of command did not end with purchase; once bought, a unit must be maintained.

Aristocratic domination of the officer corps varied over the course of the ancien régime, but in the 1780s nobles filled about 85 percent of the commissioned ranks. The proportion of non-nobles, or *roturiers,* rose at times of crisis when the monarchy needed to mobilize the wealth of all its well-to-do subjects and, thus, was more willing to give command to rich *roturiers* or *anoblis,* individuals who had only recently risen into the aristocracy by buying a title, one route of social advance for the very wealthy.

As a rule, until reforms of the 1760s, French officers poured their personal funds into their units in several manners.[87] Colonels of new regiments would raise those regiments wholly, or substantially, at their own expense. In established regiments, captains or colonels would supply their troops with equipment in expectation of being reimbursed by the crown. Even if paid in full for their outlays, they might not receive compensation for years; this meant that they had contributed their personal credit to maintaining their troops. Considering that the monarchy could only borrow from financiers at high interest rates, the de facto free credit furnished by the officer corps proved a tremendous bargain to the monarchy. In some cases, government regulations set the amount that officers could be reimbursed for certain costs, but those costs were, in fact, much higher, so the difference came out of the officer's pocket. Recruitment bounties provide a most striking case here. Officers were allowed to offer men a bounty to enlist, but wartime created a sellers' market and recruits demanded and receive higher bounties than allowed. Captains struggling to fill their companies made up the shortfall between regulation and reality out of pocket. In addition, the cost of replacing deserters fell to officers, because authorities held that it was the officer's responsibility to guard against desertion. Company commanders might have to replace equipment damaged or lost on campaign, again because it was considered the officer's responsibility to prevent such losses. Understandably, the costs required to maintain a cavalry company exceeded those of an infantry company because of the need to supply remounts and more expensive equipment.

Thus, wealth became a prerequisite for command. Vauban once reported that "I have a poor devil of a cousin . . . a good and old officer who would have been a captain a long time ago if he had the secret of transforming bad companies into good ones without ruining himself."[88] Several generations later, in 1757, the marquis de Mailly wrote the minister of war, "It is of the greatest importance to put at the head of companies only those wealthy officers who can afford good recruits . . . and who can maintain their soldiers properly in linen, shoes, etc., and who will be in a state to remedy those accidents which happen only too frequently."[89]

It is impossible to project a figure for what percentage of the cost of the French army its officers absorbed, but it would not be unreasonable to estimate that officers bore 25–30 percent of military expenses. Since the monarchy was stretched to the limit during wartime, without this contribution by its officers, the army would have to have been significantly smaller. Thus officer outlays allowed the monarchy to maintain the large armies it put into the field.

Much is written about cheating by French officers during the ancien régime, as, for example, when they claimed more soldiers than they commanded in order to pocket extra allowances for their troops. Rather than making officers rich, such devious behavior may have been little more than a way of staving off financial catastrophe. It was bad enough that after the Nine Years' War (1688–1697) Louis granted a three-year suspension of officers' debts.[90]

Purchase and maintenance systems continued in the French army until shortly before the Revolution. In an attempt to relieve officers, the duke de Choiseul, minister of war under Louis XV, ended the maintenance system in 1762 and changed to a system of direct supply by the state. In 1776, a letter from Minister of War Saint-Germain announced an edict that eventually ended the purchase of units as well, although this was done in a phased way in order to protect the officers' investments. Each time a unit changed hands, it would lose a third of its initial value. Thus only by about the time of the French Revolution did the regiments and companies of the French army finally belong to the monarch.

These edicts constituted part of a greater reform movement designed to remove wealth as a requirement for unit command so that aristocrats could advance through the commissioned ranks unhindered by limited wealth. Viewed in a vacuum, the reforms look progressive, but put in proper context they are revealed as measures designed to preserve the dominance of the older nobility. Poor nobles from old families had long argued that financial requirements allowed richer men with only recent noble status or none at all to gain advantage over those with ancient pedigrees. Aristocratic military reformers viewed *anoblis* as the worst problem, for they had money and legal nobility, but lacked the true dedication and sense of honor that only a family tradition of military service could guarantee. Reformers sought to increase modern professionalism by reserving the officer corps to the right sort of noble applicant. By eliminating purchase and maintenance, commissioned rank could be established as a prerogative of long-established aristocratic clans. The ultimate act of this reform movement came with the Ségur law of 1781, which limited direct commissions to the rank of captain to aristocrats from families that could claim at least four generations of nobility.

Aristocratic Pursuit of Gloire

Throughout nearly all the ancien régime, the semi-entrepreneurial system thrived, but what drove French aristocrats to seek military command even when it worked to their financial detriment or even their ruin? An aristocrat might reply that he sought a commission because it alone allowed him the chance to achieve *gloire*. *Gloire* probably translates more accurately as "reputation" than "glory," but the more archaic term "glory" transmits the sense of derring-do implicit in aristocratic *gloire*. It could be won in other ways, but for the officer, it was best sought in battle.

During the seventeenth century, noblemen pursued *gloire* with a consuming passion. Madame de Sévigné, who recorded her astute observations in a voluminous correspondence, upheld *gloire* as an essential aspect of aristocratic masculinity. In 1683 she wrote, "Since one constantly tells men that they are only worthy of esteem to the extent that they love *gloire*, they devote all their thoughts to it; and this shapes all French bravery." For her, women did not share in it: "As women are allowed to be weak, they take advantage of this privilege without scruple."[91] She regarded *gloire* as definably masculine, and in the context of the army, this was essential to its nature.

Of course the pursuit of *gloire* was not restricted to officers, but also commanded kings. It clearly drove Louis XIV, who wrote of his Dutch War (1672–1678), "I shall not attempt to justify myself. Ambition and [the pursuit of] *gloire* are always pardonable in a prince, and especially in a young prince so well treated by fortune as I was."[92] Love of *gloire* was not a uniquely French obsession; the staid Dutchman William III, who became king of England as well as commander of Netherlands forces, also spoke of his glory, as did Frederick the Great.

To win *gloire*, an aristocrat had to adhere to a code of honor. This pitiless code demanded displays of courage regardless of sacrifice. In aristocratic culture, appearance counted more than essence, so it was not enough to be brave; one must be *seen* as being brave by one's peers.[93] Thus, *gloire* could only be won by demonstrating courage, and the danger of battle provided an opportunity to do so. And danger there surely was; casualty rates among officers were high. Of the 5,161 casualties suffered by French infantry at Fontenoy, 389 were officers; these men did not shrink from fire.[94] Aristocratic society compelled officers to run risks. Certainly, the aristocrat internalized his sense of honor, but its origins and sanctions came from outside the individual. Honor was a culturally defined masculine standard for the elite, with ostracism the penalty for those who failed to live up to it. Within the definitions imposed by honor, to be an officer was to earn respect from the members of one's class and to gain at least a modicum of *gloire*. In the sixteenth century, the aristocratic philosopher Montaigne wrote: "The proper, sole and essential life for one of the nobility of France is the life of a soldier."[95] And this principle still held in the eighteenth century.

This explains why young men so prized commissions, particularly unit command. Louis XIV noted the enthusiasm with which nobles raised units to serve him during the first years of his personal reign. This enthusiasm did not flag during the Dutch War, when the raising of a new regiment could cause "great joy"[96] and when it was "a marvel to see the quantity of people of high birth and others . . . who are eager to have employment [as officers]."[97] In 1693, the duke de Saint-Simon hurried to receive his first company, and to spend a good deal of money in a frenzied effort to put it back on its feet, because "I died of fear of not making the campaign that was about ready to open."[98] Lisola, a Spaniard, described France as "always filled with an idle and seething [aristocratic] youth, ready to undertake anything, and who seek to exercise their valor regardless of the expense."[99]

As a luxury good, the expenses associated with military service often had little to do with practical value. Command itself was a form of conspicuous consumption; therefore, further embellishments that advertised the officer's status should not be surprising. The excesses of officers' extravagant attire have already been discussed. Officers also demonstrated their wealth and status by providing themselves with servants and fine horses. Saint-Simon reports that "to live honorably on his own, morning and night," he required thirty-five horses and mules and two gentlemen servants.[100] Display even applied to the largesse that superior officers extended on campaign by providing a sumptuous table, the cost of which could be enormous. The memoirs of d'Artagnan advised: "One of the most essential qualities of a colonel is to provide a good table. This will serve his officers marvelously, and they esteem him all the more by this than by all the rest."[101] An ordinance of 1672 condemned officers for the "evil custom of serving in the armies meals more magnificent and sumptuous than they ordinarily serve at home" and limited the highest-ranking officers to dinners including no more than two courses of meat and one of fruit.[102] One critical memoir of 1712 declared that "our fathers would be amused at this superfluous and unworthy luxury."[103] Vauban railed against excessive luxury in clothing and table. But, here again, wise counsel and stern regulations did not end extravagance. Maintaining an elegant lifestyle on campaign could be financially ruinous, but the sense remained that this was required of a man of station.

Jean-Baptiste Primi Visconti reported that aristocratic society also promised sexual incentives to those who braved military service. Certainly, military behavior and appearance involved sexual display, but Primi Visconti took the argument further; to him, war, not power, was the ultimate aphrodisiac in a more brazen version of courtly love. The man on the prowl needed military experience to win more intimate conquests. "The other princes, in order to have officers and soldiers, are obliged to pay them a great deal; and here the King has subjects who ruin themselves vying to be in his service. It is the style, and whoever does not serve in the war is despised. The ladies do not want any other lovers."[104] Perhaps Primi Visconti's analysis verges on the frivolous, but his comments and the letters of Mme de Sévigné still hit upon a truth that we first encountered in the previous chapter's discussion of chivalry. For the code of honor and *gloire* to exert such leverage on aristocratic behavior, it had to be enforced by ladies as well as by gentlemen. His observation that passion for soldiers ruled the women in the court and in Paris suggests just how much women embraced the aristocratic code of masculine honor.[105] They very well may have played as central a role in sending men off to war as they did in sending them off to the *pré*, or dueling ground.

The Duel and Battle

Long the subject of literature and scholarship, dueling provides a window into the demands of aristocratic masculine honor that permeated the French army of the ancien régime.[106] The same values that inspired men to pursue military careers despite the physical and financial risks implicit in that vocation drove them to the field of honor. Both provided opportunity for ostentatious displays of courage in a way that recalls the complementary relationship of war and the tournament in the Middle Ages. One of the most famous duelists of the seventeenth century, Count Montmorency-Bouteville, challenged his opponents in a style reminiscent of a medieval champion: "Sir, I have been assured that you are brave: we must fight!"[107] When Vauban praised the French nobility as particularly apt for war, he cited their capacity for "taking offense easily over honor."[108] The penchant for quarrels that resulted in duels was seen as essential to the military character.[109] Because of its cost in lives, lives of men that Louis XIV needed on the field of battle, he fought his own war against dueling but to little avail. He never stemmed this tide of blood. A strange either/or logic linked the duel and war, as when the 1645 *Catéchisme royal* put the following question in the young king's mouth: "If one forbids duels, how is it that the Nobility can give evidence of their courage?" This inquiry elicited the response, "In your armies, Sire."[110] A generation later, Primi Visconti testified to the same correspondence: "That bravery the French show among themselves in single combat, the King, by his edicts against duels, has made serve in war against his enemies."[111]

Despite repeated laws forbidding dueling, to deny a challenge marked one as unworthy. The abbé de Saint-Pierre charged in 1715 that an officer who refused a challenge would "find himself forced by the other officers and by the commander himself to leave the regiment."

> One counts for nothing that an officer would rather pass for a coward . . . than to commit a mortal sin and a capital crime in formal disobedience of the law and the will of the prince; one counts for nothing that he does not want to risk his safety and the loss of the good graces of his king; he does not fight, therefore he is a coward; he is a coward, therefore he must be driven away.[112]

The explanation for duels lay much more in the symbolic than in the real, for by their nature, duels were irrational. Ultimately, the aristocracy's fighting spirit was driven by the individual's drive to prove himself within the standards of his own class and thus win *gloire*. The nobility set standards that must be obeyed, or else the individual would lose caste. As one historian of the duel insists, dueling was "another religion."[113] A duel was a human sacrifice to the god of peer opinion, and so was a battle.

In a sense, the aristocrat who faced off against his adversary with cold steel on the dueling ground helps to explain the battle of Fontenoy, or more precisely he provides one piece of the intricately interlocking puzzle that was ancien régime warfare. This chapter has collected a number of the other pieces, including fashions in clothing and thought, conventions in tactics and law, as well as values of courage and honor. They all demonstrate the essential leverage of conceptual culture on combat in that age of elegance. Discourse forced itself on reality in diverse manners.

Fontenoy, however, exposes a tension between eighteenth-century discourse and reality. Maurice de Saxe, that archetypal ancien régime soldier, whose *Reveries* became one of the great works of the Military Enlightenment, expressed his disdain for battle and his desire for rational, intellectualized war. His ideal warfare was linear—orderly and predictable—and he defined battle as an admission of ineptitude. But with all his considerable skill he could not

achieve victory without crossing swords at Fontenoy. The Enlightenment discourse on war was an idealized prescription that could not always hold its own
against necessity. The wonder is how far it succeeded in imposing itself.

There is another story about Fontenoy. The evening of the battle Louis XV
rode over the field, still littered with the dead and wounded. He cautioned his
son: "See what it costs to win victories. The blood of our enemies is still the
blood of men. True glory comes in sparing it."[114] Whether Louis ever said these
words of humane wisdom matters little; it is one more memory of the battle,
one more transformation of a bitter reality into an Enlightened maxim. But
the brutal truth was that the king lost 7,000 of his own soldiers dead and
wounded that day and inflicted perhaps twice those losses on Cumberland's
army.

Notes on the Opening Illustration for Chapter Four

In its elegance and geometric regularity, this painting of the Battle of Fontenoy by
Pierre Lenfant testifies to a particularly ancien régime conception of battle. Today
it hangs among the weapons and uniforms of that age in the marvelous Musée de
l'armée at the Invalides in Paris. It is, like the objects around it, an exemplary arti-
fact of the eighteenth century.

(Musée de l'armée)

CHAPTER FIVE

Victories of the Conquered

The Native Character of the Sepoy

GENERAL LAKE ORDERED HIS CAVALRY to charge the Maratha line, half knowing the charge would fail. These squadrons of British dragoons and native cavalry of the East India Company's Bengal army were all he had on the field that morning, and without infantry support, the horsemen were unlikely to be able to seize the formidable enemy artillery that so concerned Lake. He had left his infantry behind in his effort to catch up with the Maratha army, which was trying to reach the safety of the Mewat Hills. Lake caught up with the retreating forces near the village of Laswarree as the sun rose on 1 November 1803. Now he had a battle on his hands. The British and Indian cavalry rode down upon the enemy line with dash—jumped barriers, chased off gunners, and sabered surrounding infantry—but could not hold their ground. Lake called back the charge. It had not succeeded in taking the artillery, but it had ensured that the Marathas would not continue their march to the Mewat Hills, only eight miles off. They would stand and fight; soon Lake's infantry would reach the battlefield.[1]

Gerald Lake had begun this campaign against Maratha rulers in August. The Maratha princes, *sardars,* had boasted large forces of Western-style infantry battalions trained and led by European officers and buttressed by large numbers of well-made artillery. Maratha armies were far from being tribal rabble. Although Maratha power had declined, they still contended with the British East India Company for domination of the western Deccan north to the Ganges Valley. The Company initially clashed with them in the First Maratha War (1779–1782), little more than an inconclusive skirmish, but a decisive confrontation came with the Second Maratha War (1803–1805). Lake's victories would contribute mightily to Maratha defeat. However, he often receives little attention because Arthur Wellesley, later elevated to become the Duke of Wellington, also commanded in that struggle for empire, learning the skills he would later use to frustrate Napoleon.

When General Lake marched out of Kanpur and headed west for Aligarh and Delhi on 5 August, he led roughly 5,000 infantry and 2,500 cavalry, a small force by European standards but about right for a full Company field army. His infantry included only one British royal regiment, the 76th, and thirteen battalions of sepoys, or native Indian troops trained to fight in European fashion. Europeans were more plentiful among the cavalry, which counted three British light dragoon regiments, the 8th, 27th, and 29th, with the 1st, 2nd, 3rd, and 4th Native Cavalry Regiments from the Bengal Presidency.[2]

Before he reached the battlefield of Laswarree, Lake led his army in a series of other clashes. He first brushed away a Maratha army under a French soldier of fortune, Pierre Cuillier Perron, at Coel and took the seemingly impregnable fortified town of Aligarh on 4 September. Then advancing on to Delhi, he fought a masterful battle near that city a week later. After securing Delhi, Lake reversed course and marched east to besiege Agra, which fell to him on 17 October. Through this all, his sepoys bore much of the fighting, and they would again at Laswarree.

By the time Lake caught up with the flower of the Maratha regiments, the British had been able to drive off or buy off the European officers in service to the Marathas, so their troops were now commanded by Ambaji Ingle, a soldier of some talent. That day he led fifteen battalions of trained infantry, supporting cavalry, and seventy artillery pieces, a very large train of guns. Lake had brought only five battalions of infantry along with all his cavalry, and en route he abandoned most of his artillery because it slowed the chase. He feared the Maratha guns, so he had hoped to take the artillery by his opening cavalry attacks, but they had been in vain.

By noon, Lake's infantry finally reached the field, after a march of twenty-five miles. He first ordered these men to eat, since they had been on the road without food since 3 A.M. But within an hour he marshaled them in two lines to attack the Maratha right. Enemy cannon balls and canister ruled out finesse or maneuver, Lake's forces simply had to advance without delay. Ambaji was ready for them. When Lake first encountered Ambaji's line, it spanned between two villages, Laswarree on the Maratha right and Moholpur on their left. But realizing that Lake meant to strike at his right, Ambaji refused that flank, bending his forces around the village of Molholpur and redeploying his impressive artillery.

Now the Company infantry advanced into the hellish fire; the lead line contained the 76th and two sepoy battalions. Lake had only some "galloper guns," light artillery attached to the cavalry, to support the attack. Ambaji responded by hurling his cavalry at the advancing infantry, but the 76th repelled the attack. With the line stalled, Lake ordered his cavalry to form up and drive the enemy horsemen back. Lake was not one to let others lead a charge, and just as he had done in the morning he rode over to take command. At that point an enemy cannon ball hit and killed the horse under him. Lake's son now rode to his father's side and offered his own horse to the general. The son dismounted, and while both men stood side by side, the younger man was severely wounded and slumped to the ground. Lake could not stop to care for his fallen son but ordered the attack. It was the critical moment. His cavalry, maddened by the son's wounds and galled by Maratha artillery fire, charged forward. Despite heavy artillery and infantry fire, the cavalry swept over the guns. Maratha infantry stepped forward to defend their artillery but to no avail. Through the dust of Lake's cavalry and the smoke of the Maratha guns, his British and sepoy infantry rushed forward to seize the cannon and throw back the Maratha battalions.

The Maratha infantry pulled back, but still disputed every step with fusil and bayonet. But as the British and sepoys pushed relentlessly forward, the Marathas began to break. Up to this point, Lake's army had suffered more casualties than the Marathas; he would lose 858 men, 20 percent of his force. As the enemy lost order and began to flee, however, the British and sepoys cut them down.

The boldness of Lake, "Lucky Lake" as he was known after taking Aligarh, had received the reward of the brave, good fortune and victory. After the battle he described his enemy:

> These battalions were most uncommonly well-appointed and had a most numerous artillery, as well served as they can possibly be, the gunners standing to their guns, until killed by the bayonet, all the sepoys of the enemy behaved exceedingly well. . . . I never was in so severe a business in my life or anything like it, and pray to God, I never may be in such a situation again.[3]

Repeatedly during the campaign, he praised the conduct of his sepoy troops who overcame such foes, and they would soon proudly add the inscription "Lake and Victory" to their regimental colors.

More than any other single battle, Laswarree broke Maratha power and secured British control over the Deccan and Delhi; once again the Company had triumphed by fielding sepoy armies. Laswarree, like many fights that preceded and followed it, proved the value of indigenous troops. In fact, the East India Company's most important military invention was the "sepoy," terminology borrowed from the Persian *sipahi* for soldier.[4] At first glance, the sepoy may have seemed little more than a colonial imitation of his British comrades in arms; however, the concepts of duty, honor, and loyalty that inspired the sepoy grew out of South Asian culture, and it was these, not simply his fusil, uniform, and drill, that made "Jack Sepoy" such a fine soldier.

The older native military institutions and practices of Mughal India differed both from those of ancient India discussed in Chapter 2 and those of contemporary European powers. The specific military system that Europeans grafted onto South Asian roots in the eighteenth century developed in the hundred and fifty years prior to its importation, well after the first colonial trading posts appeared along the coasts of India. At its European point of origin, this style of warfare owed much of its potency to the close relationship between European societal and military cultures, as demonstrated in Chapter 4. For that reason, one might expect that it would have withered when transported to the foreign climate of South Asia, but it thrived in a hybrid form.

The explanation of their success lies not so much in the transplanted European forms, but in the fact that sepoys infused them with native values that made them robust. South Asian societal culture—notions of caste and calling, religion and morality, and personal and community honor—branched into a distinct sepoy military culture. In a way that European common soldiers did not, sepoys remained embedded in family and village communities. This brought considerable pressure to bear on the individual sepoy to fulfill his duties in service to the British East India Company. So critical were indigenous values and ties to martial performance that Company officials wisely fostered them and protected them from the efforts of well-meaning Christian missionaries.

While the story of combat and culture presented in this chapter fits all the Company's native forces to a large degree, it is particularly apt concerning the army of the Bengal Presidency. During the eighteenth century, the East India Company had three loci, Bombay, Madras, and Calcutta; each served as the center of an administrative area, known as a presidency, and each had its own army. Because the three armies operated independently and drew their recruits from different populations, they displayed somewhat contrasting characters. The army of the Bombay Presidency prided itself on being the force that knew best how to travel light and march fast. The army of the Madras Presidency enjoyed a reputation as that most willing to deploy by sea to meet imperial needs. The army of the Bengal Presidency, with its capital at Calcutta, ranked as the most important of the three armies by the end of the eighteenth century. It also differed in composition, for unlike the other two armies, high-caste Hindus made up the majority of its rank and file. As a consequence, the army of the Bengal Presidency obeyed the practices and honored the restrictions imposed by the Hindu religion to a greater degree than did the other forces. This army has also been the most studied of the Company's forces, but not so much because of the victories it won as because of the crisis it brought, for it alone mutinied in 1857, shaking British India at its foundations.

This chapter presents a story of fusion between European and Indian discourses on war that produced something powerful and enduring. The British would import European weaponry, tactics, and organization, but it would be the native character of the sepoy which would crown them with victory.

The Evolving Indian Military Tradition

During the millennia before importation of European military practice, the subcontinent followed a path that contrasted sharply with the evolving European art of war. Chapter 2 discussed ancient South Asian military practice and texts, and the story continues here with the Muslim conquest of India.

That conquest was facilitated by the kind of disunity and suspicion between Indian principalities imagined in the *Arthashastra* of Kautilya. The mandala theory posited in that classic text insisted on necessary hostility between neighbors. Kautilya regarded underhanded methods, including subversion and assassination, as the best means to defeat the enemy. This theme of intrigue as an essential aspect of warfare marks Indian conflicts right through the eighteenth century and would, it will be seen, also provide great possibilities for the British East India Company.[5]

The weakness of Hindu India facilitated the arrival of Islam by the edge of the sword.[6] The first Muslim conquerors were Arabs who took Sind in 711–715, but they stopped there. During the late tenth and eleventh centuries, Turks raided into the Ganges Valley from the principality of Ghazni they had established in Afghanistan. The Ghaznis were eventually defeated by other Turks, the Ghorids, who captured Delhi in 1193 and made it their base in India. In 1206, Qutb-ud-din proclaimed himself sultan, creating the Delhi Sultanate, which for the next three centuries would be the major Muslim state in India. The Mongol chieftain Tamerlane led a devastating, though passing, raid into India in 1398–1399, even sacking Delhi. Although the Delhi Sultanate survived, it never fully recovered. A century later, Babur, who claimed descent from Tamerlane, led Chatatai Turks, who first occupied Kabul and then in 1526 defeated the last sultan of Delhi at the battle of Panipat to establish the great Mughal Empire, which ruled over north India and parts of the Deccan.

Muslim invaders brought with them different military beliefs, practices, and institutions along with their new proselytizing religion. Turkish Muslims—the Ghaznids, Ghurids, and finally the Mughals—came from a military tradition that contrasted sharply with that of South Asia. They were horse peoples from the steppes of Central Asia who fought in classic horse-archer fashion. This form of combat relied on rapid mobility in fluid battle, thus differing from the massive, lumbering armies of Hindu India and from the steady and powerful lines of European infantry. Armed with a superior bow and equipped with stirrups, Turkish cavalry swept all before it. Already by the eighth century, chariots had disappeared from the Indian arsenal, giving indigenous cavalry greater importance, but the Indians failed to develop horse archers of their own before the Muslim invasions, and the lack of stirrups limited the effectiveness of Indian horsemen.

Yet, it did not take the Mughals long to succumb to the same love of elephants that had typified the Hindu states before them. Abul Fazl, a major commentator during the reign of the great Emperor Akbar (1556–1605), wrote, "This wonderful animal is in bulk and strength like a mountain, and in courage and ferocity like a lion. It adds materially to the pomp of a King and to the success of a conqueror; and is of the greatest use for the army."[7] Akbar put musketeers in the howdahs, and by the eighteenth century, elephants even carried small cannon on their backs.

This is not to say that the Mughals did not appreciate the power of more modern weaponry or that they did not adapt it over time. The center of Babur's line at Panipat was held by thundering cannon and musketeers, and the next year at Khanwa, his artillery stopped the charging Rajput cavalry. Mughals favored the very large cannon in vogue among the Ottoman Turks. In fact the Mughal term for artillery, *top,* was an Ottoman word, and the early Mughals employed Turks from Istanbul as artillerymen. The matchlock muskets, an early form of shoulder-fired small arm, used by Babur's infantry were essentially the same as those employed in contemporary Europe, although the Mughals failed to develop European close-order infantry tactics to go along with these weapons. Akbar cared enough for the matchlock that he even improved its design.

Eventually, encumbered by cannon and elephants, the swollen Mughal armies became as unwieldy as those of earlier Hindu states, although the Mughals never lost their overwhelming preference for cavalry. The last of the great conquering Mughals, the Emperor Aurangzeb (1658–1707), campaigned with an army that numbered in the hundreds of thousands. He literally took his capital into the field, forming a moving tent city thirty miles in circumference with 30,000 elephants and a half million camp followers.[8] Not surprisingly, by the time Aurangzeb turned back from his twenty-five-year-long campaign to conquer the Deccan in 1705, he had exhausted the empire, and, thus, Mughal excess prepared the way for Persian and Afghan incursions during the mid-eighteenth century and, finally, complete conquest of the subcontinent by the East India Company.

During their period of dominance, the Mughals raised their military forces in a variant of the feudal system, known as the *mansubdari* system.[9] The emperor had only a small number of paid household troops; the rest were supplied by men to whom the emperor granted wealth and rank in exchange for raising a prescribed number of troops. These powerful individuals held office, a *mansab*, so were known as *mansubdars*. Akbar, who instituted the *mansubdari* system, paid his *mansubdars* in money, but soon they received land grants, *jagirs*, as compensation for their duties. This age-old exchange of land for military service received a twist under the Mughals, for *jagirs* could not be inherited, and at the death of a *mansubdar* his *jagir* reverted to the emperor, who then reassigned it to another worthy candidate. While this concept of meritocracy would seem to be more enlightened than European hereditary feudalism, it suffered a serious drawback. Because a *mansubdar* could not retain his *jagir* within his family, there was little incentive to husband its resources, and *mansubdars* lived in wasteful luxury at the expense of the inhabitants of their *jagirs*. Local welfare suffered. By requiring that *jagirs* revert to the emperors, the Mughal emperors hoped to avoid the natural tendency for great landholders to become powers unto themselves, as happened in medieval Europe. However, despite all intention and effort, when the empire became weak, this is exactly what happened, and in the eighteenth century, powerful local rulers became increasingly independent, although still expressing loyalty to the emperor.

While the official tally of troops to be furnished by a *mansubdar* was neatly set, from 10 to 7,000 (only princes held *mansabs* larger than 7,000), the actual contingent supplied would be much smaller and of no regular size. The Mughal army, then, lacked standardized or permanent units. Moreover, the system grew steadily more inefficient with time, and attempts to regulate and reform the *mansubdari* system did not arrest its decline.

Individual Mughal warriors could be superbly capable with their personal weapons, of fine physique, and excellently mounted, but there was little drill or discipline. Units neither deployed in a regular manner nor maintained set formations; they fought as collections of skilled individuals, not as cohesive units obedient to central command. The code of the warrior ruled, that of the soldier was unknown. This explains why European observers thought little of the Mughal army; Sir Thomas Roe at the emperor's court in the early seventeenth century wrote that he saw "what they call an army; but I see no soldiers, though multitudes entertained in that quality."[10] These armies with only a rudimentary organizational structure remained very centered on their leaders, whose deaths could determine the fate of battles. R. O. Cambridge would later comment that the British could "end the battle by one discharge of a six-pounder at the Raja's elephant."[11]

European Military Innovation, 1650–1750

Western ways of war overwhelmed the traditional military forms of Mughal India in the second half of the eighteenth century. In the hundred years before the Company's conquest of the subcontinent, Europeans forged the weaponry, practices, and institutions that they later transported to South Asia. The flintlock-bayonet combination and new more mobile artillery proved to be particularly effective on the subcontinent. But of even greater importance were non-technological military practices: the battle culture of forbearance, the Western reliance upon drill, and the foundation of the regimental community.

The transition from musket and pike to the fusil and bayonet constituted an important, and perhaps essential, prerequisite of European conquest in South Asia. The new weaponry maximized the power of Company forces and would, consequently, be particularly vital when they had to fight at a numerical disadvantage, as was usually, and sometimes dramatically, the case.

At the start of the 1600s, the musket/pike combination determined European tactics. The musket employed a matchlock, which ignited the powder charge by means of a lighted "match," a cord of flax or hemp. The complicated loading procedure limited the rate of fire to one shot per minute, and even then the rate of misfire could rise to 50 percent.[12] The lighted match proved dangerous to the musketeer himself and those around him, since it might accidentally ignite the gunpowder he carried or that in his proximity. Because musketeers lacked offensive shock potential and because they could not defend themselves effectively from cavalry charges, pikemen joined musketeers. In general, the pikemen grouped together in the center files of a battalion, flanked on either side by files of musketeers. Over time, the proportion of firearms to pikes in the battalion increased, from 1:1 at the start of the 1600s to 4:1 by 1690.

From the mid-seventeenth century, the more easily loaded, more reliable, and safer flintlock fusil began to replace the older musket, and the pike gave way to the bayonet. Instead of using a lit match to set off gunpowder, the fusil used flint striking steel to generate a spark. A fusilier could load in a third fewer movements, since he need not worry about the match.[13] He could also

prime and load his fusil, set it on half-cock, sling or stack the weapon, and still
be instantly ready to fire the moment he seized the firearm. As early as 1660,
General Monck rearmed his regiment, the Coldstream Guards, with fusils,
which became common in the English army in the 1690s. The French were a
bit slower to adopt the new weapon because the cost of conversion was substantial, but an ordinance of 1699 finally prescribed the universal adoption of
the fusil.[14] About the same time, the socket bayonet eliminated the need for
the pike. A desire to give muskets some shock value for defense and offense by
turning them into short but stout pikes produced earlier and more primitive
bayonets about 1640.[15] But these "plug" bayonets fit down the barrel of the
musket, meaning that with bayonet in place, the weapon could not be loaded
or fired.[16] In 1687, the famous French military engineer Vauban created the
socket bayonet that attached via a collar that slipped around the barrel, leaving the muzzle free for loading and firing. The socket bayonet soon became
standard issue in European armies during the 1690s, and early in the War of
the Spanish Succession (1701–1714) the pike disappeared from European battlefields.[17]

Adopting the fusil/bayonet combination improved the effectiveness of
European infantry. Firepower multiplied as every infantryman carried a
firearm, and shock capacity improved because every soldier now had an effective edged weapon. The implications of this improved weaponry for Europe
were significant enough, but in a South Asian context they would be even
greater. There, infantry would often face massive cavalry forces, so the need
for entire units to form impenetrable hedgehogs of bayonets was critical.
Moreover, with the numbers of Europeans and sepoys limited, it was doubly
important that every man carried an effective firearm.

If the logic of maximizing firepower to overcome larger native armies with
smaller numbers of Europeans and sepoys applies to the fusil, it applies even
more to artillery pieces. Artillery allowed one adversary to use the chemical
energy of gunpowder to counter the human energy of his enemy's multitude.
Shipboard cannon were essential to the initial expansion of European domains
in South Asia long before the Company pushed inland, where lighter field
artillery proved vital to that task.[18] The chief physical factor that limited the
utility of cannon on the early modern battlefield was their weight. In the
1620s, the barrel alone of a 34-pounder weighed 5,600 pounds, and the cannon on its carriage required twenty horses to pull it and a crew of thirty-five
to serve it.[19] Once in place cumbersome cannon could not be shifted to adjust
to the flow of battle. However, major European states conducted quiet but

essential reforms that lightened and improved cannon in the period 1740–1780. Frederick the Great improved and expanded the artillery branch of his army, making such technical improvements as the addition of ammunition boxes to gun limbers and employing screw mechanisms instead of clumsy wedges to elevate guns in 1747.[20] Under the direction of Franz, prince of Liechtenstein, the Austrians instituted an impressive program of experimentation and innovation. The most renowned artillery reform came in France, where General Jean-Baptiste de Gribeauval brought in a new system of field pieces in the 1770s. The artillery pieces of the Gribeauval system were half the weight of earlier guns; for example, the standard eight-pounder cannon was cut from 1,028 kilograms to 580.[21] In addition, these new pieces boasted more precise manufacture. Thus, the artillery environment of the second half of the eighteenth century differed in significant ways from what had existed before.

Beyond advances in weaponry, other, non-technological, military innovations rank as supremely important. The first was the battle culture of forbearance, already discussed in Chapter 4, as a new and counter-instinctual attitude toward losses in battle. This approach to combat put a premium on maintaining discipline and order while stoically accepting casualties under fire.

The ability to perform with forbearance in the face of danger and chaos was far from natural; it had to be learned. Training of European infantrymen emphasized obedience and restraint, because it was not enough that the soldier master the tools of war; the soldier himself must be mastered. In later ages, officers would come to trust in the initiative of their troops, but during the seventeenth and eighteenth centuries, aristocratic commanders assumed a low level of honor and motivation among the rank and file. So rather than rely on the common soldier's self-control, military practice put faith only in supervision by officers. Soldiers were to remain quiet, even in the attack. Tactical directives again and again insisted that men in the ranks maintain a strict silence, all the better to hear the officers' commands.[22] Silence allowed control, which preserved order. The key to teaching both skill and obedience was drill, the repetitive practice of rigidly prescribed movements in marching and the manual of arms under the careful supervision and command of officers and sergeants.[23]

During the first half of the seventeenth century, Dutch and then Swedish armies employed new more linear formations. The intricacies of the linear tactics demanded a high level of skill on the part of the troops, and drill developed to impart this ability. Drill designed by Maurice of Nassau and further extended by Gustavus Adolphus enabled maneuver and a rate of fire unknown before. The historian Michael Roberts, seconded by Geoffrey Parker, argues that these tactical innovations ushered in a true "Military Revolution," attended by what Roberts terms "the revolution in drill."[24] The promise of tactical effectiveness lured European officers to the Netherlands and northern Germany as if it were a military academy. These new tactics reached England in the seventeenth century via the experience of British mercenaries with Continental service, and when Oliver Cromwell reformed and refashioned Parliamentary troops into the New Model Army during the 1640s, he employed Swedish advisers.[25]

Yet probably from the start, and certainly during the second half of the seventeenth century, drill benefited armies not only by imparting particular skills but also by engendering a psychology. In his *Keeping Together in Time*, William McNeill argues that communal physical movement in dance or drill enhances group cohesion through "muscular bonding."[26] Few doubt that drill encourages group cohesion, and research demonstrates the importance of such cohesion in supporting soldiers in combat and holding them to their tasks.[27] For McNeill, the unavoidable product of drill was and is esprit de corps, the forging of a group identity. Drill was essential to the physical and psychological control required by the battle culture of forbearance.

In addition to altering conceptions of the battlefield, the second half of the seventeenth century witnessed the adoption of a new form of military community, a different conception of what an army should be.[28] Epitomized in the regiment, it possessed a number of innovative characteristics; it was standardized, permanent, and male. Although it was not the first military formation or unit to serve as the focus of life and devotion for its members, the European regiment allowed for a new intensity and direction of loyalty. The regiment was a regular, standardized unit of a defined size that included one or more battalions, each containing a set number of companies of an ordained size. An officially prescribed cadre of officers with standardized ranks and functions commanded. This carefully defined chain of command established and enforced the concept and reality of a hierarchy defined by military rank rather than by social prestige or personal bonds. The regiment also had a life beyond a particular campaign, war, or commander, because this new military community was in theory a permanent one. The long life of these formations allowed the creation of a regimental culture typified by strong regimental identity and intense devotion.

A coincident and absolutely integral development was the exclusion of the vast majority of women and children from the military community. Armies of the sixteenth and early seventeenth centuries included huge numbers of camp followers. Herbert Langer mentions a 40,000-man imperial force in Germany during the Thirty Years' War accompanied by 100,000 camp followers, many if not most of them women.[29] However, this created a logistical nightmare and undermined discipline, so authorities drove noncombatants from armies during the late seventeenth century.[30] Morality was also a concern; thus in the 1680s Louis XIV banned prostitutes from his armies, as the elector of Brandenburg had a generation before. In addition, authorities discouraged or forbade private soldiers to marry. Only a small number of women, usually the wives of sergeants, were retained within the regiment to work as washerwomen, seamstresses, and amateur nurses. The regiment became an essentially male community that isolated men from other bonds and focused loyalty on the military unit, with profound implications for motivation, morale, and professionalization.

Removing soldiers from women helped to cut them off from civil society. To be a common soldier was to choose an employment of last resort, and the impoverished man in the ranks generally retained few ties with home. In the French army, even when a soldier received a rare permission to marry, he could not marry a woman from his garrison town for fear of developing local ties. In fact, the French went even further, requiring that all French regiments, except the guards, change post every year to keep soldiers from developing an identity with the civilians around them. As will be seen, this form of regimental community would be severely altered to suit the South Asian cultural and social environment.

IMPORTING EUROPEAN MILITARY TECHNOLOGY TO SOUTH ASIA

The mid-eighteenth-century importation of European military practice shaped the era of conflict that followed, but the victory of the East India Company cannot be understood by supposing that it enjoyed a monopoly of Western weapons, tactics, or organization. No informed author ascribes the conquest of South Asia by the East India Company simply to a gap in weaponry. Indians used cannon and small arms for many generations before they had to fight the British and their sepoys. The Indians lagged somewhat in technology during the seventeenth century, but when the critical clashes came after 1740, Indian military hardware soon equaled that of the Europeans.[31]

Indians possessed the requisites for manufacturing modern weapons: a generally sophisticated technological base, prodigious wealth, and good raw materials. Not only did South Asia provide superior iron, it also exported high-quality saltpeter for gunpowder to Europe.[32] Moreover, the agents of technological diffusion abounded on the subcontinent. At first, the Mughals employed Ottoman Turkish technological experts, but over the sixteenth century they turned more and more to Europeans; one contemporary estimated that 5,000 Portuguese renegades served Asian potentates from Bengal to Makassar during the early seventeenth century.[33] This tradition continued, and, for example, "Frenchmen, Germans, Portuguese, Armenians, and Topasses [individuals of mixed European and South Asian parentage]" also served, and served well, the artillery of the forces of the *nawab* of Bengal, Mir Kasim, as he battled the Company army at Buxar in 1764.[34]

It was not difficult for native rulers to secure European-style weaponry in one way or another. As Hector Munro reported to Parliament in 1772: "There is hardly a ship that comes to India that does not sell . . . cannon and small arms."[35] But the most important source of weapons was Indian arsenals. Mir Kasim supplied his Western-style battalions with excellent flintlock fusils of Indian manufacture that tests showed to be superior to British weapons, owing to superior Indian Birbhum iron and Rajmahal flints.[36] In the late 1760s, Shuja-ud-daula, *nawab* of Oudh, in an effort to create Western-style forces, founded an arsenal with a work force of over 500 under the direction of a native Bengali and a French officer; it produced light cannon, muskets, and about 150–200 flintlocks per month.[37] True enough, for too long the Indians retained a preference for heavy artillery, but, when confronted with the example of successful Company campaigns, Indian rulers secured up-to-date lighter cannon of their own, complete with the latest European refinements in artillery design, such as elevating screws.[38] Toward the end of the century, the Marathas employed a Scottish expert, Sangster, to establish the most successful Indian arms production at Agra, where five factories turned out flintlock fusils, gunpowder, and cannon at the close of the eighteenth century.[39] These were the cannon that thundered at Lake's army. No less an authority than the Duke of Wellington, who also faced these guns himself, found the "ordonnance so good and so well equipped that it answers for our service," and he incorporated Maratha guns into his own artillery train.[40] Arms production in South Asia should lead us to question claims that only Europeans could produce quality, technologically advanced weaponry in quantity. Victor Davis Hanson ascribes a special advantage to Western arms production, but it did not exist in eighteenth-century India.

THE CREATION, EXPANSION, AND SUCCESS OF SEPOY FORCES

The superficial and fleeting nature of the European advantage in weaponry suggests that Western military culture and practice were far more essential imports to the subcontinent. The critical elements included discipline, drill, tactics, and, above all, the regiment. India did not accept European military culture passively, but fundamentally transformed it into something uniquely South Asian. To provide a basic historical framework for a discussion of that cultural metamorphosis, we must first trace the history of sepoy armies, from their inception under French aegis, to their maturation under the British East India Company, to their adoption by native states. For our purposes, it will suffice to carry the story only from 1740 to 1805, although the conquest of South Asia would extend into the 1840s.

From the establishment of European trading stations on the subcontinent during the sixteenth and seventeenth centuries, these foreign interlopers employed local armed men to help defend their coastal bastions. However, these forces were limited in number and purpose. It was not until mid-eighteenth century that the French Compagnie des Indes set off the race to create Western-style infantry units manned by native recruits. At Pondicherry, located some ninety miles south of Madras, the French governor, Dumas, mustered 4,000–5,000 sepoys in 1740 as a response to the threat of raids launched by the Marathas who demanded tribute throughout much of India.[41]

Meanwhile, war clouds gathered in Europe, where the War of the Austrian Succession (1740–1748) once again pitted Great Britain against France. Truces had spared the British and French from importing their wars to India before, but in 1744, Westminster forbade any new truce. The aggressive governor Dupleix, who had replaced Dumas, used his new troops to capture Madras in September 1746. This seizure embroiled the French in a struggle with the *nawab* of the Carnatic who had forbidden the Europeans to attack one another. The *nawab* dispatched an army of 10,000 men with artillery to punish the French. Paradis, in command of only 300 French and 700 "cypayes," devoid of any cannon, defeated the Indian host at the battle of St. Thomé in

November. Paradis's victory was the first in what became a pattern of victories by surprisingly small European forces with sepoy support over far larger indigenous armies.

The East India Company responded to the loss of Madras by raising sepoys of its own. Major Stringer Lawrence created a body of 3,000 natives trained to fight in European fashion and led them at the battle of Cuddalore in 1748.[42] To Robert Clive, a clerk turned soldier, fell the honor of winning the first dramatic victories with East India Company sepoys. Although the war in Europe ended in 1748, the fighting in India continued as the two rival trading companies backed different local candidates for rule over the Carnatic. Clive led a small force of 200 British plus 300 sepoys to seize the French-sponsored *nawab*'s capital at Arcot. Soon Clive found himself besieged there, but he outlasted the 3,000 troops sent against him. By the 1750s the Compagnie des Indes and the East India Company each maintained roughly 10,000 sepoys; however, from early on, the British seem to have done better with their native troops, paying them with greater regularity and demanding and achieving greater discipline.[43]

The East India Company's sepoy army continually evolved during its first half century. Initially, sepoys formed only in companies, which, though trained by Europeans, were commanded by Indian officers. It took some years before sepoys donned military uniforms, although by 1756 the authorities at Madras reported that its sepoys were attired in a "uniform of Europe cloth."[44] Alongside the sepoys, the Company always fielded its own battalions of Europeans independent of the royal army. The Company mounted little native cavalry in regular units but employed a good deal of irregular native horsemen. Artillerymen were generally European, the Company being reluctant at first to share the secrets of gunnery with the native population. In the initial clashes between French and British, sepoys played a secondary role in support of European troops, but with the years, the numbers of sepoys and their effectiveness increased.

The next crisis came when the *nawab* of Bengal took Calcutta in June 1756. Responding to the fall of Calcutta and to the atrocities following the capitulation—including the infamous Black Hole—Clive landed in Bengal. With an army of just a bit over 3,000 troops, two-thirds of them sepoys, he defeated an enemy host 50,000 strong at the battle of Plassey, 23 June 1757. In fact, this battle was something of a put-up job, because Clive had split the enemy alliance before the battle, and most of the troops arrayed against him did not actually fight. The spirit of intrigue still ruled.

Soon after his arrival in Bengal, Clive recruited the first full battalion of native infantry, the Lal Paltan, or red battalion, because of its British-style uniforms. In 1759, an ordinance completed the conversion to battalions by grouping all sepoy companies into battalions led by a small European cadre in addition to the native officers. At this time, the army of the Bengal Presidency also expanded; in a letter of April 1760, the directors of the Company in London stipulated to Calcutta that its European forces should number no more than 1,500, but allowed "blacks at your discretion."[45] From five native battalions in 1760, the Bengal army doubled to ten in 1763.

Harder fighting against a variety of enemies followed the easy victory of Plassey. By now the Seven Years' War (1756–1763) had engulfed Europe, and the French dispatched reinforcements to Pondicherry and besieged Madras, but failed. A bitter struggle between French and British also raged in the Northern Circars, a rich area held by the French, and a Company army dispatched by Clive performed marvels there. Finally, in 1761, Pondicherry fell, and the French were finished as a major colonial power in India. Even though the Treaty of Paris in 1763 restored Pondicherry to them, it so restricted their activities that the Compagnie des Indes soon dissolved. The French would play the role of spoilers, but they would not again constitute the main threat to Company ambitions.

Indigenous rulers observed the success of the East India Company's new military units and copied them; as the decades progressed, the native powers became more and more capable of fielding European-style armies of their own. The *nizam* of Hyderabad did so in the 1750s; next the *peshwa,* leader of the Maratha confederation, lured away the *nizam's* commander in 1758 and employed him to fashion a body of 8,000 infantry. After 1760, Mir Kasim, made *nawab* of Bengal after Plassey, created Western-style infantry led by two European adventurers. When war broke out between Mir Kasim and the Company in 1763, he allied with other regional rulers, including Shuja-ud-daula, *nawab* of Oudh, but the native coalition met defeat at the battle of Buxar in 1764. This battle was probably the single most important for the Company, for by winning there, the Company secured its hold over Bengal, Bihar, and Orissa—rich territory that provided the wealth and manpower necessary for further British conquest. Shuja-ud-daula, though defeated at Buxar, had learned the value of the Company's troops, and created his own Western-style infantry soon after the battle; however, his army disappeared with Shuja's death in 1774. The raja of Banaras also created such forces, which the Company defeated and dissolved in 1782.

From 1780 to 1799 the Company engaged in a struggle with Mysore, led
by the gifted military adventurer, Haider Ali, until his death in 1782, and then
by his son Tippoo Sultan.[46] Haider Ali showed no great partiality for
European-style infantry, although he maintained a body of European mercenaries. However, Tippoo Sultan raised a sizeable force of native infantry armed
and trained in European fashion with the guidance of European, mainly
French, drillmasters. However, Tippoo staffed his new regiments *(cushoons)*
and brigades *(chucheris)* with salaried native officers, rather than with
Europeans. Tippoo gave his "sepoys" uniforms, insignia, and drill manuals,
although the language of command was Persian.

After the final defeat and death of Tippoo Sultan, the East India Company
faced its most severe challenge in the Marathas. Maratha power dated back to
the close of the seventeenth century when their legendary leader, Shivaji,
fought Aurangzeb to establish Maratha independence. After Shivaji's death in
1680, the Marathas fractured, with a *peshwa* enjoying theoretical leadership,
but with several Maratha rulers, or *sardars,* exercising their own independence.
One *sardar,* Madhaji Sindia, seemed likely to reunite the Maratha confedera-
cy in the late eighteenth century. A cornerstone of his authority was a new
European-style infantry army forged with the aid of a Savoyard mercenary,
Benoit de Boigne, who had once led native troops with the Company army.
Sindia hired de Boigne to form two battalions in 1784 and later expanded this
force into the four brigades of the army of Hindustan, totaling 27,000 troops
drilled according to British manuals and armed with weapons manufactured
by his arsenal at Agra. De Boigne recruited a polyglot band of European officers, many of them British, to train and command this impressive force. In
1794 death cut short Sindia's efforts to reunite the Marathas. The far less able
Daulatrao Sindia succeeded his great-uncle, and de Boigne returned to
Europe, leaving in command his subordinate, Pierre Cuillier Perron, who
would later face Lake at Coel.

A moment of Maratha cooperation preceded their political demise. Late in
1794, the young *peshwa* summoned the Maratha *sardars* to join in a war against
the *nizam* of Hyderabad. Daulatrao Sindia committed his army of Hindustan.
At the battle of Kharda, the Marathas triumphed over the *nizam,* whose army
of 130,000 boasted 12,000 sepoys under Raymond.[47] The key clash in the battle took place between Perron's infantry and Raymond's troops, as the two
opposing forces fired volley after volley in fine eighteenth-century style.

The Company army that would soon confront the Marathas was larger and
more highly evolved than that of Clive and Munro. Further regularization and

TABLE 5.1 **Size of the Armies of the East India Company Presidencies at the Close of Major Wars**

	Bengal	Madras	Bombay
1763	6,680	9,000	2,550
1782	52,400	48,000	15,000
1805	64,000	64,000	26,500

Based on Callahan, *The East India Company and Army Reform,* p. 6.

reorganization arrived via the army reform of 1796 that replaced the older brigade organization of sepoy forces with regiments composed of two battalions each.[48] A complement of forty-two European officers commanded each sepoy regiment. Each sepoy company would also be led by a *subadar* aided by a *jemadar,* which resulted in a dual chain of command, one British and one South Asian. The reformed army was expanding as well; the above table details the increased numbers of permanent sepoy and European troops.

The Second Maratha War pitted the Company against the disunited Marathas. The British exploited a civil war among Maratha leaders by offering protection to the threatened *peshwa.* The *sardars* entered the fray piecemeal, so at first only Sindia buttressed by some allies took the field against the Company. The British undermined the army of Hindustan before the real fighting started by offering substantial bounties to its European officers who would come over to the Company. Perron mishandled the situation by not extending a counterbid; on the contrary, he made things worse by dismissing all British and Anglo-Indian officers in his brigades, because he now regarded them as untrustworthy. This stripped his units of the majority of their veteran officers at the moment of crisis.

There would still be much bitter fighting ahead, although the fact that the Marathas did not concentrate their forces put them at further disadvantage. As Lake undertook his victorious campaign, Arthur Wellesley commanded his own army of 6,000 at the battle of Assaye on 23 September 1803. There he defeated a Maratha army of 60,000, including Sindia's First Brigade, which along numbered about 6,000. Wellington would later call Assaye "the bloodiest [battle] for the numbers that I ever saw."[49] The *sardar* Holkar entered the war after Assaye and Laswarree, but those battles determined the fate of the Marathas.

After defeating the Marathas, the Company faced only one more great rival on the subcontinent, the Sikhs, but victory in the Second Maratha War, in addition to the earlier conquests of Bengal and South India, gave the Company such overwhelming wealth and manpower that the Sikhs were doomed to defeat in the Sikh Wars of the 1840s.

The narrative of the conquest provides no simple formula that prescribed victory for the East India Company. It enjoyed no monopoly over modern weaponry, and the diffusion of European military practice, though begun by the French and British, later spread to native powers who enthusiastically copied Western ways of war. Learning was a two-way street, and the Company discovered much through its South Asian experience. The British became adept at South Asian politics, characterized by divisive intrigue as well as sheer power. As Pradeep Barua concludes, vis-à-vis British maneuvering against the Marathas, "What is surprising is the degree to which the British had . . . mastered these Indian stratagems."[50] East India Company armies developed real competence at difficult aspects of military campaigning in India, notably logistics. But any explanation of the Company's success must take into account the contributions of the sepoys, and any consideration of their victories must recognize the fact that the sepoys maintained, and the Company fostered, South Asian values that reinforced the performance of these indigenous troops. Therefore, we must go beyond cataloging the formation and growth of Company regiments but also comprehend the South Asian traditions that inspired them.

BUILDING UPON INDIAN MILITARY VALUES

The ability to create a highly effective South Asian army that in its externals seemed so European depended not on the similarities between the British soldier and the sepoy but on the profound differences between them. Weaponry and uniforms, organization and command may have all had their origins in Europe, but the passion, resolve, and loyalty of the sepoy had roots in South Asian society and culture. Thus, in terms of the most important springs of martial action—motivation and morale—the sepoy units of the Company army were essentially South Asian, not mere imitations of the British.

The Company benefited from an indigenous culture that produced an optimal religious and social climate for the professional soldier of the pre-nationalist epoch. Before the onset of the French Revolution, European officers embraced military service willingly for reasons of their own, as explained in Chapter 4, but the rank and file remained outside this matrix of motivation and reward.[51] In contrast, South Asian culture explained the necessity of, and bestowed honor upon, military service by the common soldier. To glimpse the sepoy's *mentalité* requires some understanding of social and religious belief and practice on the subcontinent. This chapter, with its focus on the army of the Bengal Presidency, accordingly features Hindu tradition.

In its ancient form, the religious and social caste system in India elevated the warrior to high status, one that, in an important sense, the warrior preserved into the twentieth century. As mentioned in Chapter 2, in the traditional *varna* system of caste, which dates back to ancient Vedic times, the highest caste, *brahmans,* were priests, but the second caste, *kshatriyas,* were warriors and rulers, followed by *vaishyas* (commoners, merchants and landholders) and *shudras* (menial workers, peasants).

On the operative level of daily existence, the fairly simple caste schema of *varna* was far more varied and complicated by the principle of *jati,* literally "birth." *Jati* defined occupation and status by lineage. Moreover, one's *jati* determined not only one's profession but who one could marry; thus, *jatis* were limited regional endogamous groups throughout India. Each *jati* claimed to belong to one of the classical *varnas*. On a ritual level, the Hindu religion is much concerned with pollution and purification, and to eat, smoke, or drink with an individual of a lower-ranked *jati* or caste would pollute the higher-caste Hindu. Even accepting water drawn by the wrong caste endangered the individual. The definitions, status, and restrictions of *jati* varied from one area of India to another, but whatever the variants, within Hindu society *jati* was the most important reality of caste.

Hindu society saw humanity divided into groups set by birth and occupation, sanctioned by religion, governed by distinct codes of conduct, and guided by principles suited to one's condition. Overlaid on this caste society came the new profession of sepoy, soldier in service to the East India Company. Effectively it became another *jati,* if not initially defined by birth, then ultimately established by calling. The identity as sepoy fit well into a world defined by function and community, and now, added to his civilian identity came the new military collectivities he served: company, battalion, and regiment. Sepoys easily assumed an approach that regarded the individual as a representative of a community, which required the individual to be faithful to its standards. Group identification and loyalty are nearly omnipresent aspects of military motivation, whether it be in the form of primary group cohesion or esprit de corps. (Modern theories of group bonding will be discussed in Chapter 7.) However, the difference in India was the impressive level of religious and social sanction attached to group and occupational identity.

In a *jati*, right conduct was defined in terms of living by the dictates of that particular *jati:* The highest virtue for the sepoy was to fulfill the role of soldier. His most fundamental loyalty would not, then, be to the Company or to the British Crown, but to his military unit and to his own duty, or dharma, conceived of in a very Indian way.[52]

Hindu literature discusses dharma at length, and for the soldier, the *Bhagvad Gita (Song of God)* offers obvious guidance. Chapter 2 has already discussed the military morality of the *kshatriya,* but consider the subject again as discussed in the *Gita.* This sacred text, described by one author as "the most typical expression of Hinduism as a whole," dates from the first or second century A.D.[53] It is a dialogue between the hero Arjuna and the great god Krishna, who appears as the driver of Arjuna's chariot. The interchange comes before the climactic battle of Kurukshetra between the related but rival Pandavas and Kauravas. Arjuna, the leading prince and champion of the Pandavas, sees his kin in the opposing army, shows humane compassion for them, and expresses his desire to throw down his arms rather than fight. But Krishna insists that this course of action would be sinful, for by it Arjuna would fail to fulfill his dharma as a *kshatriya.*

Krishna first argues that because of the cycle of birth, death, and rebirth, Arjuna should not think that he is killing a foe by slaying his body; moreover, bodily death is inevitable as well as irrelevant. "Never, indeed, was there a time when I was not, nor when you were not, nor these lords of men. Never, too, will there be a time when we shall not be." (2.12)[54] And thus, "He who regards him [i.e., the soul] as a slayer, and he who regards him as slain—both of them do not know the truth; for this one neither slays nor is slain." (2.19) Krishna follows with an appeal that Arjuna's dharma requires him to fight, and he must accept this because of his *kshatriya* caste. "For a *kshatriya* there does not exist another greater good than war enjoined by dharma." (2.31) "But if you do not fight this battle which is enjoined by dharma, then you will have given up your own dharma as well as glory, and you will incur sin." (2.33) So Arjuna has a moral duty to fight because of his caste, and the consequences of battle will be positive for him whatever his fate: "Either, being slain, you will attain heaven; or being victorious, you will enjoy the earth. Therefore arise . . . intent on battle." (2.37) Krishna next explains that morality lies in the action itself, not its fruits. By extension, the proper standard by which to judge personal morality in combat is not the violence and destruction of war, but the fulfillment of the warrior's dharma.

The Hindu community's great reverence for the *Gita* derives from its discussion of dharma, rather than its specific reference to conduct in war; nonetheless, the *Bhagavad Gita* preaches a powerful warrior's code. The combatant has a duty to fight because it is the proper duty of the warrior. Since death is both inevitable and is followed by rebirth, the warrior need not feel guilt for the death of his enemies. To die in battle is blessed, and to be victorious wins earthly rewards. The morality of personal martial action is best understood as separate from the consequences of that action, a proposition that could be interpreted as measuring a soldier's right conduct in terms of warrior values—prowess, courage, self-sacrifice—rather than in terms of the interests and aims of those for whom he fights.

While the notions of caste, action, and duty examined above are definably Hindu, these conceptions influenced the Muslim and Sikh communities of South Asia as well; Indian notions of honor are even more completely shared. In discussing martial morality and motivation, there is no more complex cultural concept than honor. We have already discussed aristocratic masculine honor in Chapter 4, but that does not exhaust the possible varieties of honor. It can refer both to an individual's highly personal, internalized code of behavior and to the reputation that individual enjoys within a group or community.[55]

To this inherent complexity, Indian society adds another layer of meaning, which distinguishes between personal honor, *izzat,* and community honor, *rasuq.*[56] *Izzat* corresponds to Western notions that an individual's actions earn praise or condemnation for himself. The definitions of honorable action may differ, but the consequence is still focused on the individual. Beyond this, *rasuq* is community honor, meaning that the community, be it a village or a *jati,* holds to a standard that it expects of its members and that their actions will bring honor or disgrace to the community as a whole. In terms of *rasuq,* the individual represents his community and the community pressures the individual to live up to its standards.

Another distinctly South Asian attitude with great implications for the code of the warrior was the Indian concept of being "true to one's salt." Salt, *namak,* implied sustenance and a compact between a person who grants sustenance and an individual who accepts it. The latter must feel great loyalty to the former. This was more than simply a quid pro quo between employer and employee; it involved a covenant that asserted strong moral force on an individual compelling him to give not only service but fidelity to an institution or authority that paid and fed him so long as the bargain were kept on the other side. Perhaps this code of loyalty grew out of the frequent changes of masters, particularly political masters, in South Asia; perhaps it was an extension of the values expressed in the *Bhagavad Gita*. In any case, it gave leverage to any institution that possessed the resources necessary to hire troops to further its interests. Such an institution could expect more of its servants than a hireling's sense of giving a day's work for a day's wage. Not surprisingly, the Company made reference to salt in the oath administered to new recruits in 1766: "I, _____, do swear to serve the Honorable Company faithfully and truly against all their enemies, while I continue to receive their pay and eat their salt."[57]

THE EAST INDIA COMPANY'S EXPLOITATION OF NATIVE TRADITION

The Company learned to create an environment for its sepoys that fostered native concepts of *jati,* duty, honor, and loyalty. Because these demanded high standards, the Company had a stake in allowing the sepoy to remain integrated into his original community as much as the demands of military service allowed. Battalions, and later regiments, became communities themselves, but these benefited from association with their sepoys' civilian identities and bonds.

The emphasis placed upon Hindu texts and *jati* in the preceding discussion applies to all three Company armies, but it best fits the crucial Bengal army, because it was overwhelmingly composed of high-caste Hindus. The other presidency armies also contained a large percentage of Hindus, because it was the majority religion of South Asia. However, the high-caste nature of the Bengal army was unique. Madras, for example, had no *kshatriyas,* and its *brahmans* were so adamant about their orthodoxy and special position in society that they did not serve in the army. While complete records are not available, existing evidence all stresses the high-caste nature of the Bengal army, which was recruited predominately in Bihar and Oudh. A Benares regiment raised in 1814–1815, for which a detailed account exists, lists 696 *brahmans* and Rajputs *(kshatriyas)* and only 108 Hindus of lower castes along with ninety-two Muslims.[58] This seems to have been the pattern as early as the administration of Charles Cornwallis, governor-general and commander-in-chief, 1786–1793.[59] It seems reasonable to assume that high-caste *brahmans* and *ksha-*

triyas were most likely to take to heart the classical outlook of the *Bhagavad Gita*, although all Hindus lived in a world defined by *jati*.

The Company provided a menu of incentives to the sepoy that would seem effective in any army, but were enhanced in a South Asian context. In the period discussed in this essay, pay, promotion, and pensions mattered most. The rate of pay offered by the Company to a sepoy was not particularly hand-some, but it was enough that men sought Company service.[60] The basic pay of a sepoy was seven rupees per month, while a *jemadar* earned seventeen rupees and a *subadar* fifty-two rupees. In addition to base pay, the Company added allowances, known as *batta,* when a soldier was on the march, in the field, or posted at a distance from his home base. While pay was sustenance, it was also a bond among a soldiery pledged to be true to its salt.

Promotion provided additional incentive. Common soldiers within a European regiment, Company or royal, had little or no chance of attaining an officer's commission; however, promotion to Indian rank in a native battalion depended only upon seniority. The recruit could advance from sepoy to *naik*, to *havildar,* to *jemadar,* and finally to *subadar,* the highest-ranking Indian offi-cer in a company. To be sure, the climb up the ladder took a very long time; a young man entering the service at age sixteen could probably not expect to become a *naik* until he reached age thirty-six, and would have to survive to sixty before rising to *subadar*.[61] Since not only authority, but pay and pensions as well, increased with promotion, a jump in grade was much desired.

The Company also instituted regular pensions for men who had served a minimum of twenty years, a period later reduced to fifteen. A pensioner received half his pay rate, and even the smallest pension, when supplemented by a minimal income in the village, allowed a man to live in a tolerable con-dition. In 1852, Viscount Gough declared, "The pension is our great hold on India."[62] There is no question that the pension was a considerable draw for recruits. From 1782, the Company in Bengal offered a small land grant, a *jagir,* as an alternative to a straightforward monetary pension in order to ease the strain on the Company treasury.[63]

Beyond these obvious compensations, the life of the sepoy brought to bear rewards and sanctions specific to Indian society. The creation of a high-caste army in the Bengal Presidency may have been an accident of regional politics and the operation of the manpower market in northeast India, but the British quickly came to terms with this reality and encouraged it.[64] Before the Mutiny of 1857, the Company catered to caste by creating single-class battalions, that is battalions composed of men of the same ethnicity, religion, and caste. Incidentally, the preference for high-caste recruits in the army of the Bengal Presidency also played into the hands of the *brahman* peasantry, particularly in Bihar, where that peasantry used this leverage to strengthen their claims for elevated status.[65]

It should be noted that *brahmans* who did not occupy positions as priests could farm the land and, obviously, could be soldiers. However, even when serving in other roles, they were required to fulfill the demanding customs and ceremonies of their caste.

The Company accommodated the religious scruples of the sepoys and facilitated maintaining ties with their home communities by allowing native battalions to live in a manner very different from that imposed on European Company troops and those royal regiments posted to India. European regimental culture strove to isolate the soldier from his personal background and from the population of the towns where troops were garrisoned. The soldier himself tended to be an economic cast-off and was held in low repute by society and his officers. Cornwallis wrote in dismay about European recruits for the Company armies, "I did not think Britain could have furnished such a set of wretched objects," and went on to condemn them as "contemptible trash."[66] Two particular eighteenth-century trends increased the isolation of soldiers in Europe; on the one hand, they were more and more consigned to barracks, and, on the other hand, only a minority were allowed to marry.

While European soldiers in India continued to live in barracks, troops of native battalions inhabited small huts. An individual sepoy built this simple accommodation on a spot of ground assigned him. Soldiers living without families might share their space with a fellow sepoy, but married men were likely to have wife and children with them and perhaps other relatives. Europeans tended to regard the huts as dirty and "unmilitary," but they were a sensible adjustment to the needs of South Asian troops.

Family obligations figured prominently in sepoy life. Even if wives were not physically present in the cantonment, married sepoys could hardly forget their duties to them. A sepoy with wife and family was expected to remit part of his salary back home to his wife, and should he fail to do so, sepoys from his own village would condemn him.[67] Sepoys living with their families regularly brought wives and children with them when they changed stations.[68] The presence of women and children, as well as the bazaar peddlers necessary for supply in India, meant that armies traveled with great numbers of noncombatants. When troops marched from Bengal to Bombay in 1778–1779, the 103

Europeans and 6,624 sepoys were accompanied by 19,777 camp followers plus an additional 12,000 bazaar people.[69] Such crowds, once common in Europe, had disappeared in the male world of eighteenth-century professional armies.

Whereas European troops messed together, Hindu practice insisted that a man of higher caste could not eat food prepared by one of lower caste. In practice, Hindu restrictions on high-caste individuals required each sepoy to prepare his own food, rather than eating in a common mess. By European standards this arrangement was hopelessly confused, but it was a religious and social necessity in India, and authorities respected this.

Such regard for religious practice was a matter of policy intended to avoid unnecessary friction between Company and sepoy, but the by-product was to reinforce religion and traditional martial values within the Company army. Cornwallis wrote in 1789, "We cannot too forcibly impress on you the important light in which we view an attention to objects connected with the means of indulging these religious prejudices. . . . "[70] In 1793, a general order specifically sanctioned religious festivals: "The Commander-in-Chief has no objection to the native troops amusing themselves at the celebration of their festivals according to their respective rites and customs. . . . "[71] In the late eighteenth and early nineteenth centuries, British officers even took part in Hindu ceremonies, notably in the annual blessing of the battalion's weapons and flags. Custom commanded each *jati* to celebrate the tools of its appointed trade, and the sepoys grafted this practice into battalion life. In this effort to tolerate, even foster, native religion so as to avoid alienating its sepoys, the government and army even deflected well-meaning Christian attempts to convert the troops. When the bishop of Salisbury approached Cornwallis in an effort to foster missionary activities, Cornwallis rebuffed him.

> It is likewise a matter for serious considerations how far the impudence of intemperate zeal of one teacher might endanger a Government which owes its principle support to a native army composed of men of high caste whose fidelity and affections we have hitherto secured by an unremitted attention not to offend their religious scruples and superstition.[72]

While parrying missionary efforts, so careful was the Company to respect the caste of its Bengal soldiers that it supplied them only with *brahman* and *kshatriya* prostitutes.[73]

In order to ensure that its officers respected the men's language, customs, and religion, the Company tried to ensure that its officers became knowledgeable about them. As early as 1768, the Company directors in London declared that "no Officer should rise to the Command of a Battalion until he has made himself sufficiently Master of the Language to acquit himself in his Duty without the Assistance of an Interpreter."[74] A generation later, Cornwallis insisted that "a perfect knowledge of the Language, and a minute attention to the prejudices of the Sepoys" were absolutely essential for all officers of native troops.[75] Sita Ram testifies that in his early days as a sepoy, ca. 1815, officers spoke Indian languages well, lived with Indian women, and took part in the entertainments of the sepoys.[76] Capt. Thomas Williamson gives first-hand testimony that young officers, "attach themselves to the women of the country; and acquire a liking, a taste, for their society and customs."[77] The dual chain of command within battalions, one European and the other native, ensured that even if a British captain fell short in understanding his men's values and customs, the *subadar* and *jemadar* could inform the officer and serve as a buffer between him and the sepoys. Officially, any European officer outranked any Indian officer, so the greenest of subalterns from England could order about an experienced *subadar,* but one would think that older heads advised young men new to the army to respect the senior Indians.

Maintaining a soldiers' religion meant maintaining his relationship with his home community. Amiya Barat concludes, "by enlistment he gained status in his society to which he continued to retain his allegiance. He therefore remained a civilian at heart through becoming a soldier by profession."[78] Recruitment conspired to reinforce family and village ties. When the East India Company first formed native armies, the men who presented themselves for service were mercenaries similar to those who had offered their swords to native rulers, but the Company soon evolved its own system of recruitment, and in Bihar and Oudh this produced respectable young sepoys who arrived with their families' blessings. Pensioners who returned to their villages with a red coat and a comfortable income demonstrated the generosity of the Company, and their stories of adventure whetted the appetites of the young. The army introduced a furlough system that sent soldiers home to their villages periodically. One contemporary officer endorsed this practice as a means by which the "good feelings of their families continue through the whole period of their service to exercise a salutary influence over their conduct as men and as soldiers."[79] It was hoped that men on furlough would bring back recruits.[80] The autobiography of Sita Ram tells how he was recruited by his uncle, a *jemadar* in the infantry, who was on furlough to visit his family.[81]

While returning to camp, they were joined by two sepoys from the uncle's regiment, one of whom brought his brother to enlist. Such new recruits were given no housing allowance at first, because it was expected that they would share the hut of a relative or friend during the first year of their life in the ranks. Amiya Barat interprets this last practice as "another example of the way in which the army authorities encouraged the growth of family or village ties within the army."[82]

Over time, regiments became not only extensions of peasant villages but communities in their own right, taking on some of the characteristics of a village. Braithwaite, commander-in-chief of the Madras army, wrote in 1793, "In native corps of any standing, the ties of caste and consanguinity are . . . strong and numerous, from frequent intermarriages."[83]

Families had good reason to encourage a son to enlist. Of course, salary and pension promised life-long income in an honored profession, but added incentives also lured the high-caste Hindus who so dominated the ranks in the army of the Bengal Presidency. Such families were often landowners, and from 1796 to 1815 official policy gave preference to the pleadings of sepoys; thus a family could gain real advantage if a son served in the ranks.[84] These benefits could extend to other dealings with civil authority. Again, the story of Sita Ram reflects this. His mother lamented his wish to become a sepoy, but his father approved because he had a case pending concerning a disputed mango grove, and he knew that he might reap a benefit in court once his son was in uniform.[85] The fact that a family might expect to enjoy advantages from the military performance of a son put all the more pressure on sepoys to conduct themselves with honor.

My emphasis upon the strong bonds between sepoy and community runs counter to the thesis advanced by Steven Rosen in *Societies and Military Power: India and Its Armies*. There he insists that the success of the British sepoy army was due to "a form of military organization that increased the cohesion of the army by divorcing it from society."[86] I argue the contrary, that European regimental culture only succeeded in South Asia by being profoundly altered so as to link the military unit with family, village, *jati,* and religion. Cohesion and motivation within native battalions depended on focusing the force of indigenous community identity and honor. In the absence of patriotism, the army exploited identification with the battalion or regiment, to be sure, but it also took advantage of the wider set of societal and religious norms sepoys brought with them from their civil communities.

DIFFUSION, STABILITY, AND MOTIVATION

The success of the sepoy suggests a great deal about the role of culture in war and about the diffusion of European military practice to the non-Western world. For transplanted practice to take root and bear fruit it must ultimately be compatible with indigenous culture. Such a conclusion would seem straightforward. However, imported practice can rarely if ever be expected to fit a new environment without being modified. Therefore, successful diffusion and integration requires 1) the realization that elements considered essential to effectiveness in one cultural environment can be irrelevant or counterproductive in another and 2) the wisdom to recognize which elements can be altered, and to what degree, without detracting from the primary goal of effectiveness.

In the case of the East India Company's sepoy battalions, the match between European regimental forms, as modified, and South Asian culture far exceeded mere compatibility. A great affinity for the new regimental system synergized innovation and tradition, creating native forces that were far better than they would have been as an awkward Indian duplicate of the contemporary British army. The result was neither intended nor expected; it can only be explained as a fortunate convergence. History tells the fascinating tale of how European regimental culture metamorphosed into a form that optimized South Asian values in the service of a colonial power.

From the 1740s, European trading companies, first the French and then the British, expanded their military presence in South Asia by adding sepoy troops. This primary diffusion imported not only European fusils and artillery but Western discipline, drill, and battle culture. Above all, the colonial British instituted standardized, permanent units in imitation of European regiments. The full flower of the East India Company's system could only be expected to bloom with time; successful transplantation was a process, not an event. Passing years allowed the system to mature. In the first decade of fighting, sepoys primarily played a supportive role to European troops in the Anglo-French struggle for south India. Clive would not lay the foundations for the army of the Bengal Presidency until the 1760s, and the greatest enemies of the Company, Mysore and the Marathas, would not really take the field against the British until the 1780s and later.

By this point the British appreciated the benefits to be had by letting well enough alone. It is worth noting that the East India Company had been on the subcontinent for well over a century before they created sepoy infantry, and the British had already learned to adapt in order to survive in India.

When the Company first raised sepoy units it did so precisely because Europeans were so scarce on the subcontinent. The shortage of European officers and the experimental nature of the first sepoy companies dictated that they be commanded by Indians, and apart from the specifically tactical aspects of their duties, drill and training for example, sepoys enjoyed their own style of life under direct supervision of indigenous leaders. When the Company reformed and expanded sepoy units in later years, it imposed European officers as company, battalion, and regimental commanders, but left religious and community aspects of sepoy life to continue in an Indian pattern. Military and political leaders, exemplified by Cornwallis, clearly appreciated the wisdom in doing so.

Agents of the East India Company in South Asia enjoyed considerable flexibility in dealing with native troops, more, in fact, than with European soldiers who, because of their higher cost, were of greater concern to the directors back in England. As a private, or at least quasi-private, trading company, the Company was insulated from royal government interference during the formative period of the sepoy army, although the Crown became much more directly involved with the subcontinent through the India Act of 1784. In any case, the greatest guarantee of Company flexibility regarding its sepoy army was probably distance and unconcern. London was a very long voyage away, and, at any rate, the handling of sepoy regiments was hardly a priority there.

After European trading company armies demonstrated the ability of their sepoy forces in battle, native states created Western-style armies of their own. This secondary diffusion copied the pattern established by the East India Company, and, in fact, hired Europeans to direct the transformation. Stewart N. Gordon points out how the involvement of indigenous elites with traditional forms of landholding, wealth, and honor inhibited the adoption of Western-style infantry by native states; nonetheless, several important Indian rulers forged such armies.[87] Measured by the quality of their weaponry, the precision of their drill, and the character of their organization, the adoption of European military technology and practice by these princes was a success. However, measured by victory and defeat, indigenous diffusion failed, for no native army could stand for long against the Company.

Thus arises an apparent paradox. If the East India Company sepoy's success depended more upon his South Asian values than upon his Western weaponry, why were not native rulers, particularly those who adopted Western tactics such as the Marathas, far more effective on the battlefield? Should not they have been in a better situation to understand and draw upon the wells of

South Asian culture? The logic here is attractive, but it is also misleading, for mobilizing the military potential of the sepoy required an institutional stability that no South Asian power enjoyed during the eighteenth century.

Certainly, its political and territorial base provided the East India Company with an ability to tap money, materiel, and manpower over the long haul, and without this it could not have conquered the subcontinent. However, indigenous powers were not lacking for these assets. Neither the richness of British coffers nor the numbers of sepoy armies can alone explain the conquest. Company armies were generally outnumbered on campaign, and against the Marathas they were matched in the number of Western-style troops and outgunned by superior artillery.

In contrast to native powers, the Company's institutional stability freed it from the fates of individual leaders and, in terms of the sepoy army, provided the time needed to develop the concert between military innovation and traditional culture. While South Asian states remained at the mercy of shifting feudal loyalties and the survival of particular rulers, the Company endured and prospered. After the East India Company initiated the use of Western military practices by native troops, this stability bought time for sepoy battalions and regiments to develop identities and for bonds to grow between the sepoys and their surrounding and supporting communities, for *rasuq* to multiply *izzat*. The Company's permanent European-style military units benefited from Indian military values in a way that the irregular and transitory forces of the older South Asian pattern could not, and while some native states imitated European-style forces, these lacked the constancy and longevity required to maximize their effectiveness. In this unique manner, the political environment determined the fusion and fruition of a new military culture, a new discourse on war which combined European and South Asian elements.

The triumph of the Company's sepoy armies during the Second Maratha War involved a great deal more than the introduction of European weaponry to the subcontinent; the Marathas who faced them were as well armed or better, particularly in artillery. In fact, the spread of European technology was the least interesting and the least important aspect of the conquest of South Asia by the British East India Company in the second half of the eighteenth century. Importation of European military weapons and practices owed its great success to the synergy between innovation and tradition. The sepoy fought so well because even though he carried European weapons and wore a European uniform, he was inspired by very South Asian ideals. European military culture merged with South Asian religious, social, and village values and practices to produce a new military culture unique to India and the sepoy. At Laswarree, General Lake relied upon this fusion, and was not disappointed.

Another commander of that war, the future Duke of Wellington, said of his victory at Assaye: "I assure you that the fire was so heavy that I much doubted at one time whether I should prevail upon our troops to advance . . . and all agree that the battle was the fiercest that has ever been seen in India." And he added, "Our troops behaved admirably; the sepoys astonished me."[88]

Notes on the Opening Illustration for Chapter Five

This image of a sepoy and his wife dates from 1797. Drawn in Tanjore style, it tells us much about the native soldiers who served the British East India Company. The presence of his wife, with her adoring gaze, hints at the integration of the sepoy into his own society and of the role of native pride. His uniform mixes South Asian elements with his red coat, just as he retains his own values and practices even in service to the Company.

(Oriental and India Office Collections, The British Library)

CHAPTER SIX

The Sun of Austerlitz

*Romantic Visions of Decisive Battle in
Nineteenth-Century Europe*

ABOUT 9 A.M., DRUMMERS BEAT THE CHARGE, and French attack
columns emerged out of the mists that had hidden their presence from the
enemy. Astride the Pratzen heights, the opposing Austro-Russian army, which
minutes before had enjoyed such confidence of victory, now faced disaster.
Surging up the slopes of the Pratzen with irresistible momentum advanced the

bayonets of two French divisions. That cold morning of 2 December 1805 near the town of Austerlitz, Napoleon achieved his masterpiece, and in doing so changed the European concept of battle itself.

A whirlwind campaign built to this climax. Faced by a coalition of Austria, Russia, and Britain, Napoleon marched against Austria during the last days of August. Taking Ulm by means of a brilliant maneuver, Napoleon opened the Danube. But by then it was mid-October, a time when an ancien régime army would have gone into winter quarters. Napoleon, however, pressed on to Vienna, because he needed to drive Austria out of the war before the coalition could convince Prussia to join it. Yet even after Vienna fell, the Habsburg Emperor Francis I held on, so Napoleon played a high-risk gambit. He advanced north in numbers weak enough to convince the coalition forces that they could attack him with advantage, and this induced them to fight at Austerlitz.

On the eve of battle, Napoleon baited another trap by presenting his enemies with an under-manned right flank. This successfully lured the allies into an ill-considered attack that required them to denude their own center on the Pratzen, where Napoleon intended to strike. Early the next morning French troops who had marched through the night arrived to buttress Napoleon's right, holding off the allied assault. Meanwhile, morning fog, thickened by smoke from thousands of campfires, hid the two divisions Napoleon would hurl at the enemy center. Finally, as the sun broke through over Austerlitz, burning away the fog, he launched them against the Pratzen, where they overcame desperate resistance to dominate the heights by noon. This blow proved mortal to the coalition army, although fighting continued throughout the afternoon. By nightfall, coalition forces had lost 27,000 casualties in so shattering a defeat that it robbed the Austrians of their will; Francis I capitulated two days later. By driving Austria from the coalition, the battle of Austerlitz effectively ended the war on the Continent after a campaign of little more than three months—in contrast to the endless wars of Louis XIV or Frederick the Great.

Austerlitz was not Napoleon's first victory, but it was the clash that more than any other gave tangible reality to the ideal of decisive battle, a concept that would haunt the nineteenth and twentieth centuries. General Bonaparte's astounding campaign of 1796–1797 in Italy certainly led to triumph, but not by a single battle. In fact, the key actions involved the French attempt to take the fortress of Mantua and the Austrian attempts to relieve it. Bonaparte's expedition to Egypt in 1798 may have produced some dramatic tactical victories, but his inability to take Acre doomed his strategy. While the French viewed him as a conqueror when he returned to France in October 1799, the troops he left in Egypt eventually surrendered. Certainly Bonaparte scored an essential victory at Marengo in 1800, but he came close to losing the battle, and the war against Austria continued until Moreau won at Hohenlinden six months later. In contrast, Austerlitz marked a turning point, confirmed by Napoleon's elimination of the Prussians at Jena-Auerstadt in October 1806 and his final defeat of the Russians at Friedland in June 1807.

Not long before Austerlitz, the military pundit Antoine-Henri Jomini had counseled "give battle only when great advantages are to be derived, or the position of the army makes it necessary."[1] This reluctant endorsement of battle echoes the Military Enlightenment. However, after Napoleon's victories of 1805–1807, Jomini argued that campaigns should be designed "for the purpose of bringing [the enemy] to battle."[2]

This chapter deals with two important watersheds in military history, one in the real world of combat and the other in the conceptual world of military theory. As I have argued throughout this volume, reality and discourse relate to one another in complex interplay of influence and feedback. In this case, the new reality of war after 1789 was in part the result of conceptual changes, while the new theoretical perspectives of the nineteenth century were in large part products of the surprising success of national armies and the French emperor on campaign. In addition, the evolution of the discourse on war also reflected a shift in major European intellectual paradigms, from the Enlightenment to Romanticism. Military intellectuals looked at war differently for some of the same reasons that their civilian counterparts viewed art and philosophy in new ways. Countless volumes describe how Romanticism permeated expressions of high culture; this chapter argues that it fundamentally altered military thought as well, creating what will be termed here "Military Romanticism." Like Chapter 2, these pages deal with the cerebral world of military thought at its most elevated level. And yet while focusing on the discourse, we will nonetheless confront the question of how conception not only perceived but influenced the real world of combat.

Works of Military Romanticism enshrined Napoleon's victories as standards to guide future military practice, but, more basically, this intellectual movement mined Napoleonic experience to gain essential insights concerning the very nature of war. Military Romantics rejected Enlightenment faith in rules and principles patterned after the natural sciences and, instead, emphasized human psychology, redefined genius, accepted chance and loss, and put battle at the center of war. This reconsideration borrowed heavily from the works of major cultural figures of the time, including Immanuel Kant. Within the body of military writing, no single individual fashioned Military Romanticism. However, Carl von Clausewitz, author of the classic *On War*, towers above other Military Romantics, so much so that lesser contributors practically disappear from view, particularly from the vantage point of the twenty-first century. Yet to understand Clausewitz better, we must put him back into the contexts of time, circumstance, and community.

Military Romanticism, although clearly a product of the last decade of the eighteenth century and the first decades of the nineteenth, continues to impose its discourse through *On War*. The longevity of that vision of conflict deserves its own history, and this chapter will eventually offer some thoughts on that matter. But first it is necessary to consider the impetus toward change coming out of the revolutionary and Napoleonic wars.

REVOLUTION IN WARFARE, 1789–1815

European warfare underwent a transformation during the era beginning with the French Revolution in 1789 and extending through the Napoleonic Era. Political and social revolution in France changed the relation of the people, or the nation, to war; this, in turn, altered the conduct of war, including recruitment, command, logistics, tactics, operations, and strategy. This transformation in warfare, advanced and exploited by Napoleon, constituted one pole in a new dialogue between reality and discourse that produced Military Romanticism.

The Course of the Revolution

The French Revolution grew out of the monarchy's attempt to reform its tax system in order to solve its chronic financial distress. Once begun, however, the process of reform escalated into revolution when the people's representatives insisted that they constituted a National Assembly empowered to assert popular control over the government. Louis XVI balked, but the storming of the Bastille in Paris on 14 July 1789 ensured the survival of that revolutionary body.

The National Assembly called for a new political and social order, outlined in the Declaration of the Rights of Man and the Citizen. This essential document abolished traditional privileges and ushered in a new constitutional regime of legal and political equality. The French would enjoy "careers open to talent," rather than see offices reserved for the wellborn—a move much to the benefit of the middle classes. Soon the Assembly went beyond even this and undermined the last legal vestiges of serfdom. Peasants gained full legal equality immediately and would soon claim ownership of fields they had held from feudal landlords. Most fundamentally, French men and women became citizens instead of subjects.

Revolutionary parties shifted steadily to the left, particularly after war broke out in the spring of 1792. During the most extreme phase, the Reign of Terror, idealism justified repression in the name of preserving and advancing revolution. At this time the radical government, led by the Committee of Public Safety, mobilized French manpower, patriotic sentiment, and material resources as never before in the name of national defense. The Terror came to an abrupt halt in July 1794, and a more moderate, but also more corrupt, regime followed. Yet it too preserved the great accomplishments of the Revolution.

In 1799, the brash and victorious young general Napoleon Bonaparte exploited his military reputation to seize power in a coup that set up a more stable but more authoritarian republican government, the Consulate. Finally, in 1804 he carried his dictatorship one step further, metamorphosing the republic into the empire, with himself as its crowned head. Yet Napoleon knew he could not turn the clock backward, so while he gathered political power into his own hands, he also retained fundamental gains of the Revolution, codifying them in new laws that bore his name, the Napoleonic Code.

Without reference to the political and social revolution, the transformation of warfare, 1789–1815, defies explanation, for the sine qua non of this metamorphosis was the direct engagement of the entire population in warfare and the creation of the dedicated citizen soldier.

The Citizen Soldier in Reality and Theory

The army created to defend the Revolution profoundly changed in character and composition between 1789 and 1794. The style of army prevalent in Europe from the mid-seventeenth century through the onset of the French Revolution can be termed the "state commission army."[3] State rulers exerted much more control over this force than had been the case in the past. Officers of a state commission army received commissions from rulers to recruit standardized regiments that were raised and maintained as stipulated by the state, which closely regulated its army and imposed high standards of obedience and hierarchy on its officers. Voluntary enlistment provided the bulk of the necessary manpower for these larger armies, although many a "volunteer" was tricked or bullied into the ranks. Voluntary enlistment in a highly stratified society filled the ranks with cast-offs of society. There was little identification with a people or a cause in such armies, and states often recruited foreign regiments or hired regiments from other countries to fight their battles.

A new form of "popular conscript army" replaced the state commission pattern, first in France and then in other European states. It was a "popular," or people's, army in that it drew exclusively upon the state's own population, and citizen soldiers in the ranks were expected to feel a commitment to the people and fatherland. In order to maximize French manpower, the Revolution turned to conscription, because initial drafts of volunteers fell short of military needs. The most famous act of conscription, the *levée en masse,* called upon *all* of French society to contribute to the war effort in August 1793.

> From this moment until the enemy has been chased from the territory of the Republic, all the French are in permanent requisition for the service of the armies.
>
> Young men will go to battle, married men will forge arms and transport supplies; women will make tents, uniforms, and serve in the hospitals; children will pick rags; old men will have themselves carried to public squares, to inspire the courage of the warriors, and to preach the hatred of kings and the unity of the Republic.[4]

In a real sense, the *levée en masse* announced the return of that civic militarism extolled by Victor Davis Hanson. Other aspects of his Western Way of War reappeared, including the emphasis on decisive battle and total war, but this resurgence came only after an absence that stretched back to ancient Rome.

By the summer of 1794, when the tide of war had turned decisively in the direction of the French Republic, an army of at least 750,000 men actually under arms, or about 1,000,000 on paper, defended France.[5] This force reflected the composition of French society in the ranks. Moreover, the officer corps, now a meritocracy open to talent instead of an aristocratic preserve, contained but few nobles.[6]

On the battlefield, Republican troops displayed real dedication to the survival of the new regime and to the ideal of the French nation. This does not mean that they were fanatics; it did not require fanaticism to understand that defeat of the Republic and return to the pre-revolutionary monarchy would rob the common citizen of his or her rights, opportunities, and in many cases, possessions. The great bulk of the French people and the army belonged to a peasantry that detested the old burdens of serfdom and that would be loath to return their lands to the lords. Consequently, the people of France and the soldiers who issued from the people had a stake in the new regime. Revolution also gave form to French national identity, to patriotism, that gave an emotional commitment beyond rational social and political self-interest. The nation was the people and the army was now a representative and a defender of that people. In short, the soldier of Revolutionary France had become a citizen soldier.

So integrated was the ideal of the citizen soldier to the Revolution that it might seem to be entirely a product of the turbulent events of 1789, but such a conclusion would miss an essential fact: Men of letters and men of war focused on the notion of the citizen soldier long before the fall of the Bastille. Thus, this essential revolutionary ideal provides an illustrative case study in the way that conception can provide a template for reality.

The concept of the patriotic, public-spirited citizen soldier took form as an intellectual construct no later than the mid-eighteenth century. Consciousness of ancient military institutions, particularly those of republican Rome, predated the eighteenth century, and the Enlightenment picked up the discussion of Roman farmer/warriors. That political philosopher of immense status, Montesquieu, extolled the virtues of the citizen soldier in *Reflections on the Causes of the Grandeur and Decline of the Romans* (1734). Although he believed that such examples of sacrifice for the public good were limited to ancient republics, he still praised them as a goal and standard. At mid-century, contributors to the great *Encyclopédie* of Denis Diderot repeatedly lauded Roman citizen soldiers.[7]

The passing years brought even greater praise of this warrior ideal. In his 1772 *Considerations on the Government of Poland*, Jean-Jacques Rousseau (1712–1778) condemned European standing professional armies, which he saw as "good for only two things: to attack and to conquer one's neighbors, or to enchain and enslave one's citizens." As an alternative to forming such forces, Rousseau counseled the Poles: "I know that the state should not remain without defenders; but its true defenders are its members. Each citizen should be a soldier by duty, none by profession."[8] Military authors also dreamt of a radically different future. The most famous expression came from the pen of Jacques-Antoine-Hypolite de Guibert (1743–1790), who published his *General Essay on Tactics* the same year that Rousseau's *Considerations* appeared.

After describing the decline of ancient warrior traditions and lamenting how modern states had bogged down in wars of attrition, Guibert postulated a radical contrast. "Let us suppose," he asked his reader, a people with "austere virtues and a national militia" and who could "make war at little cost by subsisting on their victories." Such a people could "subjugate its neighbors, by overthrowing feeble constitutions, like the north wind bends frail reeds.⁹ This, the most oft-quoted excerpt from the *General Essay*, would require citizens to accept military service in a "national militia." After these famous musings about a martial people, he conceded: "This people will not arise, because there remains in Europe no nation at the same time powerful and new. . . . They all have governments destructive of all sentiments of patriotism and virtue."¹⁰ Only revolution would produce a state both "powerful and new," but he could not have known that in 1772. Guibert enjoyed a wide audience and won considerable praise. No less a figure than Voltaire himself saluted the *General Essay* as "a work of genius."¹¹

The discussion of the citizen soldier continued. In 1780, Joseph Servan published *The Citizen Soldier*, a detailed program for army reform that included a call for universal conscription. Servan would later serve briefly as minister of war for the revolutionary government in 1792. Jacques-Louis David (1748–1825) gave this appeal a visual conception in his *The Oath of the Horatii*, a painting that hung in the Paris salon of 1785 and incited considerable comment. This work portrayed the three Horatius brothers pledging to their father to fight as champions for Rome. They were willing to turn away from family bonds and to sacrifice their lives in the name of the people and the state.

The citizen soldier was more than simply a theoretical concept before the French Revolution. Of course, there was the remote, but revered, real example of republican Rome, but there was also the immediate, albeit idealized, example of revolutionary America. The two often merged: "Already the cry of 'Our Country' makes itself heard, already the citizen has taken for a device this maxim, *Dulce et decorum est pro patria mori*. . . . Every colonist is another Curius, ready to leap into the gulf to save his country. . . . His blood belongs to her."¹² French involvement in the struggle for American independence had both political and emotional dimensions, for while the government considered its support essentially as retaliation against a traditional foe, many of the progressive intelligentsia in the salons and the Masonic lodges felt fervently attached to the American cause in the name of Enlightenment ideals. No concept could be as easily projected onto American reality as that of the citizen soldier, because it so closely matched actual practice, particularly in local militias.

The ideal of the citizen soldier demonstrates how commentators drafted the outlines of a desirable new future, a vision their readers then shared well before it became reality. Later, when the Revolution created a favorable situation, historical actors could impose this pre-existing template on reality. As the first rush of Revolution overcame France, men of influence asserted that the soldier was a citizen and therefore must not threaten liberty. Already in July 1789, Camille Desmoulins addressed French troops: "You are no longer satellites of the despot, the jailers of your brothers. You are our friends, our fellows, citizens, and soldiers of the Patrie."[13] Next year, Maximilien Robespierre could proclaim to the National Assembly "soldiers are citizens."[14] After war struck, the converse became critical; the citizen must become a soldier in order to swell the forces defending the revolutionary state. So while the *levée en masse* responded to the crisis of summer 1793, this call to arms did so in a way that conformed to the now triumphant ideal. Even before the National Convention declared the *levée* in Paris, local authorities in the north imposed a levy of their own with the following justification: "A war of tactics will not suffice to drive off our enemies; it is necessary that all citizens capable of bearing arms, . . . that the entire body of the people, rise in mass to crush them."[15]

Imperatives of internal security and national defense within the context of a great transformation of society and politics would have brought about critical changes in military institutions during the French Revolution even without a pre-existing literature on the citizen soldier. One of these would have to have been a new definition of the relationship between citizenship and military service. However, the Enlightenment discussion of the citizen soldier gave particular definition to that relationship and made it instantaneously applicable to Revolutionary France.

The template of the citizen soldier not only influenced institutions but also affected perceptions and determined expectations. French troops suffered and sacrificed for the good of fatherland and hearth, and doubtless a great many, probably the majority, harbored true love of country and devotion to their new society. But beyond this reality, it is equally clear that the ideal of the citizen soldier cast the recruit into a role that he was then required to perform. He must be the self-sacrificing hero of the republic, as in ancient Rome. The revolutionary journal *Père Duchesne,* to which the common soldier was "the flower of the Republic," boasted, "You must see with what courage they endure cold, heat, fatigue and hunger. Days of combat are for them days of celebration, and they march to battle like they go to a ball, singing and dancing."[16] Such an exaggerated evaluation must be seen as a perception born of expectation overlaid upon the brutal experience of war. Once this portrait of the revolutionary citizen soldier gained credence, it became a standard by which civilians judged soldiers and by which even soldiers themselves measured their conduct.[17]

This ideal recognized and extended the nation's involvement in armed struggle, changing everything. At the critical juncture of the battle of Valmy, 20 September 1792, where French forces turned back a Prussian invasion bent on snuffing out the Revolution, their commander, François-Étienne Kellermann, rallied his troops with the cry, *Vive la nation!* The great German writer Johann Wolfgang von Goethe (1749–1832), who was present at Valmy, proclaimed, on the evening after the battle: "From this place and from this day forth commences a new era in the world's history."[18] Clausewitz would identify the fact that war became "the concern of the people as a whole" to be the essential watershed.[19]

Battlefield Implications of the Citizen Army

As French civil and military authorities came to believe that the troops of the Revolution possessed a high degree of dedication, this perception helped to father a new reality on campaign. Aristocratic officers of the ancien régime regarded men in the ranks as devoid of honor; therefore, these officers placed little trust in such troops, placed them under constant supervision, and demanded little beyond obedience. However, much more could be asked of the revolutionary soldier, and the new officer corps, much closer in origin to the troops it led, expected dedication, enthusiasm, and initiative from the rank and file.

The tactical consequences of the new soldiery led to triumph.[20] Rigid linear infantry formations dominated battle during the ancien régime, but the French now implemented a new flexible tactical system. The line remained for situations in which its massed firepower was still valuable. However, for maneuver and assault, the French turned to the more mobile column. In order to unsettle an enemy army and prepare the way for a column attack, or to take advantage of broken or wooded ground that precluded close-order formations, French troops dispersed as individual skirmishers who chose their own cover and targets. Officers had mistrusted such open-order, light infantry tactics in the ancien régime, for they feared it would only lead to desertion. Now it brought victory. The French army expected all battalions to fight in line, in column, or as skirmishers to fit the needs of the battlefield. This gave them a great tactical advantage over their enemies. At first Revolutionary French forces were not trained as well as other armies and suffered for it, but the dedication of the citizen soldier displayed itself not simply in combat, but in drill as well, and the troops improved quickly. Training already bore fruit by 1794, but as the years went by, the French continually gained finesse as well as flexibility on the battlefield. The Grande Armée of Napoleon reached a pinnacle of effectiveness because it saw the tactical elements pioneered during the Revolution employed by a superbly trained and led veteran army.

It has long been fashionable to ascribe the victories of the French during the Revolutionary Era to numbers rather than to tactical ability, but by stressing only brute strength, this view falls short.[21] In fact, French troops won when they were outnumbered as well as when they brought more troops to the field; the battle of Tourcoing, 18 May 1793, provides a notable example. However, the stress on numbers correctly reports the ability of revolutionary governments to mobilize manpower and materiel as never before. During the high tide of 1794, the new regime doubled the number of men under arms that the old regime was able to put into the field.[22] Citizen soldiers simply arrived in greater strength than had the hirelings of the past, and the government used its powers of requisition to equip and feed its battalions.

Greater numbers allowed the French to pay less attention to losses. Commanders in the past had often regarded trained soldiers as costly capital that should not be risked lightly, but now, with far more "assets" available, they could be more freely invested in the bloody business of battle. In addition to losses in combat, desertion continued to drain manpower, but at a lower rate far smaller than had afflicted armies of the ancien régime.[23]

This larger army supplied itself in the field if need be. In the past, believing that its professional soldiers would only stay with the colors if they were well supplied, and unwilling to disperse troops to forage on campaign out of fear that they would desert, ancien régime armies relied upon a cumbersome supply system that carted food to armies, but limited their mobility. The revolutionary regime expected its citizen soldiers to do without, if need be, but of greater importance, it trusted its troops to supply themselves by foraging in the field. As long as French troops kept moving and could exploit rich country, they could march fast and far, giving them unsurpassed operational potential. This ability emerged under the Revolution and reached its peak under Napoleon, most notably in the campaign of 1805.

The military transformation initiated by Revolutionary France was all the more impressive because it occurred at a time of relative technological stability in the basic weapons of infantry, cavalry, and artillery. To be sure, the late eighteenth century brought improvements in the quality and mobility of field artillery, while multiplying the number of guns, but these reforms can in no way account for the revolution in warfare. No, its fundamental origins were political, social, and, it should be noted, cultural.

Napoleon achieved unprecedented success with the military instrument forged by the Revolution. By 1805, battlefield experience had tempered the veterans of Revolutionary France and honed the army to a sharp edge. Professionalism joined forces with patriotism. The Grande Armée surpassed any other European army in its mobility and striking power, and Napoleon exploited these advantages with a virtuosity unmatched by any other commander in modern European history. As at Austerlitz, he accelerated campaigns and brought conflicts to conclusion through decisive battle, altering the face of war.

ROMANTICISM

While change in military institutions and practices provided one essential context for Military Romanticism, the emergence of a new intellectual climate in Europe supplied the other. Trying to confine Romanticism within the bounds of a few sentences is not an easy task. Of course, attempts to box in any cultural era run the twin risks of reductionism and distortion, but the lines are particularly blurred in discussing Romanticism. Standard accounts date that movement from about 1790 through 1850, but focusing on different media and different locales varies the boundaries in time. For Ludmilla Jordanova, the end of the Enlightenment and the onset of Romanticism "was bound up with the rise to power of Napoleon Bonaparte."[24]

To a considerable degree Romanticism grew out of a reaction to the rational tidiness of the Enlightenment, and thus scholars sometimes label early forms of Romanticism as the "Counter-Enlightenment." The Enlightenment posited a rational world that could be examined, understood, and controlled by reason. The methods and principles of natural science were to be applied to the full range of human experience, including the moral universe, to reveal the rational simplicity of reality. But Romanticism rebelled against this, to insist upon diversity and complexity in human experience, where psychology must be understood as comprising emotion and creativity as well as reason. For the Romantics, the moral universe defied formulae. Romanticism also emphasized nature and forces beyond the bounds of reason. Concern for the nonrational and disdain for order fostered a legitimation of struggle, from intellectual turmoil to outright violence, that ran against Enlightenment preferences for harmony. Chance, a threat to the predictable and the regular, which had existed as an unwanted stepchild during the Enlightenment now became a major factor, an unavoidable and accepted determinant. Romanticism gave far greater sway to genius and the extraordinary individual across the spheres of human activity, from art to politics. If the *philosophes* sought the universal, their successors reveled in the unique and different. One expression of this change was a taste for the exotic, often the Oriental, but a more lasting impact was an emphasis on contrasting national cultural characters and, thus, on nationalism within Europe.

These textbook generalities probably define Romanticism as well as any, but charting its development and classifying major cultural figures within its fold is very tricky. Because Romantics exalted the individual and eschewed system, it is hard to make things fit nicely. As Victor Hugo proclaimed, "All systems are false; only genius is true."[25] Also, the full-blown Romanticism of the period after 1790 grew out of movements usually classified as late Enlightenment or pre-Romantic; there was no sudden shift. For example, Rousseau certainly questioned the sway of reason and found that emotion and morality were more essential to defining the uniqueness of the human race. Immanuel Kant (1724–1804) built upon Rousseau's challenge to develop his own critique of reason, although in a rigorous philosophical form. Rousseau was both part of the Enlightenment and a figure pointing the way to Romanticism; Kant could be seen as a consummation of the Enlightenment or as a wellspring of German idealism.

The artistic community carried Romanticism to extremes that the military community would not. Virtuosos of pen and brush exalted the emotional over the rational, to champion what Kenneth Clark defined as a "consciousness of the sublime."[26] England gave birth both to the poet Wordsworth's joy in natural beauty, and Blake's fascination with the terrors of natural and supernatural power: "Tyger, tyger, burning bright." Painting combined power, violence, and tragedy: Géricault's masterpiece of shipwreck and despair, the *Raft of the Medusa,* and Delacroix's *The Massacre of Chios,* which combined death with Oriental exoticism. In such themes disillusionment accompanied a penchant for dramatic intensity. There is no accident in the title of Freidrich's painting of icy disaster at sea, *The Wreck of the "Hope."* Wordsworth, who spent much of the period 1790–1792 in France as a witness to the Revolution, found it intensely invigorating:

> For mighty were the auxiliars which then stood
> Upon our side, we who were strong in love!
> Bliss was it in that dawn to be alive,
> But to be young was very heaven![27]

But personal loss, as well as the excesses of revolution and war, converted him into orthodox conservatism as an Anglican and a Tory. The exuberance of the Romanticism of the artists gave in to disillusionment and melancholy.

Interpretation of war from a Romantic perspective would not display such artistic self-indulgence, because it had to obey a discipline imposed by reality. War witnessed tragedy worthy of the Romantics' darkest musings, but it was not this that would occupy those theorists of war who tried to make sense out of the Napoleonic experience.

MILITARY ROMANTICISM

That observers writing in the first decades of the nineteenth century would offer explanations of Napoleon's victorious campaigns was inevitable, but that these explanations took the form of Military Romanticism was not—that was a cultural exercise. The Romanticism of literature and art could not translate whole into military theory, but that intellectual movement influenced the formation of a new discourse on war. Romanticism represented an important intellectual paradigm shift that might have spawned a different conception of combat even had the reality been static, but, of course, it was anything but.

This was military discourse of a very sophisticated kind, produced by and meant for professional officers. Certainly, it grew out of the world of high civilian culture; notably its major spokesman, Carl von Clausewitz, was immersed in the intellectual life of Berlin at a very exciting time. But it also was fostered by the emergence of professional military education beyond the level of the military academies for cadets. The great work of Military Romanticism, *On War*, soon became a staple of war colleges. The new discourse on war was tied into the increasing professionalism of European armies and the rise of the general staff in Prussia.

Important contrasts distinguish Military Romanticism from the earlier Military Enlightenment. Classics of the Military Enlightenment dealt with wars of kings and discussed popular passions little, if at all, while Military Romanticism embraced wars of peoples. If the Military Enlightenment stressed a particularly rational concept of war and sought formulaic rules and principles, Military Romanticism was more at home with those factors in war that could not be contained within neat guidelines. Instead of viewing war as primarily obedient to the logic of science, Military Romanticism identified war as a human phenomenon ruled by psychology and will. The Military Enlightenment defined the talent, the genius, of the commander primarily in terms of his ability to work within the rules and principles of war; for Military Romanticism the creative genius of the commander ranged far more broadly, and played a much more critical role. Enlightenment rules promised a time-less universality, but to Military Romanticism, the conduct of war was best considered a historical phenomenon that differed in detail from age to age and place to place. Therefore, Romanticism recognized new aspects of wars, such as the rise of patriotism in people's wars. In place of universal rules governing the predictable aspects of war, chance, an aspect of warfare abhorred by the Military Enlightenment, found its proper place in Military Romanticism. If it embraced chance, it also accepted casualties in contrast to earlier military thought that had hoped to avoid losses through skill. With risk and loss an acceptable price for gain, Military Romanticism stressed battle, and conflict in the open field replaced sieges as the paradigm contest.

Adherents and Opponents

A number of individuals helped shape Military Romanticism as examples, proponents, or foils. Napoleon provided the great example, but that epitome required explanation for a Europe that had lived through, but not necessarily understood, the great transformation of warfare. Napoleon also commented on his conduct of war, but he scattered his observations about and never craft-ed them into a consistent whole. In fact, the great practitioner offered con-tradictory statements that can be quoted to different purposes. He combined a respect for ill-defined rules and principles with many Romantic tenets—for example, an emphasis on creative genius. In any case, study of his campaigns and his writings required generation after generation to confront Military Romanticism, if only in the words of Clausewitz.

Georg Heinrich von Berenhorst (1733–1814) probably deserves the title of the first Military Romantic. His *Reflections on the Art of War* (1796–1799) grew out of the intellectual environment of Germany in the first rush of Romanticism. While not well known today, he enjoyed quite a following at the time; one contemporary attested that "no book was as widely read as *Reflections*."[28] It drew hostile fire as well as praise; Massenbach wrote a critique of Berenhorst in 1802, to which he replied with his *Aphorisms* of 1805. Friedrich Constantin von Lossau (1767–1848), like Clausewitz a student of Scharnhorst and a Prussian reformer, published his volume *War* in 1815. Lossau built upon the work of Berenhorst and developed themes that would later be extended by Clausewitz, such as the influence of human psychology and chance.[29] John Mitchell, author of *Thoughts on Military Organization* (London: 1838), declared himself "a humble follower" of Berenhorst and brought him to an English audience.[30]

So central was Carl von Clausewitz (1779–1831) to Military Romanticism that this chapter must confront his theory repeatedly and at length. So over-powering and convincing has been his work that he is often presented as utter-ly original and completely unique, but it is important to realize that he expressed a trend in military thought that did not begin with him and which had several proponents.

Jomini (1779–1869) also helped define Military Romanticism, although by contrast rather than concord. He enjoyed an extensive readership during the nineteenth century, and his analysis lived on into the twentieth century, although as interpreted and updated by others.[31] Azar Gat, whose important works on culture and military thought have strongly influenced this chapter, credits Jomini with "penetrating and fertile" commentary on Napoleonic war-fare and argues that it was their approaches that most basically separated Jomini and Clausewitz: Jomini accepted and pursued the assumptions and arguments of the late Military Enlightenment, while Clausewitz worked in the new intel-lectual environment of Romanticism.[32] Most of Jomini's interpretation is "sci-entific," maintaining a strong emphasis on tidy, often geometric, operational rules, as did works of the Military Enlightenment. He insisted that operations "may be regulated by fixed laws resembling those of the positive sciences."[33]

While Clausewitz died at age fifty-one, before he had completely revised his great manuscript, Jomini survived to ninety, devoting his long life to pro-moting his reputation. Over the decades, his conceptions evolved little, and while he read Clausewitz's *On War,* Jomini seems to have been hardly affected by it.[34] These two theoreticians of warfare observed the same watershed, but through very different lenses.

The Character of Military Romanticism

Central tenets of Military Romanticism cut to the heart of war. Works of the Military Enlightenment through most of the eighteenth century concentrated on tactical matters; later, Henry Lloyd switched his and subsequent authors' attentions to operational principles, thus rising from the conduct of battles to the conduct of campaigns. Military Romanticism commented on both tactics and operations, but the vital center of the discussion moved to strategy, that is the conduct of wars, and to the nature of war itself. Thus there was a movement from the lesser to the greater issues, from those elements of war most bound by the particular circumstances of technology and organization to those more easily generalized. Paradoxically, the Military Enlightenment assumed universal principles but discussed aspects of war that would prove to be transitory, while Military Romanticism accepted change over time and eschewed the universal but discussed themes most likely to travel well—thus the present-day popularity of Clausewitz.

Military Romanticism recognized the coming of a new age, that of peoples' war, the citizen soldier, and nationalism. Guibert's dream took form in reality, although not as he would have wished. Clausewitz described it:

Suddenly war again became the business of the people—a people of thirty millions, all of whom considered themselves to be citizens. . . . The people became a participant in war; instead of governments and armies as heretofore, the full weight of the nation was thrown into the balance. The resources and efforts now available for use surpassed all conventional limits; nothing now impeded the vigor with which war could be waged, and consequently the opponents of France faced the utmost peril.[35]

In accord with philosophical and artistic Romantics who rebelled against the scientific rationality of the Enlightenment, Military Romanticism questioned the constant eighteenth-century insistence on neat and universal rules and principles. Napoleon himself admitted that there were "no precise or definite rules."[36] At base, Napoleon was a rebel against the formulaic warfare of Enlightenment theory, so although he occasionally said positive things about principles, he perseverated on genius, accident, and chance. Clausewitz denied the efficacy of scientific laws applied to the highest level of war. Of such attempts he wrote, "Efforts were therefore made to equip the conduct of war with principles, rules or even system . . . but people failed to take adequate account of the endless complexities involved."[37] In contradiction, he argued that "all principles, rules, methods . . . will increasingly lack universality and absolute truth the closer they come to being positive doctrine."[38] He saw the fruits of theory not as laws but as "aids to judgment."[39]

The Romantics agreed with the conclusions of Immanuel Kant that while the natural world obeyed scientific laws and was thus a fit subject for the methodology of science, human feelings and actions were unsuited to such precision. Because war was a complex human activity, its study could not promise scientific conclusions. Berenhorst characterized his own work as Kantian, and Azar Gat regards Clausewitz as fundamentally affected by Kant's theory of art.[40] Art was a realm in which some principles might aid creative genius, but in which genius operated independently. The debate over whether war is a science or an art has raged for centuries and may be unresolvable, but clearly the Military Enlightenment defined it primarily and ideally as a science, while Military Romanticism saw it as an art.

In place of mechanical rules, Military Romanticism explored the role of human psychology and personality. In one of his most famous statements, Napoleon claimed, "In war, morale and spirit count for three quarters, the matter of numbers counts only for the remaining quarter."[41] Berenhorst already stressed the role of human personality, and Clausewitz stressed will and genius. "War," Clausewitz argued, "is an act of force to compel our enemy to do our will."[42] As a contest of wills, resolve and reaction were everything.

Within the interactive and unpredictable contest of war, human genius played a decisive role for the Romantics. The Military Enlightenment had discussed genius as well. Those analysts and observers were usually men of practical experience, so while they may have hoped to produce scientific rules and principles of war, they were wise enough to know that campaigns presented commanders with unique and confused situations. Consequently, commanders must interpret and apply rules and principles through intelligence and talent—that is, genius. Hence, for the Military Enlightenment, rules circumscribed genius. Jomini, writing in the tradition of the Military Enlightenment, proclaimed, "Genius has a great deal to do with success, since it presides over the application of recognized rules."[43]

Military Romanticism greatly expanded the realm and importance of individual knowledge, judgment, and creativity. Kant placed genius above and outside of rules: "*Genius* is the talent [natural endowment] that gives the rule to art. . . . Genius is a *talent* for producing something for which no determinate rule can be given."[44] Napoleon insisted, "The art of war on land is an art of genius, of inspiration."[45] For Clausewitz, genius was the only way to overcome the confusion of reality in war; "A sensitive and discriminating judgment is called for; a skilled intelligence to scent out the truth."[46] Literary

Romanticism created not only a cult of genius but a cult of *the* genius, an individual of exceptional virtuosity, often in conflict with convention. Although this tendency had some influence on Clausewitz, he did not restrict genius to the rare individual; it was more generalized. Genius comprised the ability to act with intelligence and creativity in an endeavor that could not be defined by rules and in which chance and confusion complicated reality.

In opposition to universal and eternal rules, Military Romanticism comprehended that the conduct, if not the nature, of war changed from age to age. True to the Military Enlightenment, Jomini claimed, "The fundamental principles upon which rest all good combinations of war have always existed. . . . These principles are unchangeable. . . . For thirty centuries there have lived generals who have been more or less happy in their application."[47] With a much more historicist approach, Clausewitz replied, "Every age has its own kind of war, its own limiting conditions and its own peculiar preconditions."[48] Military Romantics were far more willing to see the past in its own terms, but this means they were also willing to recognize the novelty of their own present.

The fundamental preoccupation of the Romantics with the particular and, eventually, with the folk led to their concern with national character and nationalism. French patriotism that rose during the Revolution sprouted from political and social roots, but as it spread to other countries, nationalism grew from more cultural origins. Napoleon could take advantage of French national identification, but he also spread the cult of the nation outside France. Italians at first welcomed the Republican army as liberating the Italian people from foreign domination. Many would later question the degree to which the French had liberated the Italians, but they would hold fast to a Romantic ideal of an Italian people and Italian nation. In opposition to the French, Germans sought a new identity in their traditions. The cultural nationalism of important figures in early Romanticism, such as Johann Gottfried von Herder (1744–1803), helped to inspire German resistance to the French in the War of Liberation, as did the call issued by Fichte in his *Addresses to the German People* (1808). In Austria the younger brother of Habsburg Emperor Francis I, Archduke John, "was deeply influenced by Romanticism and inclined to idolize the German people as the personification of virtue, had also been attracted to the nationalist cause."[49]

Military thinkers soon recognized the power and importance of nationalism. The Prussian reformer Scharnhorst backed social reform as a way of encouraging the people to identify with the state. Clausewitz would see patriotic sentiment as a potent genie loosed by the French Revolution and now impossible to put back into the bottle. For him, wars of peoples not only inspired devotion but produced destructive passions.

Rejection of the predictable certainties of the Enlightenment opened the door to chance. In a military context, "chance" is a complex word. It might refer to slipshod planning and preparation, as in leaving something to chance that should be taken care of by concentration and application. In this sense Napoleon abhorred chance: "If I take so many precautions it is because my habit is to leave nothing to chance."[50] However, Military Romanticism extolled chance in the sense of the unpredictable reality of war. Napoleon insisted on the important and transitory nature of chance, and the crucial link between chance and genius: "War is composed of nothing but accidents, and, although holding to general principles, a general should never lose sight of everything to enable him to profit from these accidents; that is the mark of genius."[51] Berenhorst discussed the importance of chance, and Clausewitz's discussion of it constituted one of the crucial contrasts separating his great opus from the works of the Military Enlightenment. The interaction between adversaries made war unpredictable by nature, even with the best of fore-thought and planning. "War is the realm of chance. No other human activity gives it greater scope."[52]

One of the reasons the Military Enlightenment so wished to avoid chance was in order to limit casualties; war entailed financial and manpower losses that states wished to keep to a minimum. But Military Romanticism was more willing to accept, even if it did not welcome, losses as unavoidable in pursuit of decisive military operations. Napoleon uttered some callous words about the lives of his troops. "A man like me," he was supposed to have boast-ed to Metternich, "troubles himself little about the lives of a million men."[53] In 1817 he tossed off the disturbing judgment, "Troops are made to let them-selves be killed."[54] He could offer a more thoughtful explanation of his will-ingness to suffer casualties by stressing that saving life should not be a gen-eral's primary aim: "In giving battle a general should regard it as his first duty to maintain the honor and glory of his arms. To spare his troops should be but a secondary consideration."[55] Of course, a less flattering observer could equate such callousness with butchery, as did Marshal Augereau in 1814, who charged Napoleon with "having sacrificed millions of victims to his cruel ambition."[56] But Clausewitz insisted repeatedly that to shrink from carnage was to disarm yourself: "If one side uses force without compunction, undeterred by the bloodshed it involves, while the other side refrains, the first will gain the upper hand."[57]

For Military Romanticism, a chain of conceptual necessity, reinforced by Napoleonic experience, exalted the decisive battle as the essence of war. Denial of a "science" of war and, thus, of predictability led to a recognition of chance as a major factor and to the acceptance of losses, and these tenets made the risk and cost of battle acceptable, even desirable, in contrast to the Military Enlightenment. Clausewitz paraphrased this Enlightenment perspective in *On War,* deriding how "This line of thought had brought us almost to the point of regarding, in the economy of war, battle as a kind of evil brought about by mistake . . . to which an orthodox, correctly managed war should never have to resort." Praise went to "generals who know how to conduct a war without bloodshed," and the role of military theory was "to teach this kind of warfare."[58] Those eighteenth-century commanders associated with great battles did not really break the contemporary mold. Marlborough spoke of battle as preferable, but he actually fought few battles, while he conducted a great many sieges. Frederick the Great may have exploited battle in the Seven Years' War, but he had little choice if he was to hold off the mighty alliance arrayed against him, and his battles did not lead to decision; they just bought him time.

Napoleon demonstrated the potential of decisive battle to break the will of the enemy through defeat. Battle became his preferred, essentially his sole, means to victory, and, therefore, it was to be sought rather than artfully avoided. Napoleon set out to confront and defeat the main forces of the enemy. "There are many good generals in Europe, but they see too many things at the same time. I see only one thing, the mass [main body]; I try to destroy it, sure that secondary matters will fall into place on their own."[59] He insisted, "It is upon the field of battle that the fate of fortresses and empires is decided."[60] It can be overstated how much Napoleon turned his back on fortifications, because he did recognize their importance, but battle clearly replaced the siege as the archetypal European clash of arms.[61]

For Clausewitz, war was essentially battle—"There is only one means in war: combat."[62] While Jomini also sought to understand Napoleonic warfare, he did not place as great an emphasis on battle: "Battles have been stated by some writers to be the chief and deciding features of war. This assertion is not strictly true. . . ."[63] For Clausewitz, although actual battle may be a rare occurrence in war, it is fundamental, defining. In a phrase that caught the eye of another major figure in the creation of nineteenth-century ideologies, Friedrich Engels, Clausewitz proclaimed, "The decision of arms is for all major and minor operations in war what cash payment is in commerce."[64] The grand direction of war, strategy, must embrace combat: "Strategy . . . is nothing without battle, for battle is the raw material with which it works, the means it employs."[65]

By viewing the Revolutionary and Napoleonic experience through the lens of Romantic sensibilities, a new interpretation of war emerged from the late 1790s through the 1830s. Usually this development in military thought is not dealt with as a school of opinion but as the work of one exceptional individual, Carl von Clausewitz; however, by presenting certain basic tenets as Military Romanticism, this chapter seeks to present Clausewitz as part of a trend. Nonetheless, the particular formulation of his analysis in the classic *On War* went beyond what he held in common with others as both culmination and extension of Military Romanticism. Therefore, after considering shared fundamentals, the honest eye must turn to his unique contribution.

CLAUSEWITZ AND THE REVEALING COMPLEXITY OF *ON WAR*

As Napoleon reflected and reordered his world, Clausewitz reflected and reordered our understanding of it. Clausewitz explained that during the Revolutionary and Napoleonic Era, "War itself, as it were, had been lecturing"; in *On War* he offered his commentary on those lessons.[66] Clausewitz shared much with other proponents of Military Romanticism, but he remained distinct and, ultimately, overpowering. Even items of the agenda he shared with others took on a new sophistication and significance in his hands. Clausewitzian analysis, even if often only partially applied, influenced Western conceptions of warfare in the second half of the nineteenth century, although partisans still dispute how profound that influence was. After World War II, and then even more after the Vietnam conflict, *On War* established a new preeminence among works on the nature of war. Measured by its historical and contemporary significance, no other work compares.

Often, great minds cannot easily be tailored to fit intellectual categories, and this is all the more the case with Romanticism, which put a premium on individuality and originality. Clausewitz was part of the Romantic movement, but not because he displayed the full range of characteristics expressed by philosophers, writers, and artists of his day. He belongs to the Romantics because his ideas were influenced by them and because his discussion of war stresses themes that reflect their ideas. Clausewitz adopted only some arguments whole. Thus, while *On War* shares much with other Romantics and Military Romantics, it also proposes a unique analysis. The previous section considered elements of Clausewitz's conception that he held in common with others, but now we turn to arguments specific to Clausewitz.

Understanding *On War* and employing its insights to examine political and military questions have provided one of the richest wellsprings of historical and analytical literature for a century and a half. Several particularly impressive studies have appeared in recent decades. In his *Clausewitz and the State* (1976), Peter Paret contributes so intelligent a biography of the man and analysis of his ideas that it is impossible to study Clausewitz without coming to terms with Paret. Although Paret provides rich detail on the intellectual environment of Clausewitz, he leaves his reader with the impression that the key to *On War* is not the context of the work but Clausewitz's direct and profound understanding of timeless military reality. For Paret, Clausewitz is whole, consistent, and right. Yet in *The Origins of Military Thought: From the Enlightenment to Clausewitz* (1989), Azar Gat undermines this view by exploring the historical evolution of Clausewitz's own conceptions, particularly the revelation he experienced in 1827, when he recognized that he must account for limited as well for Napoleonic total war in his theory. For Gat, *On War* is not internally consistent but suffers from fundamental internal contradictions. In *Penser la guerre, Clausewitz* (1976), Raymond Aron also saw inconsistencies but ascribed them to the fact that the work was left in an unfinished state owing to the untimely death of the author. For Gat, however, the internal struggle within *On War* stems not from the lack of a final revision but from problems inherent in Clausewitz's ultimate conception of war. The treatment of *On War* here owes much to Gat, although the brevity and limited purpose of this chapter do not do full justice to the complexity of his arguments. In contradiction to Clausewitz's insistence that war is politics, the much-read John Keegan has asserted that war is culture; this essay simply hopes to demonstrate that Clausewitz is culture.[67]

Life of Clausewitz

Born in 1780, Carl von Clausewitz entered a Prussian infantry regiment at the age of twelve to begin his apprenticeship to arms. His father had served as an officer under Frederick the Great during the Seven Years' War but had been retired with the demobilization that followed. After seeing some action in the wars of the French Revolution, Clausewitz attended the Institute for Young Officers in Berlin, where he came under the influence of Gerhard von Scharnhorst (1755–1813), the military intellectual and reformer. Scharnhorst guided the young Clausewitz, who called him "the father and friend of my spirit."[68] After three years of studies, Clausewitz graduated at the head of his class and then remained in Berlin as adjutant to Prince August, cousin to the king. As the prince's adjutant, Clausewitz took part in the campaign of 1806, during which he and the prince fell prisoner to the French. Clausewitz returned to Berlin late in 1807 and joined Scharnhorst as his close personal assistant. In 1810 he was attached to the staff as a major. This year also witnessed his marriage to the well-born and intellectual Marie von Brühl, in what proved to be a wonderful union of souls. By now Clausewitz was writing and lecturing at the Kriegsschule, or War College, as well as fulfilling duties as the military tutor of the crown prince. His animosity to French domination over Germany and his desire to fight it inspired him to leave Prussian service in 1812 and accept a Russian commission. Even after the Prussians entered the war against Napoleon in 1813, the king found it difficult to welcome back Clausewitz, and he returned to the Prussian army only in April 1814. The next year he returned to the general staff. During the Waterloo campaign he served as chief of staff with Thielmann's corps and in this capacity fought at Ligny and Wavre.

With the return of peace he took on duties as chief of staff for General August Wilhelm von Gneisenau (1760–1831) at Coblenz until, in 1818, Clausewitz received both the rank of major general and the post of director of the War College, a position he held until 1830. This was a not-very-demanding administrative post that left much of his time free for writing. By this point he had already written many shorter pieces, but during his tenure at the War College he would draft the manuscript of *On War*. He generally wrote in Marie's rooms rather than in his office, which he reserved for his administrative duties; this physical proximity with his wife mirrored their intellectual partnership. In 1830 he left the War College to serve as the head of a Prussian artillery division, but when the Prussians mobilized to intervene in Poland, he once again joined Gneisenau as chief of staff in 1831. However, a cruel enemy, cholera, struck down both Gneisenau and Clausewitz that year. Clausewitz had began a major revision of *On War* pursuant to his conceptual enlightenment of 1827, but the task had not progressed far when he bundled up the manuscript before going into the field. After his death, Marie, assisted by her brother, count von Brühl, and two of Clausewitz's friends, assembled, edited, and arranged for publication of her husband's manuscripts. The first volume, which included books I–IV of *On War*, appeared in 1832, followed by seven more before Marie herself died in 1836; the final two came out in 1837.

Clausewitz in the Romantic Community

The modern stereotype of the military man portrays him as intensely practical and focused, living in a world separated by subject and slant from the high culture of the day. In contrast, Clausewitz read, met, and associated with important intellectuals and cultural figures throughout most of his adult life.

Clausewitz began reading serious literature as a teenage soldier. Early on he consumed works by Goethe and Schiller, both contributors to the *Sturm und Drang* (Storm and Stress) movement in German literature. When Clausewitz first met his highly intelligent and well-read wife-to-be in 1803, they discussed Goethe's *Sorrows of Young Werther*.[69] Paret notes that Clausewitz mentioned Schiller more than any other figure in his correspondence.[70] In particular, Schiller's concern with the heroic individual and with genius affected Clausewitz.

Marie von Brühl may ultimately rank as his most important intellectual contact. Highly intelligent, immensely well-read, and intellectually active in the cultural life of the day, she unquestionably served as a conduit between Clausewitz and the intelligentsia of Prussia, but her influence went far beyond this. He shared and discussed his ideas and his writings with her.

Although Clausewitz never met Immanuel Kant, he accepted the Kantian critiques of reason applied to human affairs and the psyche, to say nothing of the soul. As a student at the Institute, Clausewitz studied under Johann Gottfried Kiesewetter, who popularized Kantian philosophy. Clausewitz's mentor Scharnhorst was another soldier-intellectual steeped in Kant.

Captured after the Prussian defeat of 1806, Clausewitz journeyed to France with Prince August when the French forbade them to return home immediately. After a sojourn there, he spent two months in Switzerland at the house of Mme Germaine de Staël (1766–1817), whose *On Germany* (1810) played a key role in transporting Romanticism from Germany to France.

During the hiatus between Clausewitz's return to Berlin and his entry into Russian service in 1812, he partook of the rich intellectual life of that city. Through her contacts, Marie seems to have introduced her husband to Achim von Arnim (1781–1831), an important Romantic folklorist, dramatist, and poet, and to Wilhelm von Humboldt (1767–1835), philosopher and educational reformer. These two urged Clausewitz to join the Christlich-Deutsche Tischgesellschaft (Christian-German Symposium), a group that met for discussions every two weeks. A list of its active participants reads like a who's who of the Berlin intelligentsia, including Johann Gottlieb Fichte, Friedrich Schleiermacher, Heinrich von Kleist, Adam Müller, Clemens von Brentano, and Friedrich Bury.[71] Later, when Clausewitz returned to Berlin to head the War College, he met still other major cultural figures including Georg Wilhelm Friedrich Hegel (1770–1831), the pivotal philosopher. Achim von Arnim also came back into Clausewitz's life with his wife, Bettina (1785–1859), a considerable Romantic author and editor in her own right.[72] Sometimes these two incredibly gifted couples, the Clausewitzes and Arnims, would pass a day or evening in each other's company.

Clausewitz did not simply rub shoulders with major authors of his day, he read and discussed their works. Moreover he was immersed in an avant-garde intellectual environment. As Paret put it: "Such thinkers as Kant, Herder, and Fichte inspired him not only directly through their works but also through the filter of German historical writing that was influenced by them."[73]

Clausewitzian Theory

A reader who knows little or nothing about Clausewitz probably recognizes his definition of war as "a continuation of political intercourse, carried on with other means"—usually quoted by journalists as "War is the continuation of politics by other means."[74] Yet although this concept is necessary to Clausewitz's ultimate formulation of *On War,* Gat argues that this acceptance of political primacy resulted from his acceptance of limited war very late in the development of his thought and after he had drafted most of his manuscript.

More fundamental and of older vintage in Clausewitz's personal intellectual history was his focus on the violence and destruction of war. As both witness and participant during the wars of the French Revolution and Napoleon, he was most concerned with that transformation of warfare, with the unleashing of new powerful forces in war. Not surprisingly, his first goal was to understand and interpret the changes that engulfed him. It seemed as if this era had exposed the full, brutal potential of war. Battle became the means to inflict the "destructive principle" upon the enemy's forces. "We simply want to establish this dominance of the destructive principle."[75] It was the fury of total war that revealed the true nature of war, and it drove to that extreme by logical necessity.

Only in 1827 did Clausewitz experience the epiphany that he must analyze the dynamics of limited war as well as those for total war if his theory was to approach a universal understanding; he had to account for Frederick the Great as well as for Napoleon. This represented a critical shift in his thinking, and would require a thorough revision of *On War*. Raymond Aron describes this as a shift from a monist to a dualist conception of war, and he believes that because Clausewitz had only started along the path of revision when he died, *On War* remained imperfect and contradictory.[76] In fact, Aron considered that only chapter one of Book I fully realized Clausewitz's intentions and potential. Azar Gat makes even more of Clausewitz's revelation: Clausewitz's overriding concern with war as driving toward untrammeled destruction could not really be reconciled with limited war as directed by reasoned politics. To do so he had to create the duality of absolute war and real war and then further bifurcate real war into total and limited conflict. Political concerns restrained the full, and natural, destructive intensity of war in limited conflicts. Gat convincingly makes the case that even by creating his dualities Clausewitz could not accommodate his argument that war necessarily tended toward extremes with his new recognition of limited war. The result was an inescapable contradiction that explains some of the complexity and apparent confusion in *On War*. Clausewitz himself admitted the threat posed by the concept of limited war to his notion of untrammeled violence: "All imperatives inherent in the concept of war seem to dissolve, and its foundations are threatened."[77] He then put aside this warning, but his reader should not. From 1827 until his death, his ideas were in constant flux working out the implications of his lately adopted dialectic.

Begin with his notion of perfect war driving to extremes. *On War* grants conflict a nature and momentum of its own. Clausewitz postulated that in the unfettered world of theory, war could attain "perfection" in an absolute state—that is, war without constraint, in which each contestant exploits all his means with all his will. So strong are the forces that strip away limitations that "to introduce the principle of moderation into the theory of war itself would always lead to logical absurdity."[78] One must match the effort of the other, and "a reciprocal action is started which must lead, in theory, to extremes."[79] Because war "is not the action of a living force upon a lifeless mass . . . but always the collision of two living forces," interaction both creates unpre-

dictable situations and a tendency to go further and further.[80] The state of
absolute war is never reached in fact, however, because the real world presents
obstacles and imposes limitations. It is worth noting that Clausewitz spoke of
absolute war as if it were a higher form, or even more desirable, at least from
a theoretical point of view. Such seeming praise creates an almost unavoidable
conclusion that it is to be striven for, not simply relegated to a land of theoretical speculation.

Yet, while he insisted on the distinction between absolute and real war, at
other points he credited real war with near absolute intensity. He argued that,
"The more powerful and inspiring the motives for war, the more they affect
the belligerent nations and the fiercer the tensions that precede the outbreak,
the closer will war approach its abstract concept."[81] In fact, Clausewitz pointed out that the revolution in warfare initiated by the French brought reality
close to the theoretically possible. "First among the French and subsequently
among their enemies," he observed, war "again became the concern of the
people as a whole, took on an entirely different nature, or rather closely
approached its true character, its absolute perfection." This new kind of conflict, "untrammeled by any conventional restraints, had broken loose in all its
elemental fury."[82] In this excerpt, Clausewitz's notions of absolute and real war
cannot be considered as entirely separate species, even if Clausewitz elsewhere
insisted that they are very different animals.

Real war is "always an *instrument of policy,*" so statesmen and commanders
must match the conduct of war to intent.[83] Viewed in the context of his age,
Clausewitz offered the state two basic types of war, which he insisted are
"quite different" and separated by "points of irreconcilability."[84] The first type
of war strives "to overthrow the enemy" and "render him politically helpless"
so that he can be compelled to accept any kind of peace, including one that
meant the extinction of the regime or the state itself. Such is total war. The
second type of war aims at much less; for example, one can fight "merely to
occupy some of his frontier-districts so that we can annex them or use them
for bargaining at the peace negotiations."[85] It is a limited war fought for discrete, but not complete, advantage. In such a conflict, one foe simply tried to
make continuing a war more unacceptable than acceding to his conditions for
peace. In this more limited kind of war, a more circumscribed effort would be
appropriate.

Clausewitz's severe statements about blood and battle appear as logical
extensions of his belief in the "destructive principle" and his definition of
absolute war as uninhibited force leading to death and devastation, but they

mesh badly with notions of limited war. The highly cultured Clausewitz sternly accepted the human costs of war:

> Kind-hearted people might of course think there was some ingenious way
> to disarm or defeat an enemy without too much bloodshed, and might
> imagine this is the true goal of the art of war. Pleasant as it sounds, it is a
> fallacy that must be exposed: war is such a dangerous business that the mis-
> takes which come from kindness are the very worst.[86]

Bloody clashes are proper, essentially necessary, steps to victory. Battles justify
their high cost, because battles decide affairs. "Our conviction that only a
great battle can produce a major decision is founded not only on an abstract
concept of war alone, but also on experience."[87] Of course, that experience
came during the wars of the French Revolution and Napoleon, which so
monopolized his consideration until 1827. Today, some commentators might
argue that to cite the blood in Clausewitz is to misinterpret a great and subtle
work; but, on the contrary, high casualties are integral to his fundamental
notions of war.

It is interesting that Clausewitz also theorized that, as opposed to the necessary extremes of
absolute war, the limitations and shadings of "real war" derive from its character as "a strange trinity—composed of primordial violence, hatred, and
enmity, which are to be regarded as a blind natural force; of the play of chance
and probability within which the creative spirit is free to roam; and of its element of subordination, as an instrument of policy, which makes it subject to
reason alone."[88] Nothing quite so much as this statement marks *On War* as a
product of its age; what, for example, is more Romantic than exalting "blind
natural force"? After recognizing the extremes of human psychology,
Clausewitz embraced the play of chance, anathema to Military Enlightenment's desire for predictability, and opens the door for the creative genius.
Finally, Clausewitz brings back reason, which is the province of policy and the
state. Paret would emphasize both reason and the state, along with realism, as
the essential Clausewitz, but in the "strange trilogy," the intellectual safe harbor of reason is outnumbered two to one.

It is interesting that Clausewitz begins with violence, hatred, and enmity,
which he believes "mainly concerns the people," for here he labels what is
clearly the most novel and pressing matter of the day.[89] The French Revolution
changed war from an affair of kings to an affair of peoples and transformed
men in the ranks from hirelings to citizen soldiers. Clausewitz recognized this

as the most critical watershed in the warfare of his day. The German reformers, Clausewitz among them, pressed the Prussian monarchy to enlist its people in the struggle against Napoleon. They identified popular commitment as
the missing, and consequently the most urgently sought, element in the
Prussian capacity for war. Therefore, Fichte's attempt to rally patriotic feelings
worked hand in hand with Scharnhorst's concrete reforms. Art and politics
mutually reinforced each other. Not long after Clausewitz returned to Berlin
in 1807, he pleaded for the program of Romanticism: "A genuine need of our
time [is] to return from the tendency to rationalize to the neglected riches of
the emotions and of the imagination."[90]

In *On War*, Clausewitz's concern for human psychology comes out repeatedly in his overriding emphasis on the human will. War is ultimately a "contest of wills" and the bloody cost of battle is simply a means to break the
enemy's will: "rather a killing of the enemy's spirit than of his men."[91] While
will can mean political will, a rational choice, it also involves the passions of
enemy peoples. After defining "the power of resistance," as resulting from two
factors, means and will, he made it clear that "subtleties of logic do not moti-
vate the human will."[92]

Clausewitz linked chance and genius in a striking manner. The Military
Enlightenment recognized the role chance could play, but sought to reduce it
to a minimum, particularly by eschewing battle. Clausewitz found chance
unavoidable and advocated battle, a theater where chance could dominate the
stage. He rejected the comfortable notion that war could be reduced to ratio-
nalistic formulas, because "absolute, so-called mathematical, factors never find
a firm basis in military calculations." Instead, "there is an interplay of possibilities, probabilities, good luck and bad." Within "the whole range of human
activities, war most closely resembles a game of cards.[93]

The critical Clausewitzian concept of "friction" constitutes a special role for
chance. As early as 1812, in a piece written for his charge, the crown prince,
Clausewitz turned to a mechanical metaphor, so appropriate in the early stages
of the Industrial Revolution: "The conduct of war resembles the working of
an intricate machine with tremendous friction, so that combinations which
are easily planned on paper can be executed only with great effort."[94] In *On
War*, he defined friction as "the force that makes the apparently easy so difficult."[95] This is essential, because, "Everything in war is very simple, but the
simplest thing is difficult." (This is surprisingly similar to Napoleon's statement that "The art of war is a simple art and everything depends upon execution."[96]) All things that complicate action in war, that go wrong or come up

unexpectedly, constitute friction. "[T]his tremendous friction, which cannot, as in mechanics, be reduced to a few points, is everywhere in contact with chance, and brings about effects that cannot be measured, just because they are largely due to chance." In another striking metaphor, Clausewitz compares "action in war" to "movement in a resistant element": "Just as the simplest and most natural of movements, walking, cannot easily be performed in water, so in war it is difficult for normal efforts to achieve even moderate results." If general friction arises from the multitude of practical problems involved in military operations and from chance, it also results from lack of knowledge of the enemy, of the battlefield, etc., and generally from war's unavoidable uncertainty and confusion, the fog of war. "War is the realm of uncertainty; three quarters of the factors on which action in war is based are wrapped in a fog of greater or lesser uncertainty."[97]

If war were a matter of rules and principles, military talent would consist, as it did for the Military Enlightenment, in simply applying the rules. However, like other Romantics, Clausewitz appreciated the role of the unpredictable and the uncertain in a particular way that made creative genius absolutely essential in war. Only genius can triumph in the face of friction and the obscurity of the fog of war. While Clausewitz explicitly argued that genius is essential, *the* genius may not be. Clausewitz stopped short of the full excess of the genius individual of Romantic literature, but there are hints. Clausewitz's views were conditioned by what he had read and discussed, and Schiller's works on historical genius figures were favorites, such as Wallenstein, Joan of Arc, and William Tell.

After passion and genius, reason returns in the guise of policy and the state. Nevertheless, Clausewitz's relationship to reason is ambiguous. Reason is an essential element of policy formation and application, to be sure, and *On War* is a work of the intellect, laid out in reasoned fashion, in which nonrational forces are subjected to rational discussion. But there is another side. In Clausewitz's notion of absolute or pure war, reason would be overcome: "[W]ar would of its own independent will usurp the place of policy the moment policy had brought it into being; it would then drive policy out of office and rule by the laws of its own nature."[98] Real war does not equal the fury of absolute war, but it can approach it, and, in any case, the role of passion in real war tends to drive toward extremes. Therefore, Clausewitz, while appreciating the fact that reason guides policy and that war is an act of policy, was only too aware that reason is constantly in danger of being supplanted. Elsewhere Clausewitz proclaimed, "The maximum use of force is in no way incompatible with the simultaneous use of the intellect."[99] This assertion seems hard to square with his statements about absolute war, and the tensions between the absolute and the real, and total and limited war appear again.

There is a tendency to stress the "truth" of Clausewitz, seeing *On War* as timeless. Such a view must relegate the historical origins of the volume to a tertiary status. Paret regards Clausewitz as very selective in his relationship with Romanticism. Its liberating influence simply set him free to see reality more clearly; Romanticism was a window to Clausewitz, not a filter. Thus, Clausewitz benefited from the cultural currents of his time but set his own course. *On War* "combines intellectual and aesthetic attributes of the age of Goethe with an uncompromising realism."[100] Gat, however, convincingly argues that we must see Clausewitz as a philosopher responding to his time and trapped in the logic and the contradiction of his own system of thought, one that drew from reality but also imposed a construct on it. Assertions that Clausewitz promises universal insight because of his unfiltered understanding of reality ought not to be accepted uncritically.[101]

READINGS OF *ON WAR*

During the fifty years following the publication of *On War*, history reinforced Military Romanticism, as peoples' wars culminated in battles that produced rapid decisions out of bloody fury in Napoleonic fashion. The 1859 war that pitted Piedmont and France against Austria climaxed at the battle of Solferino and was over in four months, playing a vital role in Italian unification. The Austro-Prussian War, with its decisive battle at Königgrätz, consumed only seven weeks in 1866. Although fighting during the Franco-Prussian War extended from July 1870 to February 1871, the battles that sealed the fate of France, Gravelotte-St. Privat and Sedan, occurred in the first seven weeks of the war. Conflicts with indigenous colonial peoples also promised quick results, in which European advantages in the tools of war sped the process. At the same time, Europeans dismissed long and brutal struggles, such as the Crimean War and the American Civil War, as the products of bumbling.

In the decades following its publication in Clausewitz's posthumous works, *On War* appeared in new German editions and reached audiences outside Germany, with the first Dutch edition in 1846, the first French in 1849, and the first English in 1874.[102] Prussian victory over Austria and France seemed to endorse *On War*, and it acquired a great reputation.[103] Max Jähns, the German military intellectual, commented in 1891, "There is something strange about Clausewitz's influence," for even though his "almost mystical" works were not as widely read as believed, Clausewitz's "opinions have spread throughout the entire army and have proven immeasurably fruitful."[104] *On War* had become an important element in the European professional discourse on war.

But even as Prussian victories justified Military Romanticism and *On War,* factors emerged that Clausewitz could not have foreseen. On the one hand, the Industrial Revolution created new technologies of transportation, communication, and, eventually, weaponry that impacted war profoundly. And on the other hand, population growth, mobilized by new political/military systems in Europe, created huge armies. By the late nineteenth century, regular armies metamorphosed into training establishments that processed recruits during a few—usually two or three—years of full-time service and then turned them out into reserve units that outnumbered the full-time army. When armies mobilized now, reserves multiplied the number of troops to be put into campaign several times over. This "mass reserve" style of army, pioneered by Prussia/Germany, replaced the older popular conscript forces.[105] In order to manage these gargantuan, railroad-based armies, another Prussian innovation of the early nineteenth century, the general staff, proved essential. After the Franco-Prussian War demonstrated the worth of the German General Staff, all major European powers adopted this institution for centralized planning and control.

Prussian victory depended on the mastery of new technologies and the creation of new institutions, and initially these could be exploited in a way that was consistent with *On War.* The great virtuoso of mid-nineteenth-century warfare Helmuth von Moltke the elder, renowned chief of the Prussian/German General Staff, 1857–1887, called himself a disciple of Clausewitz.[106] Gerhard Ritter described Moltke as "not at all a professional soldier in the narrower sense but essentially a humanist of the post-Goethe era."[107] Moltke represented the triumph of Military Romanticism because he espoused its precepts and seems to have followed them directly in actual military operations. He shared the emphasis on battle characteristic of Military Romanticism: "[W]e can limit the enemy's will if we are ready and determined to take the initiative but we cannot defeat it by any other means than . . . battle."[108] He clearly believed in a head-to-head armed collision, as evidenced in his statement of 1868: "The plan of operations against France simply consists of locating the main enemy army and attacking it wherever it is found."[109] Moltke maintained Clausewitz's respect for the unpredictable in war. Moltke believed in extensive preparations for campaign but denied that anyone could predict the course of a campaign:

[O]ur will soon meets the independent will of the enemy. . . . The material and moral consequences of any larger encounter are, however, so far-reaching that through them a completely different situation is created, which then becomes the basis for new measures. No plan of action can look with any certainty beyond the first meeting with the major forces of the enemy. . . . The commander is compelled during the whole campaign to reach decisions on the basis of situations that cannot be predicted. All consecutive acts of war are, therefore, not executions of a premeditated plan, but spontaneous actions, directed by military tact.[110]

Moltke stressed chance, believing that "no foresight can guarantee such a final result of operations." Beyond "calculable factors," the outcome depends on "space and time, but also often on the outcome of previous minor battles, on the weather, on false news; in brief, on all that is called chance and luck in human life." As a consequence, "Great successes in war are not achieved, however, without great risks."[111] For him, war remained a "system of expedients."[112] Therefore, he criticized rules and stressed genius: "In war as in art there are no general rules; in neither can talent be replaced by a rule."[113]

In one way, however, Moltke put his own interpretation on the master's words. In Moltke's "Instructions for the Senior Troop Commanders," he stated that the "objective of war is to implement the government's policy by force."[114] This sounds like Clausewitz, but Moltke twisted the original intent and asserted, "Political considerations can be taken into account only as long as they do not make demands that are militarily improper or impossible."[115] Here Moltke expresses the conventional soldier's notion that once war begins—for policy reasons, of course—then the generals ought to be allowed to direct it without political interference.

Alfred von Schlieffen, who headed the General Staff from 1891 to 1905, moved farther from Clausewitz, although Schlieffen expressed strong public praise for *On War*.[116] His famous Schlieffen Plan detailed the opening German move of World War I, sending the majority of forces through Belgium in a gigantic right hook into northern France. Schlieffen believed that the only solution to Germany's strategic problem was a battle of annihilation against the French: "The first blow must be carried out with great force, resulting in a true decisive battle. A Solferino could do nothing for us; a Sedan must be fought, or at least a Königgrätz."[117] However, Schlieffen was convinced that a carefully orchestrated offensive could so determine the enemy's response that war plans need not leave room for the unpredictable; thus, he scheduled the invasion from its beginnings at the Belgian border to its culmination in a huge battle of envelopment from Paris to the Rhine. Schlieffen's chess-like design has been called antithetical to Clausewitz.[118]

Schlieffen's options may have been restricted, however. In fact, all the major powers produced monolithic war plans devoid of flexibility for World War I. It had become immensely complicated to mobilize, supply, and direct the ever larger, multi-million-man armies that now must move by railroad. Confronted with tasks of management and coordination that would have been daunting enough in our computer age, general staffs were then working in a pen-and-paper epoch. Producing plans with multiple alternatives may have been beyond the means of European armies by 1900.

Other aspects of Clausewitzian analysis remained convincing, particularly those dealing with the absolute character of war. A critical trend in military discussion immediately before World War I stressed the bloody predictions of *On War*, with its emphasis on the unavoidable costs of combat. Early-twentieth-century military literature repeatedly reminded readers of Clausewitz's dictum:

> We are not interested in generals who win victories without bloodshed. The fact that slaughter is a horrifying spectacle must make us take war more seriously, but not provide an excuse for gradually blunting our swords in the name of humanity. Sooner or later someone will come along with a sharp sword and hack off our arms.[119]

Col. F. N. Maude, a soldier-intellectual who wrote the introduction and notes to a 1908 English edition of *On War*, declared in his own work on infantry tactics, "Success in the assault is all a case of how you train your soldiers beforehand 'to know how to die or to avoid dying,' if the latter, then nothing can help you, and it would have been wiser not to go to war at all."[120] He was not alone in this brutal conclusion. The German theorist Friedrich von Bernardi declared, "The dread of losses will always ensure failure, while we can assume with certainty that those troops who are not afraid of losses are bound to maintain an enormous superiority over others who are more sparing of blood."[121]

The French, most notably Ferdinand Foch, read Clausewitz as raising moral factors far above material ones. Will, a strong element in *On War,* became the touchstone of Gallic theory. The French, who had at first ignored Clausewitz, took him up after being humiliated in the Franco-Prussian War. Not surprisingly, they reattached Napoleon to Clausewitz. Commandant Maillard at the École Supérieure de Guerre and Captain Gilbert discussed Clausewitz at length, and a new French translation of *On War* by Vatry appeared 1887–1889.[122] Even Jean Jaurès, the great socialist politician and historian, noted "the breadth of spirit and the objectivity of Clausewitz."[123] Foch, who taught at the École Supérieure from 1895 and became its director in 1907, studied Clausewitz in its full complexity, but Foch self-consciously simplified his own theory to emphasize rational thought and spiritual will.[124] In his *Principles of War* (1903), he also argued for the need to prepare for absolute war, à la Clausewitz. Foch believed that "national war" had been created by the French, but "we ignored that radical transformation among our neighbors" that paralleled the French creation. But "the whole of Europe has now come back to the national thesis, and therefore to armed nations," and as a result, "we stand compelled today to take up again the *absolute* concept of war, such as it results from history."[125]

CONCLUSION

When the Germans launched their invasion of France in August 1914, the Schlieffen plan at first swung forward with menacing efficiency. The equally monolithic offensive Plan of the Third Republic, which amounted to little more than a rush into Alsace Lorraine, absorbed most French troops and attention, so they did not respond in strength to the German advance until almost too late. But on the Marne, French forces aided by their British allies stalled the German offensive and forced back that gray tide. By November the lines stabilized and entrenched from the North Sea to the Alps; there they would remain with only slight alterations until the spring of 1918. All the fighting in the initial offensives had not brought decisive victory to either side on the Western Front, but casualty lists swelled to about one million on both sides by Christmas. Battle's promise had failed; only the price remained. Over the next several years, all armies proved that their troops knew "how to die" and that officers were prepared to send them to their deaths.

In 1916 the Germans and French grappled at Verdun in what proved to be the longest battle of the war (21 February–18 December). Verdun served as a metaphor for World War I, because this fight was not about breakthrough or territorial gain but only about slaughter. The chief of the German General Staff, Falkenhayn, attacked Verdun with no other goal than to draw as many French defenders as he could into the range of his artillery so as to blast them into oblivion. Mass death, he hoped, would undermine the French will to continue the war. Endless barrages of massive shells killed, buried, disinterred, and scattered the fragments of young men. In the end, though they smashed many French bodies, the Germans could not break French resolve in 1916. The final toll at Verdun appalls, nearly 550,000 French dead and wounded, almost matched by 430,000 Germans—and all to no purpose.

Measuring the exact impact of *On War* upon this terrible military reality is next to impossible; that should not lessen our appreciation of the power exerted by the conceptual sphere of warfare. *On War* was known by so many that it would be impossible to dismiss it as an influence. Even those who did not study it in depth could hardly escape it, for they had learned its language and insights second hand, and Clausewitz had many interpreters. Of course, we must bear in mind that the influence of a great work of theory upon practice is further complicated by the fact that it can be read for meanings secondary to, or even unintended by, the author. Circumstance can radically change the interpretation of theory. In addition, at the extremes a discourse on war can operate in two directions. It can produce the war it predicts. Certainly it shaped a highly conventional form of warfare for the Greeks, and by the same token it prepared the Germans to impose "blitzkrieg" in 1939–1941. But at the other extreme, strong adherence to a discourse on war can also disarm a military, as did French concepts of methodical defense and offense in 1940. Did a fairly well-defined discourse on war set up Europe for the tragedy of World War I?

After the war, when military intellectuals sought to explain the inconclusive and costly character of military operations, they found many targets; one was Clausewitz. Perhaps his most bitter critic, B. H. Liddell Hart condemned Clausewitz as the "Mahdi of Mass" and accused generals of becoming "intoxicated with the blood-red wine of Clausewitzian growth."[126] Liddell Hart blamed *On War* for teaching the necessity of great numbers and of great casualties. In recent decades, Liddell Hart himself has drawn a good deal of fire for that attack on Clausewitz. But is it so easy to dismiss entirely the charge that

Clausewitz inspired some of the savagery of that war? *On War* certainly supplied language and categories of military analysis, which at least helped to determine expression and may have also shaped perception. Did, as is so often the case, ideas filter the view of reality? And if they did, cannot conception have selected or colored the rationale utilized to make and justify military decisions? Were, for example, those who predicted the high cost of modern warfare inoculated against "the dread of losses" by the bloodier passages of Clausewitz? John Keegan offers his answer to such questions: "And although this catastrophic outcome must not be laid at the door of Clausewitz's study, we are nevertheless right to see Clausewitz as the ideological father of the First World War, just as we are right to perceive Marx as the ideological father of the Russian Revolution."[127]

The issue of Clausewitz's influence before World War I remains, and recent decades lead us to ask similar questions concerning his influence on current defense thought. Clausewitz fell out of favor between the world wars, but defense intellectuals returned to him after World War II, this time for his comments on limited war, not for his advocacy of decisive battle in the cause of total war. The impact of the Vietnam conflict only accentuated this tendency, as *On War* became standard issue for students at U.S. war colleges. The Naval War College adopted it as a key text in 1976, to be followed by the Air War College in 1978 and the Army War College in 1981.[128] Paret's magisterial biography of Clausewitz—itself evidence of this revival—explains Clausewitz's commanding prestige by his realism.[129] Paret would have us accept that Clausewitz did not impose himself and his own intellectual construct on reality but simply penetrated and portrayed the truth of it all. But this contention seems at odds with the character of his work; in fact, it runs counter to the very nature of intellectual endeavor. If Clausewitz must be seen as a product of his time and circumstance, his current popularity is worth pondering. Today, someone whose primary concern was the total warfare of the Napoleonic Era and who defined war most fundamentally in absolute terms has become the guru of limited warfare.[130] Computer-age pundits with peacekeeping operations on their minds seek guidance from a son of Romanticism who took the field against Napoleon. Such is the perseverance of the professional discourse on war nurtured by Romanticism and articulated by Clausewitz in an attempt to explain the radical nature of Napoleonic warfare. We still expect the sun of Austerlitz to burn away the fog.

Notes on the Opening Illustration for Chapter Six

This detail from the massive painting of the Battle of Austerlitz by François Gérard portrays the moment of victory. Surrounded by his entourage amidst the debris of battle, Napoleon accepts the surrender of Russian General Repnine. Breaking through from the left, the sun of Austerlitz illuminates the genius-hero on his white horse. Napoleon would regard this sun as symbolizing his brilliant destiny.

(Copyright Réunion des Musées Nationaux/Art Resource, NY)

CHAPTER SEVEN

The Merciless Fight

Race and Military Culture in the Pacific War

AFTER TWO DAYS OF BOMBARDMENT by heavy naval guns on the morning of 15 June 1944, Marines of the 2nd and 4th Divisions assaulted the beaches on the southwest coast of Saipan. General Hideki Tojo, prime minister of Japan, had boasted three months earlier, "I personally guarantee with 'a large seal' the defense of Saipan!"[1] But the U.S. invasion force nulled that guarantee. The fleet standing off Saipan included seven new and eight old battleships, fifteen large aircraft carriers, cruisers, destroyers, and myriad other vessels loaded with 71,000 troops. Yet with all this power, it would still be a tough fight.

The landings did not go as scripted. Americans confronted 32,000 Japanese troops on Saipan, not the 12,000 estimated in May. Marines had yet to confront such a large garrison. Preparatory operations tipped off the defenders, under Lieutenant General Yoshitsugu Saito. Although the long aerial and naval bombardment left much in ruins, it failed to void the Japanese defense of the beach. Marines came ashore on amphibious tracked landing craft, known as LVTs or amtracs, supported by modified armored LVTs mounting 75 mm howitzers. Plans called for the amtracs to continue inland to the high ground before disgorging their troops. Enemy fire crashed down on the first wave of over 700 LVTs carrying 8,000 Marines as it approached to within 800 yards of the beach. Some rounds found their targets, but the amtracs clawed over the reef and climbed up onto the shore. However, the underpowered craft could not negotiate the rubble-strewn and cratered beaches, so the Marines disembarked short of their intended objectives. Marines of the 2nd Division landed 900 yards north of their assigned beaches, creating a gap between them and the 4th Marine Division, and it would take hard fighting to close the breach. By the end of the day, 20,000 men held the beachhead, but they had already suffered 2,000 casualties, and in the three days it took to achieve the objectives scheduled for the initial day, some infantry battalions experienced 30 percent casualties.

Much bloody combat awaited the Marines, soon joined by the army's 27th Infantry Division, as they moved north, but they advanced fast and forcefully enough to keep the Japanese from consolidating effective new defensive lines. Instead of talking of success, the Japanese talked more and more of honorable death. Early in the battle Major General Keiji Igeta radioed Tokyo: "By becoming the bulwark of the Pacific with 10,000 deaths, we hope to requite the imperial favor."[2] American power proved unstoppable, and on 6 July Saito issued a farewell message calling for a final fight to the death: "As it says in the *Senjinkun* [Battle Ethics]: 'I will never suffer the disgrace of being taken alive,' and 'I will offer up the courage of my soul and calmly rejoice in living by the eternal principle.'"[3] Saito, Igeta, and Vice Admiral Chuichi Nagumo, who had led the attack on Pearl Harbor, committed ritual suicide, *seppuku*, together the next morning. That same day, at least 3,000 remaining troops carried out a suicidal charge. Some had only grenades or sharpened bamboo poles, but they broke through two battalions and were stopped only by desperate measures. Many of the Japanese wounded later committed suicide.[4] At the end of the battle, the Americans counted only 921 prisoners; 97 percent of the Japanese garrison died defending Saipan.

But the horrors extended beyond the troops. Fed endless stories from authorities who warned that the barbaric Americans raped, tortured, and killed Japanese captives, and true to a romantic code of death before dishonor, hundreds if not thousands of Japanese civilians committed suicide. At Marpi Point on the northern extreme of the island, families gathered around grenades to blow themselves up. Others waded into the sea together to drown or hurled themselves and their children off cliffs. William Manchester described one recorded suicide: "A brief strip of jerky newsreel footage, preserved in the island museum, shows a distraught mother, her baby in her arms, darting back and forth along the edge of the precipice, trying to make up her mind. Finally she leaps."[5] Americans could not comprehend such suicidal carnage and did what they could to stop it. American interpreters and Japanese prisoners shouted through bullhorns urging individuals to surrender and promising good treatment; U.S. naval craft pulled many from the sea who had jumped from seaward cliffs but survived the fall.

During the Pacific War, Americans and Japanese regarded each other's values and behaviors as incomprehensible, even as less than human. On Saipan, Americans faced death to achieve military victory, while the Japanese chose death to elevate physical defeat into moral triumph.

It was as if Americans and Japanese were more than enemies, but rather entirely separate species. A vast cultural gulf separated them, but both interpreted this difference as racial. In his much-praised *War Without Mercy: Race and Power in the Pacific War,* John W. Dower exposes and emphasizes the racial dimensions of the conflict.[6] Craig M. Cameron, in his *American Samurai: Myth, Imagination, and the Conduct of Battle in the First Marine Division, 1941–1951,* takes the thesis into the realm of more traditional military history.[7] Ronald Takaki, the revered practitioner of multicultural history, carries on the theme in his *Hiroshima* and the more recent *Double Victory: A Multicultural History of America in World War II.* Takaki concludes, "Unlike the fighting in Europe, the armed conflict in the Pacific was a race war, powered by mutual hatreds and stereotyping."[8]

Racial analyses of U.S. history have long been central to the study of the American past, particularly by academic scholars. Not surprisingly, then, over the last decade, racial conceptions and animosities in the Pacific War have been widely discussed, and that discussion probably ranks above all other culturally focused examinations of American military history. So central are the issues addressed in Dower's work that they demand to be examined in this book on war and culture. Because of the complexity of the subject, this chapter must span matters from battlefield atrocities to racist American legislation to the rationale for bombing Hiroshima and Nagasaki. The chapter centers on the origin, character, and impact of American racism on the battlefield. While Japanese racial attitudes and military culture are considered, sometimes at length, they are discussed mainly as context and counterpoint. Above all, this is an examination of the American discourse on race and war.

Let us accept the fact that Americans and Japanese portrayed each other in racist propaganda and treated prisoners, the wounded, and the dead in barbaric ways made conscionable by racist attitudes. Doubtless, racism framed many of the attitudes held by American troops and was a strong feature of their experience of war and of the way in which they would later remember those years. Given the penchant of cultural historians for studying opinion and memory, these scholars understandably embrace the racial interpretation of the Pacific War as being self-evidently essential to our understanding of the war. But as an inquiry into military history, this chapter questions the centrality of race and racism to the *conduct of war* as opposed to the *experience of war* as lived by soldier, sailor, or Marine. Dower himself challenges his readers to measure the impact of race: "We can gain an impression of its importance, however, by asking a simple question: when and where did race play a significant role in the war?"[9] This chapter responds by answering that it did not exert much influence on American pursuit of that conflict.

While racism and racist legislation in the United States drove America and Japan to the brink of war before 1921, American racism ceased to be at the forefront of international tensions after that date, although Japanese resentment of U.S. racial policies was always in the background. American racism colored some judgments and actions that led to war in 1941 but was not a primary factor. A better case could be made for Japanese racism as an influence driving Japan's foreign policy from 1931. American strategy and combat doctrine show virtually no stamp of racism. Both strategy and doctrine responded to the geography of the Pacific and the technology that set parameters to logistics and weaponry. While U.S. soldiers, sailors, and Marines used racist language and committed racist atrocities, there is good reason to deny that race hatred played a dominant role in combat motivation among men in the field. Finally, although it is frequently argued that racism was a critical factor in the decision to employ atomic weapons against Japan, this chapter strongly questions that verdict and argues instead that the attacks were fully justified by military necessity. In most ways, then, the U.S. pursuit of the war would have been very much the same had the American public and its armed forces been free from racial hatred toward their Japanese foes.

UNDENIABLE HATRED

In his 1946 essay, "How We Felt About the War," the Pulitzer Prize–winning historian Allan Nevins testified that, "Probably in all our history no foe has been so detested as were the Japanese. The infamy of Pearl Harbor was enough; but to it were soon added circumstantial accounts of Japanese atrocities at Hong Kong, Singapore, and finally and most appallingly, upon American prisoners in the Philippines."[10] Bitter racist feelings typified American attitudes toward the Japanese and Japanese views of their American opponents. Moreover, both governments played the race card to stiffen resolve among the civilian population and among the troops. Dower lays bare these unfortunate realities, forcefully establishing this tenet of the race thesis.

Outrage over what the American people condemned as Japanese "treachery" at Pearl Harbor seemed to justify stereotypes of wily and deceitful "Orientals." The *Los Angeles Examiner,* a Hearst paper, declared, "The war in the Pacific is the World War, the War of Oriental Races against Occidental Races for the Domination of the World."[11] The language of color and the imagery of contempt instantly appeared in newspapers and magazines. A week after the Pearl Harbor attack, *Time* claimed that "the people" exclaimed in response to "the mightiest evil of their time": "Why, the yellow bastards!"[12] *The New Yorker* published a story by Edward Newhouse in which a character referred to the Japanese as "them yellow monkeys."[13]

Because hatred against Japanese rose to such a pitch on the morrow of Pearl Harbor, *Life* magazine published a "helpful" guide to racial identification, "How to tell Japs from the Chinese: Angry citizens victimize allies with emotional outburst at enemy."[14] The editors hoped this would spare the "75,000 U.S. Chinese, whose homeland is our staunch ally," from suffering at the hands of Americans unable to tell them from the Japanese.

Political cartoons portrayed the Japanese as gorillas, apes, and monkeys. One offering by the well-known British cartoonist David Low portrays a bespectacled, grinning monkey hanging by its tail behind three unsuspecting burly fellows representing the United States, Great Britain, and the Soviet Union; the monkey clutches a knife and is in the act of deciding which back to plunge it into.[15] A *Punch* cartoon of January 1942, titled "The Monkey Folk," showed long-armed apes with submachine guns slung around their backs and wearing Japanese helmets advancing by swinging from jungle vines. A drawing in the *New York Times Magazine* gave a giant Japanese figure the attributes of King Kong, a slump-shouldered giant with round eyeglasses and teeth that invoked both a gorilla and the buck-toothed stereotype of the Japanese. In his hairy paw he clutched hapless victims. The caption read, "How Tough Are the Japanese? They are not tougher than other soldiers, but brutality is part of their fighting equipment."[16] Another cartoon run by the *New York Times* in 1943 shows a slavering guerrilla labeled "Murderers of American Fliers," with the caption "Let the punishment fit the crime."[17]

Less outrageous but still demeaning images of the "Jap" included the bespectacled, round-faced, buck-toothed little man, who appeared not only on editorial pages but in everything from Bugs Bunny cartoons to advertisements. Philco Corporation ran a series of ads in *Life* that invariably showed Hitler, Mussolini, and Tojo. Hitler and Mussolini were caricatured as individuals, but Tojo was treated as a racial type. The real Tojo did wear the scripted round eyeglasses, but he was neither round-faced nor buck-toothed; still, the ads showed him as such.[18]

Somewhat more sophisticated, but still guilty of selling a brutal stereotype, *Life* ran a series of articles designed to teach its readers about the Japanese enemy. Its first portrayal of the Japanese army in January 1942 was one of brutal beastliness. An article entitled "Its Soldiers Are Veterans" claimed: "It is a cruel and ruthless army. . . . Their cruelties do not come singly, but in the indescribable hundreds of thousands."[19] Later articles on Japanese culture continued to portray the Japanese as devious and fanatic. "The Japanese Language: A national secret code, it is perfect for hiding facts or saying what you don't mean" implied that the very character of the language encouraged deceit.[20] (It also explained the stereotypical image of the Japanese in glasses as a product of eyestrain from reading Japanese characters.) The national game, Go, became a lesson in conquest: "Go: Japs play their national game the way they fight their wars."[21] A piece from 1943 on the classical tale of the *ronin*, or lordless samurai, announces its own bias: "The 47 Ronin: The most popular play in Japan reveals the bloodthirsty character of our enemy." "Their blind loyalty to their superiors," claimed this article, "seems to be matched only by their fanaticism in the face of death."[22]

The racial insults even extended to song. One tune bore the title, "There'll Be No Adolf Hitler nor Yellow Japs to Fear," and another boasted "We're Gonna Have to Slap the Dirty Little Jap."[23]

Yet even from the start, race hatred did not take the form of dismissing the Japanese as inferior warriors. In fact, the spate of victories in the first six months of the war at first lent the Japanese soldier an air of invincibility. The image of the Japanese superman posed a threat to American confidence. *Yank,* a U.S. army paper, credited the Japanese soldier as "a 'born' jungle and night fighter."[24] Joseph Grew, U.S. ambassador to Japan at the start of the war, announced grimly, "The Japanese will not crack."[25] But American media counterattacked in print even before the United States mounted its first offensives. A March 1942 issue of the *New York Times Magazine* included an article "Japanese Superman? That, Too, Is a Fallacy."[26] More than anything else, naval victory at the battle of Midway and the costly conquest of Guadalcanal revealed shortcomings of the Japanese in combat. Of Guadalcanal, Herbert C. Merillat wrote in 1943, "Here the myth of Japanese invincibility was destroyed."[27] Still Americans never discounted the Japanese as weak or irresolute.

A recognition of his ability, perhaps fiendish ability, made the "Jap" even more to be feared and hated. *Life* published an interesting fictional interview with General Tojo's "cousin," dubbed "Admiral Quasi Tojo" by *Life,* in a clever play on the fact that he was not quite Tojo and was in some ways hideous, as in Quasimodo. This piece, "Your War with Japan: Fictitious Jap Admiral gives you the enemy point of view but he hasn't got all the answers," cautions the reader not to dismiss the admiral: "He is not an ignorant, ill-educated man who has been misled by propaganda. He is one of Japan's carefully trained military rulers. He is an able and intelligent barbarian and he knows what time of day it is."[28] Another *Life* piece, "How Strong Is Japan?" presented a series of contrasting statements with photographs; one read "Japan's army looks sloppy, dirty and stupid BUT it is intelligent, united, faithful."[29]

Japanese Racism: The Other Side of the Coin

The Japanese also harbored and encouraged racist attitudes toward the Americans and toward other peoples of Asia. Just as he does for American opinion, Dower deals with Japanese attitudes in illuminating detail. The Japanese saw themselves as a specially blessed people with a great role to play; they referred to themselves as the "leading race," the *shido minzoku.*[30] In 1940, one industrial and political figure of note, Nkajima Chikuei, claimed, "There are superior and inferior races in the world, and it is the sacred duty of the leading races to lead and enlighten the inferior ones."[31] Chikuei held the Japanese to be "the sole superior race" owing to the fact that they were pure-blooded and related to the gods. Not surprisingly, a pamphlet distributed to Japanese troops, "Read This and the War Is Won," declared the war to be "a struggle between races."[32]

Not only did the Japanese regard themselves as being superior to Americans, but they played the race card with Asian populations against white imperialists. In 1943, Ba Maw, who initially supported the Japanese in Burma, declared to delegates at the Assembly of the Greater East Asiatic Nations in 1943: "My Asiatic blood has always called to other Asiatics. . . . This is not the time to think with our minds; this is the time to think with our blood, and it is this thinking with the blood that has brought me all the way from Burma to Japan."[33]

While the Americans often caricatured the "Japs" as monkeys, the Japanese commonly portrayed the Americans and British as devils and demons. Americans were also depicted as having animal hindquarters, a sign of ridicule. Just as did the American use of the monkey, the Japanese portrayal of Westerners was intended to paint the enemy as subhuman.

In fact, the sense of Japanese solidarity with other Asians was warped by a strong sense of Japanese superiority over their neighbors. They preached the language of anti-imperialism while they acted brutally toward inhabitants of lands held by Japan. In a violent response to the 1923 earthquake, Japanese police and mobs tortured and slew 6,000 Koreans resident in Japan—a display of vicious, mindless racism.[34] The strategic writer Kanji Ishiwara might claim, "It is Japan's divine mission to assist the Chinese people," but he proposed doing so by taking Manchuria.[35] Ba Maw eventually testified of the Japanese: "The brutality, arrogance, and racial pretensions of these men remain among the deepest Burmese memories of the war years; for a great many people in Southeast Asia these are all they remember of the war."[36] He described the attitude of what he called the Japanese "Korea clique." "They had learned in Korea, Manchukuo, and China to believe that the Japanese were the master race in Asia and to deal with the other Asian races on that footing."[37] During the war the Japanese appealed to Indian independence and created the Indian National Army from Indian prisoners of war captured with the fall of Singapore. The first Indian organizer of this force, Mohan Singh, quickly became disillusioned with the Japanese and lost his post. Subas Chandra Bose would take over after Singh, but the Japanese continued to mishandle the Indians.[38]

The harsh treatment that alienated Asian populations within Japanese occupied territories does not necessarily prove Japanese hypocrisy. Ample evidence demonstrates the sense of a Japanese calling to drive Western imperial powers out of Asia. Those who predicted war with America saw Japan on a mission to free and unify Asia; Ishiwara even saw the end of this process as an apocalyptic war between the United States and Japan that would, through Japanese victory, lead to the salvation of mankind.[39] However, those who spoke of a liberated Asia saw the Japanese as the clear leaders with a marked superiority over other Asian peoples. As the Japanese came to rule from China to the Philippines, three factors undercut their ability to realize good intentions: 1) Japanese dominance came as conquest, and where the Japanese met resistance they were merciless warriors; 2) confidence in their own superiority gave them a sense of mission, but also led them to be condescending and autocratic; and 3) material needs in wartime forced them to be rapacious in demanding goods and labor.[40]

The worst excesses of abominable Japanese behavior while using the language of Asian self-determination came in China. The atrocities committed in Nanking have come to symbolize the viciousness of Japanese conquest. Iris Chang's *The Rape of Nanking* provides an unforgettable narrative of the murder of as many as 300,000 captured Chinese soldiers and civilians there. Her work has come under some criticism, but her basic narration of events is accurate and her outrage legitimate.[41] Hapless, disarmed Chinese troops were taken out in small groups and executed, many used for bayonet and sword practice. Perhaps 20,000 women of Nanking—no one can know for sure—were repeatedly raped and then killed in a crescendo of brutality. It may not have been a holocaust for an entire national group, but it was holocaust for one city.

Japanese troops treated the Chinese with omnipresent brutality. Imperial soldiers throughout China regarded rape as a prerogative.[42] They seemed to regard cruelty with relish. One corporal home on leave from China in 1942 reported: "While out foraging for supplies we got hold of a pregnant woman. We stuck our bayonets in her huge belly, skewered her like a piece of meat. . . . I wiped oil on my sword blade so the Chink's blood wouldn't stick when I cut a coolie's head off with one stroke."[43] In parts of China where the Communists operated, the Japanese would adopt the infamous "three-all" policy, *sanko seisaku*, "kill all, burn all, destroy all." The Japanese came supplied with contempt for the Chinese as part of their basic equipment. Chang tells that before the war, Japanese schoolboys were taught contempt for the Chinese. She relates one story of a lad whose reluctance to cut up a frog in class brought on this tirade from the teacher: "Why are you crying about one lousy frog? When you grow up you'll have to kill one hundred, two hundred chinks!"[44]

American Race Hatred on Campaign

American soldiers, sailors, and Marines harbored hatred for the Japanese adversary, dehumanizing that foe just as the Japanese did their enemies. Regrettably, U.S. servicemen harbored a contempt for Japanese troops that not only reflected but intensified the racial animosities expressed by the population at large. In an article "The First Ten Days of the War at Sea," *Life* quoted a sailor's letter: "Dear Mother, Don't be worried. I am all right. We are not killing people, we're just cleaning the scum off the ocean."[45]

From the outset, racism against the Japanese mixed a sense of grievance with bigotry. Fury against an enemy that had attacked Pearl Harbor without warning became "racialized" to be expressed as a condemnation of an entire people as subhuman. Sergeant Joe Smith, who fired on the Japanese attackers in the Philippines, declared, "I never had any harsh feelings toward Japanese before, but I learned to hate them right then."[46]

The language of certain prominent military commanders in the Pacific War dripped with racist contempt. Probably the most outlandish official statements came from the mouth and pen of Admiral William ("Bull") Halsey, who adopted the imagery of anti-Japanese propaganda, calling his enemies "monkeymen,"[47] declaring his desire in attacking New Georgia "to get some more Monkey meat."[48] For Halsey, "These yellow bastards are beasts alright."[49] He even proposed a solution right out of the barnyard: "emasculation for all the males and spaying for the females."[50] Since in his opinion, "The only good Jap is a Jap who's been dead six months,"[51] he encouraged his men to "Kill Japs, kill Japs, kill more Japs."[52] In October 1944, after the victory in Pelileu, Halsey addressed the victorious Marines: "The sincere admiration of the entire Third Fleet is yours for the hill blasting, cave smashing extermination of 11,000 slant-eyed gophers."[53] It is true that after the war Halsey claimed that he employed his virulent racist language to undermine the idea of Japanese invincibility.[54]

Many other military voices spoke as harshly, although less colorfully. The Australian General Sir Thomas Blamey echoed Halsey's themes in addresses to his troops in New Guinea: "Your enemy is a curious race—a cross between the human being and the ape. And like the ape, when he is cornered he knows how to die."[55] Blamey also commented to *The New York Times,* "We are not dealing with humans as we know them. We are dealing with something primitive. Our troops have the right view of the Japs. They regard them as vermin."[56]

Observers who had witnessed American attitudes toward the German enemy commented on how much more American troops detested the Japanese. The famous war correspondent Ernie Pyle left Europe for the Pacific early in 1945 and after talking to troops there reported, "In Europe we felt our enemies, horrible and deadly as they were, were still people. But out here I gathered that the Japanese were looked upon as something subhuman and repulsive; the way some people feel about cockroaches or mice."[57] About the same time, *Science Digest* published an article entitled "Why Americans Hate Japs More than Nazis."[58]

There is absolutely no question that U.S. troops harbored more virulent feelings toward their Japanese foes than toward Germans, and the classic study of motivation and sentiment sponsored by the U.S. army, *The American Soldier: Combat and Its Aftermath,* offers cold statistical evidence of burning hatred.[59] Researchers asked U.S. army recruits how they would feel about killing an enemy soldier. The four possible responses were: "I would really like to kill a [Japanese or German] soldier"; "I would feel that it was just part of the job without either liking or disliking it"; "I would feel that it was part of the job, but would still feel bad about killing a man even if he was a [Japanese or German] soldier"; and "I would feel I should not kill anyone, even a [Japanese or German] soldier." The most common response, 51 percent, confirmed that they would "really like to kill a Japanese soldier." However, the recruits tested showed far less delight at the prospect of killing Germans; here the average fell to 7 percent. The majority, 51 percent, regarded killing a German as duty "without either liking or disliking it." And, not surprisingly, U.S. recruits expressed more misgivings about killing Germans, as 36 percent of recruits admitted they "would still feel bad about killing . . . a German soldier"; however, the parallel response concerning a Japanese soldier fell to only 17 percent.

The undeniably deep racial animosity felt by U.S. troops toward their Japanese enemies in the Pacific spawned atrocities. These excesses of hatred fell upon Japanese who attempted to surrender or were already held as prisoners and upon the bodies of their dead.

It is not hard to assemble a catalog of brutality. Especially early in the war, neither side in the Pacific took many prisoners. Soon after landing on

Guadalcanal, Marines shot down unarmed Japanese laborers, or "termites," according to a U.S. intelligence report:

> Contacts with termites were also witnessed, and more of these laborers might have been taken alive if eager Marines had not shot them as soon as spotted. One group of about 20 were seen to be mowed down with M[achine] G[un] and rifle fire as they came to cross a stream with evident intention of surrendering. But such ruthless precautions were perhaps not unwise in view of Japanese tactics met with elsewhere.[60]

Denis Warner reported his own later experience on Bougainville in 1944, where General Robert Beightler overruled pleas to accept the surrender of wounded Japanese: "You heard me, Colonel, I want no prisoners. Shoot them all."[61] The Marine battle cry on Tarawa was: "Kill the Jap bastards! Take no prisoners!"[62] During Charles Lindbergh's visit to the Pacific theater in mid-1944, one American colonel put it succinctly: "Our boys just don't take prisoners."[63] When commanders made it clear that they wanted prisoners, as Lindbergh reports happened in August 1944, then troops produced them.[64]

American Marines and soldiers collected grisly souvenirs from Japanese victims: teeth, ears, scalps, and skulls.[65] There was no secret that U.S. troops scavenged the bodies of Japanese. *Guadalcanal Diary,* published late in 1942, presented such comments as: "They say the Japs have a lot of gold teeth. I'm going to make myself a necklace."[66] Such statements might simply exemplify grisly bravado meant to dispel fear. But much was in deadly earnest. E. B. Sledge tells of a Marine anxious to pillage a still-living Japanese soldier and "with a slash cut his cheeks open to each ear" to pry out his gold teeth with a knife.[67] An article from *Leatherneck* in 1943 mentioned one Marine who carried eleven ears from slain Japanese in his pocket and then went on to say "It was not disgusting . . . it is quite common for the boys to gather this kind of 'souvenirs.'"[68] Taking scalps resurrected another racial battle, the fight against Native Americans.[69] Marines described jungle combat as "Indian fighting."[70] Skulls became macabre mementoes. *Life* magazine ran photos of skulls used to decorate U.S. military vehicles and of one sent to an American girl as a souvenir by her navy fiancé.[71] Such souvenir taking was known and tolerated, although not always condoned. An issue of *Leatherneck* in 1945 included a cartoon that condemned those who pillaged the dead.[72]

In the February 1946 issue of *Atlantic Monthly,* Edgar L. Jones summed up the horrors:

We shot prisoners in cold blood, wiped out hospitals, strafed lifeboats, killed or mistreated enemy civilians, finished off the enemy wounded, tossed the dying into a hole with the dead, and in the Pacific boiled the flesh off enemy skulls to make table ornaments for sweethearts, or carved their bones into letter openers.[73]

Race hatred undeniably produced atrocities, but it should be noted that these occurred on the peripheries of combat. The victims were those attempting to surrender, those held as prisoners, and the bodies of the dead—not those engaged in the fight. This should not be surprising, because actual combat is almost always distinct from the dark realm of atrocity. In battle, armed opponents face each other, dealing out deadly violence with a justice born of self-defense—kill or be killed. Atrocity is the province of the strong against the defenseless, of the armed against the unarmed. Thus the victims of atrocities are those entirely outside the battle, such as unarmed civilians, or those who have given up the fight, individuals who are attempting to surrender, have surrendered, or lie wounded or dead on the field. Racist cruelty preyed upon such helpless individuals.

Did Race Hatred Cause or Guide the War?

American propaganda used racist images to condemn the Japanese, and U.S. troops committed barbaric acts that displayed a virulent racist contempt for their enemy in the field. These regrettable facts would seem to justify Takaki's judgment that the Pacific War was a "race war."[74] But what does that mean? What impact did racism actually have on the cause and conduct of the war? As awful as are the visions of American race hatred in the Pacific, the influence of "racialized rage" was far less than would be expected.[75] While racism certainly shaped the "experience of war" for soldiers, sailors, and Marines engaged against the Japanese, it did not cause the war, determine overall U.S. strategy, or shape combat doctrine. Let us first briefly consider these aspects of the Pacific War, to leave us free to concentrate on two areas in which critics insist that racism was fundamental: the combat motivation among American troops in the field and the bombing offensive against the Japanese home islands, eventually leading to the use of atomic bombs on Hiroshima and Nagasaki.

The Experience of War vs. the Conduct of War

In explaining the course of the war in the Pacific, racist thoughts and deeds fall mainly within what we can call the "experience of war" rather than the "conduct of war," although there is certainly some overlap. To discover the experience of war we turn to the stories of common servicemen and people back on the home front. It is history from below, that of the lesser folk rather than of the decision makers. To today's sensitivities this may seem very humane, but it can suffer severe limitations. At its weakest it becomes rather like those news stories that ask people how they feel about an event instead of trying to uncover the causes and the actors. Certainly, better examples of the genre give a sense of being there, of getting into the heads of those on the ground. For this reason, explorations of the experience of war have been a mainstay of popular military history. Works such as Cornelius Ryan's *The Longest Day* or Stephen Ambrose's *Band of Brothers* fall into this category. Such studies are also particularly engaging when turned into visual narratives in movies and TV, as have both Ryan's and Ambrose's efforts. At its most sublime, such as in John Keegan's *The Face of Battle,* the experience-of-war approach demonstrates that by looking at military history from the bottom up, rather than from the top down, we learn that we ought not to reduce military units to geometric symbols on a map, but rather we must see them as assemblages of real people with real fears and desires—and real pain.

The experience-of-war approach also tells us how those involved in a war, either in the front lines or in the rear, will remember that conflict, and to be sure, memory has its impact on future opinions and actions. For good reasons, cultural historians pay a good deal of attention to memory. The ways in which people recollected World War I, for example, had important consequences for society, politics, and culture during the interwar period. In fact, those memories partially explain the onset and course of World War II in Europe.

However, a historian of World War II must go beyond the experience of war to explain the causes and conduct of the war and, I would argue, even its character. In particular, American racism cannot supply the fundamental answers to certain key questions, although race hatred may be involved tangentially. Why did the war break out in the first place? What strategies guided American armed forces to victory? How did Americans form and apply combat doctrine? Such matters belong much more to the causes and conduct of war than to the experience of war, and racial hatred was not the decisive influence in those matters.

American Racism and the Coming of War in 1941

What does it mean to call a conflict a "race war"? If this terminology requires that explicit race hatred brought on the clash, then the armed struggle that began with the bombing of Pearl Harbor does not qualify as one. Americans had a long history of bigotry toward the Japanese, particularly immigrants to America, but by 1941 this did not exert much influence on foreign relations. Still, it is worth surveying that history.

Americans, particularly in California, were guilty of a lamentable series of racist laws and actions against Asian immigrants to the mainland from the 1880s into the 1920s. These at first focused on excluding the Chinese from the country; however, in 1906 the cutting edge of racism turned against Japanese immigrants. That year the U.S. attorney general stipulated that courts were not to naturalize Japanese immigrants. Then, as an aftershock of the great 1906 earthquake, the San Francisco Board of Education ordered that Japanese children attend the "Oriental School." The Japanese government read such segregation as an insult and protested strongly. In California violence escalated as hooligans attacked Japanese-owned businesses and anti-Japanese riots broke out.

Relations between the U.S. and Japanese governments, which had been essentially friendly since the visit of Commodore Perry in 1853, now quickly turned sour. A worsening of relations was essentially inevitable, because the United States and Japan had become rivals for empire. In 1898 the United States began in full earnest its imperialist career in the Pacific. The United States declared war on Spain in April of that year and soon scored a victory in Manila Bay. The Treaty of Paris that ended the Spanish-American War in December awarded the United States the Philippines, Guam, and Puerto Rico. During that war, the United States also formally annexed the once independent Hawaiian Islands. When the Japanese confronted Russia in a bid for influence and territory on mainland Asia, they felt slighted by the treaty that President Theodore Roosevelt brokered to end the Russo-Japanese War. In this atmosphere, the slap in the face by the School Board threatened to ignite a war. Roosevelt did all he could to avoid conflict by "speaking softly and carrying a big stick," which in this case was the U.S. Great White Fleet of battleships that he sent round the globe in 1907–1908 with a stopover in Japan. This first crisis ended when Roosevelt negotiated the "Gentlemen's Agreement" with the Japanese government in 1908. By this act, the Japanese promised to prohibit the emigration of Japanese laborers to America.

Race hatred, at times bordering on hysteria, continued. The Hearst newspapers trumpeted a call to arms against the "Yellow Peril," and popular alarmist writers predicted Japanese troops charging ashore on the West Coast.[76] Tensions flared up for real again in March 1911, when U.S. troops and ships maneuvered on Mexico's border and coast in response to revolutionary turmoil there. *The New York Times* reported that many believed that this show of strength was really directed against a Japanese plan to secure naval bases in Mexico. Baron Uchida, the Japanese ambassador to Washington, felt compelled to issue a statement denying any such plan.[77]

Not yet at ease about the presence of Japanese newcomers, the California legislature continued on its racist course by making it illegal in 1913 for "aliens ineligible for citizenship" to own real property. In reaction, anti-American demonstrations broke out in Japan, and the Japanese government formally protested. The U.S. army and navy revisited their plans for war and advised that the president deploy the fleet to the West Coast.[78] President Woodrow Wilson did what he could to defuse the crisis, and once again the incident stopped short of fighting.

The bad times were not over yet; when the Japanese joined the struggle against Germany in World War I, Japan expected imperial gains. After forces of the Rising Sun seized the German Pacific colonies in China and the Pacific, the Japanese imposed an ultimatum on China, the Twenty-One Demands, in May 1915. The United States protested ineffectively. At the same time news broke that the Japanese battle cruiser *Asama* was off Baja California. Hearst papers sounded the alarm again.[79] Rumors spread concerning a secret alliance between Mexico and Japan. The commander of the Pacific Fleet requested more ships, while the U.S. cruiser *New Orleans* sailed to investigate.

Had war come in the tense decade 1905–1915, it might reasonably have been called a race war because overt racist language and legislation in American would have pushed Japan and the United States into taking up arms. However, after World War I, the governments of both countries followed a course guided by a determination to avoid the storms of war. It is true that one more racist law threatened to scuttle good relations in 1924. A U.S. immigration act passed that year essentially excluded all Japanese immigration. Once again crowds demonstrated and newspapers protested in Japan, but the Japanese government limited its response to some formal notes.[80]

The 1920s were the era of Shidehara Diplomacy, so-called after its guiding hand, Foreign Minister Kijuro Shidehara, who strongly desired good relations with the United States. The era began with an important set of accords between the great powers, including Japan. A series of agreements signed in Washington in 1921–1922, known collectively as the Washington System, redefined international relations in the Pacific and put limits on naval competition. The decade generally brought prosperity, peace, and improved relations. Japan enjoyed its most successful form of parliamentary government, Taisho Democracy, named after the Emperor Taisho, father of Hirohito. U.S.-Japan rivalry did not disappear, nor did all racial resentment dissipate, but they did not bring the adversaries to the brink of war.

However, relations between the United States and Japan became hostile again in the 1930s, although American racism did not cause the deterioration. The Depression hit Japan hard, and a shrinking world economy gave the Japanese fewer markets and options. Overpopulation, limited agricultural production, and scarcity of industrial raw materials became more oppressive. These problems perceived through the prism of Japanese nationalism, with its religious and racist sense of destiny, led many to see the answer to Japanese problems in expansion on the Asian mainland. This thrust would destroy the limiting and supportive system of the Washington System. Radical army officers were first to embrace an ultranationalist solution. At this point Japan maintained forces in Manchuria, the Kwantung army, to guard the Japanese-run railroads. In 1931 ultranationalist Kwantung officers staged an attack on a railroad near Mukden and blamed it on Chinese extremists. Claiming that the Japanese must defend their interests, the Kwantung army seized all of Manchuria, where they soon installed a puppet government. This seizure marked the beginning of what the Japanese call the Fifteen Year War, 1931–1945.

Japanese militarism inflicted casualties at home as well in China. In May 1932 ultranationalist army officers assassinated Prime Minister Inukai, and such acts of political terrorism continue through 1936, when young officers attempted a coup d'état in Tokyo, sacrificing other military and political leaders on their altar of Japanese grandeur.

The Japanese expanded their war in China. On 7 July 1937, Japanese troops in Beijing, where the Japanese had stationed some troops ever since the Boxer Rebellion, clashed with Chinese soldiers near the Marco Polo Bridge. Japan responded by undertaking a full-scale invasion. Estimates of Chinese deaths in the ensuing war range from 15,000,000 to 35,000,000.[81] Japanese forces advanced quickly beyond the Yellow River. An amphibious operation struck

Shanghai in August, and Chinese resistance finally collapsed there in November. Japanese forces now advanced on Nanking, which they reached in mid-December and committed an orgy of murder and rape.

The Japanese hardly expected a long war in China, but the Chinese refused to capitulate. Expanded and seemingly endless conflict in China made Japan's lack of natural resources, particularly oil, all the more apparent.

Faced with Japanese aggression, the United States initially did no more than issue self-righteous complaints. An increasingly isolated Japan paid little attention and sought allies elsewhere. Already in 1936 Japan had signed an anti-Comintern pact with Nazi Germany. Then Tokyo joined the seemingly invincible Germans, forming the Rome-Berlin-Tokyo Axis in September 1940. At this point, the Japanese began occupying the French colonial possession of Indochina.

Japanese alliance with Nazi Germany, the occupation of Indochina, and the implied threat to British and Dutch imperial holdings, which were also a source of raw materials for America, alarmed the U.S. government. President Franklin Delano Roosevelt resolved to protect British and Dutch holdings in Asia and edged America closer and closer to war with Japan. Finally, the United States impounded all Japanese assets in America in July 1941, and then put an embargo on vital oil shipments to Japan in September.

As early as July 1941, the Japanese cabinet resolved to strike south for needed resources, particularly the oil and rubber of the Dutch East Indies. Establishment of the Greater East Asia Co-Prosperity Sphere would solve the Japanese resource crisis and realize the anti-colonial rhetoric of the ultranationalists, if the United States refused to reach an accommodation.[82] A government shift elevated General Tojo as prime minister in October. Americans read this as the militarization of the government, but many in Japan welcomed Tojo as someone loyal to the emperor who could restrain the all-powerful army. This new cabinet soon decided to attack the United States at Pearl Harbor and in the Philippines if Washington did not concede Japanese Asian hegemony by 25 November.[83]

This final crisis was not about race, although the outbreak of war reinvigorated American domestic racism. The consummate insult to the Japanese-American community came in the spring of 1942, when Japanese-Americans on the West Coast found themselves rounded up and shipped off to relocation camps. Authorities regarded as dangerous those Japanese-Americans living in Military District 1, a band of territory running from Washington state to Arizona on the Pacific Coast and the border with Mexico. The commander of the district, General John L. De Witt, wanted all those of Japanese ancestry out; "A Jap's a Jap," he proclaimed.[84] Against the counsel of J. Edgar Hoover, who told him that all the Japanese, Germans, and Italians worth worrying about were already in custody, President Franklin D. Roosevelt signed Executive Order 9066 in February 1942.[85] The War Relocation Authority constructed ten relocation camps and took in 110,000 Japanese-American detainees, in violation of their constitutional rights.[86]

In 1942 an international crisis brought on a monumental act of prejudice, but it was not American racism that brought on the war itself. This reversed the previous relationship between cause and effect, for it was American prejudice that precipitated international crises in 1906–1907 and 1913.

Strategy and Doctrine

Proponents of explaining the Pacific War in terms of race do not concern themselves with the technical aspects of American strategy and doctrine, with the exception of the bombing of Japanese cities. They make no claim that racism influenced such detailed military matters, but this need not be a given. In fact, a case can be made that racial stereotyping by the Japanese shaped their strategy and doctrine against the United States. Most fundamentally, the Japanese believed Americans to be soft, self-indulgent, and incapable of serious sacrifice; therefore, Americans would tire and withdraw from a contest with the far tougher and committed Japanese.[87] In what ranks as a monumental misperception, just before the battle of Midway, Mitsuo Fuchida, the air commander of the raid on Pearl Harbor and again to command at Midway, wrote a report dismissing the Americans as lacking the will to fight.[88] Without this prejudiced and fatally incorrect conviction, Japanese war plans did not make sense, since Tokyo always realized that the advantages of numbers in manpower and materiel always rested with the United States.

This certainty of spiritual superiority also led to doctrinal miscalculations. The Japanese did not alter their convictions even after being badly beaten by Soviet forces at Nomonhan in 1939. Instead, the army further stressed spirit in lieu of retraining on a Western model.[89] The Japanese paid a great price at Guadalcanal and elsewhere by grossly underestimating the fighting stamina of U.S. troops because of unrealistic racial/cultural stereotypes. This failing was particularly disastrous in submarine warfare. As historian Ronald Spector explains, "The Japanese thought that American submarines were inferior to theirs and that American sailors were too soft and luxury-loving to stand the rigors of undersea warfare."[90] One effect of this misperception was that the Japanese gave inadequate attention to anti-submarine warfare, at tremendous cost to them.

Therefore it is not beside the point to ask if racism played a role in defining American strategy and doctrine. Should we find evidence there, we might conclude that the conflict was, indeed, a race war. But the evidence does not exist. When war broke out, the United States applied a strategic blueprint that it had been drafting for over three decades. These plans were not dictated by racial bigotry but by geographical and technological imperatives. The same can be said for crucial elements of doctrine.

The U.S. navy outlined its first plans for a war with Japan during the crisis of 1906; Theodore Roosevelt asked the navy if it had studied the possibility of war with Japan, and the answer was a sketchy and partial Plan Orange.[91] In the nomenclature of U.S. "color plans," orange stood for Japan. The plan went through a number of permutations over time, but certain constants endured. It aimed at protecting U.S. interests in the Pacific, although it nearly always assumed that America would lose the Philippines early in the war and be forced to drive across the Pacific to reconquer them.

From the start, the United States planned to take on Japan in a naval campaign rather than committing to a great and costly land war in Asia. Geography dictated island-hopping operations across the central Pacific from the West Coast or Hawaii to the Philippines, which the plan assumed America would lose early in the struggle. The cruising range of warships and the need to secure sea lanes from enemy attack made it necessary for the navy to secure harbors along the way and deny them to the enemy. All this would require seizing islands under enemy control. When the fleet reached the Philippines in strength, it would begin the final phase of the plan, closing the ring around the Japanese home islands. Once again the United States would advance by taking islands, with Okinawa inevitably on the list. However, Plan Orange did not prescribe an actual invasion of the home islands, because this would be too costly. Instead, American forces would wear down Japan by naval blockade and, after 1928, by aerial bombardment. Over the years, planners extended the time frame of Plan Orange; pre-1914 scenarios predicted success in six to twelve months, but in the 1930s this had increased to three or four years. The goal, however, was always the same—total victory.

Plan Orange assumed a one-on-one contest between the United States and Japan, but after the outbreak of war on the European continent in 1939, it was clear that should the titanic struggle engulf the United States, it would enter the conflict as part of an alliance locked in combat with multiple enemies. Thus in 1940, the United States formally shelved the old "color plans" in favor of new Rainbow plans. However, the outline of Plan Orange survived in the Pacific under the name Rainbow 5, since geography and the old political assumptions remained regarding the Pacific.

The only contributor not dealt with by Plan Orange before 1940 was Australia, and the most significant early difference between Plan Orange and actual operations was the addition of a second axis of advance under Douglas MacArthur in New Guinea. In a later divergence from Plan Orange, George Marshall and the Combined Chiefs of Staff concluded in July 1944 that blockade and bombardment would not suffice to defeat Japan, and an invasion would be necessary.[92] Absolute victory, now expressed in the words "unconditional surrender" of Japan, remained the goal.

Over the decades, military doctrines and tactics were developed to carry out Plan Orange. Of all forms of combat studied and practiced before the attack on Pearl Harbor, amphibious warfare was most specifically designed to deal with a Japanese foe in the Pacific. As such, it is worth at least a glance to see if the race thesis plays out at all in this critical military preparation for war with Japan.

The necessity for the Marines to master amphibious operations arose, like Plan Orange itself, as a consequence of the imperial acquisitions of the United States in the Pacific. Defense of the U.S. Pacific empire would require a chain of naval bases, but the islands America held west of Hawaii were insufficient for such purposes. Therefore, from the first, U.S. planners realized that their forces must be able to establish temporary bases by seizing islands and building facilities during a conflict. These were known as advanced bases. The Marine Corps was fully engaged with the advanced base mission in Plan Orange even before the United States entered World War I.

Soon after John Lejeune rose to the post of commandant of the Marine Corps in the summer of 1920, he turned his attention to the potential conduct of operations against Japan, which had gained new island possessions during the war. He charged an intellectually brilliant but personally flawed officer, Earl "Pete" Ellis, with studying the problems implicit in the advanced base role of the Marines and proposing a plan of campaign. Going into monastic seclusion at Marine Corps Headquarters, Ellis produced a fundamental document, "Advanced Base Force Operations in Micronesia." Although much would change in the technology of landing operations in the next twenty

years, Ellis worked out a tentative method and sequence for landings and propounded certain basic doctrinal statements, concluding, for example, that
"the landing will entirely succeed or fail practically on the beach."[93] On 23 July
1921, Lejeune accepted Ellis's work as Operational Plan 712. Armed with a mission and aspects of doctrine, the Marine Corps tested the techniques of
amphibious operations, first in the early 1920s and then in landing exercises
that took place every year from 1935 to 1941.

Many important details remained to be ironed out, but the Marine Corps
had guessed right and prepared for the kind of fighting that awaited it on
Pacific islands. The preparation of the peacetime Corps is one of the great success stories of prewar planning and training, but it had little to do with defining the enemy as specifically Japanese. No derogatory assumptions about the
Japanese influenced these plans. It is true that Americans made some mistakes
that can be ascribed to racial stereotyping, such as dismissing the quality of
Japanese aircraft before the rude awakening, but these were peripheral to the
prosecution of the war.

American race hatred for the Japanese tells us only a bit about the cause of
the Pacific War and almost nothing about the way in which the United States
intended to fight it, as witnessed by strategy and doctrine. However, it is fair
to say that the primary proponents of a race thesis would probably not disagree too much with these conclusions. They generally look elsewhere to discover the role of racism: to combat motivation and to conduct the bombing
offensive against Japan, climaxing in the use of atomic weapons. The remain-
der of this chapter will deal with those two important matters.

Race Hatred, Military Culture, and Combat Motivation

It seems logical, even instinctual, to conclude that troops are more ferocious
in using deadly force if they hate their enemies. Such a conclusion would lead
one to believe that American racism drove U.S. soldiers, sailors, and Marines
in combat during the Pacific War. When Ronald Takaki charges that the fighting in the Pacific was "powered by mutual hatreds and stereotyping," he is
insisting that these hatreds moved men.[94] Is it then fair to assume that racism
served as a fundamental element of U.S. combat motivation against the
Japanese? Takaki and Dower more imply than prove that it did. Cameron supplies such a convoluted and speculative treatment of motivation in the 1st
Marine Division that it is at times hard to know exactly what he is saying. But

their verdict remains that racism was an important factor in "powering" the fighting.

Combat, however, is not like a feud against a known and familiar foe. A good deal of research suggests that most Americans in combat fought *for* and *with* their comrades rather than *against* their enemies. In fact, there is little evidence to demonstrate that combat effectiveness under fire improves with strong hatred. Let us return to the very nature of racism, see how this reflect-ed contrasting military cultures, then consider how that contrast affected American troops, and finally confront combat motivation.

Racism at the Front

Pacific War racism involved a great deal more than a matter of skin color and eye shape; it focused on cultural stereotypes. Of course, ultimately that is what racism is about—the attaching of derogatory stereotypes to a people of com-mon physical characteristics or ethnicity. Almost inevitably, the racist feels that his or her race, as defined by that individual, enjoys superiority over oth-ers. Racism allows little room for individuality, because the individual becomes a representative member of a group and fully guilty of its condemned traits. Linking those cultural traits with blood, racism believes the flaws to be essentially immutable because they are determined by biology.

Americans denigrated the Japanese not simply because they were Asians but because they were believed to think and act in ways that Americans saw as incomprehensible or barbaric. After all, the United States claimed other Asian peoples as allies, such as the Chinese and the Filipinos. Despite refer-ences to the "Yellow Peril" in earlier years, the immediate enemy in the Pacific was not simply yellow, but Japanese.

Racism also connotes unjustified attitudes on the part of the racist, who may be driven by irrational hatred to commit unreasonable acts. Popular con-demnation of racism charges that stereotypes ascribed to race have little if any basis in fact, that they are only imagined. But the perception of difference in military culture and behavior in the Pacific had real foundation. Moreover, actions in the Pacific were not simply a product of unprovoked racial hysteria but inspired by an understandable desire to survive on a vicious battlefield and a very regrettable, but perhaps inevitable, drive to exact retribution for bar-barous acts against one's own comrades in a perverted sense of justice. Certainly acts of self-defense and retaliation were "racialized" in that they were directed against "Japs," but not all were irrational, particularly the reluctance to take prisoners. Fighting in the Pacific witnessed a true clash of military cultures that was racialized in virulent terms because both adversaries already tended to see things in terms of race.

What Did the Japanese Do and What Did Americans Think They Did?

It is worth asking what the Japanese actually did and what U.S. troops thought them guilty of. Abominable behavior of Japanese troops toward the Chinese would not have been part of the immediate experience of U.S. troops fighting in the Pacific. They would not have known first hand of killing and rape of a friendly population until they reached the Philippines. However, they were told of such abuses by magazines and newspapers even before Pearl Harbor. *Life* ran images of the war in China, including a famous photo of a burned and abandoned Chinese baby in a bombed-out Shanghai railroad station. A story on the "Rape of Nanking" in early 1938 emphasized the fate of prisoners of war. "Suspected [Chinese] soldiers were executed in droves. In one building . . . 400 men were tied together and marched off to be shot." Swords and bayonets were, and were known to be, means of execution. One unforgettable photo in the Nanking story showed a bloody, decapitated Chinese head, with the caption, "Chinese head, whose owner was incorrigibly anti-Japanese, was wedged in a barbed-wire barricade outside Nanking."[95]

Of course, U.S. public opinion regarded the Japanese attack against Pearl Harbor on 7 December 1941 as an unforgettable and unforgivable act of treachery—"a date which will live in infamy," in the words of President Roosevelt. That "stab in the back" alone would inspire hate and resentment. But there would be more, much more.

There is no question that the Japanese abused and butchered prisoners of war and that Americans believed that they did. A *Life* article published in January 1942 charged that the Japanese troops "are absolutely convinced that they are right and their prisoners are beneath contempt. They burn prisoners alive, rape and disembowel captive women, pillage and slaughter as though an atrocity were the most natural thing in the world."[96] The most infamous crime against Americans under Japanese captivity was the Bataan Death March, an ordeal that killed as many as 24,000 Americans and Filipinos. Although the death march took place in the spring of 1942, it did not become common knowledge until the publication of a U.S. government report in January of

1944. *Life* ran a story about U.S. prisoners in the Philippines in February. It told how, "We were to see Americans tied up and tortured in full view of the prison camp, beaten and battered until they were no longer recognizable as human, before they were finally removed for execution without trial."[97] Early 1944 may have been well along in the war, but still before the U.S. campaigns on Saipan, the Philippines, Iwo Jima, and Okinawa. In fact, the Japanese showed themselves particularly ruthless if they believed prisoners might be liberated. On the Gilbert Islands, one commander beheaded twenty-two American prisoners; at Ballale ninety were bayoneted; at Wake ninety-six were machine-gunned; and at Palawan 150 were jammed into an air raid shelter doused with gasoline and ignited.[98] On Formosa, a Japanese headquarters journal detailed "extreme measures" to be taken: "In any case, it is the aim not to allow the escape of a single one, to annihilate them all, and not to leave any traces."[99]

Japanese were also known to mutilate the dead, and, in fact, were charged with cannibalism. There are numerous sworn reports of Australian and American bodies found carved up during the fighting in New Guinea. Private First Class E. H., for example, was found on 25 January, 1943. According to the records his "abdomen had been opened by two criss-cross slashes. Flesh had been removed from the thighs and buttocks."[100] Such verified reports of mutilated comrades can only have infuriated troops in the field.

Perhaps the most common criminal abuses of the Japanese as perceived by Americans involved feigned surrenders that resulted in death or injury to Americans. Belief that the Japanese were guilty of such treachery would understandably lead Americans to deny to Japanese who might have wanted to surrender the right to do so; thus, the implications are great. The first Marine offensive against Japanese troops on the ground on Guadalcanal provided "proof" of Japanese deceit and brutality. On the night of 12 August 1942, Japanese infantry wiped out a patrol of twenty-five men led by Lt. Col. Frank Goettge. Marines believed that this patrol had been lured to its destruction by a Japanese prisoner who promised that his comrades were ready to surrender. A later investigation contested the story of treachery, but that was too late; Marines had already accepted the tale.[101] The incident provoked a strong reaction among Marines: "This was the first mass killing of Marines on Guadalcanal. We were shocked. Shocked . . . because headquarters had believed anything a Jap had to say. . . . The loss of this patrol and the particularly cruel way in which they had met death, hardened our hearts toward the Japanese. The idea of taking prisoners was swept from our minds. It was too dangerous."[102] This last quote suggests that the perception of Japanese treachery against the Goettge patrol grew out of existing racist contempt for the Japanese, but once the tale became "fact," it fueled even harsher hatred for the enemy.

Reports of treacherous surrenders were certainly not limited to this one important, but questionable, instance. Samuel Eliot Morison, the famous historian of the naval war in the Pacific, wrote: "There were innumerable incidents such as a wounded Japanese soldier at Guadalcanal seizing a scalpel and burying it in the back of a surgeon who was about to save his life by an operation; and a survivor of the Battle of Vella Lavella, rescued by PT-163, pulling a gun and killing a bluejacket in the act of giving the Japanese sailor a cup of coffee."[103] Two Marine veterans of Iwo Jima told cautionary tales. One confided, "They always told you take prisoners but we had some bad experiences on Saipan taking prisoners, you take them and then as soon as they get behind the lines they drop grenades and you lose a few more people. You get a little bit leery of taking prisoners when they are fighting to the death and so are you." The other reported, "Very few of them came out on their own; when they did, why, usually one in the front he'd come out with his hands up and one behind him, he'd come out with a grenade."[104]

Given the facts that the Japanese committed atrocities and that Americans believed that they did, the actions of U.S. soldiers, sailors, and Marines can be better understood, although this does not excuse senseless barbarism. Some months after Pearl Harbor, Bull Halsey warned the Japanese: "We have good evidence of your atrocities and know where they were perpetrated. They'll be properly repaid!"[105] A Marine, Frank O. Hough, put it almost poetically:

[The Japanese] did possess at the outset one great advantage: complete lack of inhibiting battle ethics, as defined by modern civilization and the precepts of the Geneva Convention. . . . Nothing delighted him more than killing our wounded lying helpless. . . . What we did not realize at the outset was that we were fighting what was essentially a medieval nation, with the medieval conception of total war, total destruction. . . . once they showed us the way, there was nothing for it but to play the game as they wanted it played.[106]

Is it any wonder that officers might warn their soldiers against taking prisoners? Before Tarawa, one address to the troops cautioned, "And let me repeat again what the general said. If you have to run any chances whatsoever to get a prisoner, then don't get him!"[107]

But perhaps the most fearsome transgression of the Japanese against American standards of military conduct was not atrocity, but the Japanese conviction to fight to the death. Japanese soldiers who refused to surrender imposed their own principles of combat on their American foes, even though such fanatical dedication lay outside the American concept of duty. Surrender is a release, not only for the individual who surrenders but for his captor. The fighting is over, we will both survive, for now. The Japanese military culture denied that respite to the American GI or Marine. As one Marine testified:

> It was always taught to hate them in the Marine Corps, to detest them, and that they were animals, we were the men, they were the animals. By the same token, we were taught that they would die for the emperor, and we weren't taught to die for our president. And to fight or to come against an individual who wants to die or doesn't care about dying is a tough thing to combat in your mind. We wanted to live, we wanted to kill him, but we wanted to survive.[108]

The Japanese soldier trapped in a cave who refused to surrender forced his American enemy to take the risk of burning or blasting him out, or, far worse, of going in after him. The American was caught in a life-and-death struggle he did not want.

Western militaries considered surrender an acceptable recourse in difficult situations. The taking of aristocratic prisoners was fundamental to chivalric warfare; although a prisoner may have been bested in combat or trapped in an irretrievable situation, surrender did not dishonor him. Europeans developed elaborate codes for the treatment of surrendered troops during the early modern period. Some kinds of surrender could amount to a calculated military policy. A garrison that surrendered its fortress quickly enough could bargain to gain the right to march out to rejoin their own forces in the field. In such a case, surrender could be used to maintain the size of armies. Even in the West, governments and commanders issued fight-to-the-last-man orders, as was the case with Hitler and Stalin in their great ideological/racial struggle. However, Western troops normally followed a tradition of honorable surrender.

There was a consciousness among American troops that the Japanese fought by a different set of rules, that they had an essentially alien military culture, although the young and hardened Marines in the field would not have used that terminology.

Japanese Military Culture

Japanese military culture did, indeed, differ sharply from the American. At the summit of the Japanese martial code stood loyalty to the emperor. This was a societal, not simply a military, standard, reinforced by the state's emphasis upon the Shinto religion, a creed seen as uniquely Japanese and that gave the emperor divine status. Within the armed forces, loyalty was reflected in obedience. Military manuals and regulations repeated phrases like "absolute obedience to superiors."[109] For officers, obedience was a very nuanced concept, because it allowed *gekukojo,* a kind of moral autonomy among the middling ranks of officers that justified independence or disobedience in the name of a higher morality. Thus, officers might adopt rogue or rebellious courses of action so long as the officers were motivated by high principle. Firmly believing that they were acting in the best interests of the emperor and the empire, soldiers assassinated political and military leaders in Japan and precipitated war in Manchuria and China during the 1930s.

However, for the vast majority of men in the armed forces, lower officers and men in the ranks, obedience and discipline meant harsh physical treatment. Even when conforming to orders, superiors regularly hit their subordinates, a practice called *bentasu,* defined by historian Yuki Tenaka as "the routine striking and bashing of soldiers." The navy had its own disciplinary policies known as *tekken seisai* (the iron fist) and *ai-no-muchi* (the whip of love).[110]

Harsh discipline, however, did not mean an army of uninspired automatons; to the contrary, Japanese doctrine stressed spirit, particularly "the spirit of attack."[111] It is not uncommon for a military that is conscious of a material disadvantage to emphasize its moral or psychological advantage, but the Japanese did so to excess. It was entirely in character for Foreign Minister Shigemitsu to reassure the Japanese Diet in early 1944:

> What America and Britain rely on most is their material strength. The importance of material strength in war cannot be denied. But is it a factor that decides the ultimate outcome of a war? . . . Our assurance of victory is based neither on number nor volume, nor on geographical advantage. It is born of the exuberant fighting spirit and the complete unity of the nation.[112]

A perversion of the traditional Japanese code of the warrior, *bushido,* called upon the Japanese soldier to treat his own life with disregard, to despise surrender, and to embrace suicide. Originally *bushido* was a chivalric code that incorporated humanity, modesty, and consideration, as well as bravery and prowess, but Japanese military culture from the end of World War I through World War II stripped it down to a few deadly virtues. The soldier was to sacrifice his life willingly, a principle taught from an early age in school curricula. An elementary school reader published in 1904 contained a story in which son and father talk. After the son declares, "I'll be trained and when war comes, I will not be afraid to die," the father responds, "Don't be afraid to die. . . . And you must be faithful to the Imperial Precepts to Soldiers and Sailors." Another text from the more liberal 1920s has a mother admonishing her son who did not participate in a battle: "Your life is to be offered up to requite your obligation to our benevolent Emperor."[113] A hit song of 1932, "Marching in Pursuit of Bandits," ends:

> If it must be, so be it—
> I am a fighting man of the land of the rising sun:
> I have little regret to have my corpse decay in the grass.[114]

Soldiers were to find reward in death; when necessary, they were to achieve *gyokusai,* or glorious self-annihilation. To be sure, many armies have employed phases like "Death Before Dishonor" or "Death or Glory" as mottoes, but the Japanese took this idea to its extreme.[115] Again, this aspect of military culture penetrated society as a whole. A particularly disturbing example comes from the recollections of Besho Makiko, who as a little girl put notes in small packages her family sent to troops at the front. A typical one read, "Please fight well and die a glorious death."[116]

Surrender was unacceptable. The 1941 Field Service Code commanded: "Do not be taken prisoner alive." A commentary designed to make the code more understandable told the story of Major Kuga, who, while fighting in Shanghai in the 1930s, was wounded, fell unconscious, and was taken prisoner by the Chinese. After his release he committed suicide to atone for becoming a prisoner. The example concluded, "This act typifies the glorious spirit of the Imperial Army." The 1908 military criminal code declared that commanders who surrendered their units "without fighting to the last man" would be executed.[117]

Suicide to avoid being taken alive was mandatory, and accounts of Japanese soldiers committing suicide with rifles or grenades during the war are legion. Better yet was the suicide attack when troops could no longer resist effectively, such as the hopeless mass banzai charges on Saipan. This tendency for suicide in battle was epitomized in the kamikaze pilots.

Viewed in the context of this military culture, what at first may seem senseless acts of cruelty appear more like distorted extensions of the Japanese warrior code, their military culture. Soldiers were beaten by their own superiors, so why should these same soldiers not abuse enemy civilians and prisoners of war under their authority? Imperial troops despised surrender per se, so why should they not denigrate enemies who surrendered? Japanese soldiers showed scant regard for their own lives in battle, so why should they hold those of their prisoners sacrosanct? Intent on dying a meaningful death, why not try to kill as many of the enemy as possible in a last suicidal act, even attacking would-be caregivers or using the ruse of surrender to kill enemy troops?[118]

Living Up to the Code

Japanese repeatedly lived up to their demanding code. Garrisons demonstrated their willingness to die rather than surrender, producing casualty rates that bore no relationship to those known in the West. Imperial soldiers achieved their goal of death before dishonor in a way that shocked Americans. At Tarawa in November 1943, only eight Japanese survived from a force of 2,571; at Roi-Namur in February 1944, fifty-one were captured out of some 3,500 defenders; and on Kwajalein, again in February, Marines took seventy-nine Japanese prisoners from among the 4,938 defenders.[119] These are fatality, not casualty, rates of 98 percent and more. Compare this with the surrender of 130,000 British and empire troops at Singapore or 76,000 Americans and Filipinos at Bataan in 1942. There is no question that U.S. Marines shot prisoners, but if U.S. behavior bears responsibility for these high death rates among Japanese troops, there would have to have been repeated mass slaughters of captives, and these did not occur. Shooting those who were willing to give up or had already surrendered did not encourage capitulation, but U.S. atrocities simply cannot explain the proportion of Japanese troops who refused to outlive defeat. It was a matter of Japanese honor not American atrocity.

Japanese suicidal resolve awed and dumbfounded Western military observers. Marine General Alexander Archer Vandegrift reported: "I have never heard or read of this kind of fighting. These people refuse to surrender. The wounded wait until men come up to examine them . . . and blow themselves and the other fellow to pieces with a hand grenade."[120]

The kamikaze offensives that began in the fall of 1944 struck the Americans with renewed awe and fear. In the waters around Okinawa during the spring of 1945, Japanese suicide pilots inflicted the greatest damage that the U.S. fleet suffered during the entire war, sinking thirty ships and damaging 223, many so badly that they never saw action again. Among their victims were eleven aircraft carriers, and although none sunk, several, including *Bunker Hill, Franklin, Enterprise,* and the new *Yorktown,* sustained severe damage and left the fleet. Kamikaze planes were essentially cruise missiles with human guidance systems. By World War II standards, the kamikazes were extremely deadly. Nearly 5,000 sailors perished off Okinawa, a figure disturbingly close to the 7,000 American soldiers and Marines killed in ground combat on the island. Suicide raids were not limited to aircraft; the greatest battleship in the Japanese navy, the *Yamato,* made a suicide run against the American fleet as part of a "naval special attack force," only to be sunk by U.S. carrier-borne aircraft.

Behaviors Outside the U.S. Discourse on War

While American troops stated it crudely, they clearly recognized the difference between their own concepts of war, combat, and soldierly ethics and those held by their Japanese foes. In the language of this volume, both Americans and Japanese recognized that each embraced a discourse on war sharply different than the other. Japanese brutality in war can be seen as a product or perverse extension of their own discourse; American excesses resulted not from the logic of their own discourse, but from a rejection of it, at least in regard to enemy prisoners, the wounded, and the dead. The conduct of the Japanese was so alien to Americans that they could not comprehend it; it was not at all war as it was supposed to be. Rejection of the Japanese as true soldiers and what they did as "real war" led Americans to form a different, an alternative, discourse on war, free of all conventions and restraints at least as regards the treatment of Japanese combatants. The result was what I have termed an "extreme reality," in this case war without restraint or compassion toward enemy fighting men. In more acceptable circumstances, American troops would have conformed to the conventions regarding the taking and treatment of prisoners, the care of enemy wounded, and the respect of enemy dead.

In the extreme reality that they accepted, and guided now by a vicious alternative discourse, American troops cast aside conventions and believed themselves justified in doing so.

In an important sense, U.S. troops came to see enemy combatants as something other than human and to regard American inhumanity on the battlefield as required by the logic of survival and justice. To Americans, the Japanese were, indeed, unspeakable bastards, and Americans racialized the language of their contempt and fear, making the Japanese "yellow bastards." It was not their color, however, but their actions and American beliefs about their actions, that explains racist acts committed by U.S. men in the field against the Japanese.

We should also distinguish between the kinds of abuses, or atrocities, committed by Americans in the field. Refusal to take prisoners can be seen as an act of survival in a fight to the death that Americans did not choose. Japanese generally refused to surrender—its own special threat—and when some Japanese did show a white flag, Americans feared this to be a ruse designed to kill Americans. A kind of deadly logic justified the reluctance to take prisoners, but the same logic did not apply to other atrocities. Shooting prisoners already taken, abusing the wounded, and maiming the dead were acts of brutal retribution, of real barbarity. Such cruelty was not about combat, because it was inflicted upon individuals entirely removed from the act of fighting. Still, reluctance to take prisoners and other atrocities shared something in common: They were attributes of an extreme reality of war, war without limits and without mercy. It is also worth noting for comparison that Americans were, in fact, also capable of abuses against enemies they did not see in racist terms. Dower argues that "It is virtually inconceivable, however, that teeth, ears, and skulls could have been collected from German or Italian war dead and publicized in the Anglo-American countries without provoking an uproar; and in this we have yet another inkling of the racial dimensions of the war."[121] Concerning the publicizing of souvenirs, he is certainly right, but not concerning the taking of bodily souvenirs. One private who jumped into Normandy with the 82nd Airborne Division reported: "We had all been issued yellow horsehide gloves. This fellow had on red gloves, and I asked him where he got the red gloves from, and he reached down in his jumppants and pulled out a whole string of ears. He had been ear-hunting all night and had sewed them on an old bootlace."[122] Certainly, it is hard to believe that such conduct was common, but it did occur. Americans also shot prisoners; one such incident was presented to the American TV audience in the series *Band of Brothers,* when a trooper of the 101st Airborne tommy-gunned captured Germans. Robert Rush, studying the horrendous fight in the Hürtgen Forest in November and December 1944, discovered that both sides, unable to deal with prisoners in the confused and desperate fighting, shot them. One veteran of the U.S. 22nd Infantry Regiment explained: "What are you going to do with prisoners? If you try to take them back you're taking your life in hand twice. . . . So a lot of them never reached the rear that way."[123] The issue is not that U.S. troops went against convention only in the Pacific, but that they did it with so much greater frequency that it was a qualitatively different phenomenon.

MOTIVATION IN COMBAT

It is a big step from the world of atrocity to the world of combat; what led a Marine to mutilate a dead Japanese soldier was not what inspired the same Marine to storm an enemy position in the extraordinarily tough environment of island warfare. The literature on combat motivation is quite extensive, and by now it breaks down into three different, but not necessarily incompatible, approaches. The first stresses the strong bonds formed between men in small units; this is primary group motivation. The second argues that when units suffer heavy casualties and incur a high turnover in personnel, the old small groups disintegrate, and men must agree to work together to accomplish the task at hand in a given situation, giving rise to situational motivation. The third argues that when small group bonds decay in certain highly ideological armies, shared ideas of purpose in oneself or contempt for the enemy can hold men to their tasks, or ideological motivation.

Studies coming out of the experience of World War II stressed the role of bonds formed between individual soldiers in the confines of small units, such as squads or platoons, which sociologists termed primary groups.[124] Within the primary groups, individuals support each other physically and psychologically. In most circumstances, soldiers bond and come to see each other in almost familial terms. "We few, we happy few, we band of brothers." The primary group exerts its own force and serves as a conduit for values and standards; in other words, the individuals in the primary group hold each other up to certain codes of conduct and performance. It takes some time to form these essential bonds and for newcomers to a group to win the confidence, and thus the sense of obligation, of the other members of the primary group.

Discussions of primary group motivation have more to do with positive characteristics—concern for comrades, desire for respect, acceptance of responsibility—than they do with baser matters of hate and viciousness. In his classic study of American troops in combat during World War II, S. L. A. Marshall answered the question of why men fight bravely in the following terms:

> The only answer which comes to me as supportable in all that I have seen of man on the battlefield is that he is persuaded largely by the same things which induce him to face life bravely—friendship, loyalty to responsibility, and knowledge that he is a repository of the faith and confidence of others.[125]

In this context of responsibility to one's comrades, hatred can play a dangerously negative role if it inspires an individual to take unnecessary and ill-considered actions that expose his comrades to death or injury. Nearly all militaries praise the ability to keep a cool head in battle.

At times the literature on group cohesion has equated it directly with effectiveness—if a unit possesses combat cohesion, it must perform well in combat. This is excessive, because units can be cohesive and still fail due to other factors. In studying Arab armies after World War II, Ken Pollack concludes that Arab troops were indeed cohesive but were ineffective in combat because of poor leadership that lacked initiative.[126] Cohesion may not guarantee success, but does lack of small-unit cohesion lead to defeat?

Robert Rush argues that devotion to task can be more of a factor than buddy-bonding in units that are heavily engaged. He reaches this conclusion in his study of the 22nd Infantry Regiment in the Hürtgen Forest, 16 November to 4 December 1944.[127] Although this battle lasted only eighteen days, it was so intense that the regiment suffered 2,803 killed, wounded, and missing, that is 87 percent of its strength on the first day, 3,210 men. In order to keep the regiment in the field, it received 1,645 replacements during the fighting.[128] With such losses and replacements the primary groups within the regiment dissolved and there was no time to reconstitute the group bonds considered so vital in combat. His micro-history of this one unit suggests that group effectiveness quickly came to depend on the soldiers' shared sense of task and situation—their desires to defeat the Germans and end the war . . . and to survive. These feelings were strong enough to make the units work as long as veteran junior leaders remained. Rush does not deny the power of primary group bonds; in fact he feels that bonding and confidence between junior leaders is always important. He argues only that bonding cannot explain combat effectiveness among the rank and file in units that suffer heavy casualties and receive numerous replacements in prolonged combat.

Omar Bartov, whose work influenced Rush, studied a very different army, the Nazi Wehrmacht on the eastern front.[129] The German army traditionally emphasized and tried to maintain the identity and integrity of primary groups in its recruitment, training, and replacement policies. And the German forces that swept across Poland, the Low Countries, and France, 1939–1940, kept this pattern. The staggering losses suffered during the invasion of Russia in 1941, however, and the continued drain after that made it impossible for the Germans to continue their preferred policies. High casualties and the influx of replacements eroded primary groups and the bonds they engendered between men. In this situation, the intense ideological message of the Nazi Party, with its doctrines of German superiority, racial hatred for Jews, gypsies, and Slavs, and anti-Bolshevism, gave German troops something around which to rally. The Germans also buttressed ideology with deadly discipline; the Wehrmacht executed 15,000 troops for desertion and other infractions. This provided a kind of negative incentive.

Someone wishing to argue that American racism toward the Japanese provided the impetus for American combat cohesion and effectiveness in the Pacific might well appeal to Bartov, but there are good counterarguments. First, Bartov deals with an army from a heavily indoctrinated society and army, which heavily propagandized the troops to ensure ideological dedication. American troops were never receptive to concentrated ideological indoctrination. Second, German discipline was severe, if not oppressive. In contrast to the German record, the U.S. army only executed a single soldier for cowardice in Europe, Eddie Slovik.

Third, to argue that racial hatred explains the strong performance of U.S. forces in World War II creates a particular bind, because Americans fought hard in Europe as well as in the Pacific. While U.S. troops in the Pacific racially villainized their Japanese enemies, those Americans deployed to Europe did not harbor ethnic hatred against the Germans. But then what was the consequence of this difference in motivations? Were the Marines and soldiers who landed on Saipan in June 1944 any more dedicated or effective than the soldiers who stormed the beaches of Normandy on the other side of the world at the same time? The answer to this question is no; therefore we should question how much the racist component of the experience of war in the Pacific can tell us about combat motivation.

Fourth, there are reasons to see primary group and situational motivation at work. Examination of combat in the Pacific and the testimony of participants bolsters the notion of primary group cohesion among American forces, although this was most likely supplemented and at times replaced by situational cohesion in longer campaigns. Of course, no island campaigns equaled the sustained combat and slaughter of the Eastern Front; for the U.S. Marines, Guadalcanal came closest, with the 1st Marine Division landing in August of 1942 and being relieved in December. But it is important to remember that Rush's example concerned a fight of only eighteen days. Guadalcanal, New Guinea, and Okinawa almost certainly corresponded in a large degree with his paradigm, although only detailed studies such as his could establish that. Among the island hopping of the Central Pacific, Saipan (28 days), Guam (20 days), Pelileu (32 days), and Iwo Jima (26 days) all lasted as long as or longer than Hürtgen Forest. In any case, heavy fighting in the majority of the Central Pacific campaigns was of short duration, as at Makin (four days), Tarawa (five days), Kwajelein (ten days), Eniwetok (ten days), and Tinian (eight days). Troops withdrew, replenished, and retrained between island campaigns, giving them time to re-form groups and bonds even after heavy fighting.

Studies of Americans in combat during World War II indicate that the vast majority of troops found the reason to fight in their own comrades and cause, not in hate for the enemy.[130] William Manchester, a Marine in the Pacific, offers anecdotes from his personal experience of war that lead us to question the necessity of racial hatred for killing and to stress devotion to the primary group. His disturbing account of the first time he killed a Japanese soldier shows that he certainly did not kill with any delight.

> There was a door . . . which meant there was another room, which meant the sniper was in there . . . I smashed into the other room and saw him as a blur to my right. . . . His . . . rifle was strapped on in a sniper's harness, and . . . the harness sling had trapped him. . . . My first shot had missed him . . . but the second caught him dead-on. . . . I kept firing. . . . Then I began to tremble, and next to shake, all over. I sobbed, in a voice still grainy with fear: "I'm sorry." Then I threw up all over myself.[131]

Manchester also supplies the most eloquent statement of the affection and responsibility that compelled men in combat on Okinawa. He had been hit early, receiving that "million-dollar wound, the dream of every infantryman," and had been moved back to a field hospital. However, he deserted the hospital to return to his unit, where he was wounded very seriously before long.[132] He later described what had driven him back to the front:

> I understand, at last, why I jumped hospital . . . in violation of orders, returned to the front and almost certain death.
>
> It was an act of love. Those men on the line were my family, my home. They were closer to me than I can say, closer than any friends had been or ever would be. They had never let me down, and I couldn't do it to them. I had to be with them, rather than let them die and me live with the knowledge that I might have saved them. Men, I now knew, do not fight for flag or country, for the Marine Corps or glory or any other abstraction. They fight for one another.[133]

This second anecdote is hardly unique, and it demonstrates the need to fulfill a sense of responsibility to one's fellows.

History provides numerous examples of soldiers who fought each other aggressively and resolutely without feeling great personal hatred for the enemy. Lack of intense hatred between white troops during the U.S. Civil War did not stop the slaughter. In a series of charges back and forth at Antietam in 1862, Lee lost 13,700 casualties and McClellan 12,400 in a single day, as brother fought brother. Tolerance, verging on soldierly comradeship, existed between foes during World War I in the trenches where men lived in unspeakable conditions and plied diabolical tools of war against each other. On Christmas day 1914, along part of the line manned by British and Germans, troops left the trenches to mingle in no man's land. Only the intervention of their officers broke up the camaraderie. Tales of the trenches in World War I often tell of greater hostility for men of one's own army with safe billets in the rear than for the enemy who shared the horrors of life at the front.

Before leaving this discussion of racial hatred and combat motivation, one last possibility deserves consideration. Racism may have served a purpose among American troops very different from its supposed role of inspiring troops to fight harder. It may aid a soldier to define the enemy as a subhuman "other." Dehumanizing the enemy through racism or by other means can provide psychological distance and relief to those who must confront their own sense of guilt and anxiety in killing or trying to kill another human being. It probably matters less in easing the act during the heat of combat but is more valuable in times of repose, when soldiers must deal with what they have done and how it fits in their moral universe. If this is the case, and I believe it is, then it may set Dower's argument on its head. Instead of being a *cause* of killing, the blatant discussion of race may be a *consequence* of combat, something useful in coping with the deadly results of war. Certainly the racist discussion began before troops encountered the enemy, but its real value may still have been greatest in allowing soldiers, sailors, and Marines to live with the necessary horrors of war. Of course, this suggestion is merely speculation, but it may explain as well why anti-Japanese racism could lose its virulent excess immediately after the return of peace.

The history of war through the ages indicates that hate for the enemy is not a necessity for combat effectiveness, and it can be a liability when it leads to unnecessary but dangerous actions in battle. Good troops have plenty of motive without holding their enemy in contempt. In fact, respect for the enemy avoids the cardinal sin of dismissive overconfidence. Evidence convinces us that racial feelings festered in the Pacific, that they defined a major aspect of the experience of war, but the same evidence cannot make the case that racism increased the resolve or effectiveness of U.S. troops in combat against the Japanese.

RACE AND THE BOMB

We are now left with one last, and essential, question concerning the military effect of race hatred in the Pacific War—did racism figure heavily in the decision to employ atomic bombs against Japan at the close of the conflict? Many scholars, including John Dower, Ronald Takaki, and Craig Cameron, think so. Takaki speaks of a "racialized rage that would lead to . . . the atomic bombing of Hiroshima." Cameron concludes that "American willingness to exploit to their fullest potential technologies of mass destruction was driven by a dehumanizing, racist ideology."[134] Yet the highly regarded student of the Cold War John Lewis Gaddis has recently restated the opposite interpretation: "Having acquired this awesome weapon, the United States used it against Japan for a simple and straightforward reason: to achieve victory as quickly, as decisively, and as economically as possible."[135] This chapter must confront and weigh these two positions. If the race thesis explains, or largely explains, the final resort to atomic weapons, then it reasserts itself as essential to our understanding of the Pacific War, if not in its cause and conduct then certainly in its conclusion.

The literature on the Bomb dwarfs most other World War II debates; only the discussion of the Holocaust in Europe surpasses it. Here we are concerned solely with the degree to which race mattered to decision makers at the time. However, in order to weigh the importance of racism, we must consider alternative explanations, so there is no way to avoid walking over some of the same ground repeatedly trod since 1945. Such a review of the determinants and decisions leads to a conclusion that the race thesis fails to account for the arrival of the Atomic Age in the blinding dawn over Hiroshima.

The Descent into Area Bombing

Before looking at the particular circumstances that prepared the way for dropping the atomic bomb on Hiroshima, it is necessary to consider the technical and moral evolution, or devolution, that led to area bombing of cities. Recourse to the atomic bomb did not come in a vacuum.

To begin with, let us discard a canard that sometimes intrudes into discussions about the dropping of the Bomb. The ill-informed may suggest that the Bomb would never have been used against the Germans but only against the hated Japanese. In fact, the Manhattan Project came into being because scientists in the United States believed that the Germans were developing an atomic bomb and the United States had to beat them to the punch. The driving concern was "white" Germany, not "yellow" Japan, although at one time the Japanese as well as the Germans considered developing an atomic bomb. There seems little question that if a bomb could been created in time, it would have fallen on Germany. The authoritative Gerhard Weinberg writes, "In that effort, there was a built-in assumption that, when ready, such bombs would be used against Germany."[136] Germany surrendered on 8 May 1945, however, and the first test of the atomic bomb did not occur until 18 July. Only defeat spared Nazi Germany from the new weapon.

The central facts are that bombing doctrine and practice evolved during the war and that area bombing of cities, including mass fire bombings, first struck German urban centers. Before the war, there was a long tradition of trying to impose conventions on bombardment through international agreement. Hague Conferences of 1899 and 1907 forbade artillery bombardment of "undefended" towns, meaning that one could attack a fortress town or one housing a hostile army.[137] But if this was to extend to the new technology of airplanes in addition to the old one of cannon and mortars, what would "undefended" mean? Another meeting at the Hague, 1922–1923, drafted an agreement that would more expressly protect civilian targets. Article 22 expressly prohibited "aerial bombardment for the purpose of terrorizing the civilian population," and article 23 declared, "Aerial bombardment is legitimate only when directed at a military objective." This article provided a broad definition of a military objective—"an object of which the destruction or injury would constitute a distinct military advantage to the belligerent."[138] However, to abide by these guidelines, aerial bombardment would have to be highly accurate. Technology and tactics alone could guarantee compliance.

Limitations of aircraft and bombing technology in World War II, however, often made true precision visual sighting techniques impossible. The British tried daylight bombing at the start of the war, but suffered unacceptable losses in planes and crews, so switched over to night bombing, which, while safer for the bombers, promised far less accuracy. In 1940 Bomber Command instructed that "the attack must be made with reasonable care to avoid undue loss of civilian life in the vicinity of the target."[139] Crews took this seriously. But as much as they might want to comply, they were not capable of anything close to accurate bombing. Bomber Command came to realize that its planes could not depend on hitting anything other than the largest targets, that is, cities. As a consequence, it issued a directive in February 1942 stating that its efforts "should now be focussed on the morale of the enemy civil population and in particular, of industrial workers" and explicitly targeting the "built-up areas" of cities.[140] At this time, Sir Arthur Harris, "Bomber" Harris, took over Bomber Command and instituted the policy euphemistically known as "dehousing" German workers. The British committed themselves to area bombing, because they could do little else, and, of course, for many of the British, German attacks on English cities during the Blitz of 1940–1941 justified taking revenge. Fact and fury led to the same conclusion.

Bomber Command came to fully appreciate the value of incendiaries for raids against German cities. On the night of 24–25 July 1943 the RAF carried out an incendiary raid against Hamburg; this began fires stoked on 25 July and 26 July in daylight raids by American bombers. Then on the night of 27–28 July the RAF returned with a massive raid of 787 planes. The accuracy, because the bombers could aim at fires already burning below, was considered excellent. Still, only 325 of these planes dropped their bombs within *three miles* of the aiming point; such were the limits of accuracy. This attack began a firestorm which raged through the city. Bombing continued through 2 August, but the real killer was the firestorm set ablaze by the 27–28 June raid. The week-long bombing operation, which rained down 9,000 tons of bombs, proved to be the deadliest of the European theater, killing about 42,000 Germans.[141] This cataclysm truly lived up to Churchill's declaration: "We need to make the enemy burn and bleed in every way."[142]

On 14–15 February 1945, Dresden suffered a similar fate in raids by the American Eighth Air Force and RAF Bomber Command; the fires killed about 25,000 people. The raids employed a total of 1,299 bombers dropping 3,907 tons of bombs, of which 1,476 tons were incendiaries.[143] It was found that high explosives increased the effects of incendiaries in Europe, by "opening" buildings of sturdy construction.

Initially, the Americans disagreed with the British philosophy of bombing. With faith in the accuracy of the Norden bombsight, U.S. planes bombed in the daylight, so they could see their targets. The problem is that although tests worked well in the calm and clear desert skies of the American Southwest, combat conditions and, above all, cloudy European weather limited the effectiveness of American bombers. Technology for precision, all-weather bombing simply did not exist, as the Americans reluctantly came to realize. They were compelled to adjust their expectations of bombing and, as a consequence, their parameters of morality in combat—important aspects of their discourse on war. The Americans supplemented visual sighting with radar sighting in 1943; however, dropping bombs by radar was far less accurate than using the Norden. By the end of the war in Europe, over half the tonnage of bombs dropped by the Eighth Air Force had been guided by radar sighting. Americans retained the language and much of the intention of precision bombing against military targets throughout the war, but reality was a very different thing.

Freeman Dyson, the distinguished physicist, testifies to the moral compromise, even corruption, brought by the bombing campaign against Germany. During the war he served in operations research for Bomber Command in the RAF.

Bomber Command was an early example of the new evil that science and technology have added to the old evils of soldiering. Technology has made evil anonymous. Through science and technology, evil is organized bureaucratically so that no individual is responsible for what happens. Neither the boy in the Lancaster aiming his bombs at an ill-defined splodge on his radar screen, nor the operations officer shuffling papers at squadron headquarters, nor I sitting in my little office in the Operational Research Section and calculating probabilities, had any feeling of responsibility. None of us ever saw the people we killed. None of us particularly cared. . . .

Since the beginning of the war I had retreated step by step from one moral position to another, until at the end I had no moral position at all.[144]

The weather problems that hindered accuracy and effectiveness in the European bombing offensive also complicated the aerial offensive against Japan. But in addition, before the Americans could begin to bomb Japan, they had to solve the problems imposed by the long distances involved. Finding solutions would put off an air offensive against Japan until late in the war, when many of the technical and moral issues of bombing had already been confronted in Europe. The flight from London to Berlin was only about 600 miles, but that from Saipan to Tokyo was about 1,200 miles. Land-based bombers used in Europe lacked the range to fly against Japan, and the United States had to await the new B-29, which could manage the greater distances. Even then, Americans still had to take reasonable bases for them. Attempts to operate from China, beginning in June 1944, proved too difficult and gave limited success. Gasoline for the great bombers had to be flown in from India, and this meant far more planes were devoted to fuel than to bombs. Moreover, Chinese bases could be overrun by Japanese offensives. American bombers, however, did help to fight the Japanese in China. The first mass incendiary bombing by B-29s in Asia hit not Japan but the Chinese port city of Hankow, December 1944.

Only the capture of the Marianas gave the U.S. suitable bases for bombing Japan proper. The first raids from the Marianas began in November 1944, but these, too, were ineffective for a long time. Soon, the innovative and relentless Curtis LeMay assumed leadership of the bombing campaign. He learned his craft in Europe at first, and in July 1944 took command of the 20th Bomber Command in China at age thirty-seven; from there he went to the Marianas where he became chief of the 21st Bomber Command in January 1945. When he first arrived, continued attempts at high-altitude precision bombing of military targets in Japan achieved only limited success and recourse to radar sighting in bad weather turned these raids into area bombings of cities.

Forced to seek quick results, LeMay changed tactics, combining a number of innovations to launch devastating fire raids. He would send his bombers in at low altitude at night. The B-29s strained their engines less by staying low and saved considerable fuel by not climbing to altitude, and since Japanese lacked an effective night defense, he stripped planes of machine guns and gunners. The weight saved in fuel and guns could be put into an increased load of the new M-69 bomb, a product of experiments with incendiary weapons in Utah held during 1943. Weapons engineers meticulously built German- and Japanese-style structures to test the different bombs, and the result was the M-69, a cluster of small 6.2-pound gel-filled packages that dispersed to ignite a large area. Even after the first incendiary raids, planners still weighed the military value of targets and continued to try to attack relatively small industrial facilities, but area bombing by incendiaries was a powerful alternative in the destructive menu.

In fact, Japanese cities were tailor-made incendiary targets waiting for a match, and Americans realized this even before Pearl Harbor and the virulent anti-Japanese feelings it inspired. Billy Mitchell, the controversial American air power advocate who was court-martialed in the mid-1920s for strident public criticism of the War and Navy Departments, had declared Japanese "wood and paper" cities to be "the greatest aerial targets the world has ever seen. . . . Incendiary projectiles would burn the cities to the ground in short order."[145] Just before the war began, in mid-November 1941, George C. Marshall warned the Japanese, "we'll fight mercilessly. Flying Fortresses will be dispatched immediately to set the paper cities of Japan on fire."[146]

LeMay now inaugurated his new devastating tactics in a fire raid on Tokyo during the night of 9–10 March 1945. LeMay sent 334 B-29s, carrying 2,000 tons of incendiaries against Tokyo.[147] The number of planes and the tonnage of bombs did not approach that deployed against Hamburg, but the tinderbox flammability of Tokyo made the effects far greater. Fire devastated nearly sixteen square miles of Tokyo, killing 83,000 men, women, and children, a death toll from a single raid second only to the roll of the slain at Hiroshima. LeMay defended area bombing of cities on the basis that they attacked the work force of Japanese war industries and those industries themselves, because much of war production had been dispersed to workers in their own homes.

John Dower writes of the bombing offensive against Japan:

It was in this frenzy of violence that the kamikaze were born in October 1944, the consummate symbol of the pure spirit of the Japanese that would turn back the demonic onslaught. It was in this atmosphere that precision bombing of Japanese military targets was abandoned by the United States and the "madmen" and "yellow vermin" of the homeland became the primary targets. The atomic bomb, born at Alamogordo in July 1945, was in this setting but a more efficient way of killing, and its use marked the beginning of the end of the long, unnecessary death agony.[148]

This subtle paragraph says little specifically, but implies much that is questionable. After contrasting the "pure" personal sacrifice of the Japanese kamikaze with the mass slaughter inflicted by the Americans, Dower implies that "frenzy" caused the change from precision bombing to area bombing. But area bombing with incendiaries evolved first in Europe, not over Japan. Dower implies that the Americans abandoned precision because they now fought the "yellow vermin" of Japan, thus supplying a clearly racial motive. Yet as stated already, the German populace also suffered from Allied raids on their cities. Perhaps race hatred made Japanese casualties more conscionable, but it certainly did not justify Hamburg and Dresden. Dower may well be right that to those who used the atomic bomb, it was simply a more effective bomb. But it was this increased effect that U.S. strategists hoped would shock the Japanese into surrender, which it did. Who was responsible for the "long, unnecessary death agony"? That is another question that will be dealt with in the following pages.

Surrender or Continued Warfare

To an observer today, applying Western standards of reasonable behavior, the situation Tokyo faced in June 1945 looks hopeless. A virtually unbroken series of defeats going back as far as mid-1942 grew in momentum and gravity. Once the U.S. navy had built up its fleet to overpowering proportions in 1944, its Central Pacific juggernaut rolled on rapidly. The Marshal and Gilbert Islands fell in January and February. Americans took the Marianas from June to August 1944, and this victory toppled the Tojo government and brought in General Hideki Koiso as prime minister. MacArthur invaded the Philippines in October 1944 and retook Manila by March 1945. Iwo Jima fell to U.S. Marines in bitter fighting in February and March 1945, and the even more costly fight for Okinawa raged from April to June. Bombers flying from the Marianas rained death on Japan, inflicting the apocalyptic fire bombing of Tokyo. Koiso's policies met with such failure that he resigned on 5 April to be replaced as prime minister by Admiral Kantaro Suzuki. On the same day, the Soviet Union declared it would abrogate its treaty of neutrality with Japan.

Germany surrendered on 8 May, freeing the allies to concentrate on defeating Japan. In June, Americans secured their hold on Okinawa and commenced the buildup for an invasion of the home islands as the bombing raids continued. Certainly the Japanese should have realized that they should capitulate immediately before things got worse, but this was not their intent. This was, after all, a land that despised surrender; here military culture may well have trumped diplomacy.

The Japanese did make efforts to end the war in June and July, but these attempts were neither realistic nor pursued with the necessary vigor. The fact is that there are many ways to end a war, from winning a decisive victory to accepting an abject surrender. The Japanese realized they would not be able to gain the former but were a long way from submitting to the latter. Up until the use of the *second* atomic bomb on Nagasaki, the Japanese government still sought to gain what it considered favorable terms. By the summer of 1945 the Japanese definition of favorable terms had changed radically from what it had been in 1942, but these terms still fell short of what the U.S. reasonably considered to be acceptable.

In Japan at this time, the critical war/peace decisions were in the hands of the Supreme Council for the Direction of the War, also known as the Big Six, and the emperor, counseled by his immediate personal advisers, notably Marquis Kido, keeper of the privy seal. The military dominated the Big Six. Prime Minister Suzuki was a retired admiral, Admiral Mitsumasa Yonai headed the Ministry of the Navy, General Korechika Anami headed the Ministry of the Army, Admiral Soemi Toyoda commanded the Naval General Staff, and General Yoshijuri Umezu headed the Army General Staff. Such men could be trusted to understand the needs and accept the values of the military. Only Foreign Minister Shigenori Togo had not held flag rank in the military. Within the government, the army wielded more power than the navy. During the last months of the war, Suzuki and others worried that they must not alienate the army for fear of a coup. Suzuki's caution is not hard to understand; he had nearly died in the 1936 attempted army coup, when a band of zealots broke into his house and shot him several times.[149]

The Big Six and the army continued to believe that Japan could exact acceptable conditions to end the war with some honor if it could score one last triumph in battle. As early as the summer of 1944, after the fall of the Marianas, the *War Journal* of the Imperial Headquarters noted the following conclusion:

We can no longer direct the war with any hope of success. The only course left is for Japan's one hundred million people to sacrifice their lives by charging the enemy to make them lose the will to fight.

In judging the situation . . . there is unanimous agreement that henceforth we will slowly fall into a state of ruin. So it is necessary to play for a quick end to the war.[149b]

As late as March 1945, Kido believed that after one more victory, the emperor could support peace, but one more win was necessary.[150] Foreign Minister Togo reported later that when Suzuki came to power in April, the new prime minister spoke in terms of continuing the war for two or three years.[151] Until the Japanese defeat on Okinawa in June, the emperor maintained his conviction that victory in the field might still produce a good peace settlement. The army drafted plans for the defense of the home islands, Ketsu-Go or Decisive Operation, finishing the task early in April. These plans, particularly for the defense of Kyushu, hoped to throw back the first wave of invaders, but even if unsuccessful at repelling an invasion, they aimed at inflicting such damage that the war-weary Americans would agree to a negotiated peace. Field Marshal Hata, in command on Kyushu, believed that the coming struggle there would be "the last chance to change the war situation in our favor."[152] Consequently, there was no contradiction in the notion that Japan wanted to bring the war to an end but at the same time saw a need to inflict a bloody price on the enemy. There were also army die-hards who preferred to see Japan extinguished rather than surrender, but the Big Six sought what they considered terms favorable enough to bring the fighting to an end.

While the Japanese prepared for defense, they made only weak and poorly conceived diplomatic efforts. The historian Akira Iriye remarks that the surrender of Germany in early May provided an excellent opportunity for Suzuki to press for terms from the Americans, but he did little. "If, as he later claimed, he was then secretly working for peace, he failed to send any encouraging signal either to people at home or to the enemy countries."[153] Thus, Iriye identifies what he continues to see in the diplomatic effort—a go-slow policy that showed an entirely inappropriate lack of urgency that would end in disaster. When the government finally began to consider peace terms formally, the ruling clique desired a settlement beyond what the United States would have been willing to consider. On 9 June, Marquis Kido decided to draft a peace proposal and share it with the emperor, but his conditions were practically bizarre given the circumstances.[154] Japan, he stated, would give up the European colonial territories it held, but only when they were granted liberation by the European imperial powers. The armed forces could be cut back to have only a "minimal defense," but Kido did assume the preservation of the Japanese military, at least on a reduced level. At this time, defeat on Okinawa dashed the emperor's last hopes for victory, and he affirmed Kido's proposals.

As the situation worsened, the Japanese government better defined what conditions the United States would have to offer before Japan laid down its arms. The emperor must retain his position and his prerogatives, but this was not the only necessary term. Japan must not be occupied by the Americans or their allies.[155] In a meeting with the Big Six, Anami further insisted on a formula that would justify the claim that Japan was not actually defeated.[156] This would hopefully avoid the disarmament of Japan and war-crimes trials. A properly constructed peace would allow the military to retain its honor and perhaps its power. Such an end to the war, however, was mere wishful thinking. Because the United States regarded Japanese militarism as a primary cause of the war, allowing the militarists to keep their prestige and influence was out of the question. The parallel with interwar Germany can only have been too obvious; there the army denied that it actually lost World War I and insisted that it had been stabbed in the back. Even after the bombs fell on Hiroshima *and* Nagasaki, the Big Six did not concur that surrender would be possible if *only* the United States accepted the emperor; they wanted more.

When the Japanese finally sought a diplomatic solution, they did so by trying to negotiate with the Soviets, an unrealistic, almost foolish, course of action. During meetings held in mid-May, the Big Six began discussing the goals and methods of ending the war through negotiations. But again, the wheels turned slowly. Suzuki charged former Prime Minister Koki Hiroto to conduct talks with Soviet Ambassador Yakov Malik in Tokyo beginning on 3 June and extending until 24 June, but they accomplished nothing. The Japanese fervently wanted the Soviets to remain neutral and perhaps even to offer some aid to Japan so as to curb U.S. power. Meanwhile, the resolution to continue the war if necessary remained strong. On 6 and 8 June, the Supreme War Council met with the emperor and renewed the decision to fight to the end if necessary. It was only after these meetings that Kido drafted his plan for peace. At the end of June, Togo ordered the Japanese ambassador in Moscow, Naotake Sato, to contact Foreign Minister Molotov to prepare the way for negotiations. Protesting the action as pointless, Sato met with

Molotov on July 11 to no avail. Sato informed Togo that negotiation with the Soviets, whom he suspected of already being in league with the Americans and British concerning Japan, would go nowhere.

While the Japanese were talking to the Russians, American intelligence listened to virtually every word, because it had long ago cracked the Japanese diplomatic codes, as well as mastering much of the military traffic. These intercepts, known as Magic and Ultra, left the U.S. government well-informed of Japanese intentions. Much has been made of the desire of Ambassador Sato to accept American terms and achieve peace. American intelligence was well aware of his attitudes but also knew that Togo did not share them. In fact, Sato's sensible desire for peace simply highlighted the inflexibility of the Japanese government. This becomes very clear in the discussion between Sato and Togo concerning "unconditional surrender."

Takaki insists that "Truman's rigid and fierce insistence on unconditional surrender," inspired by a "racialized remembering of Pearl Harbor," prolonged the war and brought on the tragedy of the atomic bomb.[157] Key to the argument that "unconditional surrender" was the great roadblock to peace is the idea that if only the Americans had declared a willingness for the Japanese to keep their emperor as a symbolic monarch, peace would quickly have followed. This is far from the case, however; until the second week of August Japanese minimum conditions required a far more than symbolic emperor in addition to other serious demands, as mentioned above.

A key record of the Magic intercepts, the Magic Diplomatic Summary, only became available to historians in 1995; through it, we can follow illuminating critical exchanges concerning this point. On July 18, the wise Sato advised Togo, "Except for the matter of maintenance of our national structure [keeping the emperor], I think that we must absolutely not propose conditions. The situation has already reached the point where we have no alternative but unconditional surrender."[158] To Sato's advocacy of "unconditional surrender provided that the Imperial House was preserved," Togo replied that preservation of the imperial office was *not* enough:

> With regard to unconditional surrender we are unable to consent to it under any circumstances whatever. Even if the war drags on and it becomes clear that it will take much more than bloodshed, the whole country as one man will pit itself against the enemy in accordance with the Imperial Will so long as the enemy demands unconditional surrender.[159]

This reply indicates that Japanese conditions went beyond the emperor. Sato was not the only Japanese diplomat who talked of realistic peace terms before Hiroshima, and Washington knew of such proposals thanks to Magic. However, the U.S. government also knew that Tokyo was holding firm against them. The Suzuki government was not in search of someone to whom it could capitulate; it was pursuing its own unrealistic agenda.

The last best chance to forestall the American atomic assault came with the Potsdam Declaration of 26 July. The terms of this declaration were debated within American diplomatic circles. Joseph Grew advised a specific guarantee of the emperor, but this was judged unacceptable to an American public that had been told for years that Hirohito was a war criminal. Nonetheless, the declaration was worded in such a way as to leave the door open, since it promised the Japanese a government "in accordance with the freely expressed will of the Japanese people."[160] The only mention of unconditional surrender came in article 13, which called for "the unconditional surrender of all the Japanese armed forces." When Truman's critics mention only the stipulation for unconditional surrender, as is the case with Takaki, they skew the actual sense of the Potsdam Declaration.[161] We need to consider a fuller version of the peace conditions:

(6) There must be eliminated for all time the authority and influence of those who have deceived and misled the people of Japan into embarking on world conquest—for we insist that a new order of peace, security and justice will be impossible until irresponsible militarism is driven from the world.

(7) Until such a new order is established and until there is convincing proof that Japan's war-making power is destroyed, points in Japanese territory to be designated by the Allies shall be occupied to secure the achievement of the basic objectives we are here setting forth.

(8) The terms of the Cairo Declaration shall be carried out and Japanese sovereignty shall be limited to the islands of Honshu, Hokkaido, Kyushu, Shikoku and such minor islands as we determine.

(9) The Japanese military forces, after being completely disarmed, shall be permitted to return to their homes with the opportunity to lead peaceful and productive lives.

(10) We do not intend that the Japanese shall be enslaved as a race or destroyed as a nation, but stern justice shall be meted out to all war criminals, including those who have visited cruelties upon our prisoners. The

Japanese government shall remove all obstacles to the revival and strengthening of democratic tendencies among the Japanese people. Freedom of speech, of religion, and of thought, as well as respect for the fundamental human rights shall be established.

(11) Japan shall be permitted to maintain such industries as will sustain her economy and permit the exaction of just reparations in war. To this end, access to, as distinguished from control of raw materials shall be permitted. Eventual Japanese participation in world trade relations shall be permitted.

(12) The occupying forces of the Allies shall be withdrawn from Japan as soon as these objectives have been accomplished and there has been established in accordance with the freely expressed will of the Japanese people a peacefully inclined and responsible government.

(13) We call upon the Government of Japan to proclaim now the unconditional surrender of all the Japanese armed forces, and to provide proper and adequate assurances of their good faith in such action. The alternative for Japan is prompt and utter destruction.

The tone and promises of the Potsdam Declaration demonstrate that it was hardly trying to impose a Carthaginian peace on Japan and that it did grant conditions, at least in principle. The declaration pledged Japan democracy, national independence, a revived economy, and departure of U.S. occupying forces as soon as the conditions were met. In fact, the U.S. government, regardless of extreme language by some, did not intend to eliminate Japan. In September 1943, Hugh Borton, a member of the Far Eastern area committee in the State Department, advised, "[If] the terms of surrender and the subsequent agreements and treaties provide for the impoverishment of Japan and its reduction to economic impotency, permanent peace in the Pacific will be seriously threatened."[162] A State Department position paper drafted by E. R. Dickover in April 1944 insisted: "It is believed that peace and security in the Pacific can best be assured by creating a truly democratic Japan."[163]

Sato informed Tokyo on 29 July that he regarded the terms as acceptable and certainly better than those offered to Germany; in the following days he continued to press for acceptance.[164] Iriye argues that the government should have accepted the Potsdam Declaration, "for it gave them just what they were seeking, 'a peace on the basis of something other than unconditional surrender.'"[165] The official response of the Japanese government was dismissive, however; Suzuki declared, "it would not be necessary to take the declaration seriously."[166]

U.S. intelligence had little reason to think that the Japanese government was on the eve of surrender. On the one hand, Magic intercepts showed that while terms were under discussion, the government in Tokyo rejected surrender on any basis acceptable to the Americans. On the other hand, the message traffic from the army made it clear that the military was still pressing on with its preparations for a desperate defense. These preparations demonstrated the army's firm resolution to live up to its principles by fighting to the last in the home islands, and the U.S. considered the army to be the dominant force in Japan.

The Perceived Necessity to Invade

Given what U.S. leaders knew about the Japanese government's unwillingness to surrender, leading American strategists concluded that nothing short of invading the home islands would end the war. At the same time, there was good reason to expect a last-ditch suicidal defense of Japan, given the fanatical resistance of Japanese troops throughout the Pacific campaign. Therefore, as long as the enemy's will remained firm, the planned invasion threatened to be brutal and bloody no matter how few resources were left the Japanese.

How could U.S. forces defeat such opponents? It was not expected to be easy; those who shaped American strategy generally estimated that the war against Japan would probably continue for one year after the fall of Germany. Military means available to compel the Japanese to surrender came down to three alternatives, and these were hardly any secret. Even the *Life* story with the fictional Admiral Quasi Tojo got it right: "First you must understand that there just three ways to beat us. You must invade Japan itself. Or you must destroy us by bombing. Or you must blockade us till our military machine breaks down." [167]

Evidence of determination to fight to the last convinced U.S. commanders that an invasion would be necessary. At a meeting of U.S. and British commanders in the Combined Chiefs of Staff held on 14 July 1944, General Marshall concluded, "[A]s a result of recent operations in the Pacific it was now clear to the United States Joint Chiefs of Staff that, in order to finish the war with the Japanese quickly, it will be necessary to invade the industrial heart of Japan." The Combined Chiefs formally decided to "force the unconditional surrender of Japan" by wearing down the Japanese with blockade and bombardment and then "invading and seizing objectives in the industrial heart of Japan."[168]

Demonstrated Japanese devotion to and sacrifice for the national and imperial cause gave American strategists good reason to believe that blockade alone would not compel surrender, or at least would not for a long time. In fact, the famine that struck Japan in late 1945 and 1946 showed that the Japanese could subsist on the most meager of rations for a surprisingly long time.[169] Conventional bombing had yet to drive the Japanese government to the peace table. As awful as it was, the 9–10 March firebombing of Tokyo had not changed Japanese policy, and by midsummer the U.S. bombing offensive was running out of targets. In the words of Michael Sherry, "Much of LeMay's bombing simply made the rubble of Japan's war economy bounce."[170]

The fact that the Japanese were still not at the peace table in June justified the resolution of the Combined Chiefs of Staff to invade. A crucial meeting held in Washington on 18 June focused on the fate of Japan. Attending were President Truman, the Joint Chiefs of Staff, the secretaries of the army and navy, Assistant Secretary of War John McCloy, General Ira Eaker, sitting in for General Hap Arnold, and Admiral William Leahy, personal adviser and chief of staff to the president. The invasion of the home islands, known now as Downfall, would come in two phases. The first, Operation Olympic, would put U.S. troops ashore on Kyushu in November, and the second, Operation Coronet, would land American and Allied troops on Honshu in 1946. George Marshall, reinforced by an endorsement from MacArthur, strongly supported the invasion; minutes of the meeting report: "General Marshall said that it was his personal view that the operation against Kyushu was the only course to pursue."[171] Admiral Ernest King supported preparations for Olympic, but he harbored doubts that the landing would actually be necessary. King knew that the commander of the Pacific fleet, Admiral Chester Nimitz had withdrawn his support from an invasion by late May, because he believed it would be too costly.[172] Leahy always had reservations about Downfall, but did not openly oppose it. Therefore, while some at the 18 June meeting might have been less enthusiastic than others, the minutes of the meeting recorded unanimity: "THE PRESIDENT said that, as he understood it, the Joint Chiefs of Staff after weighing all the possibilities of the situation and considering all possible alternative plans were still of the unanimous opinion that the Kyushu operation was the best solution under the circumstances."[173] In this diplomatic and military context, Truman and his advisers would next face the decision to unleash atomic weapons.

A Matter of Numbers: U.S. Casualties and the Bomb

Much of the after-the-fact controversy about the dropping the atomic bomb in 1945 comes down to an argument over the number of casualties that U.S. forces would have suffered in an invasion of the home islands. On the surface, this is an argument about sparing lives based on the assumption that it may have been reasonable to drop the Bomb if it saved enough lives, either among the attacking Allied forces or among the Japanese defenders as well. However, the tallies of casualty projections serve a more basic cause for the critics of Harry Truman; it is all about trying to catch the president in a lie. If Truman's numbers are bloated, his detractors reason, and he knew they were inflated, then he was misleading the world in order to camouflage more complex and insidious motives. Numbers become a proof of motive. The accusation that Truman deceived the nation comes out in a great deal of scholarship and polemic. A recent issue of that bounty of book reviews, *The Times Literary Supplement,* offered a commentary by Gore Vidal entitled "The Greater the Lie. . . . Pearl Harbor, Hiroshima and the Origins of the Cold War: Three Myths That America Is Ruled By," in which he proclaims as the second great myth, or lie, of recent American history "that Harry Truman . . . dropped his two atom bombs . . . because he feared that a million American lives would be lost in an invasion."[174]

Any discussion of casualty projections must begin with the understanding that no one could predict with any certainty how much an invasion of the home islands would have cost. All was surmise. In such a circumstance, one would expect a variety of estimates. Also, casualty estimates have to be put in context; different individuals or agencies presented different figures at different times based on changing goals and circumstances. Figures were skewed to make cases for or against invasion during the war. After World War II, some individuals played the numbers game in order to buttress their arguments in support of one branch of the military or another during the debates about the reorganization of the armed forces and creation of the Department of Defense. For example a figure such as Admiral King, who backed invasion during the war, might argue that blockade alone—that is, the navy—could have won the war handily without the Bomb or invasion—that is, the air force or the army. To pick any single statement out of the air to justify a conclusion distorts reality.

Admittedly, Truman made confusing statements concerning the losses expected in an invasion of the home islands, but he did not rely on a figure of

1,000,000 dead, although some threw around that number. In a letter to air force historians written in January 1953, he reported that Marshall told him at the Potsdam Conference that invasion would cost 250,000 to 1,000,000 casualties.[175] In 1955, the ex-president wrote in his memoirs, "General Marshall told me that it might cost half a million American lives to force the enemy's surrender on his home grounds."[176] To be sure, he should have been more consistent and more careful using the term "casualties," which includes wounded as well as killed, and the term "lives." The figure of 1,000,000 also crops up independently of Truman. In 1947, Henry Stimson, secretary of war during World War II, testified that he had been told that the price of invasion would be 1,000,000 total American casualties,[177] and Churchill went even further putting the potential butcher's bill at an astronomical figure, "a million American lives and half that number of British."[178]

A full history of the evolution of casualty estimates is beyond the scope of this chapter, but it is key to consider where these estimates stood in mid-June and how they had increased by late July. To prove his point that dropping the Bomb was not a military necessity, Ronald Takaki latches on to the number Truman provided in his memoir and compares them to those presented at the meeting of 18 June:

> In response to Truman's request for estimates, the Joint War Plans Committee prepared a report for the Chiefs of Staff, dated June 15, 1945. They gave the following estimates of casualties:
>
> Southern Kyushu, followed by Tokyo Plain
>
> | Killed | Wounded | Missing | Total |
> |--------|---------|---------|--------|
> | 40,000 | 150,000 | 3,500 | 193,000 |
>
> . . . The estimate for the total number that would be killed was not 500,000 but 40,000.[179]

Takaki seems to believe these figures amount to a smoking gun. He devotes only three pages of his *Hiroshima* to "proving" that Truman was lying about the numbers, but these pages are the absolutely necessary logical predicate for the other 150 pages of the book, which proposes a varied series of speculations as to why Truman *really* dropped the Bomb. These run the gamut from the rather old argument that we actually wanted to awe the Russians to the more avant-guard notion that Truman did it to demonstrate his masculinity, which had always been challenged. But sandwiched among these is the strong contention that dropping the Bomb was to some, or a large, degree the result of American racism. However, if the numbers did justify Truman's decision and his words, then Takaki need not have gone on the long intellectual journey he took to find the *hidden* causes.

Indeed, the 18 June meeting was an important discussion of casualty projections in response to a request from Truman. The figures quoted by Takaki and others were considered, but they were not the only predictions on Truman's mind or on the table during that meeting. A planning document of 30 August 1944 had concluded that "it might cost us half a million American lives and many times that number wounded—in the home islands."[180] Based on such estimates, draft calls were notably increased, as *The New York Times* announced in January 1945: "The Army must provide 600,000 replacements for overseas theaters before June 30, and together with the Navy, will require a total of 900,000 inductions by June 30."[181] A draft paper of 25 April 1945 adopted by the Joint Chiefs of Staff and based on actuarial figures from the Surgeon General of the Army provided ratios of casualties per 1,000 men per day in Pacific and European campaigns. According to this, Pacific experience produced a rate of 7.45, while European losses only stood at 2.16.[182] Using the Pacific rate with an invasion force of 766,700 men for Olympic over a ninety-day period would have produced about 500,000 casualties. This same ratio and ninety-day span applied to the 1,026,000 troops slated for Coronet would add another 687,933 losses, projecting 1,202,005 total casualties for Downfall.[183] The President clearly knew about the draft calls, although he was probably ignorant of the June projections. However, such shocking predictions reached him by another route. Former President Herbert Hoover, who opposed an invasion, sent Truman two memos in May 1945 that projected the cost of an invasion at 500,000 to 1,000,000 dead. There is reason to believe that Hoover had inside information when he reached these dismal conclusions. We now know that Truman read these memos and took them seriously enough to circulate them among his top advisers.[184] Hoover's estimates met with varying reactions, but the president was definitely mindful of his predecessor's grim tallies.

Meanwhile, different military authorities were proposing their own projections. On 13 May, Nimitz presented an estimate of losses for Olympic at

49,000, included the lightly wounded, for the first thirty days.[185] A month later, in response to a request from Marshall, MacArthur estimated 50,800 casualties for the first thirty days and a total of 105,000 casualties for ninety days, although he did not count men whose wounds would be light enough to return to duty. If these are included the number might reach 149,000.[186] At the end of the process, Marshall presented the combined figures for Downfall quoted by Takaki—193,500 casualties.

But this was not the only estimate discussed on 18 June. Olympic most concerned the policy makers at the meeting, because there was some doubt whether Coronet would be necessary after success in Olympic. Casualty projections took into account two basic facts, the 766,700 U.S. troops committed to the invasion of Kyushu and the 350,000 Japanese expected to oppose them. As the minutes of the meeting state, Truman expressed his deep concern to avoid "an Okinawa from one end of Japan to the other."[187] Earlier in the meeting Leahy had reminded his colleagues that casualty rates on Okinawa had reached a bloody 35 percent of the troops committed, and that this was a reasonable ratio to apply to Kyushu.[188] Such a formula would project about a quarter million casualties for Olympic alone. In response, Marshall and King countered that fighting on Kyushu would differ fundamentally from that on Okinawa. Okinawa was a narrow island that compelled U.S. troops to engage in frontal attacks, but Kyushu would allow maneuver tactics that would result in fewer losses. Marshall came up with an extremely low estimate of something between 31,000 and 41,000 for the first thirty days.[189] It is worth noting that Leahy opposed invasion and Marshall supported it. King noted after the meeting that the experts attending the meeting never actually gave Truman a clear and direct answer as to what level of losses to expect.

In any case, the events of the next several weeks made the 18 June estimates null and void. Military intelligence soon revealed that earlier predictions had grossly underestimated the Japanese forces that would contest the island. In March 1945, Charles Willoughby, MacArthur's intelligence officer, estimated Japanese troop strength in all the home islands at 937,000, but this projection increased to 1,865,000 in mid-July. By early August the Joint Intelligence Committee expected the Japanese to marshal 2,600,000 men to oppose Downfall.[190] Moreover, Ultra intercepts revealed that the Japanese were building up forces at an alarming rate on Kyushu. Based on monitoring Japanese message traffic, U.S. intelligence continually raised its estimates of troop strength on Kyushu. These projections hit 545,000 by August 2 with more Japanese forces en route. In fact, Japanese plans slated 900,000 men for the defense of that island. By late July it was also clear that these forces were not deployed in the way that American planners had expected. Instead of splitting their forces evenly north and south on Kyushu, leaving only three divisions to oppose U.S. landings in southern Kyushu, the Japanese brought down nine divisions for that purpose. Aircraft estimates also escalated. In late May, planners expected about 2,500–3,500 aircraft to oppose Olympic and Coronet; by early August this number had climbed to about 10,300. Some of this increase resulted from different counting methods, but the fact remained that there were a lot more planes than originally estimated.[191] These increases, particularly in the figures of expected kamikazes, greatly worried U.S. strategists.

By an extremely rough rule of thumb, one can expect casualties to rise at least in proportion to the increasing number of opposing troops. Thus, the figures for Olympic and Coronet that are so important to Takaki—193,500 casualties expected against perhaps 1,000,000 enemy troops and 3,000 planes—could mount to a loss of over 500,000 when Japanese resistance increases to 2,600,000 troops and 10,000 planes. In this light, Truman's claims of Marshall's late-July estimate of 250,000–1,000,000 casualties for Downfall seem entirely reasonable. The smoking gun grows cold.

Considering what decision makers believed at the time, Truman had good reason to expect heavy losses among Allied invading forces. Projected high American casualties, whatever the exact number, justified using the terrible new weapon to spare U.S. servicemen and shorten the war by months. As Gaddis observes, "In the context of 1945, it would have been difficult to justify taking *any* more casualties than absolutely necessary."[192] Also, ending the war without an invasion almost certainly spared the lives of countless Japanese defenders, and ending the war sooner also probably saved hundreds of thousands in areas of Asia occupied by Japan, although the Joint Chiefs of Staff did not factor these numbers into their calculations.[193]

The Final Acts of War

Truman decided to unleash the new American weapon on Japan by authorizing not a single bomb, but a bombing campaign intended to continue until the Japanese sued for peace. Given the severity of the decision, General Carl Spaatz requested a written order from the president to drop the Bomb. Truman drafted such an order on 24 July, and it was sent to Spaatz the next day. "The first special bomb" was to be dropped by visual sighting after 3 August . Weather would obviously be a factor. Truman listed four cities as possible targets in order of preference: Hiroshima, Kokura, Niigata, and Nagasaki. Hiroshima came first because it was the largest Japanese city not yet firebombed and was known to be an army city, with headquarters establishments and 42,000 Japanese troops. The first bomb would simply begin a series of drops: "additional bombs will be delivered on the above targets as soon as made ready."[194]

There had been some discussion of demonstrating the awesome power of the Bomb by dropping it on some unpopulated target. This came up at a 31 May meeting of the Interim Committee chaired by Stimson, but the committee rejected the idea with reasonable arguments.[195] If the weapon failed to explode, its failure would simply encourage the enemy. And what if the Japanese moved Allied prisoners into the advertised area? It was also an issue that, with only a few weapons at hand and their shock value critical, it might be too great a cost to use one to no real effect. The meeting concluded that the Japanese should not be warned and that the blast should "make a great psychological impression" on the Japanese.[196] No solely civilian target should be hit, but Hiroshima, with a sizeable military population, was considered to be an acceptable target.

In fact, the logic behind the bombing of Hiroshima approached that of Terrorism today. An overwhelmingly civilian population, despite the large number of military personnel, was to be attacked to achieve a psychological effect that would change Japanese policy to one acceptable to the United States.[197] It was a classic strategy of terror, and it worked.

The *Enola Gay* dropped Little Boy on Hiroshima at 8:16 A.M. on 6 August, and the gates of hell opened. No one can ever know for certain how many died from that blast; probably 100,000 perished immediately, and tens of thousands more from the effects of wounds, burns, and radiation.

Horror at Hiroshima would not end the atomic nightmare of Japan. On 8 August, Russian forces attacked the Japanese in Manchuria, but worse would come the next day when the U.S. dropped a second atomic weapon on Japan, immediately killing 45,000 at Nagasaki. Many reasonably ask if this second bomb was necessary. They insist that the Japanese should have been given more time before authorities made the decision to attack Nagasaki. It is not clear that leaving the Japanese more time between Hiroshima and Nagasaki would have brought capitulation after the first bomb. This was the same government that, after witnessing 83,000 die in Tokyo on 9–10 March, conducted a murderous resistance on Okinawa.[198] American intelligence knew that shortly after the blast, Japanese sources had reported to their government casualties at Hiroshima amounting to 70–80 percent of the population. The full details of the blast were only known in Tokyo on 8 August, when a Japanese inspection committee reported. All this shook the emperor, but the government failed to move immediately, and the Big Six did not meet the evening of 8 August.

A key point is that Truman had not authorized a single bomb but, rather, had set in motion a doomsday machine: an atomic bombing *offensive* intended to continue until the Japanese capitulated. The onset of this offensive was a strategic matter that required a presidential order; the timing of further bomb drops was tactical. In a real sense then, Truman had authorized the bombing of Nagasaki before the Bomb fell on Hiroshima. Originally the second dose of destruction had been intended for 11 August, but weather reports predicted a period of overcast weather beginning on 10 August, so the bombing, which had to be carried out visually, moved up to 9 August. Instead of five days between attacks, there were only three. Yet it is important to remember that the Japanese government did nothing to move toward peace in those three days.

One idea behind carrying out a second bombing so soon was to give the impression that the U.S. already possessed a stockpile of atomic bombs, so unless the Japanese came to terms a rain of terror would descend on Japan. Apparently Nagasaki made just this impression. During a cabinet meeting convened at 2:30 P.M. on 9 August, Army Minister Anami told the cabinet, "[T]he Americans appeared to have one hundred atomic bombs . . . while they could drop three per day. The next target might be Tokyo."[199] In fact, the Americans had only one more bomb completed, and delays in shipment to Tinian meant that it would not be ready to drop until after 21 August.[200] Should they be needed, additional bombs would come on line slowly after that. But they would not be needed; after Nagasaki, Truman halted the further use of atomic bombs. Henry Wallace, who had been vice president in Roosevelt's third term (1941–1945), reports that "the thought of wiping out another 100,000 people was too horrible. He didn't like the idea of killing, as he said, 'all those kids.'"[201]

There is reason to doubt that allowing more time to pass before attacking Nagasaki would have mattered, because even after that second bomb, the Big Six could not reach a consensus over accepting the Potsdam Declaration. No one was willing to agree to it as it stood. Suzuki, Togo, and Yonai demanded only that the imperial throne be preserved, but with *all* its rights and powers. The more intransigent Anami, Toyoda, and Umezu held out for four conditions: preservation of the emperor, no occupation of Japan, self-disarmament of Japanese forces, and any war crimes trials held to be managed by the Japanese themselves.[202] The military still wanted to dodge disgrace. No one but the emperor could break the deadlock, which he did in a late night meeting of the Supreme Council on 9–10 August. Early the next morning the Japanese rushed to contact the U.S. through the Swedish and Swiss.

Japan agreed to accept the Potsdam Declaration "with the understanding that the said declaration does not comprise any demand which *prejudices the prerogatives* of His Majesty as a Sovereign Ruler."[203] [Italics are mine.] However, the U.S. government would not accept this condition, but replied that the "ultimate form of government of Japan shall, in accordance with the Potsdam Declaration, be established by the freely expressed will of the Japanese people."[204] This formula opened the door wide enough that the Japanese government finally walked through and surrendered on August 14. Even then, army dissidents tried to seize the tape of the emperor's announcement of peace to his people, but they were thwarted in a battle on palace grounds. Ultimately, the army did not fight to the finish; however, the government resisted surrender beyond reason.

Truman's comments when he canceled the further use of atomic weapons betray little bloodlust; one wonders how profound his racism was by 1945.[205] In fact, American racism toward the Japanese ultimately proved to be surprisingly malleable. The cover of *The Leatherneck: Magazine of the Marines* for September 1945 already shows a transformed, although still demeaning, image of the erstwhile enemy.[206] Instead of the fierce ape, the Japanese symbol is now a peeved but passive monkey in uniform perched on the shoulder of a broad-faced smiling Marine, who cuddles his new mascot. More seriously, the character of the administration established by MacArthur was paternalistic but not vindictive. The nuancing of American attitudes toward Asian peoples would become even more apparent during the Korean War, only a few years in the future. By then, old allies, the Chinese, were new enemies, but only if they lived on the mainland, the Koreans were our friends, but only if they lived in the south, and the Japanese had become integrated into our security regime so much that we were intent on protecting them. It is worth asking if bone-deep racial hatred can perform such intellectual and emotional gymnastics.

The World War II racist discourse, with its cartoons, posters, articles, speeches, and other bombast, probably served different purposes for civilians than it did for troops. On the home front it rallied and focused resolution to unite and pursue the war against a vile enemy. But for soldiers, sailors, and Marines engaged in the war, it had additional functions. It dehumanized the enemy, making the necessary act of fighting, maiming, and killing more conscionable. Also it served as shorthand understanding of starkly contrasting cultures of war. Remove the threat of war, and race hatred against the Japanese lost its military value. The drooling gorilla became the cute monkey, still demeaning, but in a very different way.

Race forms one of the most basic themes of historical interpretation among American scholars today, so it seems natural that they have discovered, or rediscovered, race hated in the Pacific War. This chapter has extended that discussion by questioning and ultimately denying race as a primary factor in the cause and conduct of the war, even in the decision to drop the Bomb. This is not, of course, to forget the fact that U.S. troops were reluctant to take prisoners and that some American soldiers treated prisoners, the wounded, and the dead in barbaric ways—as did the Japanese. Such indelibly brutal reality undoubtedly shaped the experience of war lived and remembered by American servicemen, even if it did not shape strategy.

The contrast in military cultures is ultimately more important and, I believe, more interesting than the phenomenon of racism in combat. American emphasis on fighting and surviving, even through surrender, contrasts with Japanese fixation on glorious self-annihilation and consequent refusal to surrender. American reliance on material warfare stands apart from Japanese praise of spirit. Americans fought a war to be won for self-defense and rational political goals, Japanese a war of apocalyptic and divine struggle. In this clash of military cultures, Americans rejected the Japanese practice of combat as within the definition of war as we imagined it to be, and so Americans rejected the Japanese as human and denied them the conventions of war. In the language of this volume, American fighting men formed an alternative discourse without the limitations implicit in their traditional ideas of war, and this justified an extreme kind of violence, war without mercy.

The lack of mercy could be particularly harsh and twisted. Return to Marpi Point on Saipan as American translators and captured Japanese try to dissuade Japanese civilians from committing suicide by leaping off cliffs or swimming out to sea. A Japanese soldier, who had been sniping at Marines on Marpi Point, fired at a man and woman with four children who stopped at the brink, unable to bring themselves to making the suicidal leap. The sniper took it upon himself to decide for the family that they must accept death before surrender.

He drilled the man from behind, dropping him off the rocks into the sea. The second bullet hit the woman. She dragged herself about thirty feet along the rocks, then she floated out in a pool of blood. The sniper would have shot the children, but a Japanese woman ran across and carried them out of range. The sniper walked defiantly out of his cave and crumpled under a hundred American bullets.[207]

The sniper obeyed what to him was a sacred code embedded in Japanese military culture by "annihilating" the parents, and then committing suicide himself by boldly coming out of cover. He accepted concepts of honor and dishonor that required him to sacrifice his life and to demand the same of others. Understandably, the infuriated Marines judged the sniper's actions by American concepts of morality. They riddled the sniper not only in self-defense but as an act of justice against such a heartless murderer. At that moment the sniper and the Marines really did come from different worlds.

Notes on the Opening Illustration for Chapter Seven

Assaulting Saipan, the first wave hit the beach, taking cover behind low dunes as its amtracs clawed up the sand. These young Marines fought in pursuit of a strategy designed without reference to the intense hatreds that afflicted the adversaries. Nonetheless, the contrasting military cultures of U.S. and Japanese troops intensified racist malice, justifying war without mercy. It would be a bloody fight.

(National Archives)

CHAPTER EIGHT

Crossing the Canal

Egyptian Effectiveness and Military Culture in the October War

AT 8:45 A.M., EGYPTIAN TIME, on 5 June 1967, Israeli warplanes streaking south from the Mediterranean bombed and strafed nine Egyptian air bases in the first strike of an attack that would continue to pummel bases in the Sinai and the Nile Valley that day.[1] During the next three hours, successive waves of Israeli jets hit airfields and other military targets in Egypt. Only eight Egyptian fighters rose from the bases under attack to counter the devastating Israeli blow, and all eight were shot down. The Israeli planners chose the hour

of the attack to catch most Egyptian pilots between their homes and their bases after breakfast. Unexpectedly, the attack also found the Egyptian air force without its commander, who was airborne in a transport and unable to give commands out of concern that Israelis would locate and down his plane. In this surprise and chaos, only one commander at an airfield deeper in Egypt took the initiative to order his planes into the air to fight off the Israelis. Of these twenty planes, four were shot down in dogfights, and the rest had to crash-land because Israeli bombs had rendered the runways in the combat zone unusable. By the end of the day, Israeli air strikes had destroyed 300 of Egypt's 450 combat aircraft and killed 100 of its 350 trained pilots, eliminating the Egyptian air force as a factor in the ground war, which began soon after the first Israeli planes appeared over Egypt. Moreover, Egyptian air force commanders failed to report the effect of the strikes to President Gamal Abdel Nasser, who only learned of the disaster about 4 that afternoon. By then, Israeli ground forces had already scored notable successes.

At 9:15 A.M., Israeli troops drove into the Sinai to assault Egyptian defensive positions. In the north, along the road by the Mediterranean shore, General Israel Tal commanded the Israeli *ugdah,* a division-sized task force of armor and infantry, that now advanced on Rafah. Egyptians held heavily fortified positions there protected by deep minefields, numerous artillery, and 100 tanks. However, the Egyptian right flank rested on sand dunes that the Egyptians believed to be impenetrable. Tal held the Egyptians' attention with a frontal attack by some of his forces, while he maneuvered others through the dunes to take the position from the flank and rear. Egyptian infantry fought very hard from their fixed positions, and their artillery support was effective when firing to the front at pre-registered targets. Artillery, however, did not adjust to the unexpected flanking attacks; neither did the infantry maneuver. In their sole counterstroke, a battalion of Egyptian T-55s without infantry or artillery support lumbered straight forward into converging Israeli attacks only to be enveloped and destroyed.

The Israelis did not halt with this victory; instead, armored units began to roll westward toward El-Arish even while infantry were consolidating at Rafah. Fearful, or ashamed, to report failure, Egyptian officers at Rafah had reported success even when their positions were battered, flanked, and cut off. As a consequence, Egyptians further down the road were caught off guard by the advancing Israelis. A tank battalion drove Egyptian defenders from the Jiradi Pass and continued on toward El-Arish. However, once they had regained their equilibrium, the Egyptians retook the pass, where they fought furiously against the main body of the Israelis. The confined space of the pass compelled the Israelis to charge directly into prepared Egyptian positions, and in that kind of combat, the Egyptians fought hard and effectively, holding up the Israelis all afternoon and into the night. Only when the Israelis found a way around the Egyptian flank did they gain the upper hand over the defenders, who did not reorient their line to face the Israelis, but even then the Egyptians resisted in fierce hand-to-hand combat. Resolution and bravery, however, would not stop the Israelis.

By the morning of 8 June, three days into the war, advanced units of the Israeli forces had fought their way to the Suez Canal, and the Israelis redirected their main strength back against Egyptian armor still in the Sinai. The Egyptian situation was by now nearly hopeless, because, among other factors, the Israeli air force ruled the skies and could attack at will.

In the early morning of 9 June the Egyptians accepted the cease-fire voted by the U.N. Security Council. Their war had lasted only four days and ended in utter defeat. Israel's other Arab foes also accepted cease-fire agreements that sacrificed territory to the Israelis. Jordan, which misplayed its options politically and militarily, lost East Jerusalem and the West Bank. King Hussein accepted a cease-fire on the evening of 7 June, succumbing even more rapidly than had Egypt. The Israelis also seized the Golan from Syria and ended their fighting late on 10 June with a cease-fire, six days after the initial air strikes against Egypt.

The Six-Day War proved to be a debacle for the Arab armies that opposed Israel. At the outset they enjoyed significant, but not overpowering, numerical advantages. In the Sinai alone the Egyptians had 100,000 troops and 950 tanks, supported by an air force of 450 combat planes. Jordan had 45,000 troops and 270 tanks on the West Bank, with only a very small air force. Syria could field 70,000 troops, 550 tanks and assault guns, and 136 MiG aircraft. Against this, Israel mustered perhaps 120,000 army troops actually deployed in combat, 1,150 tanks, and 207 combat aircraft. But the Israelis tore apart the Arab armies one after the other. Although the Six-Day War represented the high point of Israeli military effectiveness, it was not simply that the Israelis were very good; the Arab armies that fought them suffered from shortcomings fatal in modern maneuver warfare.

The shattering defeat of the Egyptians in the Six-Day War epitomizes the frustration and failure that they suffered before finally engineering the crossing of the Suez Canal in 1973. This chapter examines Egyptian military culture by observing Egyptian forces in combat from the War of Independence (1948) through the October War (1973). During this quarter century, they repeatedly displayed shortcomings in mobile campaigns that can be ascribed in the main to exaggerated deference toward command hierarchy, lack of independence and initiative on the tactical unit level, and unwillingness to report unwelcome combat information to authorities. As we shall see, the central event of this chapter, the impressive crossing of the Suez Canal during the October War, succeeded not because Egyptian planners eliminated such characteristics, but rather because they identified and adjusted for them. The resultant highly effective Egyptian operation provides a striking demonstration of the way in which militaries possess unique cultural characteristics and can profit from recognizing them.

This chapter closely follows the work of Kenneth M. Pollack.[2] In his *Arabs at War* (2002), Pollack identifies the general ineffectiveness of Arab armies, seeks explanations in a number of possible failings, and concludes that the primary weaknesses have historically been in tactical leadership, information management, technical skills and weapons handling, and maintenance. He claims that these failings have been typical of "every single Arab army and air force between 1948 and 1991."[3] It will be enough for this chapter if these generalizations fit the case study of Egypt—and they do. Above all, Egyptian shortcomings in Pollack's categories of tactical leadership and information management proved most damaging. Pollack's argument is all the more convincing because the high command of the Egyptian army itself reached similar conclusions.

The methodology employed here differs from that used earlier in *Battle*. Up to this point, we have primarily relied upon written texts to discover different societies' conceptions of military ideals, projections of their own virtues, and condemnations of their adversaries' evils. Cultures usually discuss such subjects freely and extensively. However, this chapter studies obviously poor military performance by Egyptian forces for twenty years. One could hardly expect to find those failings proudly detailed in narrative accounts or expressly promoted in prescriptive literature. We discover them best by looking at what actually happened, by concentrating on the combat record itself. In turning to tactical and operational analysis, we pursue a course similar to that taken by General Ahmed Isma'il 'Ali, the hero of this chapter, who honestly examined Egyptian defeats in order to plan a victorious campaign that maximized the benefits and minimized the drawbacks of Egyptian military culture.

If the methodology of this chapter differs sharply from that of the other chapters, its theme harmonizes with the rest of the volume: the importance of conception in determining military practice. At base, this is a study of changing military doctrine, at first deficient and then revised and effective. The story told here demonstrates that campaign plans ought to build upon the particular character of the army for which they are intended. In other words, the formal exposition of military culture that is doctrine should conform to the more basic aspects of that culture as expressed in the beliefs and behaviors of its officers and its rank and file.

The exposition of performance and conception offered here differentiates between attrition warfare and maneuver warfare. This is a distinction made in U.S. Marine Corps doctrine, which we will later propose as a contrast with Egyptian plans for the October War. Attrition warfare depends on superiority in manpower and materiel to batter an enemy into submission, and is usually costly. In contrast, maneuver warfare maximizes effect by movement, with the goal of achieving greater results at far less sacrifice of blood. Maneuver warfare probes, discovers, and exploits; it seeks advantage and strikes, ideally by attacking an enemy's vulnerability with one's own hardest and sharpest edge. Modern arsenals stocked with helicopters, tanks, and other armored vehicles provide the means for rapid movement on the battlefield, but maneuver warfare is not guaranteed by or dependent upon the presence of mechanized units. Foot-bound infantry can also apply the principles of maneuver warfare to great effect.

Maneuver requires tactical flexibility and improvisation guided by accurate and timely intelligence, and Arab military culture, Pollack insists, repeatedly found these abilities to be elusive. Thus Arab armies have suffered in present-day conflicts where maneuver warfare has proven its superiority. Yet by military alchemy, the Egyptians created a set-piece battle ruled by attrition in October 1973. The conscious choice of attrition over maneuver thus speaks to the intelligence of Egyptian army chiefs and to the bravery of their troops, but the fact that the Israelis reasserted maneuver and by it won victory reveals the danger of fielding forces capable only in set-piece engagements.

The special character of Egyptian military culture, and the value of harmonizing technology and tactics with it, argues for the absolute necessity to appreciate the uniqueness of the different militaries. Concepts of a universal soldier and ideas of weaponry as dictating a single best way to fight seem naïve. There is much to be learned from the fascinating, though often frustrating, story of Egyptian experience in war from 1948 through 1973.

NINE POTENTIAL EXPLANATIONS FOR
LOW COMBAT EFFECTIVENESS

On this journey to discover military culture by way of operational and tactical analysis, greater focus can speed us to our destination. Fortunately, Ken Pollack's exhaustive study warns us of dead ends and suggests promising avenues of inquiry from the start.

Pollack is trained as a political scientist and brings that discipline's form of systematic methodology to his study of the comparative military deficiency of Arab armies since World War II. He chooses nine categories as possible explanations: unit cohesion, generalship, morale, training, cowardice, technical skills and weapons handling, logistics and maintenance, tactical leadership, and information management. These can all be seen as practical expressions of military culture.

Unit Cohesion, Generalship, Morale, Training, and Cowardice

It is best to begin by dismissing flawed explanations for the problems of Arab armies on campaign. Much has been written about poor unit cohesion within Arab armies. Perhaps the most elaborate criticisms and claims come from Edward Luttwak and Dan Horowitz, who argue that masculine Arab culture sees loyalty as so wrapped up in the family that men cannot easily extend it outside to include those beyond a very small circle.[4] Outsiders are defined in terms of enmity rather than friendship, and one can gain credit by taking advantage of them. Standards of cooperation and truth that apply within the family thus dissolve outside that circle and are replaced by more predatory behavior. This form of sharp differentiation between codes that involve the family and those concerning outsiders has been labeled "amoral familialism." This, they argue, impedes or denies the kind of bonding essential to primary group cohesion and cooperation, as discussed in Chapter 7. But Pollack gives no credence to claims of low unit cohesion. Evidence contradicts it; there are many instances of Arab units, even those without officers, fighting to the last man rather than breaking. To be sure, some Arab units have broken, but often when put under great strain by poor leadership. Unit cohesion has varied, to be sure, but its absence has not been the norm.

Arab generalship has been uneven, but not uniformly bad. Flawed staff preparation and high-level command can explain some defeats, but not all. The highly politicized armies of some Arab regimes produced some generals of strong loyalty to the ruling regime but little ability in the field. Some commanders, however, have been first-rate, including Jordan's Field Marshal Bin Shakir, Iraq's Husayn Rashid Muhammad at-Tikriti, and, of course, Egypt's Isma'il 'Ali. Staff planning has also been excellent on occasion, the prime example being the cross-Canal offensive in 1973.

Morale has also varied; low morale may explain some failures but cannot be counted as a universal factor. Often morale has been high at the start of a conflict; Arab armies that attacked Israel in 1948 were strongly motivated, as were Egyptians and Syrians in the October War and Libyans who fought Chad. Moreover, military success has not followed high morale because other factors have led to defeat. Lack of morale may have been a contributing factor in certain defeats, but high morale has been unable to ensure victory.

Some commentators have charged that Arab armies did not train for field warfare, because their real concern was to put down internal disturbances. Other critics have claimed that Arab forces simply have not trained "seriously." Certainly, some rulers who used their armies mainly to stay in power could countenance poor field ability if the troops did their primary job well. Pollack argues that, in general, major armies—Egyptian, Syrian, and Iraqi—did not train properly immediately after World War II, but became much more diligent after Israeli success in the War of Independence, and that these armies were "very professional" by the 1970s.[5] The Jordanians provide an exception to this rule, because their Arab Legion was well-trained from the start. As we shall see, the preparation of Egyptian forces for the October War was rigorous, complete, and "serious."

Claims that an enemy army displayed cowardice in the field can be an insult or a misperception more than a careful evaluation. Some have charged Arab cowardice, but there is not much to substantiate it. In some circumstances, Arab forces retreated in a precipitous and disorganized fashion; so have the forces of nearly every army I know of. These retreats were caused at times by bad orders, such as when Nasser commanded his army out of the Sinai in 1956 during an ongoing Israel attack. But on closer inspection it becomes clear that Arab forces often attacked into heavy fire, held out doggedly against attackers, and sacrificed their lives for the common good. The charge of cowardice is best discarded outright.

Technical Skills and Weapons Handling, Logistics and Maintenance

Having dismissed several invalid explanations, we can consider significant problems. Arab militaries have a checkered history in dealing with technical matters. Certain Arab armies, notably the Egyptians and Iraqis, have excelled at practical engineering feats and logistics when put to the test, but Pollack judges them guilty of a consistent inability to take full advantage of advanced weaponry on the field of battle and to maintain that equipment.

The combat engineers who devised new means to cut through the sand walls of the Canal and who assembled and repaired the bridges across the Canal performed excellently in a difficult technical and military environment. The logistic capacities of the Egyptians, Iraqis, and Libyans passed muster. Thus, Pollack concludes, "By and large, Arab armies and air forces did not suffer in combat because they lacked ammunition, food, water, fuel, lubricants, medical supplies, repair tools, spare parts, or other combat necessities."[6] The October War proves his point. Putting two armies across the Canal and keeping them there deserves respect. Iraqis also demonstrated an ability to move and supply large forces, as in their war against Iran and their invasion of Kuwait.

However, when supplied with superior weaponry, as was often the case in wars against Israel, and also in combat with Iran and the truly rudimentary forces of Chad, Arab forces could not maximize the potential of their advanced technology. Arab artillery pieces were often the best available, but they were poorly coordinated and commanded. Even successes, as in 1973, reveal core weaknesses in artillery usage, as we shall see. Arab tank crews usually were poor marksmen and maneuvered ineptly. Fighter pilots could not defeat technologically inferior enemy aircraft. Moreover, lack of technical expertise within society seems to have limited the number of those qualified to use advanced weapons. In 1956, for example, the Egyptians could muster only thirty trained pilots for their 120 MiGs. Libya boasted only twenty-five pilots for 110 Mirages in 1973, and only 150 pilots for 550 aircraft in the late 1970s.[7] Tank crews have also been in short supply; Libyans have never been able to supply trained crews for more than a third of their tanks and Syrians for two-thirds of their armored vehicles.[8]

Maintenance proved to be a serious problem almost universally. Soldiers and their officers did not appreciate routine maintenance, so that operational readiness commonly stood at 50–67 percent, with low rates of 25–30 percent not uncommon. Units possessed too few individuals capable of maintenance and repair. Foreigners have often been hired to do this essential work. The peacetime record of keeping equipment up and running was bad enough, but under fire it became worse. Tanks hit in battle were not repaired or recovered, but abandoned even with comparatively minor damage. Egyptian, Iraqi, Syrian, and Libyan air forces had low sortie rates in combat because it took so long to service planes for succeeding missions. As a rule, rates for these air forces stood at less than one sortie per day. The Jordanian air force alone remained free of these shortcomings.[9]

Such technical problems reduced military effectiveness, and if other aspects of Arab military practice and culture had been strong, one could blame failure on technical shortcomings. However, two other factors were so damning that they kept the technical problems from being decisive. After all, Arab armies may have gotten less out of their weaponry, but they possessed so much of it. Quantity can make up certain deficiencies in quality. In the 1973 war, the Israelis marshaled 310,000 troops against total Arab forces of 505,000. Israelis fielded 2,000 tanks, Arabs 4,841. The Israelis possessed 570 artillery pieces of 100 mm or more, the Arabs 2,055. Numbers could have made up for a certain amount of technical inferiority among crews. But they did not.

Inept Tactical Leadership and Poor Information Management

Critical failures that overrode all others were inept tactical leadership and poor information management. Maneuver warfare demands independent initiative by junior officers free to evaluate and respond without waiting for directives from above. Exaggerated deference to authority in Arab armies required officers to refer decisions up the chain of command. Strictly centralized command restricted the responsibilities of junior officers to carrying out explicit orders in exactly the method prescribed. In this circumstance their lack of tactical initiative is not surprising.

The relative blindness of Arab high command multiplied the problems implicit in top-down decision making during the chaos of combat. This blindness resulted from a perverted flow of orders, reports, and intelligence. In the name of appeasing authority, officers in the field agreed to orders that they knew they could not carry out. Moreover, junior officers, and even senior commanders, tended to avoid censure by denying failure or shifting blame in reporting combat situations. Thus, defeats were described as victories, enemy numbers were exaggerated to account for setbacks, and other forms of dissimulation and outright lying distorted the real course of battle. A thick fog of war obscured the view of the battlefield from the top, so that those in authority made decisions irrelevant to the actual circumstances in the field. Incorrect and false reporting reached their most flagrant during the Six-Day War, after which "the Egyptians and the Jordanians explicitly concluded that the origin of this problem lay in Arab culture and its emphasis on avoiding shame."[10]

Poor tactical leadership consistently undermined Arab military effectiveness even when a well-designed operational plan was being pursued. Dependence on orders concerning even small details in a changing situation paralyzed units or channeled them into only the simplest responses, frontal assaults and dogged, but inflexible, defenses. Arab junior officers, on the whole, failed to demonstrate initiative on the battlefield and, lacking flexible response and improvisation, condemned their troops to defeat and death. Doctrines and plans became straitjackets restraining adaptation and improvisation. Ariel Sharon berated Egyptian tactical performance in the Six-Day War: "I think Egyptian soldiers are very good. They are simple and ignorant but they are strong and disciplined . . . but their officers are shit, they can fight only according to what they planned before."[11] Pollack concludes that during that same war, "The critical Syrian failing was the unwillingness of any officer along the chain of command to take the initiative and actually execute counterattacks."[12]

The list of specific tactical limitations typical of Arab armies engaged in maneuver warfare illustrates the need to be able to cope with the unpredictable and the penalty paid by those who cannot adapt and improvise. Arab armies have clumsily handled that paladin of desert warfare, the tank. At times, their equipment has been qualitatively superior to that of their Israeli opponents, and Arab armies regularly enjoyed numerical superiority as well, but crude tactics have repeatedly voided these advantages. In the offensive, Arab armor tended to plow directly forward, instead of maneuvering to exploit the lay of the land and stalk their opponents so as to hit the more vulnerable flanks and rear of enemy tanks. On the defensive, Arab armies employed tanks as stationary pillboxes, leaving them immobile once the action began, and thus targets for Israeli tankers. Defense became passive, as Arabs failed to counterattack their foes. By such shortcomings, tactical leadership squandered the great asset of the tank, its mobility.

Artillery, another essential of modern full-scale battle, did not reach its deadly potential in Arab forces because of inflexible tactics. When executing pre-arranged patterns of fire in set-piece engagements, Arab artillery could perform very well. This required careful planning, clear orders, and pre-registered targets; and with such preparations Arab guns posed a daunting threat. The problem comes when batteries must shift fire in response to the flow of battle. In such cases, gunners were slow to respond, if at all, and by the time they reacted the situation had again changed. Moreover, if and when such fire arrived, it was notoriously inaccurate. Americans came back with interesting stories of the vaunted Iraqi artillery in the Gulf War. Before the ground offensive, allies worried about Iraqi artillery because their guns were numerous and of very high quality, but they proved to be ineffective. When the U.S. 24th Mechanized Division encountered fire from the guns of the Nebuchadnezzar Republican Guard Division, the Americans soon realized that the Iraqis had registered their fire on fifty-five-gallon oil drums they had placed in the desert. If Americans kept clear of the oil drums, they would not be hit.[13] When Maj. General Griffith, leading the 1st Armored Division, briefed his corps commander at the front, Iraqi rounds fell nearby. The corps commander expressed some concern, but Griffith simply replied, "Don't worry, that's about the fifth barrage they've fired, but they don't move it. It just goes in the same place every time."[14]

Arab pilots have also come up short in air-to-air combat. The individual skills, independent reactions, and aggressive initiative required in aerial duels seem rare in Arab air forces. As a rule, Arab pilots have been consistently poor at dogfighting, as demonstrated by the kill ratios inflicted on them by the Israelis. During the 1973 October War, for every loss the Israelis suffered, their aircraft shot down twenty to thirty Arab planes; during the 1982 Israeli invasion of Lebanon this ratio climbed to 0:82 against the Syrians.[15] Commenting on Syrian performance in that fighting, a senior Israeli air force officer observed, "The problem is that their pilots didn't do things at the right time or in the right place . . . the pilots behaved as if they knew they were going to be shot down and then waited for it to happen and not how to prevent it or how to shoot us down."[16] An American commentator concluded, "At bottom, the Syrians were not done in by . . . any combination of Israeli [air] technical assets, but by the IDF's constant retention of the operational initiative and its clear advantages in leadership, organization, tactical adroitness, and adaptability."[17]

If Arab air-to-air tactics have not stood the test of combat, their air-to-ground operations have often been still worse. Heavy reliance upon ground control direction in air-to-air operations has left less initiative to the pilot; this has been damning enough in air-to-air combat, but lack of pilot discretion and initiative can be even more of a problem in ground attacks. In the latter case, difficulties with terrain, a rapidly changing tactical situation, and the availability of targets of opportunity require pilots to adapt instantaneously to unforeseen circumstances. Here Arab pilots consistently failed; their attacks were poor, usually worthless. There have been few notable exceptions to the rule of marginal Arab performance in the air; Americans regarded Saudi pilots as highly skilled in air-to-air combat during the Gulf War. The Royal Jordanian Air Force did well in attacks against enemy ground forces during the Syrian invasion of Jordan in 1970. Jordanian aircraft flew 200–250 sorties on the day of 22 September, breaking the will of the Syrians, although the Syrian air force did not oppose the Jordanians, giving them absolute control of the skies.

Beyond particular problems in the handling of armor, artillery, and aircraft, Arab military forces have shown little ability to coordinate the different arms in maneuver warfare. Infantry, armor, artillery, and air need to work together with one another to maximize their effect on the battlefield; in combat the whole is definitely greater than the sum of its parts. Thus, without infantry support, armor becomes vulnerable to enemy foot soldiers with antitank weapons; without artillery support, attacking infantry falls victim to overwhelming defensive fire and defending infantry can be overrun by assaulting forces too large to be halted by infantry weapons. Hampered by an exaggerated form of hierarchy, confused by a poor and sometimes misleading transmission of information, and compartmentalized by an attitude that officers are responsible only for their own units, Arab armies have fallen short in coordinating the different arms in maneuver warfare.

Armies would never prescribe in doctrine the kind of failings that have afflicted Arab militaries. No one orders poor weapons handling, inadequate maintenance, ineffective tactical leadership, or bad generation and distribution of information. Consequently, we must infer conception through practice, a method that most cultural historians find comfortable. So let us now turn our attention specifically to Egyptian conduct in the field.

Egyptian Military Performance, 1948–1967

During the period from the War of Israeli Independence through the Six-Day War, Egyptian campaigns fell victim to the kind of operational and tactical shortcomings noted above. A survey of Egyptian combat performance provides a record of actions in which can be read the story of Egyptian military culture, a story Isma'il 'Ali realized held the keys to both past defeat and future victory.

1948

Although the Egyptian ruler Mohammed 'Ali (1805–1848) first created an independent Egyptian army, the origins of the forces that struggled against the Israelis really only stretch back to the 1880s, when the British took effective control of Egypt and raised local troops to support the regime. At the end of World War II, Egyptian troops had as their first concern maintaining the throne of the nominally independent ruler, King Faruk I. Thus, the army, British in equipment and doctrine, devoted itself to internal security, not to preparing for conventional war against a foreign enemy. It was hardly prepared to take on the Israelis in 1948.

However, neither were Israeli forces well-prepared at the start of the War of Israeli Independence. They possessed only about 30,000 rifles and submachine guns, 1,500 machine guns, two artillery pieces, and four tanks for 50,000 "troops." Israelis were highly motivated, but their skills at conventional war were uneven. The fledgling state had to deploy these assets in several directions against multiple enemies, not simply against the Egyptians. At the start of the conflict, 14 May 1948, the Egyptians devoted about 10,000 troops—including one armored battalion—to Palestine. In opening clashes, the Egyptians conducted unimaginative frontal assaults, which generally met defeat; their artillery and air were ineffective, and then armor coordinated poorly with infantry. The Egyptian advance stalled before Ashdod, but an Israeli counterattack failed as well. A better-planned Egyptian effort to take Nitzanin succeeded, and then the first U.N. cease-fire of 11 June brought a lull in the action. During this time, both sides beefed up their forces.

When fighting began again on 8 July, the Egyptians tried an ill-coordinated attack against Negba, which failed, and another cease-fire took hold on 18

July. The Egyptians now boasted an army of 20,000 men deployed against the Israelis, who, having succeeded against other Arab foes, concentrated more of their strength against the Egyptians.

The offensive unleashed by the Israelis after the second cease-fire strove to push the Egyptians out of the Negev but met stiff opposition around Fallujah, as the Egyptians fought tenaciously. Eventually Israelis broke the line elsewhere, but Egyptian infantry held out in the Fallujah pocket, which contracted under Israeli pressure but was never entirely eliminated before the final armistice that ended the fighting. Israeli forces prevailed in this conflict, but units of the Egyptian army showed courage and aptitude in the defense, although Egyptian officers had been unimaginative and unaggressive on the tactical level. This first clash was no walk-over for the Israelis.

1956

The circumstances of the Sinai-Suez War of 1956 differed greatly from those of the previous struggle. Egypt had undergone a revolution in 1952; a military coup swept out the British-backed Faruk and put Col. Gamal Abdel Nasser in charge. The cabal of Free Officers who came into power intended, as one of their primary goals, to create an army capable of defeating Israel. Nasser's anti-colonial and "socialist" regime arranged to purchase a sizeable quantity of Soviet arms through Czechoslovakia in 1955, a deal that allowed the Egyptians to circumvent the arms embargo maintained by the United States, Britain, and France. Included in the purchase were 230 improved T34/85 tanks, superior to armor in the Israeli arsenal. The aircraft transferred to Egypt also outclassed Israeli jets. While the Egyptians now fielded Soviet equipment, their doctrine remained British. It would be years before Soviet advisers appeared; in fact, before the outbreak of the war, Nasser called in German military advisers with experience in the Wehrmacht. In July 1956 Nasser nationalized the Suez Canal, an act that infuriated the British and the French. Israel, concerned with the growing Egyptian military potential, joined Britain and France in a military campaign designed to retake the Canal and reduce Egyptian power. With good reason, Nasser worried about an invasion by British and French forces as well as confronting the Israelis, so he stationed only 30,000 troops in the Sinai, about a third of the army. This force could not hold the entire Sinai front in strength, so the best troops concentrated at Abu Ageilah, El-Arish, Rafah, and Gaza.

The Israeli Defense Force (IDF) that struck the Egyptian positions on 29 October had grown and matured. It deployed 45,000 troops for the invasion of the Sinai; this figure included one armored and two mechanized brigades.

The Israeli offensive began when paratroopers dropped on the Mitla Pass; this bold move trumped Egyptian intelligence, which did not realize the strength of the assault on the pass for twelve hours. Nevertheless, Egyptian defenders fought back with such vigor and resolve that the IDF troops failed to secure the pass, even when Sharon's armor arrived. The Israelis bungled their first attack on the well-entrenched Egyptian position at Abu Ageilah, and the Egyptians held stoutly. Their positions at Umm Qatef resisted the Israelis until Nasser ordered a withdrawal. British and French aircraft raided Egyptian air bases on 31 October, and Nasser correctly read this as presaging a full-scale assault on Egypt itself, so he commanded his troops in the Sinai to pull back to defend the Canal and Cairo. These orders reached Egyptian commanders on 1 November, but trying to disengage from an ongoing battle is one of the most difficult of military operations, and Egyptian forces suffered badly in the process. Units around Abu Ageilah abandoned their equipment and made their way back as best they could. Egyptian armor and infantry on the northern flank attempted a fighting withdrawal from Rafah and El-Arish. Because the retreating Egyptians stuck to the roads and drove dead ahead without proper flank protection, the Israelis inflicted heavy casualties on them in a series of engagements. Some units maintained their cohesion, others broke apart. Egyptian troops finally pulled back from the Mitla Pass as well. After this costly retreat, only a single Egyptian battalion reached the Canal in shape to continue combat.

The record of particular failings is disturbing. Throughout the war, the Egyptian air force was outclassed. Although Cairo lacked sufficient pilots to fly all its new planes, this was less of a problem than it first might seem, because aircraft maintenance was so poor that the Egyptians could count only thirty to thirty-five of their MiGs as airworthy. Thus, the Egyptians flew relatively few sorties before the British and French eliminated most of the Egyptian air force on 31 October. During the first two days of the war, the methodical Egyptian pilots failed to match Israelis in the improvised tactics of dogfighting and lost several planes, while the Israelis lost none. On the ground, Egyptian forces did not coordinate and combine arms effectively. Armor fought without infantry support, and this allowed French paratroopers at Raswah and Israeli troops in the Sinai to ply antitank weapons against

Egyptian tanks with impunity. On the offensive, Egyptian armor plowed directly forward and were shot apart by Israeli tankers; on the defensive, Egyptian armor did not maneuver but fought as stationary steel pillboxes. A fog of distortion and lying occluded the view of the Egyptian high command. Field commanders grossly inflated successes and hid failures, or they excused defeats by exaggerating the forces sent against them. Moshe Dayan described how Egyptian commanders report "the presence of Israeli battalions and brigades even when they are faced only by sections and platoons."[18]

Israeli performance in 1956 was hardly invincible and the Egyptians were not humiliated. The IDF suffered a number of setbacks in hard fighting and only overcame the Egyptians after Nasser ordered his army to withdraw. In defending set positions, many Egyptian troops fought doggedly and effectively. Egypt struggled against a powerful alliance in an extremely difficult situation. While the Sinai campaign was a defeat for the Egyptians, it was not a disgrace, because they interpreted their loss as the result of facing an overpowering alliance of Israel, Britain, and France; therefore, defeat did not bring reform.

Yemeni Civil War

The next major Egyptian military action, intervention in the Yemeni civil war, showed Nasser's army in a far better light. Yemeni army officers who admired Nasser and espoused his pan-Arab beliefs overthrew the monarchy in September 1962. Nasser almost immediately committed troops to support the new regime, while the Saudis aided the deposed king, Imam Mohammed al-Badr. The joint Ramadan Offensive saw Egyptian and Yemeni republican forces carry out a great pincer movement against royalist bands in February 1963. Planned by Egyptian Field Marshal Abd el Hakim Amer, this campaign stressed maneuver both in the conception of converging thrusts and in the way that they dealt with major objectives not by driving directly into defenses but by outflanking them. For all its success, however, the offensive did not cut off the royalists from their Saudi support. Nonetheless, the Ramadan Offensive demonstrated that Egyptian planning could be very good and that staffs were anything but oblivious to the benefits of maneuver. Egyptians increased their investment to 40,000 troops over the next two years. Their Haradh Offensive launched in June 1964 showed real creativity and had some impact. As a conventional operation, the plan was good, although the actual execution was slow, but it can be questioned whether any such conventional strike was appropriate to defeat a guerrilla opponent. In any case, the Haradh Offensive ultimately failed to destroy the royalists.

With the aid of European advisers, Yemeni royalist military skills increased and scored some victories in 1965, and the Egyptian commitment flagged. Egyptian troop numbers increased to 70,000 troops before Cairo realized its failure and limited its forces to defending important towns. Egyptian numbers in Yemen decreased to 40,000 by early 1966 and declined further to 20,000 by the time of the Six-Day War. Although they had not eliminated the royalist resistance, the Egyptians could be reassured by the fact that their troops carried out large-scale conventional operations with some success; there seemed no obvious need to revamp the military. Then came the Six-Day War.

The Six-Day War, 1967

This chapter began with an account of Egyptian catastrophe in the Six-Day War, so we need say little here. The Egyptian military that fought this conflict was more influenced by political preferment and more under Soviet influence than it had been before. At the top of the military pyramid, Field Marshal Amer (the army commander), Lt. Gen. Mahmud Sidqui Mahmud (the air force chief), and General Shams Badran (minister of war) had reached the summit because of their political ties with Nasser and the Free Officers. Once in charge, they refashioned the military into their own power base. Amer put his cronies in key army commands and seems to have believed that he might use this leverage inside the army to succeed Nasser at some point.[19] It is not that Amer lacked military credentials—he enjoyed a high reputation in the army and had planned the impressive Ramadan Offensive—but in turning the army into his own reliable political instrument, he had promoted men because of their loyalty rather than their military ability. Also, to gain political credit, Amer and Badran set the army to many civil tasks. Later, General Fawzi condemned this: "The Armed Forces became involved in land reclamation, housing, the national transport system, state security, the Aswan High Dam, and many other activities . . . the growing power of the Armed Forces in civilian life was detrimental to its main responsibility which was to be a fighting force, ready for battle."[20]

At this time, Egypt relied increasingly upon the Soviets. Nasser bought great quantities of arms from them; by the outbreak of war the Egyptians had a total of 1,400 tanks. Reorganized in accord with the Soviet model, the army also selectively imported tactics and doctrine, although it never became a mere reflection of its new sponsor. Egyptians retained elements of Turkish and British approaches as well as employing their own methods. In fact, the direct involvement of Soviet personnel remained modest; in June 1967 only 500 advisers served in Egypt, and most of these were weapons instructors.

Enjoying significant numerical advantage in the Sinai, the Egyptians braced for war. Their original plans laid out a defense in depth, with main armored forces retained for counterstrokes, but Nasser overruled this intelligent plan and demanded a forward deployment. Fundamental failures of Egyptian intelligence resulted in an extremely poor understanding of the Israeli art of maneuver war.

The actual fighting began with carefully prepared and devastatingly executed Israeli air strikes during three hours on the morning of 5 June. As mentioned above, only late in the afternoon did Nasser learn that he had no air force, and Egyptian generals in the Sinai were not told until noon the next day, a full twenty-eight hours after the initial strikes.[21] By this time, Israelis had already taken Rafah, El-Arish, and Abu Ageilah.

The three axes of the Israeli attack—against Rafah/El-Arish, against Abu Ageilah, and between the two—all advanced at such a rate that their success surprised even the Israelis. Dominance of the air facilitated the Israeli blitzkrieg, which advanced so quickly that Maj. Gen. Gavish, who commanded the front, urged his three divisional generals, Tal, Sharon, and Yoffe, to draft new plans for a more rapid pursuit. On the afternoon of 6 June, Amer ordered a general retreat. Many officers who received these orders fled west. Although Amer later rescinded the retreat order, the harm was already done.

Egypt's army had not simply been defeated; it had been humiliated. Pollack insists that the dramatic course of the war came not from a decline in Egyptian forces, but from a marked improvement in Israeli ability. Critical Egyptian deficiencies were ones they had suffered from before. The strategic plans had not been that bad, but the usual tactical shortcomings condemned their army to failure, made all the worse by the elimination of the air force. Inability to maneuver, unwillingness to improvise, failure to coordinate arms beyond the bounds of set plans, and a recurrent tendency to distort information to save face hamstrung the Egyptian defense. After the debacle, Nasser called his generals to task in a series of inquiries and trials. Amer, fearing trial himself, committed suicide. Amer and his cronies deserve a share of the blame, but this chapter argues that the primary problems lay elsewhere.

RECOGNITION AND ADAPTATION: PREPARATION AND PLANNING FOR THE OCTOBER WAR

So shattering was the experience of the Six-Day War, that Nasser and, after his death in 1970, his successor, Anwar Sadat, resolved to put aside other priorities in the military and concentrate on manning, organizing, and training a force capable of besting the Israelis in the field. In a purge of 800 officers who held the rank of colonel or above, incompetent commanders fell, and more able men replaced them. The criteria for replacement would be not political but professional. Mohamed Heikal observes that "Remembering the disasters of 1967, [Sadat] was determined that the professional soldiers should be left to run their own show."[22] Based on a thorough evaluation of Egyptian military effectiveness, this new leadership would draft and execute a plan to cross the Canal and achieve a bridgehead in the Sinai.

After the Six-Day War, the first test of arms, the War of Attrition, 1968–1970, resulted in further disappointment for the Egyptians. Egyptian strategy in this conflict aimed to inflict casualties on the IDF and wear down the Israelis, who could not afford to mobilize for war indefinitely. Egyptian batteries fired the first bombardment of the new struggle on 8 September 1968, and others followed. Over the days, weeks, and months that followed, the Israelis retaliated with bombardments of their own and with raids into Egypt. These raids damaged a dam, felled bridges, destroyed radar sites, sank vessels, and killed troops. In July 1969 the Israeli air force joined the fray, attacking Egyptian bases and missile sites and chewing up the Egyptian air force when it attempted attacks of its own. Soviet involvement intensified, as they not only supplied more hardware but also piloted aircraft for Egypt. Hostilities escalated until 30 July 1970, when twelve Israeli fighters jumped sixteen Soviet-piloted MiGs, downing five of them. Things threatened to get out of hand, and within a week the United States brokered a cease-fire to contain the conflict.

The formula that would reverse the by-now familiar failure of Egyptian forces against the IDF grew out of an insightful assessment of Egyptian and Israeli strengths and weaknesses by Isma'il 'Ali, who first served as chief of staff, then as head of intelligence, and finally as minister of war. While the Egyptians would take advantage of new military technologies, the key was not in employing particular hardware but in understanding and maximizing the abilities of the Egyptian soldier. General Mohamed Abdel Ghani El-Gamasy, deputy chief of staff during the October War, testifies that Isma'il 'Ali "had developed the conviction that the human element—the quality of the fighter—and not the weapon was what counted in victory."[23] This phrase, "the quality of the fighter," is a shorthand for the cultural characteristics of Egyptian troops in combat. Isma'il 'Ali would achieve success by adapting his war plans to the military culture of his army.

He realized that his soldiers could not match the IDF in the ad hoc give-and-take of maneuver warfare, but he also recognized that the resolute and tough Egyptian infantry performed well in set-piece battles. He concluded that the Egyptians must engage in their own kind of fight, rather than letting the Israelis determine the tempo of operations. He envisioned a clash designed to impose and maintain a more methodical and less mobile style of combat. It must be a set-piece battle, limited in time and space, so that it could be controlled. He also realized that the Israelis were unusually sensitive to casualties, so a defensive battle that inflicted serious losses on them might bring them to the table with a willingness to accept Egyptian bargaining points.

With Soviet counsel, the Egyptians had devised a campaign plan for a Soviet-style breakthrough and exploitation to conquer the Sinai. This plan, "Granite," consisted of three phases: the Canal crossing, the drive from the Canal to the passes, and the conquest of all the Sinai. But when Isma'il 'Ali became minister of war he dismissed Phases II and III of this operation, and concentrated on Phase I, the Canal crossing, which he called High Minarets. This became the blueprint for the actual crossing, Operation Badr. Redrafting of Phase I was an Egyptian project undertaken under the direction of Gamasy without Soviet input and in contradiction to some cherished Soviet principles.[24] High Minarets combined the operational offensive with the tactical defensive, by driving across the Canal in irresistible strength and under the cover of deception, and then allowing the IDF to batter itself into exhaustion trying to retake what it had lost. In order to compensate for the lack of initiative and adaptability typical of tactical-level command, the offensive would be intricately scripted. High Minarets defined movement, goals, and timing down to the squad level. The voluminous script set schedules for advances and stipulated times and targets to ensure the kind of coordination between armor, artillery, and infantry that so eluded Arab armies in maneuver warfare. Once the details were committed to paper, junior officers were not allowed to improvise lest they upset the schedules. It is clear that Isma'il 'Ali concentrated on Phase I, which was minutely scripted, while plans for Phases II and III hardly existed. Isma'il 'Ali had no faith in Phase II and would oppose implementing it when ordered to do so by Sadat.

Intensive training would guarantee the success of the script. Each soldier was to learn only a single task and master it through repetitive practice. Individual soldiers rehearsed their roles hundreds of times.

> Twice a day during four years these [engineer] units assembled and dismantled . . . bridge [segments]. Similarly, every day for years all operators of Sagger anti-tank missiles lined up outside vans containing simulators and went through half an hour's exercise in tracking tanks with their missile. . . . This system was repeated right down the line the army until every action became a reflex action.[25]

To make the preparations as realistic as possible, the Egyptians constructed extensive mock-ups of their objectives. General Shazli, chief of staff during the October War, reports that the army rehearsed the entire operation thirty-five times, on top of the endless repetition by smaller units.[26]

Egyptian tanks and fighter aircraft had not done well in duels with the Israelis, so Isma'il 'Ali turned to imported technologies to counter the enemy. New Soviet wire-guided Sagger antitank missiles in the hands of infantry would now destroy Israeli tanks sent to counterattack the Egyptians. Well-trained and methodically rehearsed Sagger crews proved their worth, extracting a deadly toll from the Israelis. After the Israelis had damaged Egyptian air defenses during the War of Attrition, the Soviets supplied their ally with an impressive array of surface-to-air missiles (SAMs), most notably the mobile SA-6. With these the Egyptians would erect an umbrella of air defense across the channel far enough to cover Phase I without having to rely upon the limited dogfighting skills of their pilots. Concern over the inability of the air force to defend its bases caused the Egyptians to built hardened hangars to protect their aircraft, where, after initial and ineffective raids, the Egyptian planes waited out the war. The script did not call for much from the air force.

Along with the new equipment, the Soviets dispatched advisers; eventually 5,000 Soviet officers served with the Egyptians, a figure that allowed ten for each battalion.[27] They taught the Egyptians how to use their advanced weaponry, and their approach to warfare influenced Egyptian conceptions, but the war planners did not accept Soviet methods wholesale. As already pointed out, High Minarets was drafted without direct Soviet input. In fact, since the Soviets were interested in détente with the United States, they did

not want another war in the Middle East, and tensions between the
Egyptians and their guests escalated to the point that Sadat sent most of the
Soviets packing in July 1972. Relations mended to the extent that in early
1973 many Soviets returned, although the vast majority were weapons train-
ers and no more.

To direct the battle effectively, the Egyptian high command required the
kind of accurate front-line intelligence that they knew was not likely to come
from their own combat officers. The fact that officers regularly doctored
reports or just plain lied had become a widely known weakness of Egyptian
military culture. In 1968, Mohamed Heikal wrote in *Al-Ahram* that Egyptians
suffered "behavioral flaws resulting from lack of discipline, namely delay in
reporting the truth, if it is negative, to higher levels of authority."[28] In lieu of
honest information from Egyptian officers, the high command would moni-
tor Israeli communications, because the Israelis commonly spoke in the clear
over their communications grid, even about sensitive matters. So the
Egyptians constructed a large electronic facility on Jebel Ataqah to eavesdrop.

Successful execution of the cross-Canal operation required considerable
feats of engineering. In a society short on technical expertise, this was a problem, but the Egyptians solved it in part by compelling previously exempt college students and graduates to serve. Heikal asserts that on the eve of the
October War, 110,000 of the 800,000-man army boasted college degrees.[29]
Engineer units learned how to blast their way through the sand dunes and
mastered the construction, maintenance, and repair of bridges that carried the
Egyptians over the Canal.

Lastly, success depended on the Egyptians seizing the initiative and keeping it until they had crossed the Canal and consolidated their positions; surprise would be essential. In 1956 and 1967, the Israelis had launched preemp-
tive attacks that allowed them to impose their style of maneuver warfare, but
the Egyptians could not let this happen again. Egyptians would have to
undertake the crossing at a time when Israeli defenses were lightly held, ensuring that the IDF lacked the power to unhinge the carefully scripted assault.
The Israeli religious calendar provides such an opportunity in Yom Kippur,
the Day of Atonement, the holiest day on the Jewish calendar, when many
troops would be allowed to return to their homes for observances. This also
met the needs of Isma'il 'Ali's plan because it coincided with favorable tides
and currents in the Canal. Next the Israelis were lulled into seeing Egyptian
activity on the west bank of the Suez Canal as normal. Over the years, the
Egyptians repeatedly mobilized and deployed as if to attack. From January to

October of 1973, the Egyptians called up reserves, brought up their troops, and practiced the Canal crossing twenty-two times; so there was no particular reason to believe that mobilization on the eve of Yom Kippur meant anything more. In fact, the serious intent of this last exercise remained hidden to all but a small number of Egyptian officers as well until the morning of 6 October.[30] Meanwhile, the Egyptians planted stories that their military equipment was in bad shape and much of it could not be put into the field. For once, the Egyptians pulled off a great intelligence coup, leaving the Israelis in the dark about their intentions until it was too late to forestall the offensive.[31]

MATTERS OF DOCTRINE:
INFLUENCE AND CONTRAST

The Egyptians stood poised to combat the Israelis in ways substantially different from those that Egyptian forces tried in the preceding twenty-five years. The unique aspect of the Egyptian preparation for the cross-Canal attack lay not in the fact that they invested so much in staff planning but that their plans were so minutely detailed and allowed for no variation. The script generated under the guidance of Isma'il 'Ali adapted to the particular character of Egyptian troops and military culture rather than trying to mimic his adversaries. His offensive would embrace an attritional form of warfare, restricting Egyptian maneuver to an initial advance followed by a strict tactical defensive designed to wear down the Israelis by weight of materiel. It so centralized command that it virtually eliminated alternatives to all but senior officers, and it ensured coordination between infantry, artillery, and armor by setting out detailed and invariable schedules. High Minarets was war by the numbers in every sense of the word; it stands out in strong relief when contrasted with other modern military doctrines.

High Minarets did draw from Soviet military thought and practice, but adapted and extended its principles. Reliant on Soviet military advisers and using Soviet weaponry, the Egyptians were also exposed to their ally's doctrine. Without attempting a long description of Soviet doctrine, a few salient traits deserve mention.[32] In the name of ensuring operational success, the Soviets concentrated authority in the hands of front commanders—the term "front" being used to refer to what Western armies term an army or army group. To maximize the options available to operational high command, Soviet doctrine restricted the options of lesser commanders; in particular, junior officers were to be obedient rather than innovative. To achieve results, meticulous planning proved essential, and offensives were set out in detailed scripts. The Soviets relied on surprise and good intelligence gathering to catch their enemies off guard and then press forward rapidly. Here Egyptian plans resemble Soviet practice.

However, in key respects, Russian doctrine was different than that adopted by Isma'il 'Ali and Gamasy. Russian junior officers enjoyed more leeway in that they were trained in combat drills that gave them a menu of tactical options to choose from. Doctrine also built in flexibility by retaining large reserves to exploit opportunities, in an aggressive, offensive style of warfare designed to achieve deep penetrations. It substituted mass for skill and regarded manpower and equipment as expendable. Willing to accept heavier losses than Egyptians could afford, Russian units advanced in waves or echelons, with fresh troops moving through spent echelons to maintain pressure on the enemy. Soviet practice stressed tank warfare, and their field armies contained a high percentage of armored divisions. Within this tank-heavy form of warfare, the Soviets stressed and achieved combination of arms on a fluid battlefield.

High Minarets represented selective adaptation rather than complete adoption of Soviet ideas. This selectivity sheds light on an oft-repeated charge that Arab military shortcomings can be ascribed to their embracing Soviet doctrine whole. Egyptians such as Mahmud Hussein have blamed "reliance, from the late 1950s onwards, on Russian weapons systems and the tactics which such systems necessarily implied."[33] British commentator Jon Glassman observes, "Arab disadvantages were heightened by the application of Russian introduced tactical models that were ill-suited for the fluid situation created by Israeli deep penetration tactics."[34] In contradiction, Pollack and Eisenstadt argue first that not all Arab armies used Russian equipment or Russian doctrine and yet all Arab forces still suffered the same recurrent tactical problems. Second, Egyptian methods were not mirror images of Soviet models. And most importantly, Soviet influence probably helped rather than hurt Egypt. Western military practice assumes an initiative among junior officers that Arab armies lacked; Soviet doctrine was more in tune with Arab reality here. Soviet precedent demonstrated the efficacy of scripting operations and of careful rehearsal, and both practices made possible the Egyptians' initial victory in 1973 and, it should be noted, Iraqi success against the Iranians in 1988 as well. For good, and ultimately effective, reasons, Arab planners went *much* further than did Soviets in scripting. So to the extent that Soviet practice shaped that of the Arabs, it provided useful examples.

To put both Egyptian and Soviet military cultures in perspective, compare them to maneuver warfare as espoused by the United States Marine Corps in its doctrinal statement *Warfighting*.³⁵ The contrasts are fundamental. *Warfighting* is heavily influenced by both Clausewitz and Sun-tzu. It emphasizes Clausewitzian concepts of will, friction, and uncertainty in war. The goal is to defeat an enemy in this environment of risk not by attrition, bringing mass against mass, but by maneuver, finding and exploiting the adversary's weaknesses. "Rather than wearing down an enemy's defenses, maneuver warfare attempts to bypass these defenses in order to *penetrate* the enemy system and tear it apart."³⁶ This is not the clash of phalanxes but a war of foxes. *Warfighting* repeatedly quotes Sun-tzu, accepting Chinese ideas of the fluidity of war. "Now an army may be likened to water, for just as flowing water avoids the heights and hastens to the lowlands, so an army avoids strength and strikes weakness."³⁷

Warfighting preaches decentralized command and advocates initiative and responsibility among subordinates. "First and foremost," it insists, "*in order to generate the tempo of operations we desire and to best cope with the uncertainty, disorder, and fluidity of combat, command and control must be decentralized.*" Subordinate commanders are explicitly told not to delay action by asking for direction from senior officers: "Subordinate commanders must make decisions on their own initiative . . . rather than passing information up the chain of command and waiting for the decision to be passed down."³⁸ *Warfighting* emphasizes the relationship between uncertainty and opportunity. The nature of battle is that "plans will go awry, instructions and information will be unclear and misinterpreted, communications will fail, and mistakes and unforeseen events will be commonplace." Such "natural disorder" creates situations "ripe for exploitation by an opportunistic will."³⁹ Maneuver warfare as embraced by the Marines "requires a certain independence of mind, a willingness to act with initiative and boldness" in which the junior officer has the "moral courage to accept responsibility for this type of behavior."⁴⁰

In order to ensure independence and initiative to subordinate commanders, maneuver warfare ideally rejects elaborate and rigid plans. Instead, doctrine advocates "simple flexible plans."⁴¹ Using "mission tactics" helps free the man on the spot from the directives of the high command. *Warfighting* defines mission tactics as "assigning a subordinate mission without specifying how the mission must be accomplished."⁴² Should a senior commander lead from the front, he should not impinge on his officers' independence. "*We must remember that command from the front should not equate to oversupervision of subordinates.*"⁴³

Of course such a doctrinal statement as *Warfighting* represents combat as it should be; it prescribes a professional discourse on war—that is, one accepted by military professionals. Whether it accurately reflects reality can always be debated. In any case, doctrine generally shapes training, and, as it is often said, armies fight the way they train. *Battle* goes further and argues that armies fight the way they think. Isma'il 'Ali accepted the combat culture of his troops and rethought how to best take advantage of it. He and Gamasy consciously eschewed the kind of maneuver warfare directed by *Warfighting* and chose tactics more like, but still distinct from, the Russian blueprint. The Egyptians opted for attrition through a static defense because it maximized the strengths of their troops and officers. Isma'il 'Ali's script was his doctrine, a professional discourse on war in accord with "the quality of the fighter."

Ismai'l 'Ali's prescription for battle presents an intriguing paradox for those who adhere to theories of a Western Way of War. Israelis, a more Western force, would employ maneuver similar to that later advocated in *Warfighting*, which explicitly references the Chinese classics to eschew costly head-to-head confrontation. In contrast, Egyptians intended to form an unbroken defensive line to meet the Israelis in close combat designed to inflict heavy casualties; thus Egyptian tactics conformed more closely to characteristics Victor Davis Hanson defines as the Western Way of War. However, whether or not Egyptian plans qualified as "Western," they would achieve a major success in the first days of the October War.

THE OCTOBER WAR ON THE EGYPTIAN FRONT

The Egyptian campaign of secrecy and misinformation worked well, if not perfectly. Because the Egyptians and the Syrians intended to attack on 6 October, they mobilized and moved troops up to Israeli lines some time before, and the presence of such massive forces alarmed the Israelis. On 5 October, the Israelis moved toward a higher condition of readiness, but Prime Minister Golda Meir resisted appeals by her military advisers to take stronger action because she hoped to avoid any charge that Israel had been overly aggressive. Thus, before the Egyptian attack began, the Israelis declared only a partial mobilization, and this was too little too late. Because it struck on Yom Kippur, the Israelis call this conflict the Yom Kippur War, while to Arabs it is the Ramadan War, because it began during the Muslim holy month of Ramadan. We use the more neutral term, the October War.

At 2 P.M. on Saturday, 6 October 1973, a devastating storm of fire and steel came down upon the under-manned Israeli positions holding the east bank of the Suez Canal.[44] In the first minute of the artillery barrage, 10,500 shells crashed into Israeli lines; the initial bombardment would last fifty-three minutes. Discharging this rain of terror were 1,850 Egyptian artillery pieces, 1,000 tanks, and 1,000 antitank guns firing from the west bank. Overhead, 250 war planes streaked toward Israeli airfields and command posts deeper in the Sinai. Soviet-built FROG missiles also targeted Israeli air bases.

The attack burst on the Israelis with irresistible force and stunning speed. For the initial blow, the Egyptians committed roughly 200,000 troops and 1,600 tanks, supported by 2,000 artillery pieces, organized as five infantry divisions, three mechanized divisions, two armored divisions, and various independent brigades grouped into the Second and Third Armies. This force was supported by over 100 SA-2 and SA-3 batteries, as well as twenty to forty SA-6 batteries; all told, the Egyptians marshaled more surface-to-air missiles than existed in the entire U.S. arsenal. Against this onslaught, the Israelis could deploy only 18,000 men and 300 tanks until reserves arrived. Strong points along the Bar Lev Line, constructed during the War of Attrition, were only partially manned. Even after the fighting began, the IDF could not concentrate against the Egyptian onslaught because it had to contend with Syrian forces on the Golan Heights, where the Syrians attacked with 60,000 men, 1,400 tanks, and 600 artillery pieces.

Egyptian success would not, however, simply depend on mass, for the Egyptians conducted the cross-Canal attack with impressive coordination. As the first shells blasted Israeli positions, Egyptian rangers pushed off from the west bank in collapsible boats to lead the way for the onslaught. Fifteen minutes into the barrage, 8,000 picked commandos put their boats into the water. These attackers carried light-weight bamboo assault ladders to mount the high palisades on the east bank. The commandos pulled their rations, weapons, and packs on specially designed trolleys. Armed with advanced wire-guided antitank missiles and shoulder-fired anti-aircraft missiles, they would set up an initial shield for the Egyptian crossing. This first wave crossed the Canal in only seven minutes, avoided Israeli strong points, pushed into the desert on the other side of the Canal, and set up ambushes to destroy Israeli tanks. As these troops landed, the Egyptian barrage lifted from the bank and switched to targets further inland. At the same time, Egyptian amphibious vehicles plowed into the Great Bitter Lake and began to navigate its waters to seize the eastern shore.

To prepare the path for additional waves, combat engineers quickly cleared passages through sand walls of the Canal on the west bank at pre-arranged positions. This enabled a very rapid pace at the outset in the operation, with further assault waves crossing every fifteen minutes. On the west bank, engineers set up high-pressure water hoses to blast open gaps in the sand and earth walls of the Canal. Israelis had assumed it would take the Egyptians from a day and a half to two days to breach these walls with bulldozers, but the innovative Egyptian method accomplished the task in as little as two hours. With avenues opened, amphibious vehicles swam the Canal and tank ferries brought additional armored firepower to the assault. Meanwhile other engineers began construction of pontoon bridges for infantry and tanks. The twelve bridges along the front of the Second Army were in operation by midnight; however, the eight that would serve the Third Army took longer because of problems in cutting though the stronger Canal walls in the south. By 8 P.M., only six hours after the initial barrage, nearly 80,000 troops had crossed the Canal. Egyptian planners feared that potential casualties during the crossing could mount to 25,000–30,000, with 10,000 dead, yet only 208 troops actually died. The historian Trevor N. Dupuy praises this operation as "one of the most memorable water crossings in the annals of warfare."[45]

The Egyptian script worked. Shazli praised the crossing as "a magnificent symphony played by tens of thousands of men."[46] The *New York Times* reporter described it this way: "The Egyptian Army has doggedly adhered to a comprehensive, preconceived strategic and tactical plan. Military spokesmen insist that there have been no departures from the plan, no improvisations and no unauthorized initiative by local commanders."[47] In fact, Egyptian orders forbade junior officers from diverging from the script for the first twelve hours of the attack.[48] Any change from the plans, as when engineers of the Third Army experienced some delay breaking through the earthen ramparts in the south, had to be referred to general headquarters. In this case, Isma'il 'Ali dispatched a senior officer to re-site some of the crossings.

Once units had crossed, they set up defensive positions, consolidated, and then expanded incrementally by advancing in a 180-degree arc. The scenario proceeded as intended, without variance. First, infantry crept forward, infiltrating Israeli defenses, if there were any, and set up their weapons; then artillery unleashed a barrage behind the advanced posts, and through this protective fire, armor and mechanized infantry drove forward to link up with the infantry. Resistance remaining after the barrage was suppressed with heavy fire from tanks and infantry. After consolidating their gains, troops repeated the

process. Eventually the expanding arcs joined the various bridgeheads together into a continuous line, under a protective umbrella of SAMs. Prearranged firing orders guaranteed coordination between the different arms, as long as everyone stuck to the schedule.

The Israelis responded as expected, with aggressive but rash and piecemeal counterstrokes. In support of the troops holding the Canal, the Israelis marshaled only a single armored division commanded by Avraham Mendler. Of his three brigades, only Colonel Amnon Reshev's was immediately available; the others were stationed further to the rear and had to come west before engaging. As early as 2:30 P.M., Reshev's armored companies rushed forward in the kind of tank charges that had been so effective in 1967. However, Egyptian antitank crews were ready and immediately began to take a heavy toll. Armed with accurate wire-guided missiles, they would fire from camouflaged positions, sometimes allowing Israeli tanks to pass over and through them, and then taking the Israelis from the flank and rear. Israeli units would attack, lose tanks, pull back, regroup, and attack again. By evening, Egyptian antitank fire had knocked out nearly all Reshev's hundred tanks. Around 8 P.M., the other two brigades were coming on line and attacking in the same headlong manner. By the morning of 7 October, Mendler had only half his original three hundred tanks, and by the end of the day only one hundred remained operational.

Israeli air attacks struck the advancing Egyptians and their bridges, but at heavy cost. Israelis claimed hits on the bridges, but Egyptian engineers soon repaired the modular bridges and kept the troops coming. During these Israeli air strikes, Egyptian SAMs and anti-aircraft fire downed fourteen Israeli aircraft and hit many more. The Egyptians inflicted so much damage that the Israeli air force ordered its planes to avoid the front near the Canal.

On 8 October the Israelis committed two more armored divisions, the 162nd under Adan and the 143rd under Sharon, in a badly planned and poorly executed counterattack. Their uncoordinated thrusts failed in the face of fierce Egyptian opposition. One of Adan's brigades lost twenty tanks, half its strength, in a matter of minutes in the first attack. So ill-designed was the operation that while Adan was heavily engaged, only one of Sharon's three brigades got involved in the fighting. Dupuy called the failed assaults "without a doubt . . . the worst defeat in the history of the Israeli Army."[49]

The Israelis, however, improvised ever more effective ways of dealing with the advancing Egyptians. In order to suppress the fire of antitank Sagger crews, Adan used machine-gun fire from armored personnel carriers to force them to keep their heads down. Other IDF units called in artillery barrages to accomplish the same task. Israeli troops also learned to halt Egyptian advances by attacking their flanks, for by pinning down some troops, the Israelis could throw off the timing of the whole. The actual Egyptian attack began to lag behind the script, and the more it diverged the more this confused and further slowed them. On 9 and 10 October the Egyptian advance finally stalled short of the objectives set for Phase I; nevertheless, the Egyptians held a band of territory several miles wide along the east bank of the Canal. Isma'il 'Ali's goals had been modest for Phase I, and stopping a bit short was not lethal to the plan. What followed, however, would be.

Early victory created an air of overconfidence that carried away Shazli and Gamasy, but Isma'il 'Ali firmly resisted moving on to the vague and uncharted Phase II drive to the passes. Yet defeat of Syrian forces on the Golan led Syrian President Hafiz al-Assad to implore Sadat to continue the Egyptian offensive to take the pressure off Syria, and the Egyptian president ordered Isma'il 'Ali to push on. Reluctantly Isma'il 'Ali brought over the two armored divisions he held in reserve on the west bank, and this gave the Egyptians 800 to 1,000 tanks for a two-pronged assault toward the passes. They launched this attack on 14 October, but now there was no script to guide them and the old problems resurfaced. Poor reconnaissance, unimaginative tactics, and poor coordination of arms doomed the offensive. To make matters worse, Israeli commandos destroyed most of the equipment at the Egyptian eavesdropping facility at Jebel Ataqah on the morning of the attack and thus robbed the Egyptian high command of its best source of tactical information. In a matter of hours the offensive failed after gaining only a few miles; Egyptians lost 265 tanks in the ill-starred attack, to an Israeli loss of only forty tanks, of which all but six were repaired and sent back into action. Although generally not a critic of Arab armies, Brigadier General S. A. El-Edroos condemned the Egyptian conduct of the battles that day: "The catastrophic defeat suffered by the Egyptian tank corps reflected the inability of Egyptian commanders, from divisional to [company] level, to conduct mobile, flexible, and fluid armored operations."[50] In the simpler words of the Israeli brigade commander, Amnon Reshev, "They just waddled forward like ducks."[51]

Defeat of the 14 October offensive fundamentally undermined the Egyptian position. By committing their major reserves, the Egyptians weakened their position on the west bank of the Canal, putting themselves in jeopardy should the Israelis mount an offensive that carried them over the Canal. This was exactly what the Israelis now did. Finding and exploiting a gap between the Second and Third Armies, the Israelis established a bridgehead on the west bank just north of the Great Bitter Lake early on 16 October. Egyptian counterattacks failed, for now the Israelis dictated the style of battle. Once Israelis crossed in strength during the next days, they overran SAM sites, making it possible for the Israeli air force to come back into play. Throughout the entire war, Israelis and Egyptians clashed in fifty-two major dogfights, in which the Israelis shot down 152 aircraft for a loss of five to eight of their own—a kill ratio of 20–30:1. Although staunch Egyptian resistance halted a thrust north from the bridgehead by Sharon's division, Adan drove south with his armor all the way to Suez, cutting off the Third Army. Major fighting ended on 24 October, and in response to superpower pressure, the Israelis accepted a formal cease-fire on 28 October.

In the end, the Israelis triumphed against great odds. But the Egyptians could also count the October War a success because they had met the vaunted Israelis in battle and driven them back for several days, and by terms of the cease-fire Egyptian units continued to hold most of the east bank of the Suez Canal. Isma'il 'Ali's plan demonstrated that if they fought on their own terms, the Egyptians could win a set-piece battle; their honor had been restored. Ultimately, it can be argued that the October War led to a greater victory for both Israel and Egypt. Pride in the initial performance of the Egyptian army gave Sadat the leverage to take the political risk to reach out to Israel four years later, a move that brought peace and restored the Sinai to Egypt in a way that the October War had not.

GOING BEYOND MILITARY CULTURE

Egyptian performance in combat demonstrated inherent problems that limited effectiveness in modern maneuver warfare. Most crippling was the character of tactical leadership, which was generally inflexible, formulaic, and unimaginative. The tendency to be overly deferential to and dependent upon centralized command was made all the more fatal because of poor gathering, reporting, and distribution of military intelligence and information. Orders from above were too often based on misinformation. Beyond identifying these flaws in military culture, it is only reasonable to speculate as to their root causes. As already stated, while some have ascribed failure to the adoption of Soviet doctrine, its influence was probably more positive than negative. It seems more promising to search for fundamental explanations not within the military itself but within society as a whole.

Kenneth Pollack does not restrict his search for such answers to any one Arab state but generalizes it to the entire Arab world. In doing so, he confronts and rejects two common explanations for battlefield frustration: economic underdevelopment and the politicization of Arab militaries. The link between modern conventional warfare and sophisticated weaponry implies that economically underdeveloped countries fight at great disadvantage. Even when such states can afford to purchase armor, artillery, and aircraft, or a great-power sponsor provides them, inherent structural problems hinder effective use of this weaponry. Illiteracy inhibits the speed and extent to which new hardware can be mastered. Lack of experience with machinery does the same and leads to extremely poor maintenance of equipment, making much of it useless. So goes the argument.

There is no question that this thesis holds true to some degree in Arab armies. By 1960, literacy in Egypt stood at only 26 percent, 15 percent in Iraq, and 36 percent in Syria. By 1990, however, these figures rose to 48 percent for Egypt, 60 percent for Iraq, and 64 percent for Syria.[52] Lack of a literate soldiery was obviously a greater problem early in the period under discussion, but rising literacy rates did not overcome Arab ineffectiveness, as exemplified in the Iran-Iraq War or the Gulf War of 1991. In terms of officer education, this cannot be proposed as a problem for the Egyptians in 1973, because they brought a very large number of college students and graduates into the army. Yet when faced with more than following the script, these educated officers proved inept.

Moreover, other underdeveloped countries did not demonstrate the same problems with maintenance and weaponry. Troops from the People's Republic of China threw back U.S. army and South Korean forces in Korea at the close of 1950. The Force Armée Nationale Tchad (FANT) from Chad, one of the world's poorest states, outmaneuvered and outfought Libyan troops armed with superior advanced weaponry in 1987.

Neither can we explain combat performance simply by appeal to the politicization of Arab militaries. When a regime cares less about assuring the military abilities of its armed forces than about maximizing their political role or ensuring their loyalty to the regime, battlefield effectiveness inevitably declines. Since 1945, Arab militaries have provided numerous examples of politicization. King Hussein repeatedly employed his army and air force as palace guards to support his regime against internal enemies, most notably when he assaulted the Palestinian minority in Jordan during Black September in 1970. In Syria, from 1949 on, a series of coups installed successive military dictatorships. A 1963 coup put nationalist and secularist Ba'thist Party officers in control, a junta that then purged the army of 700 officers. Finally, after further turmoil within the ranks of the Ba'thists, Gen. Hafiz al-Assad seized power in November 1970, following his rise to power with another purge of officers. The Iraqi army played a praetorian role in the 1960s, helping to put the Ba'th Party in control, but in 1968, after a successful coup, the Ba'thists turned on the military, purged the officer corps, and put their own candidates in command. And, of course, Col. Nasser came to power through a military coup in Egypt.

Politicization may have dampened Arab military performance, but it did not define its critical shortcomings. As indicated above, Amer and his political cronies bear some responsibility for the debacle of 1967. However, even though the strain and strength of politicization was far from constant in Arab states, the problems in maneuver warfare persisted, indicating that they derived from some other cause. The Egyptians and Syrians moved away from politicized patterns as a reaction to defeat—Egyptian humiliation in 1967 and Syrian crisis in that year and in the fighting against Jordan in 1970—as did the Iraqi military after losing campaigns against Iran, 1982–1986. Reduction in politicization brought each military similar improvements in the form of good operational plans, but performance on the tactical level continued to reveal the now-familiar problems.

If underdevelopment and politicization cannot wholly account for the primary problems of Arab militaries, where should we turn for explanations? In his 1996 dissertation, Pollack pursues answers within a generalized Arab civil culture. He stresses traditions of strongly patriarchal families, oppressive deference to authority, rote education, strong group loyalties, exaggerated forms of shame, and other attributes he ascribes to Arab society as a whole. Whether or not we accept his specific conclusions, and many will not, his impulse to find the foundation of military culture in civil values strikes me as correct.

Arab civil culture is a complex matter, outside my fields of expertise. For the purposes of this chapter, it is enough to focus only on Egyptian military culture as revealed by practice. This volume has tried to avoid imposing universal patterns on our understanding of war and warriors—the universal soldier, the Western Way of War, even the Clausewitzian dynamics of war. Therefore, this chapter, which owes so much to Pollack, concentrates on one army in one campaign, rather than trying to generalize about the entire postwar Arab military experience. The lesser task is more in accord with my greater purposes.

The most compelling argument for a cultural approach to the study of the 1973 campaign comes not from the pen of any historian but from the plan for the cross-Canal offensive designed by Isma'il 'Ali. A witness to repeated frustrations and failures, he appreciated the strengths and weaknesses of the Egyptian military in combat, weaknesses that reflected vital aspects of military culture. He recognized that he could optimize the capacity of his army only by a brave and honest evaluation of his soldiers' hearts and minds. The result was the script for the crossing.

By reviewing the Egyptian record in the field, 1948–1973, we have forced history to provide testimony that establishes the primacy of Egyptian military culture beyond a reasonable doubt. Operational and tactical analysis demonstrate problems in maneuver warfare that must be traced to the warriors, not the weapons.

Isma'il 'Ali's minutely scripted High Minarets circumvented traditional shortcomings, but only for a time. In ordering Phase II, Sadat exposed the dangers implicit in relying upon strict adherence to complicated plans. Similar to the great monolithic war plans of 1914, the 1973 script attempted to control the course of the war by seizing and keeping the initiative so as to determine the enemy's reactions. However, as Clausewitz correctly insists, the unpredictable nature of war dooms such inflexible plans. Caught outside the script, improvisation and innovation became essential, and the problems inherent in Egyptian military culture reasserted themselves.

Failure to match the Israelis in traditional maneuver warfare may have had further implications by forcing Arab struggles against Israel into different channels. After thirty-four years of intermittent clashes, 1948–1982, there has not been a full-scale Arab-Israeli war for twenty years. The major Arab states of Egypt and Jordan have concluded peace treaties with Israel, turning aside from direct armed confrontation. But the region has hardly been at peace. In fact, the violence that most threatens Israel moved from the desert to the streets, as two Palestinian risings, or intifadas, in 1987–1992 and 2000 to the present, challenge the peace and future of Israel. Israeli capacity at conventional warfare has helped to foster the turn toward Terrorism in the context of rising Islamic resentment of Israel and the United States. In part because of the kinds of military limitations discussed in this chapter, warfare at the dawn of the twenty-first century does not seem likely to conform to the patterns of the twentieth century.

Notes on the Opening Illustration for Chapter Eight

This Egyptian pontoon bridge across the Suez Canal and the gap blasted through the sand berm on the far bank demonstrate the skill of Egyptian engineers as they fulfilled their part in the tightly scripted Egyptian offensive.

(Copyright Mena/Corbis Sygma)

EPILOGUE: TERRORISM AND "EVIL"

Forming a New Discourse on War at the Dawn of the Twenty-First Century

WE ALL REMEMBER WHERE WE WERE when it happened. I was writing when Andrea, my wife, came through the study door and announced that a plane had hit one of the World Trade Center Towers. Switching on the TV, I watched black smoke pour out of the north tower. Initially it all seemed a terrifying accident, and then the second plane bore down on the south tower, and it was clear this was no deadly mistake—it was Terrorism.

Like millions of people around the country and around the world I stayed focused on the images from New York as long as I could. However, pressing business at the university called me away. NPR kept me informed as I drove to campus, so I learned that the first tower had come down. That news caused me to turn around and head for home, back into the study, back to the TV that gave me my first view of the south tower in ruin and ash. Shocked by the sight and by the fate of the thousands who must have perished, I witnessed, only a minute later, an even more appalling vision, as the remaining tower began to collapse upon itself, the upper stories pulverizing those below. The dying tower bloomed as it fell, like some malignant flower. More rubble, more death—and then the cloud of debris pursued onlookers down panicked streets.

As old as the phenomenon of Terrorism might be—and in one form or another it goes back millennia—this strike was unique in our own and in human experience. Terrorists transformed huge jet planes into cruise missiles and carried out their mission as the whole world watched live on television.

That evening, when President George Walker Bush addressed the nation he immediately turned to the language of evil to express his moral revulsion at the terrorist attacks of the morning. He grieved over the dead: "Thousands of lives were suddenly ended by evil, despicable acts of terror." He explained, "Today, our nation saw evil, the very worst of human nature," and he promised, "The search is underway for those who are behind these evil acts."[1] As it soon became clear that the horrors of 9/11 were perpetrated by Osama bin Laden and al Qaeda, Bush focused this language of evil on him. At a news conference of November 2, he stated: "Osama bin Laden is an evil man. His heart has been so corrupted that he's willing to take innocent life. And we are fighting evil, and we will continue to fight evil, and we will not stop until we defeat evil."[2] Bush continued to insist on the evil of his enemies in his State of the Union Address, where he argued that Iraq, Iran, and North Korea "and their terrorist allies, constitute an axis of evil." He sternly reminded the American people that "evil is real, and it must be opposed."[3]

The president's outrage was, of course, understandable, yet there is danger in Bush's language of evil, if it is to be taken seriously. To condemn Terrorism as evil implies removing it from the category of war, and that, in turn, might lead to the kind of unrestrained response that could multiply the problem rather than capping the threat. The history of combat in past wars, as presented in this volume, demonstrates that war is usually surrounded by conventions that control or limit certain of its aspects. To conceive of Terrorism as outside the realm of war could strip away those conventions, and that would ultimately be self-defeating. *Battle* advises us to consider long and hard what Terrorism is and warns us against indiscriminate reactions fueled by moral zeal.

THE NEED TO RECONCEPTUALIZE WAR

A fundamentally different kind of military threat requires us to rethink our military policy, the purposes of our armed forces, and the nature of war itself. In short, we need to adjust our discourse on war. *Battle* has explored the relationships between discourse and reality and argued that the way societies conceive of war influences the way they deal with that reality, often forcing it into the mold of conception. Our responses to Terrorism and other modern threats cannot be appropriate and effective if our perceptions and conceptions are deeply flawed. One of the first steps in response to 9/11 must be to reexamine and re-form our ideas about war.

In the West for hundreds of years, states have been the primary actors in war; therefore, it has been most often defined as an armed conflict between states, with clashes between irreconcilable state interests and policies imposing confrontation. Clausewitz thought in this vein. The threat of Terrorism leads us to question so restrictive a definition. A brief consideration of history reveals that war has not always been an affair of states alone and that acts of war have also been committed by sub-state or supra-state actors: Medieval Europe gives us examples of sub-state conflicts in the private clashes of local lords and of supra-state wars in the Crusades. Moreover, much organized violence transcends the rational logic of the state, in whole or in part. Humankind engages in wars of conviction inspired by religious fervor, ethnic hatred, or some other intense passion. At the extreme, some societies consider it most important to fight simply for the love of it, and having a greater cause would be almost beside the point. Such organized violence becomes a cultural necessity, as it was in the tournament and the duel.

A more inclusive explanation for warfare must transcend state interest to include deep-seated beliefs and values that demand a recourse to violence to sustain them when they cannot be accommodated through nonviolent compromise. Clearly, conflicts between Greek poleis and intensely nationalistic states were compelled by cultural forces. Even contests seen as material in origin can be redefined culturally; the Japanese may have fought in the 1930s to gain control of resources, but their aggression had its roots in concepts of a greater Japan.

Organized deadly violence may be the fulfillment of policy, but policy is a statement of perception and desire.

Today, it is important to grasp that while political goals and material interests
play a part in compelling war, fundamental cultural conflicts do as well. With
9/11, it became clear that our most immediate threat seems to come from non-
state actors motivated by strong cultural/religious preconceptions. The fact that
they do not represent states or politics in a traditional sense does not remove them
from the world of war.

If our discourse on war must take into account entire new definitions of war,
it must also take into account new military roles and responses. As Philip Bobbitt
argues in *The Shield of Achilles,* "We are at a moment in world affairs when the
essential ideas that govern statecraft must change."[4]

The military challenges and tasks that face the United States differ from those
of the past. The American military likes to pride itself on its "warfighting" capacity in a major conflict against a sophisticated foe. Images of World War II and of
the Gulf War in 1991 still stand as examples; they were conflicts American forces
know how to fight and win. However, the end of the Cold War brought the pre-
ponderance of different kinds of military actions. Peacemaking and peace-keep-
ing operations, although not new to the world, have been novel and frustrating
for the United States. Peacemaking has a way of slipping into state making, a
highly challenging task that the U.S. has yet to demonstrate it can accomplish in
the developing world. (America certainly did an admirable job of state making in
postwar Japan, but that was a very different situation.) The kinds of forces necessary for warfighting may be insufficient for peacekeeping, peacemaking, and state
making. Such constabulary duties may be better performed by troops specially
armed and trained for them—troops who think in terms of minimum rather than
maximum force. In fact, the fastest-growing segment of the world's armed forces
today is of units raised and used for the constabulary duties of internal security;
these can be termed "paramilitary" forces, without the connotation of being free-
lance militias. In both China and India, such state paramilitary forces have
climbed to a million troops.[5]

Since 9/11, international Terrorism looms as the most formidable threat to
American security, both physical and psychological. Ideas about war and combat
must alter to meet this challenge. The history of American discourses on war gives
us reason to believe that we are quite capable of recognizing changes in the kind
and level of threat and adjusting our conception and conduct of war to match
them.

Evolving Discourses on War in the United States

U.S. conceptions of war and combat have evolved since World War II to differ sharply from those of the nineteenth century and the first half of the twentieth. This transformation owes much to the cloud of nuclear annihilation that has hung over civilization since Hiroshima. But while nuclear weapons prevented war between the superpowers of the Cold War, they did not bring peace. Rather, they forced war into channels that restrained escalation toward a nuclear nightmare.

Wars became limited not because of ideological tolerance but because of deadly necessity. The U.S. policy of containment ran counter to traditional American concepts of victory. In his address before Congress in 1951, Douglas MacArthur, recently removed from command in Korea, expressed his own frustration, and that of much of the American people, in a famous utterance: "In war, indeed, there can be no substitute for victory."[6] Of course, by "victory" he did not mean achieving a discrete political goal, as in Korea, but imposing abject surrender on an enemy, as the United States had done in its war against Japan, MacArthur's war. Fortunately, Truman found a proper substitute for victory in the doctrine of containment. Eventually, the dominant American discourse on war came to define success as holding the line rather than annihilating the enemy.

The conflict in Vietnam administered another shock to the American consciousness and once again shifted national conceptions of combat and casualties. At least Korea looked like a "real" war; Vietnam did not. Instead of confronting a conventional foe armed with heavy weapons along established fronts, in Vietnam America fought a lightly armed and illusive enemy along ill-defined and shifting lines—or none at all. Long years of fighting with seemingly no result radically altered American expectations in war. If the metaphor for combat before Vietnam remained World War II, Vietnam became the new image for the American people. From then on, the ever present question asked of every new conflict would be, "Is this going to be another Vietnam?"

Showing dead and wounded on the evening news, TV made the reality of war strike home as never before. Romantic elements of the discourse on war suffered as heavy a blow as did American pride, and public opinion became increasingly reluctant to accept casualties.

Since then, the American discourse on war has displayed three related tendencies: 1) abhorrence of U.S. casualties, 2) confidence in military technology to minimize U.S. losses, and 3) concern with exit strategies. In the past few decades, the

U.S. population and its political leaders seem uneasy with the idea of paying for war with American blood. The Gulf War, which to the relief of the American people conformed more to its vision of a real war, did not actually test U.S. acceptance of losses, because allied goals were achieved quickly at a cost of only 148 U.S. battle deaths. (Initial estimates of Iraqi casualties stood at 100,000 troops killed and 300,000 wounded.)[7] More revealing, when U.S. engagement in Somalia challenged American resolve, the loss of eighteen U.S. troops in operation Ranger, 3 October 1993, led to quick U.S. withdrawal. The fact that America did not intervene to stop genocide in Rwanda and was a late-comer to Bosnia reflected its unwillingness to sustain casualties in a remote and confused affair. Clearly, repelling the Iraqi invasion of Kuwait did not restore an American willingness to "pay any price, bear any burden, meet any hardship," as Kennedy exalted in his 1961 inaugural address.

The Gulf War did, however, strongly reinforce the long-established tendency of Americans to try to win through material superiority. This tendency expresses itself now through faith in high-tech weaponry, such as precision-guided munitions and stealth aircraft, along with advanced communications and computers. To those critical of this trait, it seems like Americans are only willing to fight at 15,000 feet.

The American-led NATO air offensive in 1999 brought Milosevic to his knees. However, an air war could not physically halt Serbian ethnic cleansing of Albanian Kosovars; it could only punish the Serbs for carrying it out. At least in the short run, NATO's success fell short of complete, because over 850,000 Albanian Kosovars were expelled by the Serbs *during* the NATO offensive, which lasted from 24 March to 20 June.[8] This number far exceeded the total of Albanian Kosovars who had been "cleansed" from their homeland before the offensive began. In any case, General Wesley Clark, the NATO commander on site, received instructions to avoid a land war at all costs. Eventually, Milosevic withdrew his troops from Kosovo; and American services, particularly the air force, count Kosovo as a victory for advanced American military technology. And this, the largest U.S. military operation between the Gulf War and the 2001–2002 Afghan War, was particularly high-tech; 38 percent of the bombs dropped during the air offensive were precision-guided, as compared to only 8 percent during the Gulf War.[9]

The Kosovo air offensive also exemplified the tendency for Americans to demand exit strategies before committing to combat. On the one hand, a desire to avoid "mission creep," as in Somalia, where U.S. forces went for humanitarian relief and stayed for state making, and a need to define boundaries in a limited conflict make a concern with exit strategies reasonable. Also, political leaders believe they must give voters a sense that the mission is limited in scope and time. An electorate averse to losses will not sign a blank check. However, in another sense, exit strategies approach the bizarre. It is as though the discourse now defines a proper war not as one we should enter but as one we can be sure to leave . . . on schedule. Should we assume the monumental moral responsibility of killing, maiming, and destroying for any but essential, and irreconcilable, political interests or cultural necessities? But if the causes are, indeed, essential, the real issue is getting in, not getting out.

The dominant American discourse on war evolved greatly from 7 December, 1941 to 11 September, 2001—from resolution to fight absolute war at all costs, to an acceptance of limited wars in the name of containment, to a reluctance to accept losses and the technological reliance and limited commitment such reluctance entails. Once again, American attitudes toward war must undergo a change as the nation faces a new challenge, international Terrorism. How might the cultural history of combat illuminate the potentials and pitfalls of American response to this new threat?

DEFINING TERRORISM

Creating a discourse on Terrorism begins with a process of definition, and the consequences of defining Terrorism in one way or another could be of great importance. Within this matter resides the very important question of whether we include Terrorism as a form of war or regard it exclusively as a form of moral atrocity and act of "evil."

A convincing and inclusive definition may be ultimately unattainable. Terrorism is not a cause or a country, it is a tactic employed by different individuals and groups with different motivations and different goals over time. Nineteenth-century anarchists represented one face of Terrorism, nationalist extremists another in the twentieth century, and now religious radicals show us still one more at the dawn of the twenty-first. Yet it is necessary for reasons of national and international law and policy to try to define Terrorism. An FBI definition states: "Terrorism is the unlawful use of force or violence against persons or property to intimidate or coerce a government, the civilian population, or any segment thereof, in furtherance of political or social objectives." For Walter Laqueur, "Terrorism constitutes the illegitimate use of force to achieve a political objective when innocent people are targeted."[10]

Much can be learned from comparing two other contrasting definitions of, and approaches to, Terrorism—those offered by Bruce Hoffman and Caleb Carr.

Hoffman, in his valuable study *Inside Terrorism,* offers a mainstream definition, arguing that Terrorism is "violence or, equally important, the threat of violence—used and directed in pursuit of, or in service of, a political aim" and that it is "understood to be violence committed by non-state entities."[11] Hoffman writes intelligently and authoritatively on the dimensions of Terrorism as it threatens states, societies, and economies today. His timely definition is undoubtedly useful in an immediate sense, but the different approach pursued by Carr may prove essential in reshaping our discourse on war to meet this new threat.

Caleb Carr approaches the subject on another tack. In his recent and brief *The Lessons of Terror,* Carr maintains that it is "simply the contemporary name given to, and the modern permutations of, warfare deliberately waged against civilians with the purpose of destroying their will to support either leaders or policies that the agents of such violence find objectionable."[12] Carr never proves his assertion that Terrorism always fails. However, his insistence that Terrorism can be traced back to the ancient world and that great armies and great states have engaged in attacks on civilians designed to intimidate and terrorize them is important in both obvious and subtle ways.

To supply a significant variation on Carr's theme, I would like to suggest that we would benefit from rethinking old categories about war. We would gain by recognizing that throughout history, military forces have resorted to "strategies of terror," that is violence, or threats of violence, directed against civilian populations and meant to intimidate and demoralize them in order to undermine an enemy's will to resist or in order to change the policy of that people or its leaders. Medieval *chevauchée* raids eroded confidence in a monarch; early modern sacking of cities induced other towns to capitulate without resistance. Although Clausewitz would almost certainly object, it could be argued that his emphasis on the will and on the involvement of the people in war implies the validity of strategies of terror. Area bombing campaigns carried out by the Allies and Germany in World War II targeted civilian populations. Terrorism as we know it today should also be seen as within this broader category of strategies of terror.

There is another imperative of logic that urges us to see Terrorism as war. A case can be made that Terrorism is essentially a poor man's form of warfare; certainly terrorists have argued so in their defense. This assertion ties in with Mao Tse-tung's assertion that the revolutionary armed struggle has three phases: guerrilla, mobile, and positional. Guerrilla warfare is fought by bands of guerrillas supported by the surrounding population; guerrillas are the fish in the sea, a sea that gives them sustenance and cover. As guerrillas come to be more numerous and powerful, they could create some units armed and organized as regular military forces. These operate in coordination with guerrillas in mobile warfare. This warfare is fluid and mobile because the regular units are not yet strong enough to seize and hold terrain against the enemy's main forces. As Mao writes: "The enemy advances, we retreat; the enemy camps, we harass; the enemy tires, we attack; the enemy retreats, we pursue."[13] In the ultimate stage of war, the revolutionary forces shift to positional warfare, meaning that they now control enough territory and resources to create full-scale armies and defeat the primary forces of the enemy. It could be argued that terrorist cells can precede guerrilla bands, adding a fourth stage to Mao's typology of revolutionary forces. In fact, the idea of the revolutionary *foco,* or small revolutionary band that could serve as the "focus" of revolutionary discontent, does exactly that in the writings of Régis Debray, who gives voice to the theories of Fidel Castro and Che Guevara.[14] The *foci* engage in attacks against government installations and agents, but they did not rely on the "sea" of popular support, at least initially.

Bruce Hoffman objects to classifying today's terrorist cells as harbingers of guerrilla bands. By his logic, guerrillas operate within their own countries with the object of eventually seizing power within it; ultimately they want territory and authority. Terrorist groups such as al Qaeda strike at foes in other counties; in fact, terrorists often have no "country" of their own. They aim not at ruling their own state but at terrorizing foreign populations and governments. But this is not always the case. The Italian Red Brigades launched their campaigns within Italy, where they hoped a Marxist-Leninist state would emerge. Palestinian terrorists consider lands presently occupied by Palestinians as rightfully a Palestinian state for which the terrorists hope to win full state powers. Should we also say that the Tamil Tigers are not terrorists because they fight for independence for their own lands in Sri Lanka, despite their recourse to assassination and terror? Hoffman's distinction, while useful, is not absolute.

IS TERRORISM "EVIL"?

Terrorism should be considered as military and not simply criminal. It should be incorporated within a revised and modified discourse on war, not condemned to a separate discourse on "evil." Stressing another's "evil" seems to give us the moral justification to engage in self-defeating extremes in combatting it.

Because it inflicts such terrible human costs, all war is to that extent wicked. Pope John Paul II has pronounced, "Violence is evil. Violence is unacceptable as a solution to problems. Violence is unworthy of man."[15] But in the flawed and fearsome world of reality, mankind has long accepted that violence in war is not only acceptable but necessary and that warrior traits rank as basic virtues, as hero-ic. In the common use of language, to term a tactic "evil" removes it from the moral universe of war. Also, to condemn the al Qaeda terrorists at the controls of the planes of 9/11 as "cowards," even though they knew for some time that they would undertake a suicide mission for a cause and then carried it out, denies them a claim to be soldiers. Such condemnation also assumes a moral superiority.

However, the United States is far from justified in claiming moral purity con-cerning strategies of terror. The 9–10 March 1945 firebombing of Tokyo and the later use of atomic weapons on Hiroshima and Nagasaki alone cost the lives of at least 250,000 Japanese and the maiming of tens of thousands more. Chapter 7 argues that, though horrific, these attacks were justified; nevertheless, they remain strategies of terror. Yes, the United States was at war, but certainly al Qaeda believes it is as well. It is true that the U.S. was attacking an enemy that was doing what it could to defend itself, but the Japanese were not defending themselves all that effectively by the spring of 1945. The air armada that burned Tokyo took off with 334 B-29s, only fourteen of which went down, meaning a loss rate of less than 5 percent, and several of these were more the victims of the fierce winds cre-ated by the firestorm than of Japanese actions.[16] A B-29 crew that night included eight men, so 112 flyers were lost over Japan as 83,000 died below. An aide to General MacArthur called the raid "one of the most ruthless and barbaric killings of non-combatants in all history."[17] No planes or airmen were lost in the Hiroshima and Nagasaki bombing. It could be argued that the Japanese, who had started the war and committed horrendous atrocities, called down this hell upon themselves. Yes, but certainly violent Islamic radicals see themselves as defending their people against long-standing U.S. aggression against their honor, their cul-ture, and their lands.

To recognize U.S. use of strategies of terror changes the moral framework of the argument on Terrorism, I believe. We must see strategies of terror as some-thing we have considered valid, and we cannot simply dismiss terrorists as "evil" men who commit unprecedented and unconscionable acts. They are enemies to be defeated, not moral lepers to be excised. As horrible as the events of 9/11 were, and they were so in the extreme, they were acts of war.

A prime reason to define Terrorism as war is to impose some restraint on the campaigns against Terrorism. One theory advanced in my study is that when the conduct of war cannot be reconciled with the discourse of war, it is rejected as war and defined as something else in an alternate discourse. But, as *Battle* asserts, there are conventions that limit the conduct of war; Hoffman even uses these conven-tions to define war. Such conventions and common practices dictated by a discourse on war are stripped away when violence is no longer considered to be an act of war, but an act of "evil." The result can be a more extreme form of violent response. However, this more unbridled violence can aid the terrorists by justifying their claims and winning them converts.

Such logic brings us closer to Carr's argument than to Hoffman's. Carr speaks of a dichotomy between "destructive war" and "progressive war," between a war of terror directed against civilians and a carefully controlled and disciplined warfare that strictly distinguishes between combatant and noncombatant and tries to minimize harm done to the latter. He idealizes the era of European limited warfare, which he dates from the end of the wars of Louis XIV to the onset of the wars of the French Revolution, or 1714–1792.

In earlier work, I have used different language to argue a similar need for limitation and control in warfare when one is trying to win over opinion and peoples.[18] My remarks concerned guerrilla warfare, but they apply to Terrorism as well. Ultimately, the task is to defeat the terrorists with as little harm as possible to those who are sympathetic to their cause and to the usually far larger neutral population. Killing, maiming, and destroying create their own backlash of resentment and resistance. Only if a government or occupier is willing to sustain the most total and tyrannical kind of repression can it silence opposition, but such a hideous recourse is, thankfully, outside the realm of possibility for the United States. Barred from maximum force, a fight against Terrorism must carefully choose and focus its means and methods.

Our own reaction to the attacks of 9/11 illustrates how violence creates its own resistance. While we grieve our losses, we are not disheartened but angered. We have become so resolved that we may reverse the trends of the late twentieth century and become far less risk averse and far less concerned with exit strategies in a necessary conflict, although only the coming years will show. One is reminded of the words reputed to Admiral Yamamoto immediately after Pearl Harbor: "I fear we have awakened a sleeping giant and filled him with a terrible resolve." Bin Laden has earned our undying condemnation; let us not aid him by an indiscriminate response.

To see Terrorism as war and, thus, to integrate our views toward it within our discourse on war is wiser than to reject it as war and see it only as an atrocity that justifies any reaction. The fact that terrorists may not respect conventions of war does not mean that we can afford to abandon them ourselves. It would be a mistake to respond with little discretion in the use of violence and in ways that caused unnecessary destruction and loss of life, because such responses could undermine our own campaign against Terrorism. Captured terrorists or supporters must be treated in accord with conventions toward prisoners of war. There is also a strong argument to treat suspected terrorists as criminals, but if this is the case it should also be within the practices of criminal law. In addition, if we tear down Islamic states we regard as supporting Terrorism we should invest in rebuilding them, or we will seem like the enemies of Islam that bin Laden claims we truly are.

At the same time, we should guard our own constitutional rights while combatting Terrorism. The United States has restricted rights when in the grips of war. During the Civil War, Lincoln allowed holding of suspects for extended periods by suspending the writ of habeas corpus, and the War Department further authorized arresting and holding those suspected of "disloyal practice."[19] During World War II, Franklin Delano Roosevelt ordered the internment of Japanese-Americans on the West Coast. However, the fact that Americans transgressed against civil rights in the past provides no justification to do so in the future. Justice Robert Jackson, who served on the Supreme Court from 1941 to 1955, may have said, "The Bill of Rights is not a suicide pact," but that punchy saying cannot be used to justify sacrificing our most precious heritage. Our direct involvement in the Civil War and in World War II lasted about four years in each conflict; sacrifices were temporary. A war against Terrorism is likely to last many years, perhaps decades; sacrifices would essentially be permanent. Therefore, we need to be especially watchful in guarding our political heritage, our civil rights, and our open society.

We are a multi-ethnic society of immigrants; we must not divide ourselves in the name of our own defense. It must be as honorable to pray in church, temple, or mosque—or not to pray at all—in these United States. Nevertheless, the current emphasis on multiculturalism overlooks something of paramount importance. While unity without diversity may threaten repression, diversity without unity threatens discord. A sacred motto of our country is E Pluribus Unum, or "out of many, one." This referred originally to our several states, but now it expresses a necessary realization that we are at the same time many people and one. An overreaction to Terrorism could dissolve the bonds that hold us together. The memory of our mistreatment of the Japanese-American community during World War II should caution us against such abuses in the present. Up to this point, despite some awful, but rare, instances, the American people have been wise and reasonable in the wake of 9/11.

The United States needs to revise its dominant discourse on war. Elements must remain unchanged, for example our emphasis on civil control of the military, as well as our respect for its ability, valor, and sacrifice—also our notion that violence must be contained within certain limits and guided by certain conventions. However, we must alter our notions of a military campaign. America is still an impatient country, but if a war on Terrorism is to be fought, it will have to be a long and patient struggle. It will also have a strange momentum. Not a steady drive to victory, but a pulsating campaign—at times overt and intensive, when a clear target is in view, and at times covert and subdued, when we watch for future threats. To be successful, Americans simply must accept this as a legitimate style of combat. Obviously the United States must concentrate on the most dangerous groups and the most dangerous threats, and hopefully it can identify and neutralize them. However, Terrorism probably cannot be eradicated because it is a tactic that can be used not only by as elaborate a terrorist network as al Qaeda but also by a couple of lone extremists, like Timothy McVeigh and Terry Nichols. Ultimately it is a problem that may not be eliminated but only managed. Real victory could simply be in countering the main threats, forestalling the emergence of major new dangers, and keeping lesser attacks to a minimum. That is not MacArthur's victory, but neither was containment, and it worked.

This cultural redefinition, this reshaping of the discourse on war, is necessary and inevitable. It will require clear-headed discussion, resolve, and self-restraint. While certain aspects have remained constant in American perceptions and expectations of war, the American public has reconceived of war and victory repeatedly since 1945. It must, and it will, do so again. But to do so, I believe we must abandon the language and logic of evil, for we run the risk of defeating our own efforts and sacrificing our own liberties by demonizing the foe and simplifying the challenge.

This book began with opening verses from "The Universal Soldier," and it now concludes with the last lines of that song. Buffy Sainte-Marie's antiwar anthem portrays the universal soldier with the expectation that the audience will be appalled by the timeless and faceless killer, but also will view itself as remote from and superior to him. The listeners' shock is soothed by their own self-satisfaction, even self-righteousness. But then the song reminds them that they must accept responsibility in the bloody business of war:

> His orders come from far away no more
> They come from him, and you, and me
> and brothers can't you see
> this is not the way we put an end to war.

The hope that earnest young people could put an end to war is itself a cultural relic of the 1960s, but the notion that citizens must assume responsibility for the violent policies of their country is hardly dated. To make informed decisions about such serious matters requires that we understand threats and challenges for what they are. Proper action begins with proper ideas; the discourse becomes parent to action.

Notes on the Opening Illustration for the Epilogue

A new kind of battle begins, as hijacked United Airlines flight 175 bears down on the World Trade Center's South Tower. On 9/11, al Qaeda terrorists killed 3,020 people, Americans and visitors to our shores, making this attack more costly than Pearl Harbor. Will this assault once again awaken the sleeping giant, and will that giant demonstrate not only its power but its resolve and intelligence?

(Photo by Sean Adair/Reuters)

Appendix:
The Discourse and
the Reality of War

A Cultural Model

Running throughout *Battle,* somewhat below the surface, is a theory concerning the interaction between the ideal and the real in warfare. This theory, or model, identifies some common themes between the diverse chapters and generalizes the examples to suggest ways to analyze cases yet to be explored. However, just as I have decided to avoid the specialist theory and language of cultural history as much as possible in *Battle,* I also have chosen to put aside a complete exposition of my model and its terminology in the text. Imposed explicitly on the text, it would most likely impede the reader. However, perhaps some individuals would care to look at the model full on, so I present it as an appendix.

Models are by nature simplified, and thus inexact and incomplete, but they have the virtue of clarity, a clarity created by definition and the graphic portrayal of relationships. The obvious, but key, distinction in this model contrasts the conceptualization of war, or the "Discourse on War," and the "Reality of War." We can consider war as armed conflict by groups to achieve some political, social, economic, religious, ideological, or cultural purpose. For centuries the West has seen this as an affair between states, but war can exist within or independent of the state. Preconceptions, values, ideals, and so on concerning conflict constitute the Discourse on War—war as it is supposed to be, as imagined. The objective facts of conflict come together under the rubric of reality.

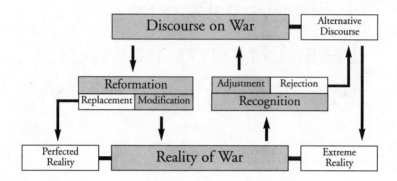

The value of the cultural model proposed here derives not from its differentiation between discourse and reality but from exploration of the relationship, and feedback, between them. Cultures try to change or control reality to fit conception, a process labeled here as "Reformation." On the other hand, through "Recognition," cultures may appreciate that conception does not suitably reflect reality, and adjust the discourse.

Reformation can lead to a process of "Modification" by which the Reality of War is altered to bring it more within certain limits, which vary from time to time and society to society. However, should a cultural need for special forms of combat be great enough and reality intractable, a society may go so far as the "Replacement" of reality with a "Perfected Reality," which better adheres to ideals within the discourse. So great is the force of discourse upon reality that it can create a special realm for violence of an ideal type, such as the medieval tournament.

In other realms of cultural assumptions, discourse often differs from reality, but there are usually few costs for this misalignment; however, in war the price paid for such misalignment can be monumental. The penalty suffered in World War I for outmoded notions of combat embraced by civilian and military sectors amounted to millions of lives lost and regimes shattered. With so much at stake, Recognition of a mismatch between discourse and reality drives a feedback process between them, and considerable incentives encourage an "Adjustment" of the discourse to fit reality better, but there are times when the nature of warfare is so at odds with the discourse that Adjustment is unacceptable; the result is "Rejection" of the violence as outside the conceptual boundaries of war. Such Rejection can engender an "Alternate Discourse," which can then justify a more "Extreme Reality" of conflict, because the formalities and limitations that often circumscribe war within the dominant discourse lose their validity. Violence outside the conceptual boundaries of war becomes not heroism but "evil" to be thoroughly condemned and utterly destroyed.

The Discourse on War

Having sketched the primary distinctions within the model, one must detail its elements. Since *Battle* primarily concerns culture, let us begin with the Discourse on War. In trying to understand the latter, we must recognize that because organized armed conflict fundamentally and comprehensively affects society, the discourse on this form of violence is generated by many different segments of that society. As a result, a culture has no single Discourse on War. Rather, a number of discourses comprise the values, expectations, etc., of varied societal groups that harbor potentially very different, and at times opposing, interests and points of view. Consequently, the conception of war will not be a monolith, but contains a greater or lesser range of attitudes and expectations. Any generalizations about these conceptions must be specific to class, gender, and—in societies with strong racial divisions—race as well. Of course, to emphasize class, gender, and race is de rigueur among historians today. However, my au courant colleagues are likely to forget that geography and borders can create important cultural distinctions as well. Moreover, profession is a relevant category here, particularly when command and planning become the province of military professionals.

Variety of interest and opinion is great enough that it is dangerous to make easy assumptions about how a culture regards armed conflict. It is also fair to say that one group's opinions about war may matter much more than do another's. The Discourse on War is a discourse on power in the traditional sense of the word, and in such matters not all segments of a society are equal. In decisions as to whether to fight or not, and when, where, and how to combat an enemy, elites usually weigh in far more heavily than do segments of society with less status.

Social, political, and military elites—often, but not always, the same in Western societies—think of warfare in ways markedly different than do lower strata. Medieval and early modern European aristocrats could view violent martial activity as an end in itself, as a necessary proof of prowess and courage and a validation of noble status, as well as a source of wealth. But often geography draws lines between elites. Even in an era with an international aristocracy, there remained differences, so late-medieval French nobles could and did hold to different principles regarding violence and military participation than did their Italian counterparts. And, of course, European peasants who had no need to justify themselves through war viewed it as an unqualified disaster leading to misery and death. Of course, even here there are exceptions, as in the case of the Swiss, who provided the most important mercenary market at the close of the Middle Ages.

Spiritual and religious communities can oppose fighting through moral codes banning violence, or at least violence directed against coreligionists. At least until Gregory VII, the papacy condemned warfare and warmakers. However, it seems that all great religions come to accept warfare on certain levels and some produced military religious orders, such as the Templars or the armed monks of Japan. There certainly have been religious leaders, like Mohandas Gandhi, who eventually came to oppose all violence, but far more common were those like the German preachers who insisted *"Gott mit uns"* or the American chaplain at Pearl Harbor who shouted encouragement to those who resisted the attack on Sunday, 7 December 1941, "Praise the Lord and pass the ammunition!"

Expansion of the public sphere and political participation multiplied the number of those whose attitudes toward war and peace had to be taken into consideration. However, at the same time that the public sphere expanded, modern military professionalism took root. To the extent that war became an affair defined and directed by military professionals, opinions held by the general public toward the technical conduct of war mattered less, even if public commitment to a particular war as a whole became increasingly important. A professional military develops its own Discourse on War. In earlier ages, this was not particularly systematic, but the rise of general staffs and war colleges in the nineteenth century generated formal doctrine. For a number of reasons, professionally generated doctrine can have a great impact on society and culture; one need look no further than the consequences of military practice at the onset of World War I.

Gender is a complicated and unpredictable variable. Modern attitudes might well expect that the historical record would reveal women resisting war and military values, while men were promoting them. And at times this has been the case, as in such movements in the United States as Mothers Against the War during the Vietnam era. However, even when women have not participated directly in the fighting, they often endorsed it through praise of warriors and condemnation of cowards. Spartan women admonished their sons to come home bearing their shields, and thus well and victorious, or on them, dead but having been resolute in battle. Medieval women adored the knight of proven prowess, and ladies of Louis XIV's court sought the attentions of brave officers. And even before our modern age of uniformed women, women regularly served in support of soldiers, as washerwomen, seamstresses, and cooks with the men, as nurses, or as war workers.

The Discourse on War often glorifies martial action. Cultures may extol prowess with arms for various reasons: Social values require masculine military performance; the consequences of victory or defeat in war are of great importance to a society; and cultural tastes generate romantic notions of valor. Praise of glory need not be foolish or ignorant. During some historical eras, societies bestowed accolades on warriors precisely because the people of those societies possessed hard knowledge, often first hand, of the labor, suffering, and danger of war. Such certainly was the case in Greek poleis. Even idealized notions of war can encompass appalling brutality, as in Nordic sagas and the medieval discourses on war.

Contemporary Western sensibilities, at least among intellectuals, are prone to prefer pacifistic discourse to more bellicose convictions. Yet, although the New Testament lauds the peacemakers as "blessed," this is not always the case. It is worth noting that post–World War I pacifism contributed to the paralysis of the Western European and American democracies in opposing the fascist menace.

THE REALITY OF WAR

The very nature of the Discourse on War dictates that it diverges from war's reality. In fact, the variety of these discourses ensures that no one reality could match the diversity of conception. But there are other factors driving a wedge between conception and reality, and they are not necessarily implied by the definition of discourse.

Different peoples can have dissimilar conceptions of war as it should be, and when they clash in battle, the fact that they are fighting by different rules creates a reality that neither adversary expected. Opponents can have different principles regarding the value of human life, the acceptability of surrender, the fate of prisoners, and the inflicting of civilian casualties. It is argued that certain Native American communities engaged in combat designed more to capture than kill the enemy, and when they confronted the more bloodthirsty conquistadors, the Discourse on War among these Native American warriors simply did not fit what they had to deal with. Similar statements are used to explain the victory of the French over Italian condottieri at the close of the fifteenth century and the start of the sixteenth.

Technical factors can also cause the real to diverge from the conceptual. Logistics provides a most important example of this; those who do not study the course of wars in history are usually surprised to realize the extent to which the necessities of supply shaped the conduct of war and the behavior of armies. For most of history, armies on the march have not been able to carry all that they needed to support themselves in the field, particularly fodder and food. Consequently they have largely lived off the country and committed excesses of theft, destruction, rape, and murder, as soldiers who foraged to find what they needed also took what they wanted. Regardless of cause or country, armies often acted like marauding bands who preyed on friend and foe alike. Such behavior became institutionalized at times, for example in the *chevauchées* of the Hundred Years' War. In order to keep soldiers and their horses fed, ideals of war had to be sacrificed, pious statements of monarchs and ministers notwithstanding.

During eras of military change, when even military elites and professionals cannot predict the full effect of innovations, war can be different than expected. In such circumstances, memories of past conflicts, particularly those tinged with nostalgia, may fail to guide a military, and they certainly mislead civil populations. New weapons and tactics can change the character of warfare before professionals and the public realize it. The longbow of the Hundred Years' War and the rifle in the American Civil War both altered conflicts with deadly results, but the impact of modern weaponry on the fighting during World War I provides the most disastrous example of a lag between the reality of killing power and the Discourse on War. Before the war, many military professionals knew and accepted the deadly effects of modern weaponry, but more did not, and the civilian Discourse on War hardly understood it.

But there is another side to the coin, at least by the twentieth century. At times discourses on war come to expect technological progress and assume that the power and accuracy of weapons is certain to increase. Such rising expectations can create a discourse that outstrips reality. The American military, and to a large degree the American public, believed in precision bombing in World War II, for example, but the shortcomings of bombsights and the difficulties imposed by weather and combat made such precision a chimera. Precision bombing of factories gave way to area bombing of cities in contradiction of dominant conceptions of warfare. Today the American military promises that precision weapons will revolutionize warfare, but despite their obvious improvements, "smart" bombs at times kill the wrong people.

Beyond the more obvious questions of technique and technology, dynamics of war defined by Clausewitz also compel real war to differ from warfare as it was intended. One such influence is the role of friction, which among other things involves the importance of chance and the unexpected. Some modern military theorists speak of the non-linearity of warfare.[1] They insist on the unpredictability of warfare and attack assumptions that war is linear in the mathematical sense—that is, that inputs yield predictable outputs. Non-linear theorists experiment with notions of chaos theory and the "new science." Projections concerning war based on linear assumptions must be frustrated in a non-linear world. Another aspect of war explored by Clausewitz is the tendency of warfare to escalate toward an absolute form, free of limitations. If one definition of a Discourse on War is an expectation of what war should be, Clausewitz would argue that it almost necessarily will be overturned by the forces implicit in real war.

Thus, for the reasons indicated above, and for still others, the Reality of Warfare differs from the Discourse on War. This disjunction is to some degree countered by efforts to make reality better conform to expectations—Reformation—and to alter discourse to better reflect reality—Recognition.

Reformation: The Imposition of Discourse upon Reality

A fundamental assertion of cultural history is that human communities impose cultural constructions upon reality, that they make the actual fit the conceptual. At the extreme, some cultural historians sometimes insist that reality is simply what is perceived, and thus culturally determined. Such an attitude in war is fatal, in the strict sense of the word. But avoiding foolish intellectual excess, this principle applies to the cultural history of war within limits set by the objective facts of armed conflict. There is a great deal of truth in arguing that human communities have tried to shape combat to fit principles imagined by the dominant discourse.

The most obvious and common form of this process is Modification, imposing the Discourse on the Reality of War. This has a long and honored history in the West. From the seventh to the fifth centuries B.C., classical Greek poleis tacitly or expressly agreed to a number of fundamental conventions in order to maintain an essentially heroic form of combat that led to quick and decisive wars. This did not mean that the actual combat between phalanxes was in any way restrained, because, once they collided, the struggle was of the most vigorous and vicious kind. Similar to most primitive warfare, Greek combat was highly ritualized and conventionalized, although Greek fighting was far more deadly.

Western warfare has usually not conformed to agreements as all-encompassing as those accepted by the classical Greeks, but military forces usually do follow certain conventions. Consider the taking and treatment of prisoners. During the early modern era, captured officers won their release on their word that they would not rejoin their army until formally exchanged. It was quite literally a gentlemen's agreement. That was a more polite age, but twentieth-century European conflicts between major states have usually been fought with rather elaborate standards as to the behavior toward prisoners of war. Although breached, these rules have remained and spread. The Geneva Conventions represent an attempt to make war become what it should be. In fact, the existence of laws of war demonstrates an important and enduring attempt of conception to master reality.

Actual fighting can also be bounded by agreements, sometimes formally recognized and sometimes implicit. In siege warfare, long a staple of Western conflicts, principles determined when a commander might surrender and how a civilian population was to be treated. Should a town hold out too long, its inhabitants could be subjected to brutal treatment, but only upon warning and according to the laws of war. In the more recent past, during World War II the Allies and the Germans avoided the use of gas, although both had stocks of this deadly poison. Here, practical fears augmented conventions in restricting any recourse to this form of weapon.

So adamantly can a society, or part of it, desire to force warfare into accepted patterns that the society may replace real war with a Perfected Reality that more completely conforms to the relevant Discourse on War. War itself cannot always be modified, and if the wall between reality and discourse is too high, then Modification gives way to Replacement. Never has such an alternate reality been more apparent than during the Middle Ages, when chivalry created the tournament as a surrogate for war. By aristocratic standards, it was ideal, as only properly certified nobles displayed their prowess before fellow warriors and their ladies. Days of danger could be followed by evenings of comfort at banquets that allowed knights to enjoy the attention of women.

Although the tournament represented the ultimate Replacement of a real with a more perfect form of combat, it was not unique. The common and enduring practice of dueling in early modern Europe did much the same, particularly the form of duel fought by groups rather than individuals. Dueling fulfilled many of the same purposes of war for elite males, for it demonstrated courage and prowess in the name of living up to a discourse of proper aristocratic masculinity.

It may seem a bit far-fetched, but modern militaries preserve practices that could be seen as replacing the reality of today's warfare with elements conforming to ideals of what war should be. Drill, ceremony, and parades project a dated but tidy and gallant image that presents the military in an artificial light that sanitizes war. Sport, particularly American football, might even be analyzed as perfected war; the American military often employs the metaphor of football and football the terminology of war. Both provide theaters of conflict for values of courage in the face of discomfort, pain, and danger.

RECOGNITION: THE IMPOSITION OF REALITY ON CONCEPTION

If lack of correspondence between the Discourse and Reality of War can stimulate an attempt to make reality more like the concept, the reverse is even more likely, in fact inevitable; the Discourse on War must evolve to take into account the actual character and prosecution of war. Thus, in the language of our model, Recognition that reality differs from expectations normally leads to an Adjustment of ideas about war.

The force driving such an Adjustment would seem to be the overwhelming need to recognize and adjust to the Reality of War in order to survive. This survival is psychological, in that by accepting reality, one is less likely to be unhinged by it, and physical, in that Recognition of reality allows armed forces to deal with and exploit changes in weaponry and military practice. Adjustment can come rapidly, particularly when a military is prepared and organized to analyze and adapt to reality. During World War I, so often used as an example of a costly misperception of reality, the German army radically changed tactics in 1917 as a result of correctly reexamining reality and producing a new doctrine, or professional discourse, and new tactics. Much the same can be said for German development of armored warfare between the wars or U.S. development of amphibious warfare and naval air power.

But discourse can also lag when elements of it are closely bound to social or political principles. Aristocratic military elites of medieval Europe may have been slower to appreciate the shifting realities of war because its aristocratic privilege was tied to its expertise in a particular kind of combat; change the style of fighting and you threatened to undercut the very justification of elite status. William's victory at Hastings in 1066 resulted from a combination of arms that took advantage both of non-aristocratic archers and of aristocratic heavy cavalry, but the elite interpreted the battle as a victory of the knight and as evidence of the impotence of infantry in the face of chivalry. During the Hundred Years' War, French chivalry fell victim at Crécy (1346) to new English tactics that took advantage of the peasant longbow in defensive positions that supported dismounted knights. A decade later the French responded at Poitiers (1356) not by confronting the problem posed by English longbowmen but by mimicking the English knights and dismounting. It was as though they could only interpret their earlier defeat as being wrought by their social equals, the English knights. The result was that the longbowmen enjoyed even better targets. Sixty years later, at Agincourt (1415), the French repeated their aristocratic mistake.

There are also cases in which the difference between reality and discourse is so fundamental that an Adjustment is not possible. This could involve either some specific aspect of a conflict or its very nature. Such an impasse leads to the Rejection of the conflict as true war and forces the creation of an alternate discourse that redefines the struggle as distinct from war, as something foreign to the dominant discourse in part or in toto. Because this alternate discourse probably lacks the limitations implicit in the dominant Discourse on War, the Alternative Discourse often justifies a more Extreme Reality of combat.

When greatly exaggerated, contempt for the enemy can drive combatants to abandon crucial aspects of their Discourse on War. The treatment of Native Americans by settlers and soldiers in North America certainly qualifies as this kind of situation, leading to massacres of Native peoples. Much has been written concerning U.S. Marines and army troops in the Pacific during World War II, who came to regard the Japanese more as animals than as men. The result was a Rejection of the usual U.S. restraints on treatment of the enemy. This may not have changed U.S. strategy, but it justified the refusal or reluctance to take prisoners and the barbaric abuse of enemy prisoners, wounded, and dead. That part of the conflict had slipped outside the Discourse on War and become a new Extreme Reality.

Throughout much of history, fighting against rebels, guerrillas, and partisans has often rejected the Discourse on War. To consider internal rebels as soldiers and their cause as a war may be unacceptable because it would seem to legitimate them. The torture of prisoners by the French in Algeria certainly qualifies as outside the Discourse on War, as may also the mutilation of French prisoners by Algerians, although native practices of fighting were traditionally cruel by Western standards. Even within a normal war, certain conduct can stand alone. French troops under Louis XIV, generally restrained in their treatment of uniformed enemy captives, committed atrocities against German partisans, *schnapphahns*, who sniped at the French during the devastation of the Palatinate (1688–1689). These *schnapphahns* were defending their homes and trying to drive out French invaders; it was war to the *schnapphahns*. But clearly it was not to the French, and they responded outside the conventions of war.

The study of history, as well as possessing its own fascination, has the power to shape the real world through informing and influencing electors, policy makers, and policies. As indicated in the Epilogue, perhaps the model suggested in these pages may offer some caution in dealing with the changes we face today both in redefining the Discourse on War and in reshaping its Reality. Most importantly, Terrorism must be incorporated in our idea of state violence in such a way that it does not tempt us to relegate it to an Extreme Reality without the conventions and limits implicit in a mature Discourse on War.

NOTES

PREFACE

1. "Universal Soldier," Words and Music by Buffy Sainte-Marie, © Copyright 1963 Caleb Music Administered by Almo Music Corp. (ASCAP) International Copyright Secured. All Rights Reserved. Used with permission. I would like to express my personal thanks to Buffy for her comments in our E-mail correspondence concerning her song.

2. Buffy Sainte-Marie's is not the only song entitled "Universal Soldier." Rapper Pastor Troy has recently released a song and album by the same name. Today, the best-known statement of popular culture using the title "Universal Soldier" is, unfortunately, a series of films by that name. The thesis of the original is that a U.S. soldier killed in Vietnam is brought back to life as a kind of animate robot. He now kills under orders, without comprehending the cause. This is anything but great art, but it gets across the notion of the individual who will "kill you for me my friend and me for you." Artist John Walker's 2000 show of etchings, "Passing Bells," carried the theme of the universal soldier. One of Martine Vaugel's pieces also has the title "Universal Soldier." There are video and war games called this as well. And assemblies of reen-actors, such as that held in September 2002 at Fort Washington National Park, go by the name. For a more serious expression of the idea of the universal soldier in a historical context see the volume by Gwynne Dyer, *War* (New York: 1985), and the PBS television series by the same name. Chapter 5, "Anybody's Son Will Do," argues that armies have been essentially the same. To make the point Dyer juxtaposes a description of training of an Egyptian, ca. 1500 B.C., and an Israeli, ca. 1970 A.D. He does not use the words "universal soldier," but that is what he is talking about. And these references are simply scratching the surface.

3. John Keegan, *The Face of Battle* (New York: 1976). Originally available through Viking Press, this wonderful study is now sold as a Penguin reprint.

4. John Keegan, *A History of Warfare* (New York: 1993), p. 12.

5. Victor Davis Hanson, *The Western Way of War: Infantry Battle in Classical Greece* (New York: 1989). It is now available in a 2nd edition with a publication date of 2000. See also his *The Soul of Battle: From Ancient Times to the Present Day, How Three Great Liberators Vanquished Tyranny* (New York: 1999) and *Carnage and Culture: Landmark Battles in the Rise of Western Power* (New York: 2001).

6. Keegan, *A History of Warfare*, p. 387.

7. Azar Gat, *The Origins of Military Thought from the Enlightenment to Clausewitz* (Oxford: 1989); *The Development of Military Thought: The Nineteenth Century* (Oxford: 1992); *Fascist and Liberal Visions of War: Fuller, Liddell Hart, Douhet, and Other Modernists* (Oxford: 1998); *A History of Military Thought from the Enlightenment to the Cold War* (Oxford: 2001).

CHAPTER ONE

1. This was not the celebrated physician, Hippocrates of Cos.

2. Thucydides, *The History of the Peloponnesian War*, trans. Richard Crawley (New York: 1950), p. 312. The account of the battle of Delium can be found in Book 4, Ch. 14, 90–98, pp. 310–315.

3. Plato, *The Dialogues of Plato*, ed. and trans. B. Jowett, 4th ed., vol. 1 (Oxford: 1953), "Symposium," p. 553.

4. Victor Davis Hanson, *The Western Way of War: Infantry Battle in Classical Greece*, 2nd ed. (Berkeley: 2000), originally published in 1989, and *Carnage and Culture: Landmark Battles in the Rise of Western Power* (New York: 2001).

5. Hanson, *The Western Way of War*, pp. 3–4.

6. Ibid., p. 5. Themistocles is actually referring to the behavior of gamecocks as a way of inspiring his troops. Another translation runs, "These birds are not fighting for their country or their fathers' gods; . . . each of the pair aims to avoid defeat and not yield to the other." Aelian, *Historical Miscellany*, Loeb Classical Library, LCL 486 (Cambridge, MA: 1997), *Varia Historia*, 2.28, p. 101. Frankly, Hanson's translation makes it read more in his sense than it would appear to be. He also translates it differently on p. 121.

7. My colleague at the University of Illinois, John Buckler, author of *The Theban Hegemony* (Cambridge, MA: 1980) and *Philip II and the Sacred War* (Leiden: 1997), objects strongly to Hanson's statements about the invulnerability of Greek agriculture. See his review of *The Western Way of War* in *JMH* 55, no. 2 (April 1991). He critiqued an earlier draft of this chapter and offered his comments in a letter of 17 March 2001.

8. I have adapted the following list from Josiah Ober, Ch. 2, "Classical Greek Times," in Michael Howard, George J. Andreopolis, and Mark R. Shuman, eds. *The Laws of War: Constraints on Warfare in the Western World* (New Haven: 1994), p. 13.

9. Hanson, *The Western Way of War*, pp. 15–16.

10. Polybius, *The Histories*, trans. W. R. Paton, vol. 4 (London: 1925), Book 13, p. 415.

11. Hanson opts for the upper end of this range; see his Ch. 6, "The Burden of Hoplite Arms and Armor," in *The Western Way of War*, pp. 55–88. However, based on his observation of armor found in museums today, John Buckler believes the armor carried to have been closer to forty pounds (letter of 17 March 2001). A good deal has been written on how much weight soldiers can carry effectively; see for example S. L. A. Marshall, *The Soldier's Load and the Mobility of a Nation* (Washington: 1950).

12. Plutarch in Hanson, *The Western Way of War*, p. 64.

13. See Plutarch, *Plutarch's Moralia*, ed. trans. Frank Cole Babbitt, vol. 3 (Cambridge, MA: 1949), Sayings of Spartans, 235.51, p. 411, and Sayings of Spartan Women, 241–242, pp. 451–469, for a number of strong sayings and actions by Spartan women and mothers demanding courage and sacrifice of their sons. A version of the more widely known statement is 241.16. "Another [mother], as she handed her son his shield, exhorted him, saying, 'Either this or upon this.'" (p. 265).

14. Homer, *The Iliad*, trans. A. T. Murray (Cambridge, MA: 1999), Book 11, p. 521.

15. Thucydides, *Peloponnesian War,* Book 5, Ch. 16, p. 392.

16. Herodotus, *The Persian Wars,* trans. George Rawlinson (New York: 1942), Book 7, Ch. 9, p. 498.

17. Hanson, *Carnage and Culture,* p. 36.

18. Ober, "Classical Greek Times," p. 15.

19. Keegan introduction to Hanson, *The Western Way of War,* p. xii.

20. Old Oligarch from *Xenophon in Seven Volumes,* ed. E. C. Marshant, vol. 7, Pseudo-Xenophon, *Constitution of Athenians,* trans. G. W. Bowersock (Cambridge, MA: 1971), pp. 475–476.

21. Victor Davis Hanson, *Carnage and Culture: Landmark Battles in the Rise of Western Power* (New York: 2001), pp. 440–441.

22. Hanson, *Carnage and Culture,* p. xiii.

23. Ibid., p. 5.

24. Ibid., p. 445.

25. Hanson, *The Soul of Battle,* p. 39.

26. Hanson, *Carnage and Culture,* p. 22.

27. Ibid., p. 328.

28. Ibid., p. 325.

29. Ibid., p. 57.

30. Ibid., p. 123.

31. Ibid., p. 444.

32. Ibid., p. 455.

33. Edward Rothstein, "Why Western Soldiers Have Always Been Such Fierce Fighters," *New York Times,* December 1, 2001.

34. Hanson, *Carnage and Culture,* p. 128.

35. John Keegan, *A History of Warfare* (New York: 1993), p. 294.

36. The best exposition of the details of Dutch use of Roman example is Geoffrey Parker, "The Military Revolution of the 1590s and the Revolution in Military Affairs of the 1990s," in John A. Lynn, ed., *ACTA of the XVIII*[th] *Congress of the International Commission on Military History* (Chicago: forthcoming 2003).

37. For example, see John A. Lynn, *Giant of the Grand Siècle: The French Army, 1610–1715* (Cambridge: 1997), pp. 472–485, for a statement of the incremental change in French infantry formations during the seventeenth century.

38. Hanson, *Carnage and Culture,* p. 363.

39. Caleb Carr, *The Lessons of Terror, A History of Warfare Against Civilians: Why It Has Always Failed and Why It Will Fail Again* (New York: 2002), p. 57.

40. Orrery in Geoffrey Parker, *The Military Revolution: Military Innovation and the Rise of the West, 1500–1800* (Cambridge: 1988), p. 16.

41. Louis XIV to Luxembourg, 5, 10, 12 August 1691, in Camille Rousset, *Histoire de Louvois,* vol. 4 (Paris: 1864), p. 510.

42. The Declaration in John A. Lynn, *The Bayonets of the Republic: Motivation and Tactics in the Army of Revolutionary France, 1791–94* (Boulder, CO: 1996; original publication University of Illinois Press in 1984), p. 56.

43. Sawyer, *The Seven Military Classics,* p. 11.

44. Keegan, *A History of Warfare,* p. 387.

45. Ibid.

46. Hanson, *Carnage and Culture,* pp. 90–91.

47. John K. Fairbank, "Introduction: Varieties of Chinese Military Experience," in Frank A. Kierman, Jr., and John K. Fairbank, eds., *Chinese Ways of Warfare* (Cambridge, MA: 1974), p. 12.

48. For a recent commentary on the influence of Vegetius, see Donald A. Neill, "Ancestral Voices: The Influence of the Ancients on the Military Thought of the Seventeenth and Eighteenth Centuries," *Journal of Military History* 62 (July 1998), pp. 487–520.

49. On the popularity of Vegetius during the Middle Ages, see Philippe Contamine, *War in the Middle Ages,* trans. Michael Jones (Oxford: 1984), pp. 210–212.

50. Vegetius, *De re militari* in T. R. Phillips, ed., *Roots of Strategy* (Harrisburg, PA: 1940), p. 172.

51. Vegetius, *De re militari*, pp. 142–143.

52. Ibid., p. 174.

53. Ibid.

54. Ibid.

55. Herodotus, *The Persian Wars,* trans. George Rawlinson (New York: 1942), Book 7, pp. 498–499.

56. This tune goes on in the second verse to make an excellent military point. "Those heroes of antiquity, Ne'er saw a cannon ball, Nor knew the force of powder, To slay their foes withall." Lewis Winstock, *Songs and Music of the Redcoats: A History of the War Music of the British Army, 1642–1902* (Harrisburg, PA: 1970), pp. 31–33.

57. Hanson, *The Western Way of War,* p. xxvii.

58. Ruskin in Kenneth Clark, *Civilization* (New York: 1969), p. 301.

59. John Buckler, "Marathon" in ed. G. Speake, *Encyclopedia of Greece and the Hellenic Tradition,* vol. 2 (London: 2000), p. 1000.

Chapter Two

1. This description of the Battle of Chi-fu rests upon the account in Sawyer's introduction to Sun Tzu, *Art of War,* trans. and ed., Ralph D. Sawyer, with Mei-chün Lee Sawyer (Boulder, CO: 1995).

2. Frank A. Kierman, Jr., "Phases and Modes of Combat in Early China," in Frank A. Kierman, Jr., and John K. Fairbank, eds., *Chinese Ways of Warfare* (Cambridge, MA: 1974), p. 5.

3. David A. Graff, "Narrative Maneuvers: The Representation of Battle in Tang Historical Writing," a paper presented at the conference Military Culture in Imperial China, 10–12 January 2003, at the University of Canterbury in Christchurch, New Zealand.

4. In Christon I. Archer, John R. Ferris, Holger H. Herwig, and Timothy H. E. Travers, *World History of Warfare* (Lincoln, NE: 2002), p. 49.

5. Kierman, "Phases and Modes of Combat in Early China," offers an interesting list of the phases of battle, pp. 30–31.

6. Ibid., p. 36.

7. Ibid., p. 43.

8. David A. Graff, *Medieval Chinese Warfare* (London: 2002), p. 22.

9. Ibid.

10. Ralph D. Sawyer with Mei-chün Lee Sawyer, ed. and trans., *The Seven Military Classics of Ancient China* (Boulder, CO: 1993), p. 11.

11. Han Fei-tzu in Patricia Buckley Ebrey, *The Cambridge Illustrated History of China* (Cambridge: 1996), p. 52.

12. Rafe de Crespigny, "Northern Frontier: The Policies and Strategy of the Later Han Empire," in New Series, no. 4 (1984), Faculty of Asian Studies Monographs, Australian National University, Canberra, pp. 94–95, a paper presented at the conference Military Culture in Imperial China, 10–12 January 2003, at the University of Canterbury in Christchurch, New Zealand, p. 4.

13. Robin Yates, "Law and the Military in Early and Imperial China," a paper presented at the conference Military Culture in Imperial China, 10–12 January 2003, at the University of Canterbury in Christchurch, New Zealand, p. 29.

14. Mark Edward Lewis, *Sanctioned Violence in Early China* (Albany: 1990), p. 107.

15. Choa Cuo in Mark E. Lewis, "The Han Abolition of Universal Military Service," in Hans van de Ven, ed., *Warfare in Chinese History* (Leiden: 2000), p. 47. See this article for an excellent treatment of Han military policy.

16. See Michael Loewe, "The Campaigns of Han Wu-ti," in Frank A. Kierman, Jr. and John K. Fairbank, eds., *Chinese Ways of Warfare* (Cambridge, MA: 1974), pp. 119–122, for the original account of Li Ling's campaign.

17. Sawyer, *The Seven Military Classics*, p. 257.

18. Yates, "Law and the Military."

19. Sawyer, *The Seven Military Classics*. All references here to Sun-tzu's *Art of War, T'ai Kung's Six Secret Teachings, The Methods of the Ssu-ma, Wu-tzu, Wei Liao-tzu,* and *Three Strategies of Huang Shih-kung* are from *The Seven Military Classics*. Sun Pin, *Military Methods*, ed. and trans. Ralph D. Sawyer with Mei-chün Lee Sawyer (Boulder, CO: 1995).

20. See the judgment in Ralph D. Sawyer, "Military Writings," in David A. Graff and Robin Higham, *A Military History of China* (Boulder, CO: 2002), pp. 97–98.

21. Confucius, *The Analects*, trans. Charles Muller, 12.22. Available on the internet at http://www.human.toyogakuen-u.ac.jp/~acmuller/contao/analects.htm.

22. *Analects*, 2.3.

23. *Tao Te Ching*, trans. Charles Muller, verse 1. Available on the internet at http://www.ede-pot.com/taoism.html.

24. Ibid., p. 45.

25. *Wei Liao-tzu*, p. 248.

26. *Three Strategies of Huang Shih-kung*, p. 304.

27. *T'ai Kung's Six Secret Teachings*, p. 56.

28. Ibid., p. 59.

29. Sun-tzu, *Art of War*, p. 157.

30. Sun Pin, *Military Methods*, p. 116.

31. *Tao Te Ching*, verse 31.

32. *Wei Liao-tzu*, pp. 256–257.

33. *Wu-tzu*, p. 206.

34. *The Methods of the Ssu-ma*, p. 117.

35. *T'ai Kung's Six Secret Teachings*, p. 71.

36. Sun-tzu, *Art of War*, p. 157.

37. *Three Strategies of Huang Shih-kung*, p. 293.

38. *T'ai Kung's Six Secret Teachings*, p. 53.

39. *Wei Liao-tzu*, p. 247.

40. *The Methods of the Ssu-ma*, p. 138.

41. Sun-tzu, *Art of War*, p. 161.

42. Ibid.

43. Ibid.

44. *T'ai Kung's Six Secret Teachings*, pp. 68, 69.

45. Sun-tzu, *Art of War*, p. 158.

46. Ibid., p. 167.

47. Ibid.

48. Sun Pin, *Military Methods*, p. 148.

49. Ibid., p. 149.

50. See Graff, "Narrative Maneuvers."

51. Graff, *Medieval Chinese Warfare*, p. 23.

52. Sun Pin, *Military Methods*, p. 231.

53. *Tao Te Ching*, verse 57, in Sawyer, *The Complete Art of War*, p. 29. The Muller translation on the web translates this part of verse 57 as "Use fairness in governing the state. Use surprise tactics in war."

54. Sun-tzu, *Art of War*, p. 168.

55. *Wei Liao-tzu*, p. 257.

56. Sun Pin, *Military Methods*, p. 197.

57. *T'ai Kung's Six Secret Teachings*, p. 65.

58. *The Methods of the Ssu-ma*, p. 113.

59. Graff, *Medieval Chinese Warfare*, p. 25.

60. The text of the *Spring and Autumn Annals of Wu and Yüeh* used here is included in Sawyer, *The Seven Military Classics of Ancient China*, pp. 151–152.

61. *Wei Liao-tzu* in Graff, *Medieval Chinese Warfare*, p. 24.

62. *Wei Liao-tzu*, p. 265.

63. Ibid., p. 267.

64. Sawyer, *The Seven Military Classics of Ancient China*, p. 290.

65. *T'ai Kung's Six Secret Teachings*, pp. 65–66.

66. *Three Strategies of Huang Shih-kung*, p. 296.

67. *T'ai Kung's Six Secret Teachings*, p. 66.

68. *Wei Liao-tzu*, p. 249.

69. *Three Strategies of Huang Shih-kung*, p. 294.

70. Sun-tzu, *Art of War*, p. 185.

71. Sun Pin, *Military Methods*, pp. 101–102.

72. Sun-tzu, *Art of War*, p. 159.

73. Sun Pin, *Military Methods*, p. 161.

74. Ibid., p. 148.

75. Thomas R. Trautmann, *Kautilya and the Arthâshastra: A Statistical Investigation of the Authorship and Evolution of the Text* (Leiden: 1971), pp. 183–184.

76. Kautilya, *The Kautilya Arthashastra*, part II, trans. and ed. R. P. Kangle (Bombay: 1972), I.I.I, p. I. This chapter employs two versions of the *Arthashastra*, the Kangle translation and Kautilya, *The Arthashastra*, trans. and ed. L. N. Rangarajan (New Delhi: 1992). Kangle presents the *Arthashastra* as written, while Rangarajan rearranges the material thematically. Kangle has a somewhat annoying practice of inserting words in brackets to flesh out passages. This explains the brackets in quotations presented here. In general, I have used the Kangle because it is a complete *Arthashastra*, but at times the Rangarajan translations are so much more artful and flowing that I have used them.

77. See Pradeep Barua, *The State at War in South Asia*, soon to be published. Pradeep has been kind enough to let me see his manuscript for Chapter 1, "Warfare in Prehistoric and Classical India." Because this is yet to be published, I cannot supply page references.

78. *Rig Veda* in Christon I. Archer, John R. Ferris, Holger H. Herwig, and Timothy H. E. Travers, *World History of Warfare* (Lincoln, NE: 2002), p. 43.

79. The *Artharva Veda* in Sarva Daman Singh, *Ancient Indian Warfare with Special Reference to the Vedic Period* (Leiden: 1965), p. 13.

80. The *Taittiriya Samhita* in Singh, *Ancient Indian Warfare*, p. 13.

81. *Rig Veda* in Singh, *Ancient Indian Warfare*, p. 93.

82. Barua, *The State at War in South Asia*.

83. *Agni Purana*, Chap. 249.6–8, vol. 28, p. 645.

84. The *Mahabharata* in Archer, Ferris, Herwig, and Travers, *World History of Warfare*, p. 45.

85. For a list of such conventions, see V. R. Ramachandra Dikshitar, *War in Ancient India* (Delhi, 1987), pp. 67–75. Also see Singh, *Ancient Indian Warfare*, pp. 50–51, 161–167. The *Manusmrti* details most of these conventions in Chapter VII, articles 88–93. *Manusmrti*, trans. Georg Bühler. The Bühler translation, which first appeared in 1889, is now in the public domain and can be found on the internet at http://members.fortunecity.com/dev3/laws_of_manu_chapter_i.htm and following.

86. Singh, *Ancient Indian Warfare*, p. 163. See also Dikshitar, *War in Ancient India*, p. 71.

87. Singh, *Ancient Indian Warfare*, p. 160.

88. *Diodorus of Sicily*, C. Bradford Welles, trans., vol. 8 (Cambridge, MA: 1963), p. 373.

89. Arrian, *Indica* in Francis R. B. Godolphin, ed., *The Greek Historians*, vol. 2 (New York: 1972), p. 744.

90. John W. McCrindle, *Ancient India as Described by Megasthenes and Arrian* (Calcutta: 1926), *Indica* of Megasthenes, p. 141.

91. Barua, *The State at War in South Asia*.

92. For example, see *Ancient Indian Tradition and Mythology Series*, vols. 27–30, *The Agni Purana*, trans. and ed. N. Gangadharan (Delhi: 1984–1987), Chap. 249.20–29, vol. 28, p. 646.

93. Arrian, "The Indica" in *Anabasis of Alexander, Together with the Indica*, E. J. Chinnock, trans. (London: 1893), Ch. 16.http://www.shsu.edu/~his_ncp/Indica.html.

94. Barua, *The State at War in South Asia*.

95. Ibid.

96. Ibid.

97. Ibid.

98. Chinese traveler Chau Ju-Kua quoted in Sastri, *The Cholas*, pp. 457–458, in Barua, *The State at War in South Asia*.

99. *Arthashastra*, Kangle, ed., 2.32.4, p. 177.

100. Ibid., 2.2.13, p. 60.

101. Priyadarsan Sensarma, *Military Wisdom in the Puranas* (Calcutta: 1979), p. 50.

102. *The Nitisara or The Elements of Polity by Kamandaki*, Rajendralatat Mitra, ed. (Calcutta: 1982), p. 328. This number is often cited as 6,000 horses. Barua believes that this was the original intent of the source, rather than the 600 in the Mitra translation.

103. Ibid.

104. See *Arthashastra*, Kangle, ed., 2.33.5, p. 180, 7.8.27, p. 348, and 10.1.7–9, p. 434. The form of the list presented in this chapter is based on the discussion and terminology in *Arthashastra*, Rangarajan, ed., pp. 683–684.

105. *Arthashastra*, Kangle, ed., 6.1.15, p. 316.

106. Ibid., 5.3.35–36, p. 304.

107. *Nitiprakasika*, Gustave Oppert, ed. (New Dehli: 1970), p. 20. *Nitiprakasika*, VI, 58.

108. Sukracraya in Chakravarti, *The Art of War in Ancient India*, p. 86.

109. These are Chapters 5 and 6 of Book 10. In his treatment of Kautilya, Rangarajan insists that "Kautilya gives an exhaustive description of how to arrange the forces for a set-piece battle" but manages to share that with his readers in eleven pages, including diagrams. In fact Kautilya does not say all that much. *Arthashastra*, Rangarajan, ed., p. 714.

110. Kautilya, *Arthashastra*, Kangle, ed., 10.5.3, p. 445. Rangarajan offers a table of ancient linear measurements translated to inches and centimeters, Kautilya, *Arthashastra*, ed. Rangarajan, pp. 763–764. His measurements are used here.

111. Kautilya, *Arthashastra*, Kangle, ed., 10.5.9–10, p. 446. See Kautilya, *Arthashastra*, Rangarajan, ed., pp. 716–720, for a diagrams that represent such units.

112. Kautilya, *Arthashastra*, Kangle, ed., 10.5.38, p. 448. Concerning formations, *vyuhas*, Kautilaya suggests four, 10.6.158–159, and *The Agni Purana*, Ch. 242, pp. 49–67, uses the same four. *The Agni Purana*, vol. 28, pp. 633–634.

113. Arrian, *Indica* in Godolphin, *The Greek Historians*, p. 744.

114. Stephen Rosen, *Societies and Military Power: India and Its Armies* (Ithaca, NY: 1996), argues that caste weakened South Asian society by segmenting it and as a side effect limited military effectiveness. As will become apparent in Chapter 5, I have serious troubles with this argument as it concerns the period 1740–1806; however, caste may have helped to undermine attention to state issues and trapped Indian discussion of war and the state at the dog-eat-dog level.

115. *Santi Parva*, Section LV, in *The Mahabharata*, ed. Pratap Chandra Roy, vol. 8 (Calcutta: 1962), p. 118.

116. *Agni Purana*, Ch. 236, lines 50–55, p. 614.

117. *Manusmrti*, VII, 98.

118. Ibid., II, 155.

119. Ibid., I, 89.

120. Ibid., II, 31–32.

121. Ibid., VII, 2–3.

122. *Matsya Purana* (Ch. 215, Sloka 68 a), cited in Priyadarsan Sensarma, *Military Wisdom in the Puranas* (Calcutta: 1979), p. 13.

123. *Manusmrti*, VII, 87.

124. A. L. Basham, *The Wonder That Was India* (Calcutta: 1991), p. 123.

125. *Arthashastra*, Kangle, ed., 14.3.35, p. 505, and 6.1.15, p. 316.

126. Ibid., 9.2.13, p. 412.

127. *Ancient Indian Tradition and Mythology Series*, vols. 27–30, *The Agni Purana*, trans. and ed. N. Gangadharan (Delhi, 1984–1987), Chap. 249.6–8, vol. 28, p. 645.

128. *Manusmrti*, VII, 47.

129. Ibid., VII, 10.

130. Ibid., VII, 22.

131. Ibid., VII, 19.

132. Aradhana Parma, *Techniques of Statecraft: A Study of Kautiliya's Arthasastra* (New Delhi: 1987), p. 210.

133. The Manusmrti and Yajnavalkya both have six kinds of foreign policy and the mandala as well; it is not unique to the *Arthshastra*.

134. *Arthashastra*, Kangle, ed., 6.2, pp. 317–320, presents the outlines of the mandala theory. See as well the discussion in *Arthashastra*, Rangarajan, ed., pp. 551–563.

135. *Arthashastra*, Rangarajan, ed., 6.2.39–40, p. 551.

136. *Arthashastra*, Kangle, ed., 7.1.1–15, p. 321.

137. Parma, *Techniques of Statecraft*, p. 207.

138. *Arthashastra*, Kangle, ed., 6.2.13, p. 318.

139. Ibid., 7.14.18–19, p. 368.

140. Ibid., 12.1.10–16, p. 460.

141. *Arthashastra*, Rangarajan, ed., p. 676.

142. *Arthashastra*, Kangle, ed., 7.6.40–41, p. 342.

143. Ibid., 10.3.26, p. 440.

144. Ibid., 10.3.1, p. 438.

145. *Arthashastra*, Rangajaran, ed., 1.12.20, p. 498.

146. Stephen Rosen, *Societies and Military Power: India and Its Armies* (Ithaca, NY: 1996), pp. 75–76.

147. *Arthashastra*, Kangle, ed., 1.10.1, p. 18.

148. Ibid., 1.10.9–12, pp. 19–20.

149. Ibid., 4.4.3–4, p. 265.

150. Ibid., 4.4.6–8, p. 265.

151. Ibid., 5.3.47, p. 305.

152. *Santi Parva*, Section LXIX, p. 157.

153. *Matsya Purana*, chap 215, in Sensarma, *Military Wisdom of the Puranas*, p. 21.

154. *Arthashastra*, Rangajaran, ed., 13.1.21, p. 455.

155. *Arthashastra*, Kangle, ed., 12.2.13, p. 463.

156. Ibid., p. 455.

157. Ibid., 11.1.6–15, p. 265.

158. Ibid., 9.6.54–55, p. 425.

159. Ibid., 11.1.34–36, p. 457.

160. Ibid., 12.2.11–14, p. 463; and *Arthashastra*, Rangajaran, ed., 12.2.14, p. 528.

161. See, for example, Caleb Carr, *The Lessons of Terror, A History of Warfare Against Civilians: Why It Has Always Failed and Why It Will Fail Again* (New York: 2002), p. 251.

162. *Agni Purana*, Ch. 242, 34–48, vol. 28, p. 633.

163. See *Arthashastra*, Kangle, ed., 9.5, "Dangers from (officers in) the outer regions and the interior," pp. 420–422.

164. Ibid., 5.1.21–22, pp. 293–294.

165. *Arthashastra*, Kangle, ed., 10.6.51, p. 453.

166. Graff and Higham, *Chinese Military History*, pp. 13–14.

167. John Keegan, *A History of Warfare* (New York: 1993), p. 387.

168. See Basil Henry Liddell Hart, *Strategy* (New York: 1991), for a reprint of his well-known study of the indirect approach, first published in 1954.

Chapter Three

1. Geoffrey le Baker, *Chronicle*, in Richard Barber, ed., *The Life and Campaigns of the Black Prince: From Contemporary Letters, Diaries and Chronicles* (Woodbridge, Suffolk: 1986), p. 44.

2. My description of the battle formation comes from discussions with Kelly DeVries, who strongly and convincingly disputes the descriptions offered by Clifford J. Rogers, *War Cruel and Sharp: English Strategy Under Edward III, 1327–1360* (Woodbridge, Suffolk: 2000) and by Jonathan Sumption in his *The Hundred Years War*, vol. I, *Trial by Battle* (London: 1990), pp. 525–532. For a printed account of DeVries's argument, see his *Infantry Warfare in the Early Fourteenth Century* (Woodbridge, Suffolk: 1996), pp. 160–164.

3. Geoffrey le Baker, *Chronicle,* in Barber, *The Life and Campaigns of the Black Prince,* p. 43.

4. Froissart, *Chronicles,* ed. Geoffrey Brereton (London: 1978), p. 86.

5. Geoffrey le Baker, *Chronicle,* in Barber, *The Life and Campaigns of the Black Prince,* p. 43.

6. The issue of whether or not the Genoese had *pavisses* at all is up for contention. Rogers, *War Cruel and Sharp,* p. 267, agrees they did. Kelly DeVries believes that they only began to carry such large shields later.

7. Froissart, *Chronicles,* p. 89.

8. See, for example, the discussion in Kelly DeVries, *Medieval Military Technology* (Peterborough, Ontario: 1992), p. 38.

9. *Chronicle of St. Omer* in Rogers, *War Cruel and Sharp,* p. 269.

10. Geoffrey le Baker, *Chronicle,* in Barber, *The Life and Campaigns of the Black Prince,* p. 43.

11. *Chronicle of St. Omer* in Rogers, *War Cruel and Sharp,* p. 269.

12. Thomas Malory, *Malory, Works,* ed. Eugène Vinaver, 2nd ed. (Oxford: 1971), p. 408. I have taken the liberty of putting the archaic English of the original into modern English throughout this chapter.

13. The most important works on the subject are Maurice Keen, *Chivalry* (New Haven: 1984) and Richard W. Kaeuper, *Chivalry and Violence in Medieval Europe* (Oxford: 1999). Other authors and works of particular value for this chapter include Nicolas Wright, *Knights and Peasants: The Hundred Years War in the French Countryside* (Woodbridge, Suffolk: 1998); Rogers, *War Cruel and Sharp,* as well as works by Kelly DeVries. The literature on medieval warfare and military values seems to be flourishing today.

14. Keen, *Chivalry,* p. 102.

15. Ibid., p. 111. On the use of Vegetius in the Middle Ages, see Philippe Richardot, *Végèce et la culture militaire au moyen âge, V^e–XVe siècles* (Paris: 1998).

16. Kaeuper, *Chivalry and Violence,* p. 47.

17. *Lancelot,* ed. Alexandre Micha, vol. 4 (Paris: 1979), p. 359.

18. Asher, trans., *Quest,* p. 137; Bogdanow, *Folie Lancelot,* pp. 119–120, in Kaeuper, *Chivalry and Violence,* p. 132.

19. Wright, ed., trans., *Historical Works,* p. 256 or 279, in Kaeuper, *Chivalry and Violence,* p. 140.

20. Philippe Contamine, *War in the Middle Ages,* trans. Michael Jones (Oxford: 1984), p. 77. For controversy over feudalism, see Susan Reynolds, *Fiefs and Vassals: The Medieval Evidence Reinterpreted* (Oxford: 1994); Thomas N. Bisson, "The 'Feudal Revolution,'" *Past and Present* 142 (February 1994), pp. 6–42; and Dominique Barthélemy and Stephen D. White, "Debate—The 'Feudal Revolution'," *Past and Present* 152 (August 1996), pp. 196–223.

21. Keen, *Chivalry,* p. 10.

22. BN, MS Esp. 33, in ibid., p. 185.

23. Llull, *Ars Brevis,* in Anthony Bonner, ed., *Selected Works of Ramon Llull,* 2 vols. (Princeton: 1985), vol. 1, p. 624.

24. Erdmann, *Entstehung des Kreuzzugsgedankens,* p. 330, in Keen, *Chivalry,* p. 71.

25. Philippe de Mézières, *Le Songe du Vieil Pelerin,* ed. G. Coopland, vol. 1 (Cambridge: 1969), pp. 531–532.

26. Vinaver, ed., *Malory, Works,* p. 75.

27. *La Bataille de trente,* ed. Henry Brush (Chicago: 1912), p. 39

28. Rupert T. Pickens, ed. *The Story of Merlin,* in Norris Lacy, ed., *Lancelot-Grail,* vol. I (New York: 1993), pp. 20, 223 in Kaeuper, *Chivalry and Violence,* p. 196.

29. *Raoull de Hodenc: Le roman des eles/The Anonymous Ordene de chevalerie*, ed. Keith Busby (Amsterdam: 1983), p. 167.

30. In J. Bumke, *The Concept of Knighthood in the Middle Ages*, trans. W. T. H. and E. Jackson (New York: 1982).

31. Pickens, trans., *Story of Merlin*, in Kaeuper, *Chivalry and Violence*, p. 221.

32. Boucicaut, *Le livre des faicts du Maréchal de Boucicaut*, ed. M. Petitot in *Collection complète de des mémoires rélatifs à l'histoire de France*, vol. 6 (Paris: 1819), p. 393.

33. *Raoul of Cambrai*, ed., trans., Sarah Kay (Oxford: 1992), p. 333.

34. Rosenberg, trans., *Lancelot Part III*, p. 267 or 275, in Kaeuper, *Chivalry and Violence*, p. 223.

35. William of Malmesbury, *Gesta regum Anglorum*, trans. and ed. R. A. B. Mynors, R. M. Thomson, and M. Winterbottom (Oxford: 1998), p. 785. This is an amusing story, but it should also be noted that the duke was hardly typical. Malmesbury called him "a lecher and a fool," p. 783, and reported that he was excommunicated for his sins.

36. In Kathryn Gravdal, *Ravishing Maidens: Writing Rape in Medieval French Literature and Law* (Philadelphia: 1991), p. 66. Gravdal concludes that "rape is an accepted male right," p. 67. This is not an isolated statement of this principle. When a lady wanted to go on a quest with Hector the ladies of court thought her foolish, "for if it happened that another knight defeated Hector, he would take you and do with you as he wished." *Lancelot*, part II, trans. Carleton W. Carroll, in Norris Lacy, ed., *Lancelot-Grail*, vol. II (New York: 1993), p. 169.

37. Llull, *Felix or the Book of Wonders* in Bonner, ed., *Selected Works of Ramon Llull*, vol. 2, pp. 668–669.

38. See, for example, "*chevalchie*," in line 7792. Paul Meyer, ed., *L'Histoire de Guillaume le Maréchal*, vol. 1 (Paris: 1891), p. 281. My inability to read Middle French with any ease forces me to use not only the original French published by the Société de l'histoire de France, as in the volume above, but, more importantly, English translations by John Gillingham and Stewart Gregory cited below.

39. Rogers makes these estimates in Clifford J. Rogers, "By Fire and Sword: *Bellum Hostile* and 'Civilians' in the Hundred Years' War," in Mark Grimsley and Clifford J. Rogers, eds., *Civilians in the Path of War* (Lincoln, NE: 2002), p. 37. He figures five leagues as 13.4 miles in modern measurements.

40. The Chandos Herald in Barber, *The Life and Campaigns of the Black Prince: From Contemporary Letters, Diaries and Chronicles*, p. 93. Kelly DeVries argues that the Chandos Herald exaggerated the destruction.

41. Petrarch in R. Boutruch, "The Devastation of Rural Areas During the Hundred Years' War and the Agricultural Recovery of France," in *The Recovery of France in the Fifteenth Century*, ed. P. S. Lewis (New York: 1972), p. 26 in Rogers, "By Fire and Sword," p. 34.

42. See the classic article by G. Perjés, "Army Provisioning, Logistics and Strategy in the Second Half of the 17th Century," *Acta Historica Academiae Scientiarum Hungaricae* 16, nr. 1–2 (1970), pp. 27–29. See also the discussion of supply in Chapter 2 of John A. Lynn, *Giant of the Grand Siècle: The French Army 1610–1715* (New York: 1997).

43. Jordan Fantosme's *Chronicle*, in John Gillingham, "Richard I and the Science of War in the Middle Ages," in J. Gillingham and J. C. Holt, eds., *War and Government in the Middle Ages* (Cambridge: 1984), p. 84.

44. I have elsewhere defined this as a medieval stipendiary army. See John A. Lynn, "The Evolution of Army Style in the Modern West, 800–2000," *International History Review* 18, no. 3 (August 1996), pp. 505–545.

45. Jean de Bueil, *Le Jouvencel,* I, pp. 95–96 and ii, p. 83, in Wright, *Knights and Peasants,* p. 40.

46. Robert Stacey, Ch. 3, "The Age of Chivalry," in Michael Howard, George J. Andreopolis, and Mark R. Shuman, eds. *The Laws of War: Constraints on Warfare in the Western World* (New Haven: 1994), pp. 34–35.

47. This useful privateer/pirate analogy comes from Rogers, "By Fire and Sword," pp. 58–59.

48. Robertus de Avesbury, *De Gestis Mirabilibus Regis Edwardi Tertii,* ed. E. Thompson (Rolls series, 1889), p. 306, in Wright, *Knights and Peasants,* p. 34.

49. Chandos Herald, *Life of the Black Prince by the Herald of Sir John Chandos,* ed. Mildred Pope and Eleanor Lodge (Oxford: 1910), p. 7, lines 236–239. We know this author only as the herald of John Chandos.

50. Henry V in Juvenal des Ursins, *Histoire de Charles VI* in J. A. Buchon, *Choix des Chroniques* (Paris: 1875), p. 565, in Gillingham, "Richard I and the Science of War," p. 85.

51. Chanson Gaydon in Daniel, *Heroes and Saracens: An Interpretation of the Chansons de geste* (Edinburgh: 1984), p. 26.

52. Jean de Venette, *The Chronicle of Jean de Venette,* tr. J. Birdsall, ed. R. A. Newhall (New York: 1953), pp. 99–100.

53. Ibid., p. 111.

54. See such admissions discussed in Wright, *Knights and Peasants,* p. 73.

55. Described in *Journal d'un Bourgeois de Paris, 1405–1449,* ed. A. Tuetey (Paris: 1881), p. 356, in Wright, *Knights and Peasants,* p. 70.

56. *Lay de guerre* in A. Piaget and E. Droz, *Pierre de Nesson et ses Oeuvres* (Paris: 1925), p. 47, lines 1–5, and p. 56, lines 307–308.

57. *Patis* was an ancestor of the practice by which hostile armies on campaign demanded "contributions" from communities in the seventeenth century and later. However, payment of contributions was far more regularized and rationalized than the demand for *patis*; moreover contributions implied protection. On contributions see John A. Lynn, "How War Fed War: The Tax of Violence and Contributions During the *Grand Siècle*," *Journal of Modern History* 65, no. 2 (June 1993), pp. 286–310.

58. Rogers, "By Fire and Sword," p. 62.

59. Bouvet in John Gillingham, "War and Chivalry in the History of William the Marshall" in Matthew Strickland, ed., *Anglo-Norman Warfare: Studies in Late Anglo-Saxon and Anglo-Norman Military Organization and Warfare* (Woodbridge, Suffolk: 1992), p. 263.

60. In Duvin, "Origines," p. 369, in Wright, *Knights and Peasants,* p. 85. There were also ordinances that forbade the use of town bells, out of fear that they would be used in a Jacquerie. See Wright, *Knights and Peasants,* p. 113.

61. See A. Blanchet, *Les Souterrains-refuges de la France* (Paris: 1923).

62. Jean de Venette, *The Chronicle of Jean de Venette,* p. 91.

63. Kelly DeVries disputes that the 1346 campaign was truly a *chevauchée,* because it was not called such at the time. He feels that its depredations resulted only from logistical necessity. I have taken my lead from Clifford Rogers, who definitely defines the 1346 campaign as a *chevauchée.*

64. Parliamentary advisory, June 1344, in Rogers, *War Cruel and Sharp,* p. 221.

65. Letters of Bartholomew Burghersh and of Thomas Bradwardine, Chancellor of St. Paul's in *Murimuth,* pp. 200–201, in Rogers, *War Cruel and Sharp,* p. 241.

66. "Acts of War of Edward III," in Barber, *The Life and Campaigns of the Black Prince,* p. 29.

67. Jean le Bel, *Chronique de Jean le Bel,* Jules Viard and Eugène Déprez, eds., 2 vols. (Paris: 1904–1905), vol. 2, p. 78, in Rogers, *War Cruel and Sharp,* p. 245.

68. Froissart, *Chronicles,* p. 75.

69. Ibid., p. 76.

70. Originally, "the toun & the subbarbus vnto the bare wallys of all thing that myghte be bore & caryed out, was robbid and despoyled." *English Brut* in Rogers, *War Cruel and Sharp,* p. 250.

71. Froissart, *Chronicles,* p. 77.

72. Ibid.

73. Edward's response in Rogers, *War Cruel and Sharp,* p. 260.

74. Johan Huizinga, *The Waning of the Middle Ages* (London: 1924), p. 56.

75. Helmut Nickel, "The Tournament: An Historical Sketch" in Howell Chickering and Tomas H. Seiler, eds., *The Study of Chivalry: Resources and Approaches* (Kalamazoo, MI: 1988), p. 214.

76. *History of William the Marshal,* trans. Stewart Gregory, with the assistance of David Crouch, lines 4837–4840. This is available on the internet at http://www.deremilitari.org/marshal.htm.

77. Keen, *Chivalry,* p. 87.

78. Ibid.

79. In Nickel, "The Tournament," p. 248.

80. Kaeuper, *Chivalry and Violence,* p. 175.

81. Concerning *pas d'armes,* see Keen, *Chivalry,* Ch. 11, and Anthony Annunziata, "Teaching the *Pas d'Armes,*" in Chickering and Seiler, eds., *The Study of Chivalry,* pp. 557–582.

82. R. Hoveden, *Chronica,* ed. W. Stubbs (RS, 1869), II, pp. 166–167, in Keen, *Chivalry,* p. 88.

83. Ferrers writing in 1386 in Keen, *Chivalry,* p. 99.

84. Geoffroi de Charny, *The Book of Chivalry of Geoffroi de Charny,* ed. Richard W. Kaeuper and Elspeth Kennedy (Philadelphia: 1996), pp. 85–91.

85. Huizinga, *The Waning of the Middle Ages,* p. 72; Kaeuper, *Chivalry and Violence,* p. 165; Barber and Barker in Kaeuper, *Chivalry and Violence,* p. 303; Nickel, "The Tournament," p. 213.

86. Girart de Borneth in Gillingham, "War and Chivalry in the *History of William the Marshal,*" p. 262.

87. Rules issued under Emperor Henry the Fowler in Nickel, "The Tournament," p. 253.

88. Ibid., pp. 251–253.

89. Keen, *Chivalry and Violence,* p. 90.

90. Another factor made the tournament much softer than war; a tournament that climaxed in a banquet posed a very different challenge from a military campaign that knew privation.

91. From C. Oulmont, *Les Débats du clerc et du chevalier* (Paris: 1911), p. 113, in Keen, *Chivalry,* p. 88.

92. Kaeuper, *Chivalry and Violence,* p. 229.

93. See Nickel, "The Tournament," pp. 235–236.

94. Charny, *The Book of Chivalry,* p. 121.

95. Jacques de Vitry, Exemplum 141, from *The Exempla of Jacques de Vitry,* ed. Thomas F. Crane (London: 1890), pp. 62–64, presented in David Carlson, "Religious Writers and Church Councils on Chivalry," in Chickering and Seiler, eds., *The Study of Chivalry,* p. 155.

96. The archbishop in Gillingham, "War and Chivalry in the *History of William the Marshall,*" p. 252.

97. *History of William the Marshal,* lines 18,483–485, in Kaeuper, *Chivalry and Violence,* p. 282.

98. *History of William the Marshal,* lines 7785–7798, in Gillingham, "War and Chivalry in the *History of William the Marshal,*" p. 255.

99. Ibid., lines 7799–7802, p. 255.

100. Ibid., lines 665–669, p. 256.

101. Gillingham, "War and Chivalry in the *History of William the Marshal,*" p. 262.

102. *History of William the Marshal,* trans. Stewart Gregory, lines 4797–4803.

103. Ibid., lines 4808–1410.

104. Ibid., line 4814.

105. Ibid., lines 4839–4840.

106. Ibid., lines 8637–8639.

107. Ibid., lines 16,883–16,886.

108. Ibid., lines 16,686–16,696.

109. Ibid., lines 8661–8663.

110. Ibid., lines 8687–8689.

111. Ibid., lines 8703–8707.

112. Ibid., lines 16,390–16,391.

113. Ibid., line 16,768.

114. Ibid., lines 16,331–16,334.

115. Kaeuper, *Wars, Justice, and Public Order,* p. 145.

116. Marjorie Chibnall, ed., *The Ecclesiastical History of Orderic Vitalis,* vol. II (Oxford: 1969), p. 121.

117. Chibnall, ed., *The Ecclesiastical History of Orderic Vitalis,* vol. IV (Oxford: 1973), p. 299.

118. H. E. J. Cowdrey, "The Peace and the Truce of God in the Eleventh Century," *Past and Present,* no. 46 (February 1970), pp. 43–44.

119. Stacey, "The Age of Chivalry," p. 30.

120. Mansi, xix, cc.483–484, in Cowdrey, "The Peace and the Truce of God," p. 44.

121. Yves de Chartres, *Panormia,* lib. XII, cap. CXLVII, dans P. L., t. XLXI, col. 1343, in Aryeh Graboïs, "De la trêve de Dieu à la paix du roi: Étude sur les transformations du mouvement de la paix au XII siècle," in Pierre Gallais and Yves-Jean Riou, *Mélanges offerts à René Crozet* (Poitiers: 1966), p. 586.

122. Andrew of Fleury, *Miracula sancti Benedicti,* ii–iv, *Les Miracles de saint xxx,* ed. E. de Certain (Société de l'histoire de France, Paris, 1858), pp. 192–198, in Cowdrey, "The Peace and the Truce of God," p. 47.

123. Council of Narbonne, canon I, Mansi, xix, cc. 593–596, in Cowdrey, "The Peace and the Truce of God," p. 53.

124. Graboïs, "De la trêve de Dieu à la paix du roi," p. 592.

125. Rules issued under Emperor Henry the Fowler in Nickel, "The Tournament," p. 251.

126. Council of Clermont, canon 9, in Carlson, "Religious Writers and Church Councils on Chivalry," p. 150.

127. Buno Scott James, trans., Bernard of Clairvaux, letter 405, in Kaeuper, *Chivalry and Violence,* p. 85.

128. Bernard of Clairvaux, "In Praise of the New Knighthood," in David Carlson, "Religious Writers and Church Councils on Chivalry," in Chickering and Seiler, eds., *The Study of Chivalry,* pp. 161–162.

129. Balderic of Dol's account of Urban's words in August C. Krey, *The First Crusade: The Accounts of Eye-Witnesses and Participants* (Princeton: 1921), p. 35.

130. Kaeuper, *War, Justice, and Public Order,* p. 146, calls the First Crusade the "safety valve for knightly violence," and Cowdrey, "The Peace and the Truce of God," p. 58, argues of Urban II that "His crusade was the complement of the Peace movement."

131. Greenia, trans., *Bernard of Clairvaux,* pp. 138, 131, 132, 143; Leclercq and Rochais, eds., *Bernard of Clairvaux,* 219, 215, 216, 213, in Kaeuper, *Chivalry and Violence,* p. 76.

132. PL CLVI, 685, in Keen, *Chivalry,* pp. 48–49.

133. Bernard of Clairvaux, "In Praise of the New Knighthood," in Carlson, "Religious Writers and Church Councils on Chivalry," pp. 164–165.

134. Joseph Bédier, *Les Chansons de Croisade* (Paris: 1909), pp. 32–35, in Keen, *Chivalry,* p. 56.

135. Ibid.

CHAPTER FOUR

1. Actually the French is stronger, "Perdue, perdue, quel est le jean-foutre qui a dit cela?" Frédéric Hulot, *Le maréchal de Saxe* (Paris: 1989), p. 171.

2. Frédéric Lacaille, "Les grands, la peinture et la guerre, galeries et grands ensembles consacrés à la représentation de la guerre en France aux XVIIe et XVIIIe siècles: Esquisse d'un inventaire" in *L'Art de la guerre: La vision des peintres aux XVIIe et XVIIIe siècles,* ed., Centre d'études d'histoire de la défense (Saint-Maixent-l'École: 1998), pp. 99–118.

3. Other painters also give us visions of Fontenoy; the most seen image is that brushed by Émile Jean Horace Vernet (1789–1863) in the Hall of Battles at the Chateau de Versailles.

4. Voltaire, *Oeuvres complètes,* ed. Beuchot, vol. 15 (Paris: Garnier frères, 1878), *Précis du siècle de Louis XV,* p. 240. In addition, Voltaire also composed a poem, published at Amsterdam in 1748, in honor of Louis XV and the battle of Fontenoy.

5. One report has Hay taunt the French: "We hope you will stand till we come up to you and not swim the river as you did at Dettingen!" Hulot, *Le maréchal de Saxe,* p. 169.

6. Both Jean-Baptiste Le Paon (1736–1785) and Félix Philippoteaux (1815–1884) made it the subjects of their canvases.

7. At the 2002 annual meeting of the Society for Military History held in Madison, WI, Scott Hendrix presented an excellent paper, which parallels many of the same themes as this chapter, except that Hendrix deals specifically with the British in the eighteenth century. It is very much worth the reading. Scott N. Hendrix, "Everybody Loves a Parade: Drill, Uniforms, Swords and Spectacle in the Mid-Eighteenth-Century British Army."

8. See the section on clothing in John A. Lynn, *Giant of the Grand Siècle: The French Army 1610–1715* (New York: 1997), pp. 169–180.

9. Turenne to Le Tellier, 22 December 1667, in Joseph Michaud and Jean Poujoulat, *Nouvelle collection des mémoires relatifs a l'histoire de France* (Paris: 1836), 3:512.

10. Letter of 28 October 1647 in Louis André, *Michel Le Tellier et l'organisation de l'armée monarchique* (Paris: 1906. Reprint Geneva: 1980), p. 339.

11. Service Historique de l'Armée de Terre (SHAT), Archives de guerre (AG), A¹221, 20 December 1668, instructions to Martinet by Louvois in Camille Rousset, *Histoire de Louvois,* 4 vols. (Paris: 1862–1864), 1:208.

12. See for example, the letter of 28 October 1647 in André, *Michel Le Tellier,* p. 339.

13. SHAT, AG, A¹279, #124, 9 October 1672.

14. SHAT, AG, A¹315, 8 April 1673, in Rousset, *Louvois,* 1:187.

15. Louvois to d'Alauzier, 11 May 1682, in Rousset, *Louvois,* 3:294n. My italics.

16. Philippe Contamine, ed., *Histoire militaire de la France,* vol. 1, series editor André Corvisier (Paris: 1992), p. 406.

17. Regulation of 26 May 1704, Victor Belhomme, *Histoire de l'infanterie en France,* 5 vols. (Paris: 1893–1902), 2:396–397.

18. Daniel Roche, *La Culture des apparences* (Paris, 1989), chap. 5 "La hierarchie des apparences à Paris de Louis XIV à Louis XVI," pp. 87–117.

19. *Mercure galant,* 23 April 1672, pp. 306–307, in Clare Haru Crowston, *Fabricating Women: The Seamstresses of Old Regime France, 1675–1791* (Durham, NC: 2001), p. 30. I would like to express my thanks to my colleague Clare Crowston for getting me thinking along these lines.

20. *Mercure galant,* 23 April 1672, pp. 308–309. I thank Clare Crowston for giving me this quotation.

21. SHAT, Bibliothèque, *Collection des ordonnances militaires,* vol. 22, #176, 25 March 1672.

22. Rousseau, "Lettre à d'Alembert," in *Discours sur les sciences et les arts,* ed. Jean Varloot (Paris: 1987), p. 213, in Crowston, *Fabricating Women,* p. 29.

23. Maurice de Saxe, *My Reveries on the Art of War,* in Thomas R. Phillips, trans. and ed., *Roots of Strategy* (Harrisburg, PA: 1940), p. 195.

24. Ibid., pp. 194–195.

25. Ibid., p. 195.

26. See Geoffrey Parker, *The Military Revolution: Military Innovation and the Rise of the West, 1500–1800* (Cambridge: 1988) and John A. Lynn, "The *trace italienne* and the Growth of Armies: The French Case," *Journal of Military History* (July 1991), pp. 297–330, as well as Ch. 16 of Lynn, *Giant of the Grand Siècle.* The best general studies of early modern fortifications are by Christopher Duffy.

27. For examples of the plans en relief, see Antoine de Roux, Nicolas Faucherre, Guillaume Monsaigngeon, *Les plans en relief des places du roy* (Paris: 1989).

28. Henry Guerlac, "Vauban: The Impact of Science on War," in Peter Paret, ed., *Makers of Modern Strategy from Machiavelli to the Nuclear Age* (Princeton: 1986), argues this.

29. The most sophisticated examination of siege warfare as systematized by Vauban is Jamel Ostwald, "Vauban's Siege Legacy in the War of the Spanish Succession, 1702–1712," Ph.D dissertation, Ohio State University, 2003.

30. Turpin de Crisse, *The Art of the War* (London: 1761), vol. 1, p. 106, in Azar Gat, *The Origins of Military Thought: From the Enlightenment to Clausewitz* (Oxford: 1989), p. 37.

31. Frederick in R. R. Palmer, "Frederick the Great, Guibert, von Bülow: From Dynastic to National War," Peter Paret, ed., *Makers of Modern Strategy* (Princeton: 1986), p. 103.

32. Denis Diderot, ed., *Encyclopédie ou Dictionnaire raisonné des sciences, des arts et des métiers,* 17 vols. (1751–1765). See John A. Lynn, "The Treatment of Military Subjects in Diderot's *Encyclopédie," Journal of Military History* 65, no. 1 (January 2001), pp. 131–165; Kathleen Hardesty Doig, "War in the Reform Program of the *Encyclopédie," War and Society* 6, no. 1 (May 1988), pp. 1–10; and Peter Aubery, "The *Encyclopédie* on War and Peace," *Transactions of the Eighth International Congress on the Enlightenment,* Voltaire Foundation, vol. 3 (Oxford: 1992), pp. 1827–1829.

33. Jean le Rond d'Alembert, *Preliminary Discourse to the Encyclopédie of Diderot,* trans. R. N. Schwab with W. E. Rex (New York: 1963), pp. 144–145, is the best English source for this. The original is in Diderot, *Encyclopédie,* vol. 1, après page liii. A comparison of editions of the *Encyclopédie* reveals that the copy at the University of Illinois differs from others; it shows the "Système figuré" slightly modified to put *art militaire* and *tactique* under "Science de l'homme," "Morale," and "Science des lois," a categorization that would have pleased the

Romantics. In this unusually altered chart, a note by *art militaire* states, "One can put these back, if one wants, to the branch of mathematics that deals with their principles."

34. For a brief introduction to Bülow, see R. R. Palmer, "Frederick the Great, Guibert, von Bülow: From Dynastic to National War."

35. Denis Diderot, "Salon of 1761," in Jean Seznec and Jean Adhémar, eds., *Diderot. Salons*, 2nd ed., vol. 1 (Oxford: 1975), p. 126. It is only fair to comment that Diderot found this symmetry monotonous.

36. The results reported here are from test data assembled by Moritz Theirbach in the late nineteenth century under very careful test conditions. Results discussed in Bert S. Hall, *Weapons and Warfare in Renaissance Europe: Gunpowder, Technology, and Tactics* (Baltimore: 1997), pp. 138–139. Hall reports the Theirbach ranges as 75, 150, and 225 meters. Theirbach's results correspond well with tests conducted by the Prussians during the Napoleonic era. They found that a French 1777 model smoothbore could hit a "large target" 75 percent of the time at eighty yards, 50 percent at 160 yards, and 25 percent at 240 yards. Peter Paret, *Yorck and the Era of Prussian Reform, 1807–1815* (Princeton: 1966), pp. 272–273. The Hall volume contains an extremely useful chapter on smoothbore ballistics, pp. 134–156, that covers far more than the Renaissance. He reports a modern test with antique weapons showing that ancien régime muskets fired at a very respectable muzzle velocity, as high as 1,750 feet per second, superior to a modern 9mm pistol that yielded results of 1,191 feet per second. Hall, *Weapons and Warfare in Renaissance Europe*, p. 136.

37. Gerhard von Scharnhorst, *Über die Wirkung des Feuergewehrs* (Osnabrück: 1973—reprint of 1813 edition), p. 96.

38. Jaucourt, "Déserteur," *Encyclopédie*, vol. 4, p. 881.

39. Saint-Germain in M. Delarue, "L'Education politique à l'armée du Rhin, 1793–1794." Mémoire de maîtrise, Université de Paris-Nanterre, 1967–1968, p. 42. Wellington, in command of a British army that maintained an eighteenth-century composition even in the Napoleonic wars, said of his troops: "We have in the service the scum of the earth as common soldiers." Elizabeth Longford, *Wellington: The Years of the Sword* (New York: 1969), p. 321.

40. Frederick II, *Militärische Schriften*, ed. von Taysen (Berlin: 1882), "Das militärische Testament," p. 205.

41. On desertion in the French army during the Revolutionary and Napoleonic Eras see Alan Forrest, *Conscripts and Deserters* (Oxford: 1989) and Isser Woloch, *The New Regime* (New York: 1994), Ch. 13.

42. See the discussion of motivation in John A. Lynn, *The Bayonets of the Republic: Motivation and Tactics in the Army of Revolutionary France, 1791–94* (Boulder, CO: 1996; original publication, University of Illinois Press in 1984).

43. Gat, *Origins of Military Thought*, p. 25. He bases this count on the impressive bibliographical guide by Johann Pohler, *Bibliotheca historico-militaris. Systematische Uebersicht der Erscheinungen aller Sprachen auf dem Gebiete der Geschichte der Kriege und Kriegswissenschaft seit Erfindung der Buchdruckerkunst bis zum Schluss des Jahres 1880*, 4 vols. (Leipzig: 1887–1899).

44. Erik A. Lund, *War for the Every Day: Generals, Knowledge, and Warfare in Early Modern Europe, 1680–1740* (Westport, CT: 1999), p. 13.

45. Le Blond, "Guerre," *Encyclopédie*, vol. 7, p. 985.

46. Paul-Gédéon Joly de Maizeroy, *Théorie de la guerre* (Lausanne: 1777), pp. lxxxvi–lxxxvii.

47. Charles in Gat, *Origins of Military Thought*, p. 99.

48. Turpin de Crisse, *The Art of the War*, vol. 1, pp. i–ii, in Gat, *Origins of Military Thought*, p. 36.

49. Concerning the enduring influence of the ancients on Western military thought and practice, see Bruno Colson and Hervé Coutau-Bégarie, eds., *Pensée stratégique et humanisme: De la tactique des Anciens à l'éthique de la stratégie* (Paris: 2000).

50. Le Blond, "Tactique," *Encyclopédie*, vol. 15, pp. 824–825.

51. Voltaire, *Dictionnaire philosophique*, vol. 3 (Paris: 1828), "Bataillon," p. 42.

52. De Saxe, *My Reveries*, p. 269; and Jacques Guibert, *Essai général de tactique*, vol. 1 (London: 1773), p. 7.

53. Claude Louis Hector Villars, *Mémoires du maréchal de Villars*, ed. Vogüé, 5 vols. (Paris: 1884–1895), 3:82.

54. Bibliothèque nationale (BN), fonds français 6257, Villars, "Traité," p. 83.

55. Louis XIV, *Mémoires de Louis XIV pour l'instruction du dauphin*, ed. Charles Dreyss, 2 vols. (Paris: 1860), 2:112–113.

56. Catinat in Jean Colin, *L'infanterie au XVIIIe siècle: La tactique* (Paris: 1907), p. 25.

57. Sébastien le Prestre de Vauban, *A Manual of Siegecraft and Fortification*, trans. G. A. Rothrock (Ann Arbor: 1968), p. 123.

58. Frederick, *The Instruction of Frederick the Great for His Generals, 1747*, in Phillips, *Roots of Strategy*, p. 379.

59. Louis XIV to Luxembourg, 5, 10, 12 August 1691, in Camille Roussset, *Histoire de Louvois*, vol. 4 (Paris: 1864), p. 510.

60. De Saxe, *My Reveries*, pp. 298–299.

61. Puységur in Le Blond, "Bataille," *Encyclopédie*, vol. 2, p. 134.

62. De Saxe, *My Reveries*, p. 298.

63. Bülow in Gat, *Origins of Military Thought*, p. 85.

64. Frederick, *Instruction*, in Phillips, *Roots of Strategy*, p. 391.

65. Caleb Carr, *The Lessons of Terror, A History of Warfare Against Civilians: Why It Has Always Failed and Why It Will Fail Again* (New York: 2002), p. 87.

66. Vauban in P. Lazard, *Vauban, 1633–1707* (Paris: 1934), p. 257.

67. De Saxe in Jean Baptiste Joseph Damarzit-Sahuguet, Baron d'Espagnac, *Histoire de Maurice, Comte de Saxe* (Paris: 1775), vol. 2, p. 496.

68. Michael Howard, "Constraints on Warfare," in Michael Howard, George J. Andreopolis, and Mark R. Shuman, eds. *The Laws of War: Constraints on Warfare in the Western World* (New Haven: 1994), p. 1.

69. St. Augustine quoted on *Breakpoint Online*, 25 February 2003, http://www.break-point.org/Breakpoint/ChannelRoot/Home/A+Fact+Sheet+on+Just+War+Theory.htm.

70. St. Thomas Aquinas, *Summa Theologica*, trans. Fathers of the English Dominican Province (Chicago: 1952), Part II of Second Part, Q. 40, article 1, p. 578.

71. Geoffrey Parker, "Early Modern Europe," Ch. 4 of Howard, Andreopolis, and Shuman, *The Laws of War*, p. 41.

72. Ibid., pp. 41–42. Parker argues a fifth foundation was reciprocity.

73. Hugo Grotius, *The Rights of War and Peace*, trans. A. C. Campbell (New York: 1901), p. 75. This translation of Grotius is available on the web at http://www.constitution.org/gro/djbp.htm.

74. Ibid.

75. Ibid., p. 363.

76. Contamine, *Histoire militaire*, 1:397. See other cartels: with Spain, dated 19 January 1669, Contamine, *Histoire militaire*, 1:397; with the Dutch, 21 May 1675, Dumont, *Corps universel diplomatique*, 7:pt 1:292–295; and with the Dutch, 29 December 1690, Dumont, *Corps universel diplomatique*, 7:pt. 2:277–282.

77. Babeau, *La vie militaire*, 1:290.

78. Grotius, *The Rights of War and Peace*, p. 363.

79. Ibid., p. 363.

80. Emmerich de Vattel, *The Law of Nations*, trans. Joseph Chitty, (Philadelphia: 1863), . 381.

81. Ibid., p. 382.

82. Ibid.

83. Ibid., p. 403.

84. See the argument of Carr, *The Lessons of Terror*, pp. 90–96.

85. Those who have read my earlier discussions of army size will note a discrepancy here. In the past I have given the maximum paper size of the French army during the Nine Years' War as about 420,000. However, rereading a critical document on size, Archives Nationales, G⁷1774, #52, I realize that it gives the size of the army in 1692–1693 as 446,612. This also means that the army topped out at that time, rather than in 1696, which I believed in the past.

86. While I have described the purchase and maintenance systems and their impacts in print for thirty years, I owe the term combining them as the "semi-entrepreneurial system" to David Parrott, "The Administration of the French Army During the Ministry of Cardinal Richelieu," Ph.D. dissertation, Oxford, 1985. In his recent and definitive study, *Richelieu's Army: War, Government and Society in France, 1624–1642* (Cambridge: 2001), he leaves the term aside and talks of "The French Rejection of Entrepreneurship," Ch. 2. However, I still find the term useful.

87. On costs of military command, see Parrott, *Richelieu's Army*, particularly pp. 313–365; Louis Tuetey, *Les officiers de l'ancien régime. Nobles et roturiers* (Paris: 1908); Lynn, *Giant of the Grand Siècle*; pp. 30, 57, 222, 233–239, 248, 253, 281, 310–312, 335, 351, 463, 511, 598, and 607. See as well John A. Lynn, "The Pattern of French Military Reform, 1750–1790," a paper delivered at the February 1974 Consortium on Revolutionary Europe, 1750–1850 and published in the *Proceedings of the Consortium on Revolutionary Europe* (Gainesville, FL: 1978); and the more sophisticated discussion by Rafe Blaufarb, "Noble Privilege and Absolutist State Building: French Military Administration after the Seven Years' War," *French Historical Studies* 24, no. 2 (Spring 2001), pp. 223–246.

88. In Rousset, *Louvois*, 1:180–181.

89. De Mailly in Tuetey, *Les officiers*, p. 130.

90. Lynn, *Giant of the Grand Siècle*, p. 238.

91. Letter of 23 October 1683, Marie Sévigné, *Lettres de madame de Sévigné*, Gault-de-Saint-Germain, ed., vol. 7 (Paris: 1823), p. 394.

92. Louis in Gaston Zeller, "French Diplomacy and Foreign Policy in Their European Setting," in *New Cambridge Modern History*, vol. 5 (London: 1970), p. 217.

93. See the discussion of honor in Bertram Wyatt-Brown, *Honor and Violence in the Old South* (Oxford: 1986), pp. 3–115.

94. Charles Grant, *The Battle of Fontenoy* (London: 1975), p. 79.

95. Michel de Montaigne (Essai, II, 7) in Maurice Keen, *Chivalry* (New Haven: 1984), p. 249.

96. SHAT, AG, A¹356, #29, 1 February 1673, Lebret to Louvois.

97. Commissaire Lenfant to Louvois in Tuetey, *Les officiers*, p. 61.

98. Saint-Simon, *Mémoires*, A. de Boislisle, ed., vol. 1 (Paris: 1879), p. 113.

99. Lisola, *Bouclier d'état* (1667) in Rousset, *Louvois*, 1:22–23.

100. Saint-Simon, *Mémoires*, vol. 1, p.33.

101. Memoirs of d'Artagnan in Babeau, *La vie militaire*, 2:175.

102. SHAT, Bibliothèque, Collection des ordonnances militaires, vol. 22, #175, 24 March 1672.

103. SHAT, AG, MR 1701, piece 15, "Traité de la guerre," of 8 June 1712.

104. Jean-Baptiste Primi Visconti, *Mémoires sur la cour de Louis XIV, 1673–1681,* Jean-François Solnon, ed. (Paris: 1988), p. 146.

105. See Wyatt-Brown, *Honor and Violence,* p. 35, on "the mother as the moral arbiter of bravery."

106. Four recent works that discuss French dueling in terms of modern scholarship are Pascal Brioist, Hervé Drévillon, and Pierre Serna, *Croiser le fer: Violence et culture de l'épée dans la France moderne (XVIe-XVIIIe siècle)* (Seyssel: 2002); François Billaçois, *Le duel dans la société française des XVIe–XVIIe siècles* (Paris: 1986); translated as *The Duel: Its Rise and Fall in Early Modern France,* trans. Trista Selous (New Haven: 1990); V. G. Kiernan, *The Duel in European History* (Oxford: 1988); and Cuénin, Micheline, *Le duel sous l'ancien régime* (Paris: 1982).

107. Jacques Boulenger, *The Seventeenth Century in France* (New York: 1963), p. 107.

108. Vauban in Albert Rochas d'Aiglun, *Vauban, sa famille et ses écrits,* vol. 1 (Paris: 1910), p. 269.

109. André Corvisier, *Les Français et l'armée sous Louis XIV* (Vincennes: 1975), 62.

110. *Catéchisme royal* by Pierre Fortin de la Hoguette in Cuénin, *Le duel,* 142.

111. Primi Visconti, *Mémoires,* 146.

112. Saint-Pierre in Cuénin, *Le duel,* 231.

113. Billaçois, *Le duel,* p. 350.

114. Hulot, *Le maréchal de Saxe,* p. 174.

CHAPTER FIVE

1. For accounts of Lake's 1803 campaign, see G. B. Malleson, *The Decisive Battles of India* (New Delhi: 1969), pp. 280–292, and K. G. Pitre, *The Second Anglo-Maratha War, 1802–1805* (Poona: 1990), pp. 109–139.

2. On the size and composition of Lake's forces see Malleson and Pitre, above, and Philip Mason, *A Matter of Honor: An Account of the Indian Army, Its Officers and Men* (London: 1986), p. 162.

3. Lake in Pitre, *The Second Anglo-Maratha War,* p. 135.

4. Persian was the official language of the Mughal Empire, thus the use of this language imported from West Asia for an institution imported from Europe.

5. Stephen Rosen, in *Societies and Military Power: India and Its Armies,* argues that the key constant in the various forms of the Indian state system remained the division of Indian society by caste and later religion, inspiring internecine warfare and limiting the ability of Indian political entities to unite. Steven Peter Rosen, *Societies and Military Power: India and Its Armies* (Ithaca, NY: 1996).

6. On medieval India, which is to say India after the arrival of the Muslims, see Jagadish Narayan Sarkar, *The Art of War in Medieval India* (New Delhi: 1984) and William Irvine, *The Army of the Mughals* (New Delhi: 1962).

7. Fazl in Sarkar, *The Art of War in Medieval India,* pp. 105–106.

8. Stanley Wolpert, *A New History of India,* 5th ed. (Oxford: 1997), p. 167.

9. See Abdul Aziz, *The Mansabdari System and the Mughul Army* (Delhi: 1972).

10. Roe in Bruce Lenman, "The Transition to European Military Ascendency in India, 1600–1800," in John A. Lynn, ed., *Tools of War: Instruments, Ideas, and Institutions of Warfare, 1445–1871* (Urbana, IL: 1990), p. 105. The original spelling has been modernized.

11. Cambridge, *Account of the War in India* (first pub. 1772) in Mason, *A Matter of Honor,* p. 55.

12. David Chandler, *The Art of Warfare in the Age of Marlborough* (New York: 1976), pp. 76–77.

13. Corvisier says the number of movements fell from 36 to 23. Philippe Contamine, ed., *Histoire militaire de la France,* vol. 1, series editor André Corvisier (Paris: 1992), vol. 1, p. 409.

14. Jean Colin, *L'infanterie au XVIIIe siècle: La tactique* (Paris: 1907), p. 26.

15. Louis André, *Michel Le Tellier et l'organisation de l'armée monarchique* (Paris: 1906), p. 344.

16. Puységur in Chandler, *The Art of Warfare,* p. 83.

17. In 1703, the French abandoned the pike altogether. Jacques-François de Chastenet de Puységur, *Art de la guerre par règles et principes,* 2 vols. (Paris: 1748), vol. 1, pp. 51, 57; Louis XIV, *Oeuvres de Louis XIV,* Philippe Grimoard and Grouvelle, eds., 6 vols. (Paris: 1806), vol. 4, pp. 396–397fn.

18. Lenman, "The Transition to European Military Ascendency in India," argues that until Buxar, naval gunfire played a key role in supporting the army.

19. These figures come from the very interesting and very detailed tables supplied by Du Praissac, *Les discours militaires* (Paris: 1622), pp. 112–130. I have called his 33–1/3 pounder a 34-pounder for convenience.

20. Lenman, "The Transition to European Military Ascendency in India," p. 119.

21. These are weights for the barrel of the gun only. Gribeauval also developed improved carriages. See comparative weights in Denis Diderot et al., *Encyclopédie,* 17 vols. (Paris: 1751–1765), 2:608; Louis Jouan and Ernest Picard, *L'artillerie française au XVIIIe siècle* (Paris: 1906), pp. 44–47; Howard Rosen, "The Système Gribeauval: A Study of Technological Development and Institutional Change in Eighteenth-Century France," Ph.D. dissertation, University of Chicago, 1981, p. 130; Matti Lauerma, *L'artillerie de campagne française pendant les guerres de la Révolution* (Helsinki: 1956), pp. 10, 16; Chandler, *The Art of Warfare,* p. 178. Weights are translated from *livres* to kilograms with the *livre* figured at 489.50585 grams. Marcel Marion, *Dictionnaire des institutions de la France aux XVIIe et XVIIIe siècles* (Paris: 1972), p. 375.

22. For simply one such insistence on silence, see Paul Azan, *Un tacticien du XVIIe siècle* (Paris: 1904), p. 65.

23. Concerning seventeenth-century drill see Chapter 15 of John A. Lynn, *Giant of the Grand Siècle: The French Army, 1610–1715* (New York: 1997).

24. Michael Roberts, *The Military Revolution, 1560–1660* (Belfast: 1956), p. 10. On the now widely discussed "Military Revolution," see Michael Roberts, *The Military Revolution, 1560–1660* (Belfast: 1956); Geoffrey Parker, *The Military Revolution: Military Innovation and the Rise of the West, 1500–1800,* 2nd ed. (Cambridge: 1996); and Cliff Rogers, ed., *The Military Revolution Debate: Readings on the Military Transformation of Early Modern Europe* (Boulder, CO: 1995). For wonderful new detail on the introduction of drill by the Dutch, see Geoffrey Parker's keynote address to the 2002 congress of the International Commission of Military History, held in Norfolk, VA.

25. James W. Hoover, "The Origins of the Sepoy Military System: 1498–1770," M.A. thesis, University of Wisconsin-Madison, 1993, p. 44.

26. William H. McNeill, *Keeping Together in Time: Dance and Drill in Human History* (Cambridge, MA: 1995).

27. There is a large literature on primary group cohesion. In particular see S. L. A. Marshall, *Men Against Fire* (Gloucester, MA: 1978; repr. of 1947 edition); Samuel A. Stouffer et al., *The American Soldier: Combat and Its Aftermath* (Princeton: 1949); and Anthony Kellett, *Combat Motivation* (Boston: 1982). For later modifications of these theories, see Omar Bartov, *Hitler's Army: Soldiers, Nazis, and War in the Third Reich* (Oxford: 1992) and Robert Sterling Rush, *Hell in Hürtgen Forest: The Ordeal and Triumph of an American Infantry Regiment* (Lawrence, KS: 2001). For a consideration of primary group cohesion in an early modern context see John A. Lynn, *Bayonets of the Republic: Motivation and Tactics in the Army of Revolutionary France, 1791–94*, 2nd ed. (Boulder, CO: 1996).

28. My good friend Geoffrey Parker would give me an argument on this, saying the development came earlier and in Spain, whereas I would date it later and in France. More than the Spanish, the French form of the regimental army became the standard for the Continent.

29. Langer in Barton Hacker, "Women and Military Institutions in Early Modern Europe: A Reconnaissance," *Signs* 6, no. 4 (summer 1981), p. 648.

30. For the French case, see Lynn, *Giant of the Grand Siècle*, pp. 337–343.

31. Rosen, *Societies and Military Power*, p. 162, judges that there existed "rough equality of British and Indian military technology."

32. See Rosen, *Societies and Military Power*, p. 165, for comments on superior Indian iron, which was exported worldwide. Hoover, "Origins of the Sepoy Military System," p. 44.

33. João Rubeiro in Lenman, "The Transition to European Military Ascendency in India," p. 103. See as well Jean-Baptiste Tavernier in Lenman, p. 102.

34. Second Report of the Select Committee of the House of Commons, 1772, p. 8, in Hoover, "Origins of the Sepoy Military System," p. 128.

35. Munro from Select Committee, H.C., 1772 in Hoover, "Origins of the Sepoy Military System," p. 126.

36. Mason, *A Matter of Honor*, p. 40.

37. Seema Alavi, *The Sepoys and the Company: Tradition and Transition in Northern India, 1770–1830* (Delhi: 1995), pp. 23–24.

38. Lenman, "The Transition to European Military Ascendency," p. 119.

39. Pradeep Barua, "Military Developments in India, 1750–1850," *Journal of Military History* 58, no. 4 (October 1994), p. 607.

40. Wellington to his brother Henry, Mason, *A Matter of Honor*, p. 161.

41. G. B. Malleson, *History of the French in India* (Delhi: repr. 1984, orig. 1909), p. 87.

42. Lawrence insisted that there, "the military, both black and white . . . behaved extremely well." Lawrence in Hoover, "Origins of the Sepoy Military System," p. 91.

43. As Dupleix's Indian assistant, Ananda Pillai, reported, native troops in French service tended to degenerate into lawlessness in cantonments. Hoover, "Origins of the Sepoy Military System," p. 77.

44. April 1756 report by the President of Fort St. George to the Company in Mason, *A Matter of Honor*, p. 62.

45. Amiya Barat, *The Bengal Native Infantry: Its Organization and Discipline, 1796–1852* (Calcutta: 1962), p. 11.

46. My approach to the campaigns against Mysore and the Marathas has been strongly influenced by the excellent article by Pradeep Barua, "Military Developments in India, 1750–1850."

47. Rosen, *Societies and Military Power*, p. 183.

48. On the process of achieving army reform in 1796, see Raymond Callahan, *The East India Company and Army Reform, 1783–1798* (Cambridge, MA: 1972). Barat, *The Bengal Native Infantry,* may overstate the case, but he makes clear the importance of the 1796 reform: "[O]nly in 1796 did the rapid, haphazard growth of Clive's original forces give way to some regularity of organization."

49. Wellesley in Mason, *A Matter of Honor,* p. 161.

50. Barua, "Military Developments in India, 1750–1850," p. 609.

51. On this see Lynn, *Giant of the Grand Siècle,* Ch. 8.

52. Dharma is subject to a number of definitions, including duty, responsibility, law, and truth.

53. Ainslie T. Embree, ed., *Sources of the Indian Tradition,* vol. 1, 2ⁿᵈ ed. (New York: 1988), p. 276. The *Gita* is interpreted in many ways that have nothing to do with soldierly conduct. The analysis here is meant not to question more elevated interpretations of the *Gita* but simply to see it in a literal sense as having a great deal to do with the ethics of the warrior.

54. The following quotations from the *Gita* are found in Embree, *Sources of the Indian Tradition,* pp. 281–286. This is a particularly accessible translation. I have inserted chapter and line notations. Conveniently, the entire text of the *Gita* is available on the internet. *Bhagavad Gita,* trans. Ramanand Prasad (1988: American Gita Society) at http://eawc.evansville.edu/anthology/gita.htm.

55. On honor see Bertram Wyatt-Brown, *Honor and Violence in the Old South* (Oxford: 1986); John A. Lynn, "Towards an Army of Honor: The Moral Evolution of the French Army 1789–1815," *French Historical Studies* 16, no. 1 (Spring 1989), pp. 152–173; and Lynn, *Giant of the Grand Siècle,* Chs. 8 and 13.

56. See the stress placed on *izzat* and *rasuq* in Pradeep Dhillon, *Multiple Identities: A Phenomenological of Multicultural Communication* (Frankfurt: 1994). In contrast, McNeill, *Keeping Together in Time,* p. 135, sees sepoys as developing European esprit de corps when exposed to Western drill, but this conclusion misses the point, I believe. While native regiments certainly developed esprit de corps, this took a very South Asian flavor for very South Asian reasons.

57. Mason, *A Matter of Honor,* p. 66.

58. Barat, *The Bengal Native Infantry,* p. 122. See as well the General observations of the court of inquiry, Barrackpore, 2 January 1825, in Barat, *The Bengal Native Infantry,* p. 121.

59. Callahan, *The East India Company and Army Reform,* pp. 3–4.

60. See Barat, *The Bengal Native Infantry,* pp. 132–143, on pay in the Company armies.

61. Ibid., p. 154.

62. Gough in ibid., p. 142.

63. Ibid., p. 51.

64. On the Hindu nature of the Bengal army and on recruitment patterns in North India see ibid. and Alavi, *The Sepoys and the Company.* See Hastings on trying to maintain caste to divide Hindus in Alavi, *The Sepoys and the Company,* pp. 44–45.

65. Alavi, *The Sepoys and the Company,* p. 51.

66. Correspondence of Cornwallis, ed. C. Ross, vol. 1, pp. 268–269, 299. See also Cornwallis's letter of 1789, in which he complains of "a great proportion" of recruits as "miserable wretches who from want of size or strength or from other causes are totally unfit for military service." *Fort William-India House Correspondence,* 21 vols. (New Delhi: 1949–1985), vol. 19, Letter to Court, 10 March 1789, #45. See as well the comments of a Major Scott, who reported in 1760 that "among the 900 raw highlanders" sent to India, "not one could speak English

or even use a firelock . . . the men's inducement to enlist was a promise that they might carry ten women in the company." Letter from Scott, 16 March 1760, in Barat, *The Bengal Native Infantry,* p. 17.

67. Barat, *The Bengal Native Infantry,* p. 177.

68. Rosen, *Societies and Military Power,* p. 179.

69. Callahan, *The East India Company and Army Reform,* p. 9.

70. Cornwallis to deputy governor and council at Fort Marlbro, 1789, in Alavi, *The Sepoys and the Company,* p. 46. See as well Pennington in Barat, *The Bengal Native Infantry,* pp. 174–175.

71. General Order of 17 March 1793, in Alavi, *The Sepoys and the Company,* p. 79. On Ramlila, a celebration of Rama's conquest over the demon Ravana with the aid of the monkey-king and his general, Hanumant, see Alavi, *The Sepoys and the Company,* p. 81.

72. Cornwallis to the Bishop of Salisbury, 1788, in Alavi, *The Sepoys and the Company,* p. 47. Cornwallis's brother was a bishop.

73. Alavi, *The Sepoys and the Company,* p. 83. This citation deals with a report dated 1850.

74. 11 November 1768 letter from Court of Directors to the President and Council at Fort William in Lenman, "The Transition to European Military Ascendency in India," p. 122.

75. Cornwallis to Dundas, 4 April 1790, in Callahan, *The East India Company and Army Reform,* p. 107.

76. Sita Ram, *From Sepoy to Subedar,* ed. James Lunt (Delhi: 1970), pp. 24–25. Controversy surrounds this work, which is supposed to be the autobiography of an old *subadar* who served in the Bengal army from 1812 to 1860. Some believe that Norgate, who published the work first in 1873, invented the story. In any case, if this is not the true story of a particular sepoy, it is a distillation of the experience of many, and is regularly used as a source by Indian historians, as it is the only detailed account of a sepoy's life.

77. Capt. Thomas Williamson, *The European in India; from a Collection of Drawings* (London: 1813), pp. 9–10. An officer might even advertise for an Indian wife, as one did in 1781, requesting a woman with "a tolerable share of beauty, a great portion of pliability of temper, of decent cast or parentage, and the useful education of country." *Hickey's Bengal Gazette,* 12–19 May 1781, no. XVII. Just how much European officers did to please native women is suggested by the story of an Indian mistress who insisted that her officer lover be circumcised as was demanded by her caste. *Hickey's Bengal Gazette,* 20–27 January 1781, no. III. I would like to credit my student Lauren Heckler for bringing these citations to my attention.

78. Barat, *The Bengal Native Infantry,* p. 126.

79. Sleeman in Mason, *A Matter of Honor,* p. 166.

80. See Barat, *The Bengal Native Infantry,* p. 126, on furloughs and recruitment.

81. Sita Ram, *From Sepoy to Subedar,* Ch. 1.

82. Barat, *The Bengal Native Infantry,* p. 130.

83. Mason, *A Matter of Honor,* p. 123.

84. Barat, *The Bengal Native Infantry,* p. 150.

85. Sita Ram, *From Sepoy to Subedar,* pp. 5, 49.

86. Rosen, *Societies and Military Power,* p. 196.

87. Stewart N. Gordon, "An Analysis of the Limited Adoption of European Style Military Forces by Eighteenth Century Rulers in India," paper sent to me by Stewart Gordon.

88. Mason, *A Matter of Honor,* p. 161.

Chapter Six

1. Antoine-Henri Jomini, *Treatise on Grand Military Operations*, trans. Col S. B. Holabird, 2 vols. (London: 1865), 1:443. I thank Azar Gat's works for pointing the way to this and a number of other quotations cited in this chapter.

2. Jomini, *Treatise on Grand Military Operations*, 2:323.

3. See John A. Lynn, "The Evolution of Army Style in the Modern West, 800–2000," *International History Review* 18, no. 3 (August 1996) and "International Rivalry and Warfare, 1700–1815," in *The Short Oxford History of Europe: Eighteenth-Century Europe*, ed. T. C. W. Blanning (Oxford: 2001), for a description of the state commission army style. My evolutionary schema posits seven styles of armies: feudal, medieval stipendiary, aggregate conscript, state commission, popular conscript, mass reserve, and volunteer technical.

4. The Declaration in John A. Lynn, *The Bayonets of the Republic: Motivation and Tactics in the Army of Revolutionary France, 1791–94* (Boulder, CO: 1996; orig. 1984), p. 56. It is worth noting that while young men were to take up arms, women were to take up needles; this represents the gender stereotypes encouraged by Rousseau, who thought sewing was particularly appropriate for women and ought to be exclusively their craft.

5. The authoritative Jacques Godechot, *Les institutions de la France sous la Révolution et l'Empire* (Paris: 1968), p. 362, credits the army with 1,169,000 men in September 1794. It has become usual to discount this to 750,000–800,000 actually present under arms. See Jean-Paul Bertaud, *La Révolution armée* (Paris: 1979), p. 137.

6. Among captains, for example, only 2–3 percent could claim aristocratic families, while 44 percent were middle class, 25 percent artisan, and 22 percent peasant. Lynn, *Bayonets of the Republic*, pp. 70–71, table of French officer corps composition.

7. See, for example, "Économie" by Jean-Jacques Rousseau and "Déserteur," "Lacédémone," and "Suisse" by Louis de Jaucourt, in Denis Diderot, ed., *Encyclopédie ou Dictionnaire raisonné des sciences, des arts et des métiers*, 17 vols. (Paris: 1751–1765), 5:337–349, 4:881, 9:152–160, 15:646–148.

8. Jean Jacques Rousseau, *Considerations on the Government of Poland*, in *Rousseau: Political Writings*, ed. Frederick Watkins (Edinburgh: 1953), p. 237. See Rousseau's similar comment in "Économie," in Diderot, *Encyclopédie*, 5:346. "Tyrants established regular troops, ostensibly to contain foreign [enemies], but in fact to oppress the inhabitant."

9. *Essai général de tactique* (1772) in Jacques-Antoine-Hypolite de Guibert, *Écrits militaires*, ed. Ménard (Paris: 1977), p. 57.

10. Ibid.

11. Guibert, *Écrits militaires*, p. vii.

12. *Coup d'oeil sur la Grande Bretagne* (London: 1776), pp. 86–87.

13. Desmoulins in Cornwall Rogers, *The Spirit of Revolution in 1789* (Princeton: 1949), p. 210.

14. Robespierre in Georges Michon, "L'armée et la politique intérieure sous la Convention," *Annales historiques de la Révolution française*, 4 (1927), pp. 13–14.

15. Service Historique de l'Armée de Terre, Archives de Guerre, B¹16, 1 August 1793, printed order.

16. *Père Duchesne*, number 321, in Jacques-René Hébert, *Le Père Duchesne, 1790–1794*, vol. 10 (Paris: 1969).

17. See Lynn, *Bayonets of the Republic*, Ch. 7, "The *Ordinaire* and Motivation," pp. 163–182.

18. Goethe in J. F. C. Fuller, *A Military History of the Western World*, 3 vols. (New York: 1955), 2:369.

19. Carl von Clausewitz, *On War,* ed. and trans. Michael Howard and Peter Paret, indexed edition (Princeton: 1984), pp. 592–593. This is now the definitive English translation of *On War.* All citations in this chapter to *On War* are from the Howard/Paret edition.

20. On the tactical system of revolutionary infantry see Lynn, *Bayonets of the Republic.*

21. See, for example, David Chandler, *Campaigns of Napoleon* (New York: 1966); Paddy Griffith, *The Art of War of Revolutionary France, 1789–1802* (London: 1998); and T. C. W. Blanning, *The French Revolutionary Wars, 1787–1802* (New York: 1996).

22. John A. Lynn, "The Pattern of Army Growth, 1445–1945," in *The Tools of War: Ideas, Instruments, and Institutions of Warfare, 1445–1871* (Urbana, IL: 1990), pp. 1–27.

23. Alan Forrest, *Conscripts and Deserters: The Army and French Society During the Revolution and Empire* (Oxford: 1989).

24. Peter Hulme and Lumilla Jordanova, eds., *The Enlightenment and Its Shadows* (London: 1990), p. 202. See also Frederick C. Beiser, *Enlightenment, Revolution, and Romanticism: The Genesis of Modern German Political Thought, 1790–1800* (Cambridge, MA: 1992), p. vii.

25. Hugo in Hugh Honour, *Romanticism* (New York: 1979), p. 22.

26. Kenneth Clark, *Civilization: A Personal View* (New York: 1969), p. 307.

27. Opening lines of his "The French Revolution As It Appeared to Enthusiasts at Its Commencement."

28. Testimony in Max Jähns, *Geschichte der Kriegswissenschaften,* in Azar Gat, *The Origins of Military Thought from the Enlightenment to Clausewitz* (Oxford: 1989), p. 152.

29. Gat, *Origins of Military Thought,* p. 185.

30. John Mitchell, *Thoughts on Tactics and Military Organization* (London: 1838), p. 12, in Azar Gat, *A History of Military Thought from the Enlightenment to the Cold War* (Oxford: 2001), pp. 279–280.

31. On this point, see John Shy, "Jomini," in Peter Paret, ed., *Makers of Modern Strategy* (Princeton: 1986), pp. 143–185.

32. Gat, *Origins of Military Thought,* p. 106. John Shy takes a very different tack with Jomini arguing that he was a fusion of Romanticism and scientific trends of the early nineteenth century. Shy, "Jomini." On the whole, I find Gat's argument more persuasive. See as well Gat's statements in his *The Development of Military Thought: The Nineteenth Century* (Oxford: 1992), p. 3.

33. Antoine-Henri de Jomini, *The Art of War,* trans. G. H. Mendell and W. P. Graighill (Philadelphia: 1862, reprint Westport, CT), p. 293. Jomini uses the term "strategy," but I have employed "operations" because that is the proper term in modern military language. He goes on to say "but this is not true of war viewed as a whole."

34. Shy, "Jomini," p. 153.

35. Clausewitz, *On War,* p. 592.

36. Napoleon in Gunther Rothenberg, *The Art of Warfare in the Age of Napoleon* (Bloomington, IN: 1978), p. 147.

37. Clausewitz, *On War,* p. 134.

38. Ibid., pp. 157–158.

39. Ibid., p. 158.

40. For example, see Gat, *Origins of Military Thought,* pp. 174–176.

41. This is a nearly impossible sentence to translate: "A la guerre, les trois quarts sont des affaires morales, la balance des forces réelles n'est que pour un autre quart." Napoleon, *Correspondence,* vol. XVII, no. 14276, 27 August 1808. It is often translated as "In war, the moral is to the physical as three is to one."

42. Clausewitz, *On War,* p. 75.

43. Antoine-Henri Jomini, *Traité des grandes opérations militaires,* 2nd ed., vol. 1 (Paris: 1811), p. 166.

44. Immanuel Kant, *Critique of Judgment* (Indianapolis: 1987), pp. 174–175.

45. Napoleon, *Military Maxims,* in Thomas R. Phillips, ed., *Roots of Strategy* (Harrisburg, PA: 1940), p. 440.

46. Clausewitz, *On War,* p. 101.

47. Jomini, *Treatise,* concluding chapter, p. 445, in Gat, *Origins of Military Thought,* p. 112.

48. Clausewitz, *On War,* p. 593. Gat, *Origins of Military Thought,* p. 191, argues that this attitude reflects Schleiermacher's historicist ideas on religion, that the spirit remains the same but that forms change through time.

49. Charles J. Esdaile, *The Wars of Napoleon* (London: 1995), p. 194.

50. Jay Luvaas, ed., *Napoleon on the Art of War* (New York: 1999), p. 66.

51. Napoleon, *Military Maxims,* p. 436.

52. Clausewitz, *On War,* p. 101. See as well, "No other human activity is so continuously or universally bound up with chance," p. 85.

53. Napoleon in Sir J. Seeley, *A Short History of Napoleon I* (London: 1899), p. 195, in Chandler, *Campaigns of Napoleon,* p. 157.

54. Napoleon in J. Christopher Herold, *The Mind of Napoleon* (New York: 1955), p. 211.

55. Napoleon, *Military Maxims,* p. 411.

56. Augereau in David G. Chandler, *On the Napoleonic Wars* (Mechanicsburg, PA: 1994), pp. 113–114. In fact, Houdaille calculates that the wars of the Empire cost 863,000 French deaths, a loss of young manhood proportionally approaching that inflicted by World War I. J. Houdaille, "Pertes de l'armée de terre sous le Prémier Empire," *Population* (January-February, 1972), pp. 27–50, concludes that the wars of Napoleon killed 20 percent—one in five—of all French men born between 1790 and 1795 (compared with the 25 percent, or one in four, French men born between 1891 and 1895 killed in World War I). See as well, Schroeder, *The Transformation of European Politics,* p. 580. Esdaille, *Wars of Napoleon,* p. 300, estimates the total civilian and military dead during the Napoleonic wars as 4,000,000.

57. Clausewitz, *On War,* p. 76.

58. Ibid., p. 259.

59. Napoleon in Pierre Berthezène, *Souvenirs militaires de la république et de l'empire,* vol. 2 (Paris: 1855), p. 309.

60. Napoleon in Herbert H. Sargent, *Napoleon Bonaparte's First Campaign, with Comments* (Chicago: 1895), p. 31.

61. For Martin van Creveld, "It was, in fact, his inversion of the relationship between sieges and battles—between the relative importance of the enemy's fortresses and his field army as objectives of strategy—that constituted Napoleon's most revolutionary contribution to the art of war." Martin van Creveld, *Supplying War* (Cambridge: 1977), p. 41. This is a provocative statement, but it goes too far. For one thing, Frederick also emphasized battle, and, second, Napoleon did not regard fortresses and siege warfare as inconsequential. In 1806, during the string of his greatest battlefield victories, Napoleon wrote, "One asked in the last [eighteenth] century if fortifications were of any utility. It is the sovereigns who judged them useless and who as a consequence dismantled their fortresses. As for me I would reverse the question and ask if it is possible to make war without fortresses, and I declare no." Napoleon to Général Dejean, 3 September 1806, *Correspondance de Napoléon Iᵉʳ,* vol. 13 (Paris: 1863), no. 10726, p. 131. See as well his letter of 1809 to his minister of war, Clarke, Napoleon demanding that works be written to educate young soldiers: "The work for the school at Metz ought to contain the ordinances on fortifications, judgments that have been incurred by all the commanders who have

too easily surrendered the fortresses entrusted to them, finally all the ordinance of Louis XIV and of our day which forbid giving up a fortress before there is a breach [in the wall] and a passage through the ditch is possible. . . . The goal ought to be to make them realize just how important the defense of fortresses is." *Correspondance de Napoléon Ier*, vol. 19 (Paris: 1866), no. 15889, pp. 540–541.

62. Clausewitz, *On War*, p. 96.

63. Jomini, *Art of War*, p. 162.

64. Clausewitz, *On War*, p. 97.

65. Clausewitz, "Bemerkungen über die reine und angewandte Strategie des Herrn von Bülow," *Neue Bellona* 9, no. 3 (1805), p. 271, in Peter Paret, "Clausewitz," in Peter Paret, ed., *Makers of Modern Strategy* (Princeton: 1986), p. 190.

66. Clausewitz, *Ueber das Leben und den Charackter von Scharnhorst*, in H. Rothfels, "Clausewitz," in Edward Meade Earle, ed., *Makers of Modern Strategy* (Princeton: 1941), p. 96.

67. John Keegan, *A History of Warfare* (New York: 1993).

68. Letter of Clausewitz to Marie von Brühl, 28 Jan. 1807, in Peter Paret, *Clausewitz and the State* (Princeton: 1985), p. 75.

69. Paret, *Clausewitz and the State*, p. 99. Paret calls Clausewitz "a forceful, exceptionally creative member of the generation of Germans whose fate was determined by Napoleon and Goethe," pp. 5–6.

70. Ibid., p. 84.

71. Ibid., p. 212.

72. Ibid., p. 316.

73. Ibid., p. 84.

74. Clausewitz, *On War*, p. 87.

75. Ibid., p. 228.

76. Raymond Aron, *Clausewitz, Philosopher of War*, trans. Christine Booker and Norman Stone (London: 1983), pp. 84–87.

77. Clausewitz, *On War*, p. 604.

78. Ibid., p. 76.

79. Ibid., p. 77.

80. Ibid., p. 77.

81. Ibid., pp. 87–88.

82. Ibid., pp. 592–593.

83. Ibid., p. 88.

84. Note of 10 July 1827 by Clausewitz in ibid., p. 69.

85. Ibid.

86. Ibid., p. 75.

87. Ibid., p. 260.

88. Ibid., p. 89. The quotation from the Paret and Howard translation is "paradoxical trinity" but I have taken the liberty to use the term "strange," which fits the original German *wunderlich* better.

89. Ibid., p. 89.

90. "Historisch-politische Aufzeichnungen," *Politische Schriften und Briefe*, p. 59, in Paret, *Clausewitz and the State*, p. 158.

91. Ibid., p. 259.

92. Ibid., pp. 77 and 78.

93. Ibid., p. 86.

94. *Principles of War*, p. 61, in Gat, *Origins of Military Thought*, pp. 185–186.

95. All of Clausewitz's statements concerning friction in this paragraph come from *On War,* Book One, Chapter Seven, "Friction in War," pp. 119–121. It is worth noting that some of the most fundamental and enlightening insights of Clausewitz take up very few words in *On War.* The concept of the trilogy consumes only half a page of print, p. 89. Friction takes up less than three.

96. Napoleon, "Précis des événements militaires arrivés pendant les six premiers mois de 1799," in *Correspondance de Napoléon Iᵉ,* vol. 30 (Paris: 1870), p. 262.

97. Clausewitz, *On War,* p. 101.

98. Ibid., p. 87.

99. Ibid., p. 75.

100. Paret, "Clausewitz," p. 186.

101. Paret also insists, "In one respect, however—purists might regard it as the only one that matters—Clausewitz differed completely from the transcendental philosophers: as has already been noted in the discussion of his writings before 1806, he accepted the reality of concrete phenomena." Paret, *Clausewitz and the State,* p. 151. Perhaps Paret's view is best expressed in a passage from Delbrück quoted by Paret: "He sees things as they really are." This is truly Rankian praise. Delbrück, "General von Clausewitz," reprinted in his *Historische und politische Aufsätze* (Berlin: 1887), pp. 218, in Paret, *Clausewitz and the State,* p. 353.

102. Eugène Carrias, *La Pensée militaire française* (Paris: 1960), p. 252. The French edition was translated by a Belgian officer, Neuens. The 1874 translation by J. J. Graham continued to appear in new editions through 1968.

103. Peter Paret, "Clausewitz and the Nineteenth Century," in Michael Howard, ed., *The Theory and Practice of War* (London: 1965), p. 29.

104. Max Jähns, *Geschichte der Kriegswissenschaften,* in Paret, "Clausewitz and the Nineteenth Century," p. 24.

105. Lynn, "Evolution of Army Style."

106. Gunther Rothenberg, "Moltke, Schlieffen, and the Doctrine of Strategic Envelopment," in Paret, *Makers of Modern Strategy,* p. 297. Moltke listed Clausewitz as the only military writer who influenced him decisively. Gerhard Ritter, *The Sword and the Scepter: The Problem of Militarism in Germany,* trans. Heinz Norden, vol. 1 (Coral Gables, FL: 1969), p. 188.

107. Ritter, *The Sword and the Scepter,* p. 189.

108. Moltke in Holborn, "The Prusso-German School," in Earle, *Makers of Modern Strategy,* p. 289.

109. 1868 Moltke plan in Rothenberg, "Moltke, Schlieffen, and the Doctrine of Strategic Envelopment," p. 303.

110. Moltke in Holborn, "The Prusso-German School," p. 289.

111. Ibid., p. 288.

112. Moltke in Rothenberg, "Moltke, Schlieffen, and the Doctrine of Strategic Envelopment," p. 299.

113. Helmuth von Moltke, *Gedanken von Moltke,* ed. General der Artillerie von Cochenhausen (Berlin: 1941), p. 13.

114. Moltke in Rothenberg, "Moltke, Schlieffen, and the Doctrine of Strategic Envelopment," p. 298.

115. Ibid.

116. See Schlieffen's praise for *On War* in his introduction to the 5th edition of the work, published in Berlin in 1905. Paret, "Clausewitz and the Nineteenth Century," p. 39, fn. 3.

117. Alfred von Schlieffen, *Dienstschriften des Chefs des Geralstabes der Armee General Feldmarschall Grafen von Schlieffen,* vol. 2 (Berlin: 1938), p. 222.

118. Rothenberg, "Moltke, Schlieffen, and the Doctrine of Strategic Envelopment," p. 312.

119. Clausewitz, *On War*, p. 260. There is a tendency for modern Clausewitz scholars to dismiss this bloodiness as inconsequential, but the definition of Military Romanticism offered here proposes that this acceptance of human loss was essential.

120. F. N. Maude, *The Evolution of Infantry Tactics* (London: 1905), p. 146 in Michael Howard, "Men Against Fire: The Doctrine of the Offensive in 1914," in Paret, *Makers of Modern Strategy*, p. 511. The edition of *On War* presented by Maude was the Graham translation, which continued to be reissued through the 1960s with Maude's introduction and notes.

121. Friedrich von Bernardi, *On War Today* (London, 1912), 2:53, in Howard, "Men Against Fire," pp. 510–511.

122. See the discussion in Carrias, *La Pensée militaire française*, pp. 278–281. Important works by Maillard include his *Étude des combats dans la bataille de Saint-Privat* (Paris: 1889) and *Éléments de la guerre* (Paris: 1891). Gilbert wrote *Essais de critique militaire* (Paris: 1890).

123. Jean Jaurès, *L'armée nouvelle* (Paris: 1915), p. 101.

124. For a brief introduction to Foch, see Stefan T. Possony and Étienne Mantoux, "Du Picq and Foch: The French School," in Earle, *Makers of Modern Strategy*, pp. 206–233.

125. Ferdinand Foch, *The Principles of War*, trans. Hilaire Belloc (New York, 1920), p. 25. Foch's most important theoretical works were *Des principes de la guerre* (1903) and *De la conduite de la guerre* (1904).

126. Basil Henry Liddell Hart, *The Ghost of Napoleon* (London: 1933), p. 21.

127. Keegan, *A History of Warfare*, p. 22.

128. Christopher Bassford, "John Keegan and the Grand Tradition of Trashing Clausewitz: A Polemic," paper presented at The Military Conflict Institute, 14 July 1994.

129. Paret, "Clausewitz," p. 186.

130. Alan Beyerchen proposes one of the most interesting but also one of the most extreme modern interpretations of *On War* in his "Clausewitz, Nonlinearity, and the Unpredictability of War," *International Security*, vol. 17, no. 3 (Winter 1992–1993), pp. 59–90. This article paints Clausewitz as a theorist who understood nonlinearity and chaos theory without knowing it. Beyerchen ascribes the complexity and indeterminate nature of Clausewitz to this appreciation of nonlinearity and his floating war between the three poles of the trinity.

Chapter Seven

1. Tojo in John Toland, *The Rising Sun: The Decline and Fall of the Japanese Empire, 1936–1945* (New York: 1971), p. 549.

2. Igeta in ibid., p. 564.

3. Excerpt from Saito message, in ibid., p. 582.

4. See account in ibid., p. 585.

5. William Manchester, *Goodbye Darkness: A Memoir of the Pacific War* (New York: 1982), p. 318.

6. John W. Dower, *War Without Mercy: Race and Power in the Pacific War* (New York: 1986).

7. Craig M. Cameron, *American Samurai: Myth, Imagination, and the Conduct of Battle in the First Marine Division, 1941–1951* (Cambridge: 1994).

8. Ronald Takaki, *Hiroshima* (Boston: 1995) and *Double Victory: A Multicultural History of America in World War II* (Boston: 2000). The quotation is from *Double Victory*, p. 168. This is an odd judgment taken out of context, because the Nazi war in Europe was more fundamen-

tally racist than was the war in the Pacific. Of course, Takaki refers only to American attitudes. Still, he ought to have been a bit more careful with such a loaded statement.

9. Dower, *War Without Mercy,* p. 4.

10. Allan Nevins, "How We Felt About the War," in Jack Goldman, ed., *While You Were Gone: A Report on Wartime Life in the United States* (New York: 1946), p. 13.

11. In Carey McWilliams, *Prejudice: Japanese Americans—Symbols of Racial Intolerance* (Boston: 1944), p. 234.

12. *Time,* December 15, 1941, p. 17.

13. Edward Newhouse, "Defense of the Islands," *The New Yorker,* December 20, 1941, p. 19, in Dower, *War Without Mercy,* p. 37.

14. *Life,* December 22, 1941, pp. 81–82.

15. Low cartoon in Dower, *War Without Mercy,* p. 182.

16. *New York Times Magazine,* May 3, 1943, p. 6. The cartoon caption is actually the title of the article by Hugh Byas.

17. *New York Times,* April 25, 1943, p. 11 E.

18. Interestingly, the Philco ads lampooning the Axis leaders did not usually show the Japanese as monkeys. One ad has all three—Hitler, Mussolini, and Tojo—as monkeys. The other three ads I have seen show them all in military uniform as petty dictators. The Philco ads were by a series of well-known cartoonists commissioned to draw them.

19. "Its Soldiers Are Veterans," *Life,* January 5, 1942, p. 34.

20. "The Japanese Language: A National Secret Code, It Is Perfect for Hiding Facts or Saying What You Don't Mean," *Life,* September 7, 1942, pp. 58–67.

21. "Go: Japs Play Their National Game the Way They Fight Their Wars," *Life,* May 18, 1942, pp. 92–95.

22. "The 47 Ronin: The Most Popular Play in Japan Reveals the Bloodthirsty Character of Our Enemy," *Life,* November 1, 1943, p. 52.

23. Dower, *War Without Mercy,* p. 81. American songs could use ethnic and racial language without much sensitivity. During World War I, a different time with different attitudes, one World War I song cheerfully exclaimed, "When Tony goes over the top, keep your eye on that fighting Wop!"; another was entitled, "Mammy's Little Chocolate Soldier." See, and hear, these songs on the web at http://www.besmark.com/ww9–2.ram.

24. Myers in *Yank,* in Dower, *War Without Mercy,* p. 112.

25. Grew in Dower, *War Without Mercy,* p. 113.

26. Nathaniel Pfeffer, "Japanese Superman? That, Too, Is a Fallacy," in *New York Times Magazine,* March 22, 1942, pp. 14, 37.

27. Advertising copy for Herbert C. Merillat, *The Island* (Boston: 1944) in Cameron, *American Samurai,* p. 101.

28. *Life,* March 6, 1944, pp. 100–102, 104, 106, 109–110, 112.

29. *Life,* August 16, 1943, pp. 87–99.

30. Dower, *War Without Mercy,* p. 203.

31. Nkajima Chikuhei in Tswrumi Shunsuke, ed., *Nihon no Hyakunen 3: Hateshinaki Sensen* in Dower, *War Without Mercy,* p. 217.

32. Dower, *War Without Mercy,* p. 25.

33. Ba Maw speech in ibid., p. 6.

34. Dower, *War Without Mercy,* p. 284.

35. Ishiwara in Ienaga, *The Pacific War,* 12.

36. Ba Maw, *Breakthrough in Burma: Memoirs of a Revolution, 1939–46* (New Haven: 1968), p. 180.

37. Ibid., p. 156.

38. On the Indian National Army, see Kalyan Kumar Ghosh, *The Indian National Army: Second Front of the Indian Independence Movement* (Meerut: 1969).

39. See Ch. 3, "The Final War," in Mark Peattie, *Ishiwara Kanji and Japan's Confrontation with the West* (Princeton: 1975), pp. 49–83.

40. See Peter Duus, "Japan's Wartime Empire: Problems and Issues," in Peter Duus, Ramon H. Meyers, and Mark R. Peattie, eds., *The Japanese Wartime Empire, 1931–1945* (Princeton: 1996), pp. xi–xlvii, for a brief exposition of the goals and the problems imposed by military overcommitment and territorial overextension in the Japanese Empire.

41. Iris Chang, *The Rape of Nanking* (New York: 1997). For a discussion and criticism of Chang's work see Joshua A. Fogel, ed., *The Nanjing Massacre in History and Historiography* (Berkeley: 2000). The figures for the dead run from 100,000 to 300,000.

42. See the discussion in Ienaga, *The Pacific War*, pp. 166–167.

43. Ibid., p. 167.

44. Chang, *The Rape of Nanking*, p. 30. Also see Ienaga, *The Pacific War*, pp. 6–7, on earlier slurs against "Chinks."

45. "The First Ten Days of the War at Sea," *Life*, January 5, 1942, p. 20.

46. "We Shoot Down the First Japs: Two U.S. Gunners from New Mexico Meet Attack on Philippine Field," *Life*, December 22, 1941, p. 29.

47. Halsey in James M. Merrill, *A Sailor's Admiral: A Biography of William F. Halsey* (New York: 1976), p. 74.

48. Ibid., p. 85.

49. Ibid., p. 65.

50. Ibid., p. 66.

51. Ibid., p. 111.

52. Halsey statements in Dower, *War Without Mercy*, p. 55. This sounds awful, but such language is not uncommon in war. The traditional French cry in the attack is "Kill, kill!" A Soviet order to its troops then besieging Nazi-held Danzig in March 1945 commanded: "Soldiers of the Red Army, kill the Germans! Kill all Germans! Kill! Kill! Kill!" Geoffrey Parker, Ch. 4, "Early Modern Europe," Michael Howard, George J. Andreopolis, and Mark R. Shuman, eds., *The Laws of War: Constraints on Warfare in the Western World* (New Haven: 1994), p. 56.

53. Halsey in Cameron, *American Samurai*, p. 1.

54. Merrill, *A Sailor's Admiral*, p. 74.

55. George H. Johnston, *The Toughest Fighting in the World* (New York: 1943), p. 228.

56. *New York Times*, January 9, 1943, p. 4.

57. Ernie Pyle, *Last Chapter* (New York: 1946), p. 5.

58. Dower, *War Without Mercy*, p. 78.

59. Samuel A. Stouffer et al., *The American Soldier: Combat and Its Aftermath* (Princeton: 1949), chart VII, p. 34.

60. Draft Intelligence Report, p. 18, in Cameron, *American Samurai*, p. 108.

61. Denis Warner and Peggy Warner, *The Sacred Warriors: Japan's Suicide Legions* (New York: 1982), p. 36.

62. Tom Bailey, *Tarawa* (Monarch Books: 1962), p. 38, in Dower, *War Without Mercy*, p. 68.

63. Charles A. Lindbergh, *The Wartime Journals of Charles A. Lindbergh* (New York: 1970), p. 881. Entry for July 22, 1944.

64. Lindbergh, *The Wartime Journals*, p. 902. Entry for August 11, 1944.

65. Dower and Cameron both discuss this barbaric quest. See as well James J. Weingartner, "Trophies of War: U.S. Troops and the Mutilation of Japanese War Dead, 1941–1945," *Pacific Historical Quarterly* 61 (February 1992), pp. 53–67.

66. Richard Tregaskis, *Guadalcanal Diary* (New York: 1942), p. 15.

67. E. B. Sledge, *With the Old Breed at Peleliu and Okinawa* (Novato, CA: 1981), p. 120.

68. *Leatherneck,* June 1943, p. 29.

69. In making this point, Ronald Takaki misinterprets a quotation. He says, "Marines frequently saw the Japanese as 'whooping like a bunch of wild Indians'" (*Hiroshima,* p. 75 and *Double Victory,* p. 171). His citation is to Cameron, *American Samurai,* p. 127, but the quotation there has a Marine describing attacking *Marines* as "whooping like a bunch of wild Indians."

70. Dower, *War Without Mercy,* p. 152.

71. *Life,* May 22, 1944, p. 35. "Arizona war worker writes her Navy boyfriend a thank-you note for the Jap skull he sent her." Using skulls on vehicles was also a German practice; see photo of a skull used as a hood ornament on an SS vehicle. *WWII: Time-Life Books History of the Second World War* (New York: 1989), p. 136.

72. *Leatherneck,* March 1945, p. 11, in Dower, *War Without Mercy,* p. 66.

73. Edgar L. Jones, "One War Is Enough," *Atlantic Monthly,* February 1946, p. 49.

74. Takaki, *Double Victory,* p. 168.

75. The term is Takaki's in ibid., p. 19.

76. Original map, "The Invasion of San Francisco, 1909, A Fictional Account," in Edward S. Miller, *War Plan Orange: The U.S. Strategy to Defeat Japan, 1897–1945* (Annapolis, MD: 1991), p. 40.

77. *New York Times,* March 11, 1911, p. 2.

78. Allan R. Millett, *Semper Fidelis: The History of the United States Marine Corps* (New York: Free Press: 1991), p. 278.

79. *New York American,* April 25, 1915 in Tuchman, *The Zimmermann Telegram,* pp. 58–59.

80. On the 1924 law see, Izumi Hirobe, *Japanese Pride, American Prejudice: Modifying the Exclusion Clause of the 1924 Immigration Act* (Stanford: 2001). Hirobe insists that the 1924 law "is recognized as one of the principal causes of the deadly clash between the United States and Japan in 1941" (p. 1). I disagree.

81. Weinberg, *A World at Arms,* p. 895. For an example, a website that offers a chronology of the Sino-Japanese War lists 35,000,000 as official casualties from the government of the Republic of China. http://www.edu.cn/history/www.arts.cuhk.hk/NanjingMassacre/NMchron.html.

82. See Policy Adopted at Imperial Conference, 2 July 1941, on http://www.ibiblio.org/hyperwar/PTO/Dip/IR–410702.html.

83. On Tojo see Robert J. C. Butow, *Tojo and the Coming of the War* (Princeton: 1961).

84. De Witt in Dower, *War Without Mercy,* p. 81.

85. Dower, *War Without Mercy,* p. 80.

86. The Canadian government also passed "Order in council PC 1486," which authorized the removing of people of Japanese ancestry from within 100 miles of the coast of British Columbia. A total of 22,000 Japanese-Canadians were given 24 hours to pack and then interned in camps. Considering the smaller population of Canada, their relocation camps represented a greater effort. It is interesting that Takaki's *Stangers from a Different Shore, Hiroshima* and *Double Victory* fail to mention the Canadian camps. One does wonder why.

87. See for example the evaluation by Edward J. Drea, *In Service of the Emperor: Essays on the Imperial Japanese Army* (Lincoln, NE: 1998), p. 32, in Richard B. Frank, *Downfall: The End of the Japanese Empire* (New York: 1999), p. 89.

88. Victor Davis Hanson, *Carnage and Culture: Landmark Battles in the Rise of Western Power* (New York: 2001), p. 342.

89. Cameron, *American Samurai,* p. 185.

90. Spector, *Eagle Against the Sun,* p. 486.

91. The Plan Orange, and later Rainbow plans, have been discussed repeatedly over the years, but the best and most complete work on the subject is of recent vintage: Edward S. Miller, *War Plan Orange: The U.S. Strategy to Defeat Japan, 1897–1945* (Annapolis, MD: 1991). The discussion of Orange in this chapter rests mainly upon the Miller volume. Steven Ross also supplies a useful collection of documents in his *U.S. War Plan 1939–1945* (Malabar, FL: 2000).

92. Frank, *Downfall,* p. 30.

93. Maj. E. H. Ellis, "Advanced Base Force Operations in Micronesia," Operational Plan 712 D, HAF 165, in Millett, *Semper Fidelis,* p. 326.

94. Takaki, *Double Victory,* p. 168.

95. *Life,* January 10, 1938, pp. 50–51.

96. "Its Soldiers Are Veterans," *Life,* January 5, 1942, p. 34.

97. "Death Was Part of Our Life," *Life,* February 7, 1944, p. 27.

98. Gavan Daws, *Prisoners of the Japanese: POWs of World War II in the Pacific War* (New York: 1996), pp. 278–279.

99. Ibid., p. 325.

100. Yuki Tanaka, *Hidden Horrors: Japanese War Crimes in World War II* (Boulder, CO: 1998), p. 116.

101. Cameron, *American Samurai,* pp. 111–112.

102. T. Grady Gallant, *On Valor's Side* (Garden City, NY: 1963), p. 297.

103. Samuel Eliot Morison, *The Two-Ocean War* (Boston: 1963), p. 273.

104. Interviews with Marine veterans for the Thames Television series *The World at War,* for "The Pacific, February 1942–July 1945."

105. Merrill, *Sailor's Admiral,* p. 73.

106. Frank O. Hough, *The Island War: The United States Marine Corps in the Pacific* (Philadelphia: 1947), p. 82.

107. Filmed address shown in series *The World at War,* for "The Pacific, February 1942–July 1945."

108. Interview with Marine veteran of Iwo Jima for series *The World at War,* for "The Pacific, February 1942–July 1945."

109. Ienaga, *The Pacific War,* pp. 48–49.

110. Tanaka, *Hidden Horrors,* pp. 202–203.

111. "A striking feature of the doctrine is its excessive emphasis on spirit." Ienaga, *The Pacific War,* p. 49.

112. Duus, "Japan's Wartime Empire: Problems and Issues," p. xviii.

113. Textbook examples from Ienaga, *The Pacific War,* pp. 24–26.

114. L. H. Gann, "Reflections on the Japanese and German Empires of World War II," in Peter Duus, Ramon H. Myers, and Mark R. Peattie, *The Japanese Wartime Empire, 1931–1945* (Princeton: 1996), p. 345.

115. Mottoes of the 1–397th Regiment (USMC) and the British 17th Lancers.

116. Ienaga, *The Pacific War,* p. 109.

117. All examples from ibid., p. 49.

118. Tanaka, *Hidden Horrors,* uses this kind of logic to account for horrendous Japanese war crimes, even the murder of German, and thus allied, civilians by Japanese land and sea forces during the war.

119. Figures from Frank, *Downfall,* p. 29.

120. A. A. Vandegrift and R. B. Asprey, *Once a Marine: The Memoirs of General A. A. Vandegrift, United States Marine Corps, as Told to Robert B. Asprey* (New York: 1964), p. 142.

121. Dower, *War Without Mercy,* p. 66.

122. Stephen E. Ambrose, *D-Day, June 6, 1944, the Climactic Battle of World War II* (New York: 1995), p. 308.

123. Robert Sterling Rush, *Hell in Hürtgen Forest: The Ordeal and Triumph of an American Infantry Regiment* (Lawrence, KS: 2001), p. 317.

124. The most important studies published immediately on the heels of World War II are: S. L. A. Marshall, *Men Against Fire: The Problem of Battle Command in Future War* (Washington, DC: 1947); Samuel A. Stouffer et al., *The American Soldier: Combat and Its Aftermath* (Princeton: 1949); and Edward Shils and Morris Janowitz, "Cohesion and Disintegration in the Wehrmacht in World War II," *Public Opinion Quarterly* 12 (Summer 1949). Extending this kind of primary group literature to the Korean and Vietnam Wars are: R. W. Little, "Buddy Relationships and Combat Performance," in Morris Janowitz, ed., *The New Military: Changing Patterns of Organization* (New York: 1964); Charles C. Moskos, Jr., *The American Enlisted Man* (New York: 1970); and Charles C. Moskos, Jr., "The American Combat Soldier in Vietnam," *Journal of Social Issues* 31, no. 4 (1975). For somewhat dated but still valuable surveys of the question and the literature see: Sam C. Sarkesian, ed., *Combat Effectiveness: Cohesion, Stress, and the Volunteer Military* (Beverly Hills: 1980); and Anthony Kellett, *Combat Motivation: The Behavior of Soldiers in Battle* (Boston: 1982).

125. Marshall, *Men Against Fire,* pp. 160–161.

126. Kenneth M. Pollack, *Arabs at War: Military Effectiveness, 1948–1991* (Lincoln, NE: 2002), pp. 578–581.

127. Rush, *Hell in Hürtgen Forest.*

128. Ibid., Table 9, p. 328.

129. Omar Bartov, *Hitler's Army: Soldiers, Nazis, and War in the Third Reich* (Oxford: 1992).

130. See, for example, John A. Lynn, *Bayonets of the Republic: Motivation and Tactics in the Army of Revolutionary France, 1791–94* (Boulder, CO: 1996) and James M. McPherson, *For Cause and Comrades: Why Men Fought in the Civil War* (Oxford: 1997).

131. Manchester, *Goodbye, Darkness: A Memoir of the Pacific War,* pp. 16–18.

132. Ibid., p. 441.

133. Ibid., p. 451.

134. Cameron, *American Samurai,* p. 166.

135. John Lewis Gaddis, *We Now Know: Rethinking Cold War History* (Oxford: 1997), p. 87. It is worth also considering Barton J. Bernstein, "The Atomic Bombings Reconsidered," *Foreign Affairs* 74, no. 1 (January/February 1995), although it is superseded by Gaddis and by Frank, *Downfall.*

136. Weinberg, *A World at Arms,* p. 884. See the similar judgment in Gaddis, *We Now Know,* p. 87.

137. Tami Davis Biddle, Ch. 9, "Air Power," in Michael Howard, George J. Andreopolis, and Mark R. Shuman, eds., *The Laws of War: Constraints on Warfare in the Western World* (New Haven: 1994), pp. 141–142.

138. Ibid., p. 148.

139. Ibid., p. 152, and Max Hastings, *Bomber Command: The Myths and Reality of the Strategic Bombing Offensive, 1939–45* (New York: 1979), p. 89.

140. Hastings, *Bomber Command,* p. 147.

141. For an account of the Hamburg bombing see ibid., pp. 232–237.

142. www.historylearningsite.co.uk/bombing.htm.

143. See the report on the bombing of Dresden prepared by the USAF Historical Division Research Studies Institute Air University on the web at http://www.airforcehistory.hq.af.mil/soi/dresden.htm.

144. Freeman Dyson, *Disturbing the Universe* (New York: 1979), pp. 30–31.

145. Mitchell in Michael Sherry, *The Rise of American Air Power: The Creation of Armageddon* (New Haven: 1987), p. 58.

146. Marshall in Sherry, *The Rise of American Air Power,* p. 109.

147. Spector, *Eagle Against the Sun,* p. 504.

148. Dower, *War Without Mercy,* p. 300.

149. William Craig, *The Fall of Japan* (London: 1968), p. 97. Toland, *The Rising Sun,* pp. 16–17.

149b. *War Journal* in Frank, *Downfall,* p. 89.

150. Frank, *Downfall,* p. 91.

151. Ibid., p. 93.

152. Major General Joichiro Sanada statement of belief of Field Marshal Hata in Frank, *Downfall,* p. 167.

153. Iriye, *Power and Culture,* p. 241.

154. Frank, *Downfall,* p. 97.

155. Wickerling report on Japanese peace plan in Frank, *Downfall,* p. 223.

156. Frank, *Downfall,* p. 227.

157. Takaki, *Double Victory,* p. 168.

158. Sato message of July 18, 1945, Magic Diplomatic Summary, in Frank, *Downfall,* p. 229.

159. Togo message of 21 July 1945, Magic Diplomatic Summary, in Frank, *Downfall,* p. 230.

160. *Foreign Relations of the United States: The Conference of Berlin, 1945,* vol. 2 (Washington, DC: 1960), pp. 1474–1476.

161. Takaki, *Hiroshima,* p. 38, provides a case of stating the facts in a highly selective way when he uses the Potsdam Declaration to demonstrate Truman's rigidity against Japan. Practically his sole words about the declaration are: "Thus, in the Potsdam Declaration of July 26, Truman issued an ultimatum to Japan to accept 'unconditional surrender,' or face the 'utter devastation of the Japanese homeland.'" Certainly the declaration is far more nuanced than that. Takaki uses almost exactly the same words in *Double Victory,* p. 168.

162. Borton in Iriye, *Power and Culture,* p. 149.

163. Dickover draft in ibid., p. 207.

164. Frank, *Downfall,* pp. 235–236. See Iriye, *Power and Culture,* p. 263, as well on the urgings of Sato and Ambassador Kase in Bern to accept the declaration.

165. Iriye, *Power and Culture,* p. 263.

166. Suzuki in ibid., p. 263.

167. *Life,* March 6, 1944.

168. Marshall's comments in CCS, 7-14-44, CCS 381 Pacific Ocean Area (6-10-43), Section 6, RG 218, NARA and directive of Combined Chiefs in CCS 417/3, 7-11-44 in Frank, *Downfall,* p. 30.

169. In 1941, average intake of the Japanese stood at 2,000 calories, by 1944 this dropped to 1,900, and in early 1945 it sank to 1,680. Failure of the 1945 rice crop made things far worse, so that by May 1945 the official ration reached 1,042, but, in fact, the amount of food consumed was even less. Frank, *Downfall,* pp. 350–351.

170. Sherry, *The Rise of American Air Power,* p. 286.

171. Minutes of 18 June 1945 meeting in Giangreco, "Casualty Projections for the U.S. Invasions of Japan," p. 555.

172. Frank, *Downfall*, pp. 146–147, draws attention to King's ambivalence.

173. Minutes of 18 June 1945 meeting in Giangreco, "Casualty Projections for the U.S. Invasions of Japan," p. 559.

174. *The Times Literary Supplement*, November 10, 2000, p. 16. This sparked a debate in letters that appeared in every issue from November 24 through December 22.

175. Letter from Truman to Cate, January 12, 1953 in W. F. Craven and J. L. Cate, eds., *The Army Air Forces in World War II*, vol. 5, *The Pacific: Matterhorn to Nagasaki, June 1944 to August 1945* (Chicago: 1953), between pp. 712 and 713.

176. Harry S. Truman, *Memoirs of Harry S. Truman: Year of Decisions, 1945* (Garden City, NY: 1955), p. 417.

177. Henry L. Stimson, "The Decision to Use the Atomic Bomb," *Harper's*, February 1947, in Frank, *Downfall*, pp. 338.

178. Winston S. Churchill, *The Second World War*, vol. 6, *Triumph and Tragedy* (Boston: 1953), p. 638.

179. Takaki, *Hiroshima*, p. 23. He uses the same figures and the same expression of surprise in *Double Victory*, p. 166.

180. JCS 924/2, "Operations Against Japan Subsequent to Formosa," 30 August 1944 in D. M. Giancreco, "'A Score of Bloody Okinawas and Iwo Jima's: President Truman and Casualty Estimates for the Invasion of Japan," *Pacific Historical Review* (March 2003), p. 100.

181. *New York Times*, 18 January 1945, p. 1, in Giancreco, "'A Score of Bloody Okinawas and Iwo Jimas'," p. 102.

182. European fighting was less intense over longer times; Pacific island warfare was very intense fighting for short periods while American forces took the island, with no fighting between campaigns. This explains the much higher Pacific rates of casualties in combat per day.

183. 25 April 1945 ratio from Frank, *Downfall*, pp. 136–137.

184. This is a major finding in Giancreco, "'A Score of Bloody Okinawas and Iwo Jimas'," which voids the claim made by Barton Bernstein, author of "A Postwar Myth: 500,000 Lives Saved," *Bulletin of Atomic Scientists* (June–July 1986) and other articles, that "No scholar has been able to find any *high-level* supporting archival documents from the *Truman administration months* before Hiroshima that, in unalloyed form, provide even an explicit estimate of 500,000 casualties, let alone a million or more." Bernstein letter in *Journal of Military History* 63 (Jan. 1999), p. 247.

185. Nimitz, draft edition of Joint Staff Study for Olympic, in Frank, *Downfall*, p. 137.

186. MacArthur to Marshall, 17 June 1945, and Frank projection in Frank, *Downfall*, p. 138.

187. Minutes in Frank, *Downfall*, p. 143.

188. Account of meeting in Frank, *Downfall*, p. 142.

189. Ibid.

190. See figures for rising troop strength in ibid., pp. 200–203.

191. For the escalation of aircraft numbers, see ibid., pp. 206–211.

192. Gaddis, *We Now Know*, p. 324, n. 14.

193. Without even counting the Japanese who might have died in an invasion of the home islands, great numbers of others were spared. It is reasonable, even conservative, to argue that Japan might very well have endured a blockade for another six months. The British planned a major campaign in September, Zipper, to drive on Singapore, and it doubtless would have been a bloody affair. But of even greater moment were the Asian deaths that occurred in areas occupied by Japan, such as the slave laborers, or *romusha*, drafted by the Japanese. Robert Newman

concludes that each month the war continued in 1945 "upwards of 250,000 people, mostly Asian but some Westerners, *would have died each month the Japanese Empire struggled in its death throes beyond July 1945*" (italics are Newman's). Robert P. Newman, *Truman and the Hiroshima Cult* (East Lansing, MI: 1995), p. 139. Frank, *Downfall*, p. 163, takes a conservative turn and posits an estimate of Asian noncombatant deaths at a minimum of 100,000 per month and perhaps as many as 250,000. If these figures have any merit, a delay in Japanese surrender for six months, would have resulted in 600,000–1,500,000 additional Asian noncombatant deaths outside Japan. And what of the famine that U.S. blockade would have imposed on Japan? As it was, even with the end of war and U.S. relief, famine hit the home islands, so that by November 1945 per-capita calorie intake fell to a ration of 1,325 and then 1,042 in May 1946. At a certain point even this meager ration was not regularly supplied. Continued bombing of the Japanese rail system, a course of action adopted by the U.S., would have multiplied the effects of blockade by leaving the distribution system in utter shambles. The cost in lives is impossible to know, but death would have stalked the home islands. Truman did not calculate these losses, but those engaged in moral outrage about the loss of life should.

194. General Thomas T. Handy to General Carl Spaatz, 25 July 1945, in Frank, *Downfall*, p. 262

195. On this meeting see Frank, *Downfall*, pp. 256–258.

196. Minutes of the May 31 meeting in ibid., p. 257.

197. The bombings clearly fall within Caleb Carr's definition of Terrorism in his *The Lessons of Terror, A History of Warfare Against Civilians: Why It Has Always Failed and Why It Will Fail Again* (New York: 2002).

198. Frank, *Downfall*, pp. 258, 268–269.

199. Anami in Lawrence Freedman and Saki Dockrill, "Hiroshima: A Strategy of Shock," in Saki Docrill, ed., *From Pearl Harbor to Hiroshima: The Second World War in the Pacific, 1941–45* (New York: 1994), p. 207.

200. Frank, *Downfall*, p. 303.

201. Henry A. Wallace, diary, August 10, 1945, reprinted in Michael B. Stoff, Jonathan F. Fanton, R. Hal Williams, eds., *The Manhattan Project: Documentary Introduction to the Atomic Age* (New York: 1991), p. 245.

202. Frank, *Downfall*, p. 291.

203. Foreign Ministry cable in ibid., p. 296.

204. U.S. reply in Iriye, *Power and Culture*, p. 265.

205. Takaki offers a nuanced approach to Truman's racial attitudes in *Hiroshima*, in fact it may be the strongest aspect of the book. As a younger man, Truman certainly made racist statements, but as an older man he advocated policies of integration and racial justice.

206. Cover of *Leatherneck* in Dower, *War Without Mercy*, p. 186.

207. Robert Sherrod, *On to Westward* (New York: 1945), p. 138.

CHAPTER EIGHT

1. Brief accounts of the Sinai campaign in the Six-Day War can be found in: Chaim Herzog, *The Arab Israeli Wars* (New York: 1982), pp. 151–206; Trevor N. Dupuy, *Elusive Victory: The Arab-Israeli Wars, 1947–1974*, 5th ed. (Dubuque, IA: 1992), pp. 219–340; and Kenneth M. Pollack, *Arabs at War: Military Effectiveness, 1948–1991* (Lincoln, NE: 2002), pp. 58–88. The details presented here concerning the Six-Day War were taken from these sources.

2. This chapter derives a great deal of its argument and its sources from the works of Kenneth M. Pollack. He published two volumes in 2002, *Arabs at War* and *The Threatening Storm: The Case for Invading Iraq* (New York: 2002). The first is extremely important for this chapter, the second is not. Also, he contributed, with Michael J. Eisenstadt, Ch. 3, "Armies of Snow and Armies of Sand: The Impact of Soviet Military Doctrine on Arab Militaries," to Emily O. Goldman and Leslie C. Eliason, eds., *Diffusion of Military Knowledge, Technology and Practices: International Consequences of Military Innovations* (Palo Alto, CA: 2003). In addition I have turned to his dissertation, "The Influence of Arab Culture on Arab Military Effectiveness," Ph.D. diss., Massachusetts Institute of Technology, 1996. When I began this book six years ago, Ken sent me his dissertation and gave me permission to draw from it. I very much appreciate his generosity and his comments.

3. Pollack, *Arabs at War,* p. 574.

4. Edward Luttwak and Dan Horowitz, *The Israeli Army* (New York: 1975), pp. 285–286.

5. Pollack, *Arabs at War,* p. 571.

6. Ibid., p. 564.

7. Ibid.

8. Ibid.

9. Ibid., pp. 567–568.

10. Pollack, "Influence of Arab Culture," p. 545.

11. Sharon in Pollack, *Arabs at War,* p. 78.

12. Pollack, "Influence of Arab Culture," p. 453.

13. Pollack, *Arabs at War,* p. 255.

14. Robert H. Scales, *Certain Victory* (Washington, DC: 1994), p. 298.

15. This chapter will call the conflict that broke out on 6 October 1973 and continued through most of that month the October War, rather than the Yom Kippur War. The focus here is the Arab rather than the Israeli experience, and as such it seems inappropriate to label the war by the Jewish holy day.

16. Anthony Cordesman and Abraham Wagner, *The Lessons of Modern War,* vol. 1, *The Arab-Israeli Wars, 1973–1989* (Boulder, CO: 1990), p. 197.

17. Benjamin S. Lambeth, *Moscow's Lessons from the 1982 Lebanon War* (1984, R–3000-AF), p. 31, in Pollack, *Arabs at War,* p. 534.

18. Moshe Dayan, *Diary of the Sinai Campaign* (New York: 1966), p. 63.

19. Pollack, *Arabs at War,* p. 58.

20. General Muhammad Fawzi in Field Marshal Mohamed Abdel Ghani El-Gamasy, *The October War,* trans. Gilian Potter, Nadra Marcos, Rosette Frances (Cairo: 1993), p. 85, in Pollack, "Influence of Arab Culture," p. 196.

21. Herzog, *The Arab-Israeli Wars,* p. 171.

22. Mohamed Heikal, *The Road to Ramadan* (New York: 1975), p. 22.

23. El-Gamasy, *The October War,* p. 157, in Pollack, *Arabs at War,* p. 100.

24. Pollack, *Arabs at War,* p. 101.

25. Chaim Herzog, *The War of Atonement, October 1973* (Boston: 1975), p. 35.

26. Lt. Gen. Saad El Shazli, *The Crossing of the Suez* (San Francisco: 1980), p. 42, in Pollack, *Arabs at War,* p. 102.

27. Total advisers hit 20,000, with 5,000 officers "saturating all of the Egyptian military organizations down to battalion and even lower in the case of tank and artillery." Badolato, "A Clash of Cultures," p. 75.

28. 28 June 1968 issue of *Al-Ahram,* cited in Raymond W. Baker, *Sadat and After: Struggles for Egypt's Political Soul* (Cambridge, MA: 1990), p. 188.

29. Heikal, *The Road to Ramadan,* p. 43.

30. Herzog, *The Arab-Israeli Wars,* p. 250.

31. Pollack, *Arabs at War,* p. 104.

32. On Soviet military doctrine and its limited impact on Arab tactics, see ibid., and Pollack and Eisenstadt, "Armies of Snow and Armies of Sand."

33. Roger Owen paraphrasing Hussein in Roger Owen, "The Role of the Army in Middle East Politics: A Critique of Existing Analyses," *Review of Middle East Studies* 3 (1978), p. 70.

34. Jon D. Glassman, *Arms for the Arabs* (Baltimore: 1975), pp. 50–51.

35. *Warfighting* first appeared in 1987 and was designated as FMFM–1; in a somewhat revised version it came out again in 1995 as MCDP–1. Although initially prepared under the auspices of General A. M. Gray, Commandant of the Marines at the time, the actual writing was done by the military intellectual Captain, now Major, John Schmitt.

36. *Warfighting,* p. 73.

37. Sun-tzu quotation in ibid., p. 69.

38. Ibid., p. 78. Italics are in MCDP–1.

39. Ibid., pp. 10–11.

40. Ibid., pp. 75–76.

41. Ibid., p. 8.

42. Ibid., p. 87.

43. Ibid., p. 80. Italics are in MCDP–1.

44. Accounts of the October War can be found in Herzog, *The Arab-Israeli Wars,* pp. 252–362; Dupuy, *Elusive Victory: The Arab-Israeli Wars, 1947–1974,* pp. 385–617; and Pollack, *Arabs at War,* pp. 98–137. The details of the cross-Canal attack presented here come from these sources.

45. Dupuy, *Elusive Victory,* p. 417.

46. Shazli in The Insight Team of the London Sunday *Times, The Yom Kippur War* (New York: 1974), p. 147.

47. Cairo correspondent of *The New York Times* in Insight Team, *The Yom Kippur War,* p. 221.

48. Pollack, "Influence of Arab Culture," p. 547.

49. Dupuy, *Elusive Victory,* p. 433.

50. S. A. El Edroos, *The Hashemite Arab Army, 1908–1979* (Amman: 1980), p. 508, in Pollack, *Arabs at War,* p. 117.

51. Pollack interview with Reshef, September 1996, in Michael J. Eisenstadt and Kenneth M. Pollack, "Armies of Snow and Armies of Sand: The Impact of Soviet Military Doctrine on Arab Militaries," paper presented at meeting, *Diffusion of Military Knowledge, Technology and Practices: International Consequences of Military Innovations,* Washington, DC, 18 January 1999, p. 21.

52. Pollack, "The Influence of Arab Culture," p. 143.

Epilogue

1. http://www.whitehouse.gov/news/releases/2001/09/20010911–16.html.

2. http://www.whitehouse.gov/news/releases/2001/11/20011102–5.html.

3. http://www.whitehouse.gov/news/releases/2002/01/20020129–11.html.

4. Philip Bobbitt, *The Shield of Achilles: War, Peace, and the Course of History* (New York: 2002), p. xxi.

5. See Sunil Dasgupta, "Internal Security and Military Organization: The Rise of Paramilitaries in Developing Societies," Ph.D. dissertation, University of Illinois at Urbana-Champaign, 2002.

6. For the MacArthur speech see http://www.homestead.com/douglassmacarthur/Congress.html.

7. http://www.cnn.com/SPECIALS/2001/gulf.war/facts/gulfwar/.

8. http://www.pbs.org/wgbh/pages/frontline/shows/kosovo/.

9. http://www.pbs.org/wgbh/pages/frontline/shows/kosovo/etc/facts.html.

10. For a selection definitions, see the site of the Terrorism Research Center, http://www.terrorism.com/terrorism/def.shtml.

11. Bruce Hoffman, *Inside Terrorism* (New York: 1998), pp. 15 and 25.

12. Caleb Carr, *The Lessons of Terror, A History of Warfare Against Civilians: Why It Has Always Failed and Why It Will Fail Again* (New York: 2002), p. 6.

13. *Simpson's Contemporary Quotations*, compiled by James B. Simpson (1988), quoted in http://www.bartleby.com/63/89/1289.html.

14. See Régis Debray, *Revolution in the Revolution?* (New York: 1967).

15. The Pope in an article on Time.com, http://www.time.com/time/daily/special/papacy/formatted/0209841.html.

16. Christopher Lew, "Trial by Fire: The Strategy of Bombing Japan," from *World War II* magazine on http://history1900s.about.com/library/prm/bltrialbyfire3.htm.

17. Jonathan Rauch, "Firebombs over Tokyo," *Atlantic Online,* July/August 2001, http://www.theatlantic.com/issues/2002/07/rauch.htm.

18. John A. Lynn, "War of Annihilation, War of Attrition, and War of Legitimacy: A Neo-Clausewitzian Approach to Twentieth-Century Conflicts," *Marine Corps Gazette* 80, no. 10 (October 1996).

19. Bruce Porter, *War and the Rise of the State* (New York: 1994), p. 262.

Appendix

1. See Alan Beyerchen, "Clausewitz, Nonlinearity, and the Unpredictability of War," *International Security* 17, no. 3 (Winter 1992–1993), pp. 59–90.

INDEX